ENCOUNTERS IN HISTORY

ENCOUNTERS IN HISTORY

Pieter Geyl

COLLINS
St James's Place, London
1963

TITLE IN BCL 2nd ED

CONTENTS

I

SHAKESPEARE AS A HISTORIAN: A FRAGMENT

Shakespeare as a Historian: A Fragment

PREFACE

I feel that an apology, or at least an explanation, is due for the inclusion in this volume of the following essay on Shakespeare.

First, because it is a fragment that will never be completed. Second, because for a discussion of Shakespeare more expert knowledge might be desired than that which I have at my command.

The essay is the result of a number of months of intensive reading—rereading of the plays and reading of such literature on Shakespeare as I could lay my hands on.

It was in the winter of 1944-45, that is to say, during the worst period of the German occupation, that I indulged in this fascinating occupation. I had been released from internment in February 1944 and had spent the spring and summer of that year writing *Napoleon For and Against*. In one respect circumstances were ideal. I had been dismissed from my professorial post. No classes, no examinations, no reading and discussing of essays. No telephone. Apart from occasional trips to Amsterdam or The Hague and animated discussions with like-minded friends on what might be made of the future, there was nothing but work to while away the months of weary waiting and sometimes excruciating suspense. So in that last winter, while famine was laying a heavy hand on us all, sitting by the one old-fashioned stove to which the dearth of fuel was compelling us to resort, the same stove on which my wife cooked our scanty meals, I read Shakespeare and about Shakespeare ; I read the French and Dutch dramatists of the seventeenth century and about *them*; and I made extensive notes, which very soon kindled in my mind the idea of a book.

The liberation came while I was in the middle of these activities. In fact I had had to interrupt them some two weeks earlier and go into hiding with my wife—just before the German military police descended on my house. On returning I recovered the Shakespeare notes from the awful mess to which what was left of my belongings had been reduced, but life had suddenly become too crowded and active again to give them much attention.

It was not until a year or more afterwards that I looked at them more closely and felt so gripped again by the promise of the subject that I sat down to work them out. But when I had written the fragment I published in the *Nieuw Vlaams Tijdschrift* in 1947, and some years later included in my volume of essays *Tochten en Toernooien*, the notes gave out, and my attention, or at least my creative powers, engaged by many more actual and pressing matters, did not allow me to resume the work where I had left off in the spring of 1945.

The fragment, then, will remain a fragment. Reviewers of the Dutch original have been kind to it; American readers of the translation have encouraged me. If I cannot compete with the experts, perhaps the spontaneous (or must I say, naïve?) reactions of a historian to the inexhaustible manifestations of Shakespeare's genius may still be of some interest.

(Utrecht, 1960)

A

Shakespeare's Attitude Towards State and Society

AN INTRODUCTORY NOTE ON THE HISTORY PLAYS

Although I shall not, in trying to delineate Shakespeare's attitude towards history and his powers as a historian, confine myself to the evidence provided by the history plays proper, a note giving some details about these plays may be useful. Of the thirty-five or thirty-six plays that may be regarded as actually written by Shakespeare, a full dozen can be so described. (As drawn up by E. K. Chambers, *William Shakespeare: A Study of Facts and Problems* [1930], the list of Shakespeare's plays contains thirty-eight titles. Of these, *Pericles, Prince of Tyre* and *The Two Noble Kinsmen* seem to me doubtful, while to *Henry VIII*, which otherwise would increase the number of history plays to thirteen, Shakespeare certainly contributed no more than a few scenes. *Henry VI, First Part*, was also at one time considered to contain no more than a few scenes by Shakespeare, while the *Second Part* and the *Third Part* were regarded as no more than recastings; I shall refer to this farther on in the text.) Apart from the twelve, history has served Shakespeare in a good many of his other plays, comedies and tragedies alike, if only to provide a background and a setting for their plots. Among these I count the Greek plays *Troilus and Cressida* and *Timon of Athens*, and even *Titus Andronicus*, a melodrama (belonging to the poet's early period) that, though it deals with a Roman theme, cannot well be described as a history play.

The twelve history plays proper fall into two groups. There are nine dealing with English subjects and three inspired by Roman history. Among the nine named after English kings are some of the earliest plays known to have been composed by Shakespeare; all nine belong to the first ten years of his career as a dramatist, the whole of which covered not much more than twenty years (1590 to 1612 or 1613). Of the Roman plays, one followed immediately after the English series, but the two others belong to a later period, coming even after the great tragedies.

Here is the entire list, with, for the reader's convenience, the years of the reigns of the kings after whom the English plays are named. The *New Cambridge Shakespeare*, edited by J. Dover Wilson, and the *New Arden Shakespeare*, edited by Una Ellis-Fermor, editions that appeared since Chambers wrote, have been consulted for the dates of the plays, some of them presumptive.

King John	(1199-1216)	1591 (?)
Henry VI, First Part		
Henry VI, Second Part	(1422-1461)	before the summer of 1592
Henry VI, Third Part		
Richard III	(1483-1485)	1593 (?)
Richard II	(1377-1399)	1595
Henry IV, First Part		1597
Henry IV, Second Part	(1399-1413)	1598
Henry V	(1413-1422)	1599
Julius Caesar		1599 (?)
Antony and Cleopatra		1607-1608
Coriolanus		1607-1608

Leaving *King John* to one side, eight English plays cover a century of history (1377-1485) which as seen by the author forms a coherent episode, significant to him and to his contemporaries. Actually, these plays fall into two groups of four, that covering 1377 to 1422 written after that covering 1422 to 1485, the reverse of historical chronology.

The downfall of Richard II, with which the poet ushered in the events preliminary to the period already treated in his first four plays, did indeed mean the end, for a number of generations, of the old legitimate royalty, which had just attained to glory under Richard's grandfather Edward III, the conqueror of France. Richard's deposition by Bolingbroke, Duke of Hereford, son of the fourth of Edward's sons, John of Gaunt, may have been explicable by Richard's incapacity and by that dreamer's self-glorification; Bolingbroke's assuming the royal dignity was nonetheless a violation of the legitimate order of succession. This tampering with the sacred order made itself felt the more painfully because, although Richard himself (who was soon murdered) left no children, there were descendants, in the female line it is true, of Edward's third son. However forceful a ruler Bolingbroke-Lancaster, Henry IV, may have been, he was severely troubled by revolts, which shook his usurped throne. His son Henry V, who won the glorious victory over the French at Agincourt, and who seemed to be reviving the great days of Edward III, was ever conscious of the wrong done to Richard II. Shakespeare revelled in the glory of that celebrated warrior, nor did he belittle the piety and virtuousness that, after his wild youth, Henry displayed when he was King.

But for all that, Shakespeare never forgot that Henry V's greatness was to be followed by the disastrous reign of Henry VI: in the epilogue to *Henry V* he recalls having already (some seven years earlier) put this on the stage. The infraction of the order must be avenged. This young and feeble king, a pious bookworm rather than a king, completely lacking his father's sanguine courage and energy, was unable to restrain the quarrels of the high nobles, his relatives mostly, until finally a party was formed under the Duke of York, grandson of Edward III's fifth son (and through his mother the great-great-grandson of the third), a party that disputed Henry's right to the crown. So it came to what is known as the feud between Lancaster and York—for the King, the descendant of Bolingbroke-Lancaster and of Gaunt-Lancaster, now was made to appear a pretender, on an equal footing with his rival, at the head of a connection of high nobles. The so-called Wars of the Roses, between the Red Rose (Lancaster) and the White Rose (York), were characterized by pitiless executions and inhuman horrors, resulting in the extermination of a large part of the highest English nobility.

In the end Henry VI became the captive of York's sons— York himself having been killed—and had to give up the crown to the elder, who thus became Edward IV. The deposed king, like Richard II sixty years earlier, was soon murdered, as was his young son. More than Edward IV his younger brother Richard, the hunchback, was the perpetrator of these crimes. Edward IV died a natural death, still in middle age, after a relatively quiet reign of twenty years' duration. But now Richard, robbing Edward's young sons of their rights, made himself master of the kingdom and (according, at least, to the reading of history universally accepted in Shakespeare's time) had the two princes, his nephews, murdered in the Tower.

After these events the conjurations and the revolts began afresh, against Richard this time, until he was defeated by Henry Tudor, Earl of Richmond, and got killed during his flight.

Richmond's mother was a direct descendant of John of Gaunt, and consequently, Richmond was a Lancaster, but he married the daughter of Edward IV, the York king, sister of the little princes murdered by Richard. Lancaster and York could thus be regarded as united under Richmond, Henry VII; at any rate, with him there came an end to the protracted and murderous civil war. With him, and under the Tudor dynasty, a new period of strong and undisputed royal power opened for England, which in Shakespeare's own lifetime seemed to be culminating in the brilliant reign of Elizabeth, daughter of Henry VII's son Henry VIII.

SHAKESPEARE'S BELIEF IN A MORAL COSMIC ORDER

Shakespeare awoke to literary consciousness at a time when the stage was much used in order to bring before the public the great events of English history. It was done in a spirit of lively national pride. As against the Continent, torn by war and civil war, England was aware of its unity and prosperity and enthusiastically accepted the Tudor kingship, both as representing and as safeguarding those boons. The writers of chronicle plays did not look for much more in history than the colourful or the shocking event, that which could be staged for the amusement of the spectators and to the glory of England. From the preceding survey of Shakespeare's eight plays, it must have become clear that he intended to do more. He subordinated incident to a conception. All the crowded variety of a century of English history he attempted to view as a unity.

This, then, is the first feature to be noted in Shakespeare's treatment of historical subject matter, distinguishing it at once from the more primitive chronicle fashion employed by most writers. Not that this approach of his was entirely original. England possessed a rich historiography, and on more than one side a reflective interpretation of events, a tracing of their connections with an all-embracing cosmic order, was being attempted. It has been customary to stress above all Shakespeare's debt to Holinshed, whose large chronicle went into a second edition in 1587. No doubt the chronicle play in general owed much to that work, and Shakespeare as well as other dramatists made use of it. But besides, he must have found mental nourishment in the ideas of more philosophically inclined and moralizing writers, like Hall and the authors of the *Mirror for Magistrates*, who addressed themselves to the intellectual élite of the day.[1]

The old classicist picture of Shakespeare as the barbarian of genius—inevitable in an age that identified all civilization with conformity to its own rules, transitory as they were—has long been assailed and sapped of its authority.[2] The critics are, however, still engaged in uncovering the cultural wealth of that amazing *oeuvre*. Of late years they have been assisted by a reaction—and a similar one is evident in Homeric criticism—against the "disintegrators," as they have been somewhat acidly described—the eighteenth- and nineteenth-century critics who splintered the unity of the Shakespeare canon as it has been handed down to us, ascribing to other writers, wholly or in part, a number of plays, especially among the earlier ones, or degrading these plays to mere imitations of lost works. It is only since, in particular, the

[1] I follow here E. M. W. Tillyard, *Shakespeare's History Plays* (1944). The spiritual background of the English plays in particular is excellently evoked.

[2] It was in France that its dominance was most complete. Voltaire, who prided himself on having discovered Shakespeare for his compatriots, did not understand him in the least. When later on other French writers had the impudence to admire Shakespeare in their own way he flew into a rage, which he wreaked upon his one time protégé. His outburst against "le sauvage ivre" has remained famous. An American writer, Thomas R. Lounsbury, has described Voltaire's eventful relationship to Shakespeare in a book that is amusing as well as instructive: *Shakespeare and Voltaire* (1902). Even Taine's sketch of Shakespeare, in his *Littérature anglaise* (1869), is little better than a caricature. Not all Frenchmen, naturally, were to that extent the prisoners of the classicist tradition. Mézières, *Shakespeare, ses oeuvres et ses critiques* (1860), has great merits, and the very able book of Stapfer, *Shakespeare et l'antiquité* (1879-80), not to mention any later authorities, excels in understanding.

Henry VI trilogy has been boldly restored to his hand, that justice can be done to the intellectual formation of the youthful Shakespeare.[3] New studies continue to bring important contributions, helping us realize that from his youth on, Shakespeare, far from being a child of nature, or a mummer who had learned to decorate his fabrications for the stage with the fine-sounding phrases of the intellectual movement of his period, took his full share in that movement and integrated it into his plays. And in truth integrated it. Ideas were so taken up in the full tide of his dramatic imaginings that only with the help of a profound familiarity with late-sixteenth-century philosophy and theology and politics and historiography—a familiarity in which earlier generations of readers and critics were deficient—can they be isolated and valued.

The belief in a moral cosmic order permeates the whole of Shakespeare's work.[4] This is the life breath of the tragedies as well as of the history plays, and when years came in which the poet seemed above all conscious of the contrast presented by harsh reality, this is reflected in an almost despairing gloom.

> As flies to wanton boys, are we to the gods;
> They kill us for their sport.

But these words of Gloucester's, by which doubt seems to be thrown on everything, are not the last spoken in *King Lear*. After the death of the unhappy old king, who was himself unable to find sense in the end to which his innocent daughters came, Kent and Edgar are still called upon to sustain "the gor'd state."

In the English history plays, at any rate, even doubt is not yet voiced, and the order reflects itself for all to see, not only in the moral world, but in the forms of earthly society. Connected with the entire ordinance of things, and supplying to

[3] See especially P. Alexander, *Shakespeare's Henry VI and Richard III* (1929). For Homer, see J. A. Scott, *The Unity of Homer* (1921). The effect of Alexander's study reminds one of that created by the child's ingenuous remark in Andersen's tale, "The Clothes of the Emperor of China".

[4] This has been pointed out particularly by A. C. Bradley in his great book, *Shakespearean Tragedy* (1904).

it indispensable support, there is in the community of man a fixed hierarchy of superior and inferior. Nowhere do we find this conception indicated more emphatically than in that well-known parallel of the solar system with which Ulysses in *Troilus and Cressida* tries to demonstrate the necessity of "degree"—*Troilus and Cressida*, which nevertheless was written in those gloomy years and gives of the Greek world an almost grotesque and certainly unattractive picture (not, in fact, taken direct from Homer, but derived from medieval adaptations).

The parallel of the solar system, however, is not meant for more than a parallel. In Shakespeare's mind, especially as it realized itself through the imagination in his dramas, the social order is neither rigid nor mechanical: it depends on moral, on human, factors, which may fail. It cannot help, therefore, but be frequently disarranged, but forever undismayed there springs from the human mind an urge to overcome these confusions. That is the drama.

SHAKESPEARE AND KINGSHIP

Shakespeare's treatment of kingship—of authority—reflects a life-like conception, a sense for the human problematics of social relationships. Kingship has a claim to recognition. In itself the claim is absolute: rebellion is a wholly unjustifiable sin. This was the general attitude of the age; the detestation of rebellion was deeply felt. In England, a sermon "Against Disobedience and Willful Rebellion" had been included in 1574 in the official *Book of Homilies*. But not in England alone; throughout the whole of Europe the intellectuals, even without the exhortations of religion, were keenly aware of the dangers that state and society might incur from rebellion, whether coming from the mob, from religious fanatics, or from turbulent noblemen. It is important to note—for without it Shakespeare's dramatic powers could not have attained their depth—that in Shakespeare's view the holder of regal authority was himself subject to the moral order. With all due reverence for the office, Shakespeare was nevertheless able to retain freedom of judgment with regard to the king's person and the king's actions: the law is valid for the king as well; he, too, is accountable for his misdeeds.

To realize the significance of this attitude and the wealth of dramatic tensions it released, contrast the doctrine proclaimed by Corneille—a doctrine that must have strait-jacketed his freedom of judgment. (It is Caesar speaking, but Corneille sides with him unhesitatingly.)

Of all these crimes of State committed to obtain the crown,
We are absolved by Heaven when it gives it to us,
And in the sacred rank where Heaven's favour has placed us
The past becomes guiltless and the future lawful.
He who can attain that rank cannot be guilty;
Whatever he may have done or does, he is inviolable.[5]

A doctrine suited to tyrants; small wonder that Napoleon (as Talleyrand assures us in his memoirs) knew these lines from *Cinna* by heart and liked to quote them.

In the absolute rejection of rebellion Shakespeare was typical of the European civilization of his age—insofar as the theory of Machiavelli did not embolden people to eliminate all moral restraints from politics, which became thereby a mere game of power—but in his freedom of judgment, which in the final reckoning discerned the human being in king and rebel alike and assigned to both their places in the same order, he was a child of his own country. In England the universal triumph of state absolutism was still accompanied by a recognition of the sovereignty of law.

In Shakespeare's own world, as he fashioned it in the untrammelled liberty of his imagination—in a play like *Measure for Measure*, for instance, where he could let his mind play with the problem of authority in a purely fanciful environment—this law assumes a broadly moral and human sense and is tempered by mercy and love. There, when the Duke of Vienna

[5] Tous ces crimes d'Etat qu'on fait pour la couronne,
Le ciel nous en absout alors qu'il nous la donne,
Et dans le sacré rang où sa faveur l'a mis,
Le passé devient juste, et l'avenir permis.
Qui peut y parvenir ne peut être coupable;
Quoi qu'il ait fait ou fasse, il est inviolable.

is concerned, or rather, a sanctimonious nobleman who, placed in the Duke's position, extends the privileges of authority to the breaking point and soon misuses them for his lust, the poet can afford to mock the entire spectacle of earthly power.

> . . . man, proud man,
> Drest in a little brief authority,
> Most ignorant of what he's most assur'd,
> His glassy essence, like an angry ape,
> Plays such fantastic tricks before high heaven
> As make the angels weep; who, with our spleens,
> Would all themselves laugh mortal.

But the historic kings of England, too, are far from being to Shakespeare the mere symbolic bearers of an inviolable right. They are men, subject not only to the moral obligations, but to the weaknesses, of men, and their being men helps us to understand their vicissitudes, even to understand the rebellions that—however unjustifiable—are sometimes directed against them. It is true that in nearly the whole of the period Shakespeare chose for his series of eight plays, the kings are themselves sired by rebellion, their titles are often doubtful, and their misfortunes can be regarded as retribution for old misdeeds, misdeeds perhaps committed by a preceding generation. In connection with my present argument, therefore, no play (with perhaps the exception of *King John*, which, however, on account of the period to which it transfers the reader, falls outside the continuity of the series) is as important as *Richard II*, the tragedy of the last indisputably legitimate Plantagenet.

King John

The two plays just mentioned, *Richard II* and *King John*, differ not a little. In *King John* the King behaves like a villain when he orders his little nephew to be killed and like a coward when he tries to throw the guilt on his henchman. His selling England to the Pope is no more surprising than that his nobles rise against him and plot with France. But although the King's person is not spared, the office of king is left uncompromised. England's humiliation and peril constitute the play's proper theme, and the character who rises above all national calamity is he who at the play's end, expressing national self-confidence no less than aversion to rebellion, utters the famous words:

> This England never did, nor never shall,
> Lie at the proud foot of a conqueror,
> But when it first did help to wound itself.
> Now these her princes are come home again,
> [The King has by then died repentant; the rebellious
>   nobles have mended their ways.]
> Come the three corners of the world in arms,
> And we shall shock them. Nought shall make us rue,
> If England to itself do rest but true.

A most remarkable character, this Bastard! Even though the picture lacks finish, he has, from his first entrance, when, with easy-tempered mockery, he glories in his illegitimate birth and the paternity of Richard the Lion-Hearted, the marks of Shakespeare's great creative powers upon him. Not the King, but *he* is the impersonation of the England Shakespeare wanted to hold up for the public's love and veneration, the merry, vital England longing for deeds, the England of his own day. It is as if, by placing that man as the true hero over and against the wearer of the crown, he gave rein to his feeling of the relative importance of "degree," in the cult of which at the same time he participated. At all events, when the Bastard finally becomes the mouthpiece of an emphatic loyalism, it is rather the English nation symbolized by the kingship than the kingship itself that supplies the animating force. With what a striking absence of respect, at once daring and simple-minded, had the Bastard given his impression of the great ones of the earth whom it had been his lot to meet: "Mad world! mad kings! . . . he that wins of [i.e., governs] all . . . kings . . . beggars, old men, young men, maids, [is] That smooth-fac'd gentleman . . . Commodity" —that is to say, interest.

King Richard II

King Richard II is constructed upon the same antithesis as *King John:* kingship as a divine institution and the king as a human being. If the play nevertheless shows sharp contrast with *King John*, which was written some years earlier, it is but a sign of the incomparable width of Shakespeare's artistic power. It is the character of the King that occupies, from the third act on at least, the central position.

At first, in a play whose outlines, forceful and vivid, impress by strength rather than subtlety, the verse heavily rhetorical, a good measure of somewhat forced metaphors and verbal ingenuity, the lines stepping purposefully, without any enjambments, the whole built up by lines, frequently rhymed —at first, Richard, too, has nothing that surpasses the ordinary. He is a tyrant, given to abuse of his power, unfair, arbitrary, thinking only of his own convenience, rude to his uncles. But when, later, he is shown in his distress, soon in his humiliation, a personality entirely his own, a personality such as only a great poet can create, breaks through that regularity, that humdrum quality, finding a voice fitted to the most unusual conception. The unbalanced weakling turns out to be possessed of the finest sensibility and imaginative power. His change from exalted belief in the saving quality of his royalty to abject prostration, from a sort of unreal rebelliousness—for it never gets beyond words, beyond fits and starts—to the meekest acquiescence, fascinates the reader from now on right to the end; and what is particularly striking is the magnificent and surprising flight of his fancy under the stimulus of those varying moods. The climax comes in the abdication scene, when the helpless King faces the cold, firm Bolingbroke, the victor, the usurper. Northumberland is hard, Bolingbroke somewhat pityingly contemptuous, and now the romantic Richard *acts* his misfortune, with the crown, with the mirror. When, at the last, he is murdered, he still, at the point of death, pronounces his royal blood to be something very particular, which will carry its shedder to hell; as for himself, his soul will mount to heaven.

Shakespeare does not polemize with that ultraroyalist view—that is not his way. Indeed, up to a point, as we know, he accepted it himself. In spite of the sanction of Parliament, Bolingbroke, now King Henry IV, felt the unlawfulness of his position as a heavy burden. Even Henry V was still conscious of the irregularity, and as a matter of fact, retribution was to come under Henry VI. And yet what the drama of Richard II most clearly conveys to our minds is that these highflying claims are untenable when advanced by so factitious a personality, at once weak and false. It is significant that Essex, on the eve of his rebellion against Queen Elizabeth, in 1601, had *Richard II* performed by his actors.[6] Shakespeare's play was certainly not intended to be revolutionary, but the idea that it made visible to contemporaries was nevertheless the possibility of a ruler, boastfully proclaiming his divine right, but hesitating, and given to listening to the promptings of evil councillors, being replaced, under the sanction of Parliament, by a more forceful figure.

And indeed, Shakespeare completely accepted Henry IV's kingship. As a matter of fact, and historically, he could not, as an Englishman, help doing so; his people's history had decided that issue. But poetically, too, we see Shakespeare making full use of the freedom thus given him, contrasting the born ruler in the usurper with the utter failure of the representative of the venerated hereditary monarchy. To Henry V particularly, still the product of rebellion, Shakespeare did homage as being the great and good King par excellence. It was only after Henry V, in whom rebellion seemed to blossom out so splendidly, that its poisonous fruit was brought

[6] J. A. R. Marriott, *English History in Shakespeare* (1918), p. 69, considers it improbable, in accordance, as he says, with most critics, that the play about Richard II performed on the eve of Essex's rebellion was Shakespeare's *King Richard II*. E. K. Chambers, *William Shakespeare: A Study of Facts and Problems* (1930), Vol. I, p. 354, and John Dover Wilson, *Essential Shakespeare* (1932), p. 102, although differing on many points, both very positively assume that it was.

[7] This is also the view taken by the modern historian; see J. H. Ramsay, *Lancaster and York, 1399-1485* (1892).

forth, and I recall the fact that Shakespeare had begun by staging that awful example.

King Henry VI

In his trilogy of Henry VI Shakespeare had indeed given a shocking picture of confusion, hatred, bloodshed, treachery. Henry VI is a good and pious young man, but he is unworldly, more at home with his books than among men; the kingship weighs heavily upon him, and he sighs for the lot of the simple husbandman; and so under him the forces of evil have free play. Shakespeare judges his kings; and not only by their human qualities, but by their fitness for the exalted office, which makes demands of its own. It is not only, however, the personal failure of the youthful King which brings about disaster. It is, above all, the far-reaching effect of the subversion of order inherent in the deposition of Richard II. It is the struggle between Lancaster and York, all descendants of Edward III (Richard's grandfather), among whom Henry VI is not, after all, indisputably pre-eminent. It is the inner division of the dynasty itself. It is all that which leads to that terrible civil war and to the impending destruction of all human values and of law. The King himself was fated to hear a father, over the dead body of his son, bewailing this dissolution of society:

> O! Pity, God, this miserable age.
> What stratagems, how fell, how butcherly,
> Erroneous, mutinous, and unnatural,
> This deadly quarrel daily doth beget!
> O boy! thy father gave thee life too soon,
> And hath bereft thee of thy life too late.

To be born is in that juncture a misfortune, and to die, a blessing. . . .

King Richard III

The terrible time Shakespeare depicted in *King Henry VI* culminates in Richard III, the misshapen tyrant, the murderer of Henry VI's son, of the small sons of his own brother Edward IV, and of one after the other of his favourites and henchmen—the virtuoso of crime. The King, chuckling over the successes of his simulations and the gullibility of his victims, relishing a sense of power when the sister of the murdered boy princes, though shrinking from their assassin, consents to become his wife, is in many ways a figure of melodrama, and indeed the entire play, with its violent contrasts and hammering verse, vigorously proceeding on its headlong way, clearly belongs—however strikingly different in this respect from the rambling construction of the three parts of *Henry VI*—to Shakespeare's early period. Yet it is a powerful piece of work.

In the last act, on the night before the decisive battle, Richmond, the heir of both York and Lancaster, and destined to become Henry VII, is shown to us refreshed by the quiet sleep of a good conscience; Richard, on the contrary, who believed his royal dignity gave him, in the hour of crisis, a claim to God's support, is startled by the apparitions of all whose deaths he had compassed. Nevertheless, on the battlefield he behaves with courage, until defeat overtakes him. His horse is slain. "A horse! a horse! my kingdom for a horse!" In that last cry, so miraculously dramatic, is expressed Shakespeare's profound sense of the relative nature of all earthly power. After that career of reckless ambition Richard is ready to give its great object, his kingdom, for a horse to save his life.

King Henry V

Of the earlier play's final sense of relativity there is little trace in *King Henry V*. Glorification of the man of action as the ideal king is the dominant note. Many admirers of Shakespeare have felt some embarrassment with respect to this play. Shake-

speare's detractors—for he, too, has detractors (there are
Tolstoy and Shaw, the improvers of the world, who measure
literature by ethical, or puritan, or practical-progressive,
standards)—his detractors fasten upon *Henry V* with zest.

Taken by itself the sketch of the leader of men is masterly.

> Gloucester, 'tis true that we are in great danger;
> The greater therefore should our courage be.

The battle of Agincourt in the fourth act, which opens with
these manly, clear-toned lines, constitutes the climax of the
play, and Henry appears as a born ruler, a true commander,
quick, firm, sure. A man who knows how to speak to his men
to win them. Not a despot, not a despiser of his subjects; on
the contrary, his influence, the impression he makes, proceed
from his humanity. He can, when talking with the soldiers,
joke about his kingship (the sense of relative values after all!)
It is an anonymous conversation, in the dark of night, when
he makes the round of the watches. He says: ". . . the king is
but a man, as I am: the violet smells to him as it doth to me,"
etc.

But even in the light of day, when the Welshman Fluellen
permits himself familiarly to express his delight that the King
does not think it beneath him to wear the leek, he replies in
homely fashion:

> I wear it for a memorable honour;
> For I am Welsh, you know, good countryman.

What a contrast when Shakespeare pictures the French! It
is in itself an indication of a typically historical awareness that
he found this contrast worth noting. After their defeat it is an
added bitterness to the herald of the French to see nobles and
commoners lying pell-mell on the field. Henry, on the contrary, in addressing the men before the battle (a rhetorical
masterpiece, that little speech, to electrify an audience of
soldiers—and of theatre-goers!) had said:

> We few, we happy few, we band of brothers;
> For he to-day that sheds his blood with me

> Shall be my brother; be he ne'er so vile,
> This day shall gentle his condition:
> And gentlemen in England now a-bed,
> Shall think themselves accurs'd they were not here.

The *appearance*, then, is there, and it never misses its effect on the stage. But as for the *essence*, it leaves one cold, doubtful, irritated even. For what purpose all that energy and that eloquence? What do they signify? Shakespeare seems to want us to regard it all as something very high and noble, but in spite of the religious flavour with which he has permeated Henry's utterances, in spite of the insistence with which he pictures him as seeking what is good and right in the eyes of God, now with the help of the clergy, then in his personal prayers or in his communings with himself, one cannot help feeling that this war was no more than a recklesss, frivolous, and fundamentally selfish undertaking.

That unctuous and would-be historical oration of the Archbishop of Canterbury in the first act, concluding with an assurance to the King's conscience that he is about to pursue a rightful claim, does not for a moment carry conviction. The impression of insincerity is thus created right from the beginning. It is strengthened by the incident of the traitors. Henry's behaviour may look very fine—at once severe and mild, each quality accurately distributed; in short, a pattern of royal justice—but one cannot guard oneself against the suspicion of calculation, and the less so because the traitors have been touched off with too careless a brush; the poet is less than fair to them.

King Henry IV

The character of Henry V had been carefully prepared by Shakespeare in the two parts of *King Henry IV*. The Prince of Wales makes a prominent appearance in both plays. He is then the loose-living youth, a disappointment to his father. Only compare him with that other Harry, the ardent fighter Hotspur, son to the Earl of Northumberland (from the literary point of view a splendid character!), how sorry a figure does Prince Hal cut, drinking and gambling in Doll Tearsheet's inn with the gang of rakes and pickpockets of whom Falstaff is the chief.

But from the beginning Shakespeare had the conception (indeed he found it ready-made in the popular legend) of the gifted youth whose wildness is only evidence of his abundant vitality and who will prove completely equal to the responsibility of power.

I confess to a feeling that the contemptible quality of the young man's chosen companions is a bar to appreciation of his person. The critics have told us that in contemplating Falstaff we must suspend the working of our moral feelings. I am afraid the demand is too much for me. Falstaff, however amusing, however incredibly alive and in his wit at times profoundly wise, remains a swindler, a braggart, and a coward. [8]

However, I am now after data to define more closely Shakespeare's attitude toward kingship, and for this purpose his treatment of Prince Hal's association with that raffish fat man is certainly rewarding. It demonstrates his sure feeling for the human quality of the occupant of the high office.

The most priceless scene of all, in which at moments Shakespeare seems to make dangerously free with majesty, is the one in which Falstaff, his head covered with a cushion for the crown, acts the part of Henry IV and addresses his young friend in fatherly fashion; after which the roles are reversed and Hal, now the King, scolds Falstaff with much harsher fatherly authority. In fact, the dignity of the royal office comes out of this scene unscathed. Unexpectedly, and with inimitable tact, it

---

[8] Bradley, in his *Oxford Lectures on Poetry* (1909), says that in Falstaff we admire "the bliss of freedom gained in humour." As a matter of fact, the effect of the character probably rests upon that illusion of amoral freedom, but cool reflection will lead to the conclusion that it *is* an illusion. The attitude postulated reminds one of that of Lamb toward Congreve, Wycherley, and company. Lamb argued that one need not be offended by their immorality since their world is but a theatrical world and has nothing in common with the true world, where standards of good and evil hold sway. Macaulay disposed of that argument in a well-known essay occasioned by Leigh Hunt's edition of Restoration dramatists.

is even brought out more clearly in this light-hearted fooling. The equilibrium is perfect.

In other passages, however, it seems to me that Shakespeare's freedom of mind as a creator of human beings was hampered by his respect for the office of king, and the damage done to the character of Henry is irreparable.

The first passage that I shall mention is an early one, where the Prince, having been shown for the first time in his familiarity with those scoundrelly companions, is made to reassure the public (for that is obviously what is intended by that monologue) and lets it be understood that he knows very well what he is doing. He compares himself to the sun, hiding behind clouds, but due soon to reappear to the greater delight of mankind.

> So, when this loose behaviour I throw off,
> And pay the debt I never promised,
> By how much better than my word I am,
> By so much shall I falsify men's hopes;
> And like bright metal on a sullen ground,
> My reformation, glittering o'er my fault,
> Shall show more goodly and attract more eyes
> Than that which hath no foil to set it off.
> I'll so offend to make offence a skill;
> Redeeming time when men think least I will.

The second passage is that of the famous, or I may say, the notorious, "repudiation" of Falstaff. King Henry IV is dead. Prince Hal's boon companions are elated at the news and hurry toward London.

> God save thy grace, King Hal! my royal Hal! . . .
> God save thee, my sweet boy!

So cries Falstaff when the youthful king and his following, the Lord Chief Justice among them, appear in "A public Place near Westminster Abbey".

K. Hen. V. My lord chief justice, speak to that vain man.
Ch. Just.   Have you your wits? know you what 'tis you speak?

Fal.	My king! my love! I speak to thee, my heart!
K. Hen. V.	I know thee not, old man: fall to thy prayers;
	How ill white hairs become a fool and jester!
	I have long dream'd of such a kind of man,
	So surfeit-swell'd, so old, and so profane;
	But being awak'd, I do despise my dream.

The scene is dramatically effective to a degree, but it sets on Henry an uneffaceable stamp of hypocrisy. Combined with the cold-blooded calculation implicit in the first-quoted passage—all the more repulsive because it concerns something so apparently spontaneous as the merrymaking of a lad loving a spree—this proceeding of the freshly-made king, too, casts on the conduct of the ripened man a most disagreeable light.

And throughout *King Henry V*, when we turn to that play again, we can now see a striving after effect, and the arts of the demagogue, where the poet invites us to admire greatness of soul and wisdom.

King Henry V (Once More)

In the third act of *King Henry V* the King summons the French governor of Harfleur to surrender the town. He dwells on his desire to save the citizenry from the horrors that would be the inevitable sequel to a capture of the town by storm. In advance he lays the responsibility upon the defenders. Now, it is true enough that in the Middle Ages, and in Shakespeare's own day, the soldiery were not, in such a case, to be restrained. It might be said, therefore, that we are faced here by one of the hard facts of life as it was then, and that the realist Shakespeare did no more than accept it. Yet in the King's speech one is struck, as in the incident of the traitors in the second act— and this without the author having apparently intended or even noticed it—by an intolerable self-assurance, and what is worse, cleverness in casting himself for the generous role. [9]

[9] The commentators are often all too anxious to whitewash Henry V both in his princely and his royal phase. Mr. Losey (who edited *King Henry IV* for one of the modern editions of Shakespeare's works), for

How is it that Shakespeare, who elsewhere was able so impressively to make us accept a higher than worldly wisdom, did not here rise above an uncritical glorification of his practical-minded and self-confident man of action?

It should first of all be remembered that Shakespeare, whose powers of feeling and of creation covered so enormous an expanse, who, moreover, never ceased intellectually and sentimentally to develop, should not be judged by one play, or identified with the mood prevailing in one play. *King Henry V* was the last English history play he wrote—it was the last perhaps for the very reason that the culmination to which the genre had led left *him*, too, in his heart of hearts, unsatisfied. Perhaps it is his own criticism of the glorification of the active and triumphant victor, of the man whom the crowd hailed for his success, that soon afterwards, in *Julius Caesar*, led him to present such a loving study of Brutus, of the unpractical idealist, great in spite of his incapacity to understand, or to get hold of, his fellow men, great in spite of his dismal failure. *Hamlet*, too, in which the chief character is ruined by the impotence of his superior mind, of his fecund imagination, of his oversensitive heart, in the face of the task imposed upon him by the stark and pitiless reality of life— *Hamlet*, too, was not far off.

---

example, finds something to admire in the Prince of Wales's seeking "low company": it is the young man brimming over with life who prefers intercourse with "the people" because it can teach him more than would the chilly sphere of the court. As if Falstaff and his crew were "the people"! They were highwaymen and gamblers.

The same Mr. Losey sees in the King's fatherly remonstrances to his son (the true King's this time: *King Henry IV, First Part*, Act iii, Scene ii) cold-blooded calculation and in that relationship finds the superiority on the Prince's side. To my mind the genuine and vigorous personality of Henry IV comes out convincingly in that scene; striking, in particular, are the reminiscences to which, in the softened mood of the moment, he abandons himself. But to a certain type of Englishman Henry V must be in all circumstances the ideal figure.

ch in times of heightened national consciousnes
always made so powerful an appeal to the Englis
caricature of Joan of Arc served up in *King Henr*
rt, is so repulsive that this is one of the reason
later generation refused to accept the play
e's work. And indeed it is hard to believe th
e in a later phase of his development could ha
e crudity of that early effort. But the way in whi
ly stage he simply followed the current Engli
ion, the war propaganda of the evil-minded wit
e less typical of a certain feature of his personali
ench generally his sketches are always in tune w
rejudice, extraordinarily clever no doubt, done w
ch, but never rising above national bias. Charact
sarcasm Joan of Arc herself is made to utter (m
ously really):

one like a Frenchman: turn, and turn again!

is especially in *Henry V* that the French are depic
terly fashion, but always to make the manly and ma
rity of the English king come out the more brillia
boastings and at the same time their fears when
out him, their incorrigible frivolity, are irresis
g, but for all that these traits remain within
s of a convention, and the poet, who at other time
o look at life and at human beings with so fre
rating an eye, here shows himself blinkered.

SHAKESPEARE AND THE PEOPLE

ar I have sketched the conservative, the assenting f
hakespeare's mind in relation to kingship, war, patri
n be observed equally well in his attitude toward the
ses. He does not merely indulge in generalities abo
essity of a stable social order.
t seems to me unnecessary (although it has frequent
ne) to depict Shakespeare as a hardened aristocrat
Julius Caesar he makes Caesar wrinkle his nose at the

SHAKESPEARE'S ACCEPTANCE OF SOCIAL
ARRANGEMENTS (WAR AND PATRIOTISM)

The above considerations, I think, touch the core of the poet's
being. But it is not on that account less necessary to observe
that this peculiar quality of *Henry V* is at the same time connected with a profound and permanent feature of Shakespeare's
attitude toward public affairs, toward the subject matter, in
other words, that he has in common with the historian.

Shakespeare had nothing of the reformer. Tolstoy and Shaw,
blind as they were to his greatness, did perceive *that* rightly
enough. He accepted the world's order as constituted, and
what he took to be its reflection in human society. In that order,
as we know, the ruler's obligation had its appointed place, a
moral obligation, an obligation with respect to God, but his
authority nevertheless remained part of the unalterable order
fixed of old. In *Henry V* Shakespeare pictured the social order
with the help of yet another image than that of the firmament
(employed in *Troilus and Cressida*).

Says the Archbishop of Canterbury:

> . . . heaven [doth] divide
> The state of man in divers functions,
> Setting endeavour in continual motion;
> To which is fixed, as an aim or butt,
> Obedience: for so work the honey-bees,
> Creatures that by a rule in nature teach
> The act of order to a peopled kingdom.
> They have a king and officers of sorts;
> Where some, like magistrates, correct at home,
> Others, like merchants, venture trade abroad,
> Others, like soldiers, armed in their stings,
> Make boot upon the summer's velvet buds;
> Which pillage they with merry march bring home
> To the tent-royal of their emperor:
> Who, busied in his majesty, surveys
> The singing masons building roofs of gold,

The civil citizens kneading up the honey,
The poor mechanic porters crowding in
Their heavy burdens at his narrow gate,
The sad-ey'd justice, with his surly hum,
Delivering o'er to executors pale
The lazy yawning drone.

This passage is not original. It follows Lyly's *Euphues and His England*, that too-famous book of 1580, whose ornate and hyperingenious style exerted so much influence over that generation, and over Shakespeare. But independently of Lyly (who was not himself, in fact, the first to use the comparison of the bees), Shakespeare's conception of human society was a static one; all thought of development or progress was alien to his mind, and so consequently was all desire for, all belief in, change. Thus Shakespeare accepted war, too, as a condition inherent in our humanity. No doubt he postulated a just war; but this justice was tested by the most conventional rules of the game of kings, laws of inheritance, honour, and such like; these rules satisfied, king and people could give themselves up whole-heartedly to the joys of conquest and glory. Through-out Shakespeare's work it is possible to trace that state of mind.

When we hear the business of war discussed slightingly, it is the sour Thersites speaking, the keen but crooked mind that likes to crab everything ("Good Thersites, come in and rail," Patroclus says laughingly).

Here is such patchery, such juggling, and such knavery! all the argument is a cuckold and a whore [this is all Thersites leaves of that famed Trojan war]; a good quarrel to draw emulous factions and bleed to death upon. Now, the dry serpigo on the subject! and war and lechery confound all!

That concentrated bitterness, too, Shakespeare was able to feel with his imagination, but that he regarded it as a whisper of the Evil One appears from the fact that (even in this play of *Troilus and Cressida*, in which one senses his own mood

---

Shakespe

must have been
into the mouth
differently does t
of war! Nothing b
Fortinbras," the N
thousand soldiers
patch of ground."
admiration.

Examples gros
Witness this a
Led by a delica
Whose spirit wi
Makes mouths a
Exposing what is
To all that fortun
Even for an egg-sh
. . . to my shame,
The imminent deat
That, for a fantasy
Go to their graves li
Whereon the number
Which is not tomb en
To hide the slain . . .

It is always necessary to gu
error of indiscriminately ascri
voiced by his characters. Perhaps
image of the beehive occurs in a
Canterbury, and most certainly
passage just quoted is to be
profoundly shaken mood, in which
up to "bloody" deeds. Yet I ven
utterances generally agree with Sha
society.

In the English history plays he al
with a satisfaction unmarred by refl
battles in which the French are defea
scruple. This is the spirit that anima

E.H.

---

through whic
this play has
public. The
VI, First P
for which
Shakespear
Shakespear
repeated th
at that ea
interpretat
is none th
Of the Fr
English p
a sure to
istic is a
incongru

But i
in a ma
superio
Their
talk al
amusi
bound
able
pene

So f
of S
It c
clas
ne

do
in

of the mob. It is true that the passage is not singular: Shakespeare's own sense of smell must have been keen. It is at any rate undeniable that he liked to show up men of the people in their stupidity and clumsiness. The ducal company in *Midsummer Night's Dream* makes mercilessly merry over the antics that Bottom and his fellow handicraftsmen perform in such deadly earnest. Audrey, the clumsy peasant girl in *As You Like It*, may have a touch of the pathetic in her callow innocence, but nobody, not even her creator, takes her seriously, and the last we hear about her is Touchstone's request to the Duke to be allowed to marry her—in this strain: ". . . an ill-favoured thing, sir, but mine own: a poor humour of mine, sir, to take that that no man else will." The masterly little thumbnail sketch of the old nurse in *Romeo and Juliet* is strikingly unkind. True, over against these, characters of a different stamp can be placed. For instance, in *King Lear*, the servant who has the courage to protest when Cornwall is about to pull out Gloucester's eyes; or, in *As You Like It* once more, Adam, the old serving man, who sticks to Orlando in his misfortunes and offers him his savings; in his turn, when their journey proves too much for the feeble old man, Orlando carries him on his back. Here, of course, it should be remembered that the aristocratic code is always ready to acknowledge the virtue of faithfulness in a servant.

One hesitates what to conclude, but what must strike every reader of Shakespeare—and in my argument it has obvious significance—is his consistent lack of sympathy for popular movements or for any meddling with public affairs on the part of the multitude or even of the middle class. Anything in that line he treats with distaste and scorn.

In Dogberry and Verges, that precious pair of self-important but endlessly blundering constables of the civic guard in *Much Ado About Nothing*, ridicule is thrown not only on small-town middle-class men, but on the entire institution they represent. When, in *Richard III*, the King and his henchman Buckingham explain to the Lord Mayor of London how they were compelled to the killing of Hastings by the victim's (purely fictitious) attempts on their own lives, the crass stupidity with which the representative of burgherdom allows himself to be bamboozled is no less striking than the false scoundrelism of the highborn murderers.

The clearest evidence, however (although even this is not always interpreted alike in the countless speculations about Shakespeare's political sentiments by modern critics), is afforded by the set scenes of riotous, or at least politically excited, crowds in *Henry IV*, in *Julius Caesar*, and in *Coriolanus*. At every new reading one is amazed at the brilliant competence of those scenes. The arts of the popular orator, the reactions of the mob—how accurately have they been observed and with what faultless efficiency noted down. The historic sense is here very manifest. But to me there can be no doubt that observation and execution were inspired by hostility.

Jack Cade in King Henry VI

Hear the followers of Jack Cade. Says John: ". . . it was never merry world in England since gentlemen came up."

"O miserable age!" George echoes. "Virtue is not regarded in handicrafts-men."

And John once more: ". . . it is said, 'Labour in thy vocation,' which is as much to say as, let the magistrates be labouring men; and therefore should we be magistrates."

This sample of crooked logic sets the tone at once. Cade himself, who pretends to be of the royal blood, talks even more wildly: "There shall be in England," he promises his followers, "seven halfpenny loaves sold for a penny; the three-hooped pot shall have ten hoops; and I will make it a felony to drink small beer. All the realm shall be in common, and [he does not forget himself!] in Cheapside shall my palfrey go to grass." To death with all lawyers, cries one among the mob, and Cade, for his part, inveighs against the rule of parchment. "Away!" he commands a little later on, "burn all the records of the realm: my mouth shall be the parliament of England." This is indeed the revolution touched off in its deepest essence. Cade is also shown as the fanatic of equality when he sentences Chatham's clerk for being able to read and write and for possessing a book with red lettering. Lord Say is a traitor: doesn't he know French? The scene of his being convicted can serve for a satire on all brutal revolutionary trials, but it is especially the illiterate at whom the satire digs. And by what means does old Lord Clifford in the end succeed in detaching the people from the impostor? Not by rational argument, but by appealing to their feelings of loyalty to the veritable King, Henry VI, and above all by working on their hatred and fear of the French, against whom only the true blood can protect them (and, too, he offers them a chance of winning rank and spoils in France under his leadership).

It is not only, then, that Shakespeare condemns Jack Cade's rebellion; that he does so is only natural. But he does not evince the slightest sympathy for the groping aspirations that were behind it; he is silent about the distress that gave rise to it; he makes it, in all its manifestations, silly and foolish.

Julius Caesar

Everybody knows the crowd in *Julius Caesar* and remembers how it let itself be swept off its feet, first by Brutus, then by Mark Antony. Brutus impresses the people by his grave and noble personality, but so little do they understand the motives of the high-principled republican that in order to show their enthusiasm they wish to crown *him*. But now the unscrupulous Mark Antony manages to rouse them to the pitch of frenzy. Soon they are all impatience to wreak their fury on Brutus, whom they had cheered but a moment before; Caesar's avenger has to call them back in order to serve up to them the argument that is to bring them over to his side for good: he had begun with an allusion to Caesar's will, but they had forgotten all about it in their excitement. How they now love to hear that Caesar has left a large part of his fortune to the people! "Mischief, thou art afoot," Mark Antony exclaims as he remains behind by himself. And that too is brought before our eyes in the biting little scene wherein the raving citizens stop a gentleman to fire the maddest questions at him. When it appears, after some rather caustic answers, which have not exactly pacified the hotheads, that his name is Cinna, there is an outcry:

Second Citizen.   Tear him to pieces; he's a conspirator.
Cinna.   I am Cinna the poet, I am Cinna the poet.
Fourth Citizen.   Tear him for his bad verses, tear him for his bad verses.
Cinna.   I am not Cinna the conspirator.
Second Citizen.   It is no matter, his name's Cinna; pluck but his name out of his heart, and turn him going.
Third Citizen.   Tear him, tear him!

Coriolanus

There is one among the Roman plays, *Coriolanus*, in which the problem of aristocracy versus democracy is posed more directly—for what dominates the interest in *Julius Caesar* is, after all, the conflict between aristocracy and autocracy. *Julius Caesar* is perhaps the first of Shakespeare's works that can, without qualifications, be called great. It opens the poet's richest period. *Coriolanus* was written eight years later, after the great tragedies, to which it can be said in a sense still to belong. No other work supplies so much relevant material to the discussion of Shakespeare's feelings toward the people, about his aristocratic, or antidemocratic, attitude.

Caius Marcius, the son of the noble lady Volumnia, is a formidable warrior, and at the same time, a despiser of the plebs. A bitter social struggle is raging in Rome. The plebeians want to have corn at a lower price than that fixed by the Senate. Old Menenius, a wise man in spite of his somewhat wordy and jolly manner, tells them the parable of the stomach and the limbs—again a comparison in which the social order appears as a thing fixed forever and the poor are taught that they must have patience. The story makes a profound impression, until the hot-blooded Caius Marcius enters and starts inveighing against the plebeians' impudence in criticizing a decision of the Senate. Meanwhile the Senate, to the intense indignation of Caius Marcius, appoints two tribunes to look after the interests of the people; these men, Brutus and Sicinius, regard Marcius as the principal adversary. Marcius, however, now wins new glory by conquering Corioli, the capital of the hereditary enemy, the Volsces, and the Senate, honouring him with the name of Coriolanus, elects him to be consul—an election, however, still to be confirmed by the people.

With the greatest reluctance, but encouraged by Volumnia, Menenius, and other friends, Coriolanus submits to ancient custom and goes to the market place to beg for votes. With thinly disguised contempt he assures the voters that it is only for the sake of their votes that he has exposed his life, and his begging cry: "Your voices . . . your voices," sounds like mockery. To bare his body in order to display his scars—that, too, required by custom—is a humiliation to which he cannot stoop. But his heroic deeds count, and the election *is* confirmed. Soon afterwards, however, while Coriolanus is being installed in the Senate, the slow-thinking crowd is beginning to realize it has been insulted; the tribunes stir up the ill feeling; and on Coriolanus's return to the Forum, his right to the office is called into question. In spite of the attempts of Menenius and some others to hold him back, he replies with bitter taunts, carefully noted down by the tribunes. At last he draws his sword, a crime for which he is exiled from the city by the tribunes, in the name of the people. Coriolanus receives that sentence with heartfelt bitterness. "I banish you"! is the rejoinder he hurls at the crowd, with scathing remarks about the reek of their breaths.

> . . . Despising,
> For you, the city, thus I turn my back:
> There is a world elsewhere.

And indeed he makes his opponents feel it. He goes straight to the enemy. The chieftain of the Volsces, Aufidius, joyfully takes him in and entrusts to him the command of a fresh attack on Rome. Rome is shaken; people and tribunes tremble at the imminent danger. They humble themselves before

Menenius, imploring him to go to Coriolanus and prevail upon
him to forbear in his revenge. Coriolanus rejects his old
friend's plea. When, however, Coriolanus's wife, and particularly, his mother, come to add their supplications, he cannot
resist any longer.

> . . . O my mother! mother! O!
> You have won a happy victory to Rome;
> But, for your son, believe it, O! believe it,
> Most dangerously you have with him prevail'd,
> If not most mortal to him. But let it come.

His was true foresight. Aufidius turns against him, and he is
killed by the Volsces.

The critics—as I hinted before—do not agree in their
interpretations of this powerful tragedy. Coleridge says that it
illustrates the wonderful philosophical impartiality of Shakespeare's political drama, and Hazlitt, in the same vein, argues
that here all is said that can be said both for the aristocrat and
for the democrat. Brandes, on the contrary, is struck by "the
physical aversion to the people's atmosphere" and by "the
absence of any humane attention for the oppression of the
poor"; it all turns on the divine greatness of the hero Marcius.
Brandes believes that Shakespeare did detest the latter's
betrayal of Rome, but of criticism of his earlier behaviour as
the virulent hater of the people he finds not a trace. Shakespeare's view of life in this play is, according to Brandes, that
"round the lonely great ones of this earth there is inevitably
a conspiracy of envy and hatred, hatched by the base and
common sort."

M. W. MacCallum,[10] overseeing these pronouncements in
1910, attempts to prove the truth of Coleridge's view. But when
he admits that Shakespeare will always, in other works no less
than in *Coriolanus*, picture the multitude as changeable, blind,
and unfit to govern, he has practically given way to those who
see in Shakespeare the aristocrat and antidemocrat. That this
does not involve hatred, that Brandes is wrong when he ascribes
to the poet the feelings of physical loathing expressed by his

[10] *Shakespeare's Roman Plays and Their Background.*

dramatic personages, may be true; I myself noted above that Shakespeare, to use MacCallum's words, "is kind enough to individual representatives" of the people and that "he certainly believes in the sacred obligation of governing them for their good"; even so, the question of what must be understood by this good that is to be promoted by the people's governors continues to present a complication of problems. And the mentality here sketched is in any case a typically aristocratic one. The effect of this on the historic truth of Shakespeare's picture of the plebs I shall indicate in a moment; my conclusion now is only, not that Brandes takes the right view, but that at least Shakespeare's politics are not so philosophically impartial as Coleridge would have us believe, and also that, if he says all that can be said on behalf of the aristocrats, he certainly does not—as Hazlitt asserts—say all on behalf of the democrats.

But indeed one has only to read the play. It is not that Shakespeare unreservedly exalts Coriolanus before he committed his high treason. Brandes commits a double error. The treason is, in Shakespeare's eyes, a much less heinous crime than we moderns would expect; but in any case the poet makes it proceed naturally from the defect of character shown from the beginning as the root of the tragic conflict: his hero's stubbornness and lack of self-restraint.

The conflict is not between two political attitudes, not between aristocrat and democrat. That struggle is no more that the occasion. In itself it did not interest Shakespeare overmuch, so confidently did he take his stand with one side. Volumnia, Menenius, the senators, all hold the same view, in no wise differing from Coriolanus's own, of the stupid people, the crafty and ignoble tribunes. Only, Volumnia and Menenius and the other friends deplore the reckless, the all too outspoken, the imprudent behaviour of the man who seemed destined to become the soul of their party. Coriolanus is great; he is noble. His nature is too noble for the world.

This is what Menenius says of him. He cannot stoop to compromise. Allard Pierson, the great Dutch critic of the late nineteenth century, compared him, very aptly, with Alceste in Molière's *Misanthrope*. Coriolanus cannot conceal the contempt that he (with all of his class) feels for the plebeians. Before Corioli, cowards as they are, they had left him in the lurch: their stupidity is equalled only by their unreliability. Even more profound is the loathing he feels for the tribunes, who flatter the crowd the better to nurse their own ambitions. Even among the plebeians some seem to take this view. Two servants laying cushions in the Capitol discuss the situation. One thinks that Coriolanus goes too far, not only does he abstain from flattery of the people, he seems wilfully to seek their displeasure and hatred. The other cannot help feeling respect for a man whose claims rest on honourable deeds: ". . . his ascent is not by such easy degrees as those who, having been supple and courteous to the people, bonneted, without any further deed to have them at all into their estimation and report." When in the fatal dispute the tribune Brutus condescendingly admits that Coriolanus has served Rome well, the latter interjects cuttingly: "What do you prate of service?"

Shakespeare gives a most striking little sketch of the tribunes Brutus and Sicinius, a sketch charged with that active dislike which the true conservative is apt to feel for democratic politicians much more than for the people. Envious and given to intrigue, it is they who goad the hotheaded hero on to his ruin. "Put him to choler straight," is the advice of the one to the other before the fateful encounter, and Menenius's whispers to Coriolanus—"Nay, temperately; your promise!" and "Is this the promise that you made your mother?"—cannot save him from himself.

There is no lack of writers who delight in the picture of false, petty, and pushing demagogues drawn by Shakespeare in Sicinius and Brutus, maintaining at the same time that nothing can be deduced from this picture as to Shakespeare's feelings about true democracy. These writers only betray their own conservative prejudice. The tribunes in *Coriolanus* are most certainly instructive about Shakespeare's antidemocratic sentiments—not, of course, because Shakespeare detests demagogues: everybody does! But because Shakespeare cannot view the advocates of the plebs as anything but abject demagogues.

Occasionally, nevertheless, the tribunes do say something of what they might have said for democracy, such as Hazlitt asserted Shakespeare made them do consistently. So Brutus snaps at Coriolanus:

> You speak o' the people,
> As if you were a god to punish, not
> A man of their infirmity.

One more word, and one that indeed cuts deeply, is spoken by Sicinius in reply to a senator who warned him that by undoing the election of Coriolanus to the consulate he risked overthrowing the city:

> What is the city but the people?

The citizens at once shout their assent:

> True,
> The people are the city.

But Coriolanus takes up the senator's warning and exclaims:

> That is the way to lay the city flat;
> To bring the roof to the foundation,
> And bury all, which yet distinctly ranges,
> In heaps and piles of ruin.

We can see in this exchange the contrast between a humanitarian, social, democratic ideal, in which pride of place gives way to the interest of the community, that is to say, of the human beings composing it; and a conservative and authoritarian ideal, in which the state, apart from its citizens and their needs and desires, is regarded as the primary interest. Here we get a glimpse of that complication of problems of which I spoke; and it is, at any rate, beyond all doubt that the second of the two alternatives is the one inspiring *Coriolanus*—insofar as the play can be said to be inspired by any political notion. The citizens had bluntly stated their needs at the outset, but neither Coriolanus nor Menenius and Volumnia give these the slightest attention, and the motif soon recedes from view. It is the state that is important, the well-being of Rome as an independent entity over against the Volsces. And just as in the case of Jack Cade's rebellion, it is the foreign danger that becomes, toward the end, the ruling factor, making even the plebeians change their minds.

So we see Shakespeare once again as a son of his country and of his age. Among the most influential and intellectual classes, newly awakened national consciousness, and pride in their own state and monarchy maintaining themselves against great Continental powers, were infinitely stronger considerations than those of social betterment or internal politics. It might be thought that one outcome of such an attitude must have been detestation of Coriolanus's treason. Naturally the deed is condemned: it is the last and worst result of the hero's defect of character, of his pride, his inability to observe measure, and it leads directly to his ruin. But it does not detract from his nobility, which is acknowledged even by the Volsces after they have killed him. To understand this it is essential, once more, to remember the many instances Shakespeare's age still offered to the observing eye of great noblemen deserting to their country's enemy out of wounded pride, or because they considered themselves wronged. It was an age of suddenly erupted national passion, but the code of honour of the great still admitted of a good deal of trifling with national solidarity.

I cannot take leave of *Coriolanus* without stating (although the remark is implied in what was said before) that it is a history play in a sense differing from the English dramas. *Julius Caesar* in this respect may be said to mark a transition. In the English history plays the *history* constitutes the real subject matter—this is true even of *Richard II* and *Richard III*, in which the persons of the kings occupy so striking a position. *Coriolanus* is more similar to the great tragedies Shakespeare had just written. Its real subject is the hero's ruin, due to the defects of his heroic personality. The history, however loving the care with which it has been treated, is an ornamental dressing.

The Tempest

He who would try to deduce Shakespeare's political philosophy from *The Tempest* must be sadly lacking in feeling for poetry; even some sense of humour should suffice to make one desist from the attempt. And yet it is impossible, when considering Shakespeare's attitude towards authority, towards the people, or towards social problems, to keep completely silent about that charming fantasy with which he concluded his literary career.

An unambiguous answer to our questions, a coherent system, we must not expect to find. What will be revealed to us is Shakespeare's mind playing with all sorts of ideas on these matters, and now and then we shall be able to surprise his involuntary reactions.

Among the varied company that, after the shipwreck caused by Prospero's magic, comes ashore on his bewitched island, the good Gonzalo is the most inclined to reflection. He expounds to his companions in the adventure how *he* would arrange matters were it given to him to rule over the island. A complete Utopia, which Shakespeare had found in Montaigne: everything in common, no riches and no poverty, no contracts and no law of inheritance, neither field nor vineyard enclosed, no trade, no magistrates, no writings, neither trade nor handicraft.

> . . . all men idle, all;
> And women too, but innocent and pure;
> No sovereignty—

It does not mean much that the bad men, Sebastian and Antonio, scoff at these imaginings, or that King Alonzo, who has in the past plotted with Antonio against Prospero, does not think them worth more than a shrug. But the contrast pointed by reality, by the reality of the fantasy, by the island such as Prospero has made it, is striking.

For Prospero, the best and wisest of men, does not scruple to exercise authority (sovereignty, as the poet calls it), nor does he shrink from resorting to harsh methods. The monster

Caliban, the slave used for the rougher kind of work, is driven with merciless imprecations and kept in order by his fear of the colics and bellyaches with which the potent magician will punish him in the event of disobedience; even Ariel, the graceful spirit of the air, who at Prospero's command directs the breezes and with their music attracts the shipwrecked men and soothes them to sleep, is forced to stay in Prospero's service only by the cruellest threats. Prospero, like his creator, accepts the conditions of our humanity, or rather, of existing social arrangements. When his daughter, Miranda, expresses the horror she feels at the sight of the wicked and common Caliban, he replies with unmitigated matter-of-factness:

> But, as 'tis,
> We cannot miss him: he does make our fire,
> Fetch in our wood; and serves in offices
> That profit us—What ho! slave! Caliban!
> Thou earth, thou! speak.

Did Shakespeare mean Caliban to represent the people, the labouring classes? The passage quoted would almost persuade one to believe it. But in that case Caliban's evil nature, his coarse materialism, his vulgarity, which is such that he will use the human language learned from Prospero only to curse, his superstitiousness, his inaccessibility to arguments other than those of punishment or pain—all this would betray a particularly unpleasant attitude in the poet. Many commentators (and one is reminded of what happened in connection with *Coriolanus*) have done their best to clear "the gentle Shakespeare" from the suspicion.

The most interesting alternative explanation is that Caliban (anagram of Can[n]ibal) represents primitive man, the savage to whom voyages of exploration were just drawing the attention of the European public. As a matter of fact, Caliban is soon shown more particularly in relation to Stephano and Trinculo, the two vulgar types among the shipwrecked, the drunken sailor and the clown; and it is then possible to construct a contrast between the natural barbarian and the dregs of civilization, a contrast in which Caliban really does not come off worst. Even then, however, it is not exactly Shakespeare's "gentleness" that reveals itself. Kreyssig remarks that in presenting his natural man Shakespeare, as it were, by anticipation, rejected Rousseau's conception. Instead of giving way to an optimistic belief in man's innate goodness, which is corrupted only by civilization, Shakespeare drew a repulsive picture of man in his natural condition, his evil proclivities needing to be curbed by a civilized society, by order, by authority. Whether or not this conception actually guided Shakespeare's mind in the creation of Caliban, it is certainly in agreement with the entire spirit of his writings. That man's nature is beset by evil inclinations, which have to be carefully restrained, and that order and punishment are indispensable to that end—Shakespeare has expressed these views not once but countless times.

Nevertheless, Stephano and Trinculo are even more contemptible than Caliban. The monster at first pays divine honours to Stephano, who treats him to wine, but in the long run he turns out to have more common sense than that base pair of topers, and in fact forswears his veneration. Indeed Stephano and Trinculo are no very edifying samples of the society existing outside the bewitched island. Is that the sailor, this drunkard with his bottle, singing songs like "The master, the swabber, the boatswain and I . . ."?

But do not let us make the mistake of wanting to explain everything symbolically. Shakespeare knew well enough that there were better sailors and that "the people," if not portrayed in Caliban, was not fully represented in Stephano and Trinculo either.

One is struck, all the same, by the difference of the treatment Shakespeare meted out, in the denouement of his idyll, to the aristocratic and to the plebeian scoundrels. Both kinds are present. There are not only Caliban, Stephano, and Trinculo; there are also Sebastian and Antonio. In the past Antonio had thrust Prospero out of his lawful inheritance, the duchy of Milan, and now he incites Sebastian to kill his brother, Alonzo, in order to obtain the throne of Naples for himself. The crime is prevented by Ariel. Prospero, who now has them all in his power, does not think of revenge. Under the stress of the helpless condition into which he has manoeuvred them, they show repentance, and this is sufficient for him to forgive them. But does the repentance go more than skin deep? Rather, Antonio and Sebastian, at the moment of punishment, behave defiantly, and once sure of their pardon, they are as breezy and arrogant as ever. Caliban, Stephano, and Trinculo, on the other hand, who also have misbehaved themselves, plotting and committing robberies, are let off less lightly in the hour of retribution. True, they are not punished again, but they are still writhing with the pains already inflicted upon them. While the gentlemen look on, and laugh, they slink away under a shower of hard words to take the loot back to where they found it. "Or stole it, rather," the unsuccessful murderer Sebastian has the impudence to add. Shakespeare clearly uses two measures: his plebeian monster is indeed treated very unfairly in comparison with his aristocratic evildoer.

The impression we already formed of Shakespeare's attitude toward state and society is confirmed. To Shakespeare, state and society were static entities, firmly settled in an order linked to the eternal cosmic order. Labour was the lot of the many, so that the few might be more complete human beings; the authority by which that order was to be protected belonged in the hands of those called to this high task by birth and culture; the task laid obligations on them, but to think that the multitude could call them to account was mere foolishness.

Attitude towards Social Reform

In Shakespeare's system the wretchedness of the poor had its place. Criticism of social conditions, in the sense of an indignant awareness of shortcomings allied to a desire to remedy them, is hardly to be found in the whole of his works. One may think of the starving apothecary in *Romeo and Juliet;* his misery is keenly observed, but it is coolly used to help Romeo to his poison. Or of Hamlet's soliloquy, in which he mentions "The slings and arrows of outrageous fortune":

The oppressor's wrong, the proud man's contumely,
. . . the law's delay,
The insolence of office, and the spurns
That patient merit of the unworthy takes.

An enumeration of social evils—and indeed Shakespeare was not blind, nor did he try to blind himself. But the thought that in a differently arranged state or society men might be spared these trials is utterly foreign to his mind. To him they belong (if I may once more use that expression) to the conditions of our humanity, so much so that half way in his little list (where the dots indicate an excision in my quotation) he mentions the "pangs of dispriz'd love"—all in the same category of inevitability.

I can remember only one passage where a different note is struck. Listen to Lear, in the storm, on the heath:

Poor naked wretches, wheresoe'er you are,
That bide the pelting of this pitiless storm,
How shall your houseless heads and unfed sides,
Your loop'd and window'd raggedness, defend you
From seasons such as these? O! I have ta'en
Too little care of this. Take physic, pomp;
Expose thyself to feel what wretches feel,
That thou mayst shake the superflux to them,
And show the heavens more just.

But if anywhere, then it is here necessary to remember that it is Lear who speaks like this, Lear in his misfortune. The expression of a feeling of kinship in suffering, including even those words "O! I have ta'en—Too little care of this," is as it were wrung from the dramatic situation. The poet's all-embracing imagination could comprehend this too. But it is no more than a cry of anguish, which leads to no consequences in the play and has no place in Shakespeare's philosophy of state and society.

It would be an error to think that the mentality here delineated was the only one possible for men of Shakespeare's age. It reigned supreme, no doubt, in political and social thinking, but not everybody accepted it as wholeheartedly as Shakespeare did; here and there not only blind sufferers but also clear-sighted thinkers contended with it. The Utopias of the age should not, certainly, be regarded as programmes of action, yet in the minds of their devisers they stood for more than Shakespeare was willing to see in that of Montaigne. More, in particular, intended a serious criticism. Erasmus, too, treated kings and their wars with a good deal less resignation than did Shakespeare. The contrast between the acquiescent conservative and the critical reformer is one of all times, and about Shakespeare's place in his generation there can be no doubt.

SHAKESPEARE AND THE PURITANS: HIS RELIGION

It is significant that Shakespeare had no use for the Puritans and liked to ridicule them. The Puritans, certainly, were not first and foremost reformers of state and society, but they regarded these with an independence that was enough to annoy Shakespeare and to rouse his scorn. That traditional order, which was to Shakespeare the immutable setting within which the human drama, the drama of good and evil, was enacted, that order which he respected and loved with all its shadings, its heights and its depths, the Puritans tested, if need be, by a command—to them, of a superior nature; but to Shakespeare, arbitrary, fantastical, arrogant. It is true that neither in *Twelfth Night* nor in *Measure for Measure* did he put the problem in those terms. He girded only against the rejection of joy of life and of natural enjoyment of the senses which struck him in Puritanism.

> Dost thou think, because thou art virtuous,
> there shall be no more cakes and ale?[11]

Of Malvolio, moreover, he made a coxcomb, and of Angelo a hypocrite. That the idealist, that is to say, the man who sets an abstraction above life, who wants to remodel the order in the image of his personal opinion, was not to Shakespeare's liking, so much is in any case clear from that scathing reaction.

[11] *Twelfth Night*, Act II, Scene III.

It will be seen that I do not express the problem of Shakespeare's attitude to Puritanism in religious terms. And indeed I do not think that that was how it presented itself to him. Much has been written about Shakespeare's religion; attempts have been made to drag him in various directions.

Dowden saw in him a Protestant.[12] But what was Protestantism to Dowden? "Energy, devotion to the fact, self-government, tolerance, a disbelief in minute apparatus for the improvement of human character, an indifference to externals in comparison with that which is of the invisible life, and a resolution to judge all things from a purely human standpoint." For the Puritan, for the Calvinist, for the sixteenth-century Protestant, that definition would have been, in essential parts, unacceptable. What Dowden had in mind was the Protestantism of his own day, a bastard of the genuine brand and of the Renaissance. The Renaissance—is not that where we should look for Shakespeare's spiritual home? "The Renaissance," says Croce, "had made earthly life a reality, and that is where he belonged."[13]

In 1922 a Catholic author, Looten, of the Catholic University of Lille, published a little book on Shakespeare's religion. According to him Shakespeare was a Catholic for a good bit of his life; all the first half of his literary output, Looten says, bears witness to this. Not until the closing years of the sixteenth century did the humanistic and Machiavellian influences of the age reduce him to doubt, and it is this that explains the gloomy, the despairing mood of the great tragedies.

No more than the others does this view carry conviction. Familiarity with Catholic attitudes is no doubt unmistakable in Shakespeare's dramas, but this was not as yet anything singular. And the attacks on Catholicism that can be observed later do not denote scepticism; they are rather typically Protestant and are directed against the papacy and the Jesuits. But such attacks were conditioned by the national temper, and even though they were conducted with weapons

[12] Edward Dowden, *Shakespeare, His Mind and Art* (1875).
[13] Cf. notes by Ralli, *A History of Shakespearean Criticism* (1932), Vol. II, p. 391.

taken from the Protestant armoury, they were not necessarily inspired by any distinct religious conviction. That much discussed gloominess of the first years of the new century, moreover, cannot be so lightly equated to despair.

Bradley has made on all this the most penetrating and the most balanced comments. "It does not seem likely that outside his poetry he was a very simple-minded Catholic or Protestant or Atheist, as some have maintained; but we cannot be sure, as with poets like Milton, or Wordsworth, or Shelley we can, that in his works he expressed his deepest and most cherished convictions on ultimate questions, or even that he had any." And Bradley goes on to suggest that one must temporarily suspend one's particular religious faith if one is to undergo to the full the tragic impression of the Shakespearean drama. This impression is made by the representation of human action within the framework of a moral cosmic order. The world is not governed by a blind and indifferent Fate: yet there is not, either, a just dispensation according to which merit is rewarded. By the morality of the cosmic order is meant that this order strives after good, exists through good, and reacts to evil by expelling and destroying it. The process of life nevertheless involves a disturbance of the order; it is attended by violence and entails the ruin and waste of much that is good and noble: this is its tragic aspect. The Shakespearean tragedy, however, is not therefore depressing. In the solution one will always observe the expulsion of evil, at the cost of however much suffering and waste; the assertion of a moral order.

In this view of Shakespeare's attitude toward religion the dogmatic contrasts within the Christian world recede into the background. And indeed it seems possible to me that here, too, Shakespeare's reactions to public life were simply conservative and national, that is to say, that he accepted the Church "as by law established" and detested the Puritans as fanatics and disturbers of the public peace.

PURITAN REACTIONS TO SHAKESPEARE:
TOLSTOY AND CROSBY

Nothing seems more natural, when the above observations
have been made, than that modern puritans and radicals (I
alluded to the fact before) are so often hostile to Shakespeare.
I mentioned Tolstoy. His very shallow and insignificant little
book (by the author of *The Kreutzer Sonata*, not by the author
of *War and Peace!*) is inspired by the Shakespearean criticism
of some nineteenth-century English writers, of Ernest Crosby
more particularly, who himself quotes Edward Carpenter.
Crosby does not go the lengths to which goes Tolstoy, who
writes off the Shakespeare cult as a ridiculous and ephemeral
phenomenon, but he does feel that the poet's lack of understanding of humble folk, or his aversion to them, seriously
detracts from his greatness. This judgment proceeds naturally
from his conviction that democracy, liberalism, faith in
progress, are requisites for the production of great literature;
it is the task of the great writer to lead mankind toward
emancipation. Edward Carpenter's indignation is roused by
Prospero's remark (which I quoted above) on Caliban's usefulness in spite of his repulsive appearance: "Who are you," he
exclaims indignantly, "pouring out sarcasm on him who gets
you bread, who clothes you, who all day and all night slaves
for you obscurely on the earth?"

Shaw

The rejection of Shakespeare by Shaw has its place in this
tradition. I must admit that I can read an early essay of Shaw's
on *Henry IV* with a good deal of agreement. It deals particularly with the figure of Henry V, who, as we know, appears
already in the plays called after his father, and who towards
the end of the second, repudiates Falstaff. One can hardly quite
forgive Shakespeare for the worldly phase in which he tried
to thrust such a jingo hero as his Harry V down our throats.

After so much uncritical acceptance of the conventional and

demagogic hero (even a generally very sensible German like
Kreyssig allowed himself to be swept off his feet and envied
the English for the possession of so patriotic a play; a sensible
German, but one who was strongly moved by the spirit of
1870, so that he could not help thinking the cheap caricature
of the French a wonderful hit), after streams of praise, Shaw's
biting criticism is indeed refreshing.

But when he wrote it, at least he still acknowledged Shakespeare's greatness. Soon he was totally to reject him.

In the whole of Shakespeare not a single hero! Only one
man in all those thirty-six big plays who believes in life,
enjoys life, thinks life worth living, and has a sincere, un-
rhetorical tear dropped over his death-bed; and that
man . . . Falstaff! What a crew they are, these Saturday-to-
Monday athletic stockbroker Orlandos, these villains, fools,
clowns, drunkards, cowards, intriguers, fighters, lovers,
patriots, hypochondriacs who mistake themselves (and are
mistaken by the author) for philosophers, princes without
any sense of public duty, futile pessimists, who imagine they
are confronting a barren and unmeaning world when they are
only contemplating their own worthlessness, self-seekers of
all kinds, keenly observed and masterfully drawn from the
romantic-commercial point of view. . . . Search for states-
manship, or even citizenship, or any sense of the commonwealth, material or spiritual, and you will not find the
making of a decent vestryman or curate in the whole horde.
As for faith, hope, courage, conviction, or any of the true
heroic qualities, you find nothing but death made stage-
sublime, sex made romantic, and barrenness covered up by
sentimentality and the mechanical lilt of blank verse.

After this wholehearted denunciation, of which the final
words are hard to forgive (especially coming from a man who
had elsewhere shown himself sensitive to the delight of the
Shakespearean verse), Shaw points a contrast; and the man he
dares to proclaim truly great, as against the hollow, romantic
Shakespeare, is a Puritan among Puritans.

All that you miss in Shakespeare, you find in Bunyan, to whom the heroic came quite obviously and naturally. . . . "My sword I give to him that shall succeed me in my pilgrimage, and my courage and skill to him that can get it." The heart vibrates like a bell to such an utterance as this. To turn from it to "Out, out, brief candle," and "The rest is silence," and "We are such stuff as dreams are made on, and our little life is rounded by a sleep," is to turn from life, strength, resolution, morning air and eternal youth, to the terrors of a drunken nightmare.

This is no more than letting off steam, I know. It is a scream of hate when understanding fails. Yet I have thought it worth quoting, because it helps to distinguish even more clearly this one aspect of Shakespeare: that his view of life has a repelling effect on the puritan, humourless mentality intent only on reform. To a sober, practical, progressive mind, to a man who regards life as a task to be fulfilled and the world as an ill-arranged muddle that he feels called upon to set right, to such a one Shakespeare is an objectionable, an antisocial, figure— like an artist who in a miserable slum thinks of the picturesque instead of falling to work with statistics and a stethoscope.

Indeed, a plan of improvement in accordance with Shaw's political or scientific principles will not be found in Shakespeare's works. Yet the picturesque effect is far from being all to him. He struggles with life after his own fashion, a purely personal struggle. The social problem does not exist, there is only the moral, and that is to say, the individual problem. The social environment certainly claims attention, for it is part of life. And life in all its forms is given, in its contrasts and unintelligibilities, in its sorrows and its joys, its love and sin, its hatred and its folly, in its light and its dark. Unceasingly changeful, this life is ever the same, glorious and terrible, repellent and beautiful. To every generation and to every human being it is set again to be lived through and to be struggled with, and whatever the puritan or the reformer may think, no wisdom, no faith, and no philosophy will ever succeed in solving its riddle.

A Dutch Marxist's View

In concluding this section I cannot refrain from offering a digression on the Shakespeare interpretation sprung from the brain of a fellow countryman of mine. Theun de Vries belongs, spiritually, to the small group of radical dogmatists, one or two of whom I have discussed already. He has tried to place Shakespeare in history. Shakespeare's rejection of the Puritans is to him a sign, not of conservative and nationalist feeling, nor of humanism and love of intellectual freedom, but of backwardness, of reactionary and unavailing resistance to the forces of the future. In that period of Shakespeare's, the period of transition from the Middle Ages, with their static conception of the world, to the age of modern capitalism, of cool, matter-of-fact and rational burgherdom—the latter represented by the Puritans and soon triumphant in Cromwell—he felt distracted. He could not let go of the poetry of the past, of the dream, the fancy, the fairy tale; yet with a large portion of his personality he was undoubtedly modern, critical, given to questioning.

Bold theories indeed! but from how distorted a view of English, and in fact of European, history do they proceed! The identification of Calvinism with middle-class capitalism is as completely unjustified as is that of both with rationalism and of the Middle Ages with poetry; and no less wrong is the opinion that Cromwell won for Calvinism and burgherdom more than a fruitless victory, a victory without a morrow. Yet these are the views, or I may say errors, that obliged Mr. de Vries, thinking on the lines of his historic-materialist philosophy, to posit Calvinism as a postulate for Shakespeare and his contemporaries. Calvinism, a critical sense, and capitalist burgherdom are one, and the future is theirs—no more need be said, for the future determines what is truth. But if, as a matter of historic reality, Calvinism was not so cool and matter-of-fact, and if its victory and the victory of the middle class represented by Cromwell was but a hollow victory undone by the Restoration and with little effect on the development of England—what remains of the argument?

Everything is error here. According to De Vries the gloom of Shakespeare's penultimate phase has to be explained by his growing awareness of the inevitable ruin of his world (even in our author's own train of thought it is surprising that a less gloomy last phase was still to come!). But apart from the fact that a poet's mood is not to be explained with greater probability by general, or social, circumstances than by personal experience, Shakespeare's world was not by any means in so bad a way; its self-confidence was far from being shaken. I do not admit that the connection of a poet's thought with the future is the only, let alone the principal, measure of his greatness, but even when that standard is applied Shakespeare will succeed. Not, however, in the way indicated by De Vries when, as an afterthought, he ascribes to Shakespeare "a premonition of a higher order more in accordance with justice, and an aspiration after such an order"; for of all that, as I have demonstrated at sufficient length, Shakespeare was completely innocent. But in his earthiness and in his humanity Shakespeare did have something strikingly modern. He has his place in a great intellectual movement that was to sweep on ever more powerfully in the succeeding centuries.

And in nothing does this modern quality of Shakespeare's mind appear more clearly than in his aversion from Puritanism. To De Vries this is nothing but the stage director's material interest, strengthened by hidebound traditionalism, loyalty to King and Church and all the established institutions. It should be observed, first of all, that this conservative attitude, far from being a spent force, was able to survive the shock of the Cromwell episode, and down to the present day has proved itself a factor to be reckoned with in English society and civilization. But besides, the aversion to Puritanism, to Calvinism, to the real (as distinguished from Dowden's imaginary) Protestantism, which Shakespeare shared with so many of the greatest minds of the Reformation period, was directed against a new dogmatism, in which there was nothing modern apart from its being new, which preached a scholastic, inexorable, inflexible morality, and which was hostile, not to the stage only, but to all free expansion of the human mind.

The one thing that De Vries has discerned in Puritanism is its doctrinaire revolutionary tendency. In his schematic view of the world and of history, that is the only progressive force, and apart from it, all that he can see is sluggish conservatism feeding on self-interest, however variously and attractively it may disguise itself. Now the doctrinaire revolutionary tendency is a permanent force in history, which has often powerfully contributed to its movement; I shall not dream of denying it. But in English history especially—not that this feature is unique in English history, but it is perhaps exceptionally marked—that force has never been able to work itself out. Has English history therefore stood still?

The fullness of life knows other contrasts. Over against the doctrinaire revolutionary spirit that De Vries unduly identifies with Calvinism, one can place the genuine devotion to religion that, although it was not the whole of sixteenth-century Calvinism, was undeniably present in it. But, above all, opposed to revolutionary doctrinairism, there is comprehension, leading to acceptance, to toleration, to compromise—the recognition of the relativity of the merely social, and of the eternity of human values. Contrasts, let me add, that are not to be equated with periods. The one is as little medieval as the other is modern. There is a struggle here that is of the essence of the history of mankind, as old as is its past, as young as is the hour in which we draw breath.

B

Shakespeare's Historical Capacity

COMPARISONS WITH DUTCH AND FRENCH PLAYWRIGHTS

In what has preceded I have tried to define the general views that helped Shakespeare give form to his history plays, his attitudes towards some of the great problems that are bound to crop up in every historic presentation—kingship and authority; rank and class; war and, generally speaking, contest or strife; poverty; religion—and I have attempted to establish a relation between those attitudes and a general philosophy of life and of the world. It is indispensable to have some notion of Shakespeare's views on these points if the history plays are to be understood. Yet from the historiographical standpoint, when we ask, as I have set out to do, what Shakespeare's qualities as a historian are, these general opinions, though they did help to make of his *oeuvre* a considerable intellectual achievement, are not in themselves the most important matter.

It is not in his general outlook that Shakespeare shows the originality of his genius. The conceptions in which this outlook expresses itself were mostly borrowed from others. This aspect of his drama proves Elizabethan civilization to have been a noble and a rich civilization in which Shakespeare had his full share. That is much; but it is not the main thing, not for us, not, I should think, for the poet either. It is not why his plays were written; those general ideas were present in his mind, but they did not supply the real motive force to his interest. Nor is his dramatic presentation dominated by them to the extent that he attempts to force them upon the reader. The reader, or the spectator, can enjoy that work without even noticing them. The poet saw and felt and wished to communicate so many other things: human beings, and the events or mutual relationships in which human beings reveal their personalities. This, after all, is the miracle in Shakespeare's historical work: the power of historic presentation, the plastic power, the power of evocation, of character exposition.

Before I try to bring this out—and here I shall do it mainly by comparison with other playwrights—I want to make the remark that in a view of the world such as I have described resides the promise of a special aptitude for historic presentation. Perhaps not for the most penetrating form of historical understanding, at least not according to modern standards, which attach so preponderating an importance to the genetic principle applied to the social body. The Elizabethans were familiar with the idea of a concatenation of cause and effect,[14] nor does Shakespeare ever lose sight of it; we saw how it gave unity to his eight English history plays. But he sees it realizing

[14] Cf. above, p. 14/15.

itself in the moral sphere, and through persons: *there* lies, for him, the intimate connection of history and drama. In the social sphere, on the contrary, where the modern historian will try most of all to apply this concept, *he* never thought of development; his conception of the community life—I have emphasized this point—is a static one, and his attitude with respect to it in the present, quiescent. His mind is fascinated in watching the varied spectacle of history, but it is not tempted to reduce it to any rigid system nor to subject the men and the events of the past to a present aim. It is a mind that is open to life.

I am far from intending to suggest that Shakespeare was capable of absolute objectivity. His glorification of Henry V and belittling of the crowd (and of the French!) were proof of the reverse. Now ultrapatriotism, then aristocratic prejudice—and other biases might be mentioned. But there remains a vast sphere in which Shakespeare manifests a divine understanding, just because he does not look upon the society of men as an object of reform but simply accepts it as the arena where the eternal conflict is waged between good and evil.

HOOFT'S HISTORICAL DRAMAS

Shakespeare's amazing historiographical power, and its connection with the state of mind that has been indicated above, are suddenly illumined when Shakespeare's history plays are placed side by side with P. C. Hooft's *Geraard van Velzen* and *Baeto*.[15]

How frequently, says Mézières in his *Shakespeare et ses critiques* (1860), has it been deplored that the French seventeenth-century playwrights left unused the subject matter

---

[15] Pieter Corneliszoon Hooft (1581-1647), son of an Amsterdam burgo-master, wrote lyrical poetry of a very high quality and devoted the last half of his life (when he was bailiff for the town of Amsterdam, in the rural district of Gooiland, and resided in the castle at Muiden) to his large-scale history of the revolt of the Netherlands. That work, a master-piece of Dutch prose, would occupy a very considerable place in European historiography if Dutch were more widely read. The dramas discussed in the text are not Hooft's greatest achievement.

offered by their own medieval chronicles; see what Shakespeare managed to make of his dry Hall and Holinshed!

In Holland that complaint would be ill-founded! Hooft read Melis Stoke[16] for his *Geraard van Velzen;* he even incorporates an archaic-sounding sentence taken from the Middle Dutch text. Hooft's *Baeto,* too, and Vondel's *Gijsbreght van Aemstel* and *Batavische Gebroeders,* all deal with national subjects. Why is it that, compared with Shakespeare, the Dutch—Hooft, and Vondel, too, as I shall show later on—have made such a poor job of it?

In a certain sense their subject matter, compared with that of the English poet, although in innumerable details promising enough, must be said to have been ungrateful and refractory. There had been too sharp a break with the past; medieval conditions had become too alien. To begin with, it could never be Netherlands, it had to be Holland, or even Amsterdam, matter. Besides, the seventeenth-century historians and antiquarians had their minds stuffed with confusing fallacies about the Middle Ages. A continuity was postulated that had no basis in reality. England had not had a similar break; the national kingship went back into the centuries and supplied a natural and close connection with the older history.

This is one explanation of the absence in Dutch literature of a living national drama such as Shakespeare was able to create. The explanation will not work for France, where, too, the kingship was rooted in a remote past and survived in the modern age; the even more complete absence of national history plays there is an indication that we must look elsewhere. For the moment I confine my attention to Hooft, and what I find first and foremost is a mental structure radically differing from Shakespeare's.

The theme of *Geraard van Velzen* is the deposition of a ruler (of the thirteenth-century Count Florent V of Holland), the theme, one might say, of *King Richard II.* The comparison will

[16] A Dutch writer of the late thirteenth and early fourteenth centuries. His *Rijmkroniek* ("Rhymed Chronicle") is particularly important for the events of his own lifetime, covering the reign of Count Florent V of Holland, murdered in 1296, and his immediate successors.

be instructive. Shakespeare was obviously gripped by his subject as such. His intention must have been, first, to bring to the stage that fragment of English history, next, to delve into the personality of the King—perhaps it is more correct to say he imagined a personality for him, and what a personality! a subtly shaded one, revealing unsuspected depths.

As for Hooft, he does not seem to care much for the piece of history that he has chosen for his subject. It is disposed of very summarily. Shakespeare gives scene after scene, thrilling, immediate, full of life, in order to build up the crisis and place it before our eyes to see; the solution is made intelligible, and again, visible. The great noblemen, their grievances, their quarrels, it all receives colour and character. In Hooft's play the course of events—Florent V's misgovernment and crimes, the conspiracy of the nobles and their internal divisions, the people's loyalty to the Count, the resulting catastrophe—is indicated only very slightly, mostly in long monologues, or even in choruses (for that device was still employed by the Dutch playwrights, and it was the occasion for some of the finest poetry of both Hooft and Vondel). There is no question of any delineation or evocation of character. Machteld (Velzen's wife, dishonoured by Florent) is mildness personified, superior to earthly passion, while Velzen is the worldling keen on honour, and breathing vengeance; but the contrast remains stark and simple, neither character is in any way individualized. Even Florent V, so rich in possibilities one would have thought, remains shadowy. Compared with Shakespeare's vivid and fascinating treatment of Richard II, there is a distressing poverty of invention here.

But indeed invention was not what Hooft was out for. His mind ran on an entirely different track. The difference here is not to be expressed in the contrast I shall draw later on between the French playwrights and Shakespeare, that is to say, between the classicist and the romantic-realist style. Hooft's dramatic work is not so severely classicist. That is to say, it is modelled on the example of Seneca rather than on the precepts of Aristotle—precepts, indeed, of which the French had made their own exceedingly inflexible system. Hooft could still permit himself realistic touches, for instance, the incident of the esquire and the soothsayer—elaborated, but in the result rather colourless and insignificant. Had he been so minded, he might have gone in for more scenes of that nature, but he preferred to use his stage time for allegoric characters like Strife, Violence, Deceit. No, what mattered to him were the constitutional and theological ideas that he expounded. The historical theme was no more than an excuse for speaking his mind on those.

I shall not maintain that no work of true literary significance can be written in that fashion. The poetic imagination can be fired in many ways. This much is certain, however: in *Geraard van Velzen* the miracle has not happened, and not in *Baeto* either. Both are completely cerebral performances. Sixty years ago the very able Dutch critic Koopmans wrote an essay in which he determined and analyzed the ideas running through these two plays. The impression created is of something very high-minded and pure. Criticism of that sort has its use, but it should be made clear that Hooft deserves this close attention from the literary critic only on the score of the totality of his work and of his remarkable and interesting personality. It is this that adds to the dramas of his youth an importance they would not otherwise possess. And in any case, that importance remains confined to the history of ideas of the period. Koopmans does not even try to test these plays on their aesthetic value, and as soon as aesthetic standards are applied (and it is by them that the true significance of a drama must be determined), it will be seen that the plays are completely impotent products, failures, nothing!

To me it seems certain that the method employed in *Geraard van Velzen* and *Baeto* cannot yield any historic perspective, any evocation of a civilization or sphere belonging to the past. Circumstances and events may differ ever so much from what Hooft in his own time was familiar with, but the personages of his dramas are exactly like those he saw around him, and they talk and argue about their problems in the same spirit and as much as possible in the same phraseology. But in fact the characters in *Geraard* and *Baeto* are hardly human beings. They are ventriloquist's puppets in fancy dress, who declaim a treatise by P. C. Hooft on authority and liberty, the right to rebel and its limitations, the importance of concord and peace, and the horrors of civil war; all in dialogues and under pretence of fighting out a dispute of the past.

What was the message of which Hooft felt he must unburden himself? He preaches a curious kind of political quietism. Before everything, he wants order and quiet to be ensured, and for this purpose he looks to a strong government. No doubt this government should be legitimate and conduct itself in accordance with the highest moral law, but if it does not, there is still nothing but submission. To pursue one's right at all costs can, like the desire for revenge, lead to nothing but misery.

Florent's misgovernment is not condoned in *Geraard van Velzen*. The poet thinks that there was much to be said for Florent's being put under restraint. Everything is, however, compromised when the conspiring noblemen definitely part with law and call in foreign (that is, English) help. The Lord of Aemstel, who represents the poet's own political wisdom, knows exactly what the law requires: to leave the matter to the assembly of the States (which was as a matter of historic fact far to seek in the year 1296). When his two comrades express doubts about whether the States will show sufficient vigour, he warns them that in that case acquiescence is the only course: to "overthrow" legality, "guarded by the best part of the people," means running the risk of getting rushed along by "the scum of citizens and of peasants."

This political creed—and the conviction that the priesthood should be kept firmly under the control of the secular authority forms an integral part of it (this is stated more particularly in *Baeto*)—is closely related to that of Shakespeare. He, too—we have seen it—was an upholder of authority and a despiser of the people, a believer in the aristocracy of the mind and of the blood. Shakespeare, too, believed that authority had to keep within the law—although, of course, with respect to the relation between aristocracy and monarchy, his position was different from that of the republican Hooft. Shakespeare, too, believed that he who resisted a tyrannical king loaded himself with a guilt that would have to be atoned for, albeit perhaps only in a succeeding generation. Bolingbroke, who deposed Richard II, remained, we know it, oppressed by the consciousness of his offence, and indeed, under his grandson Henry VI disaster came. The entire series of Shakespeare's English history plays was, as we saw, dominated by the idea that by contest about authority, by civil war, usurpation, disobedience, the eternal order is disturbed; and the moral that England can be great only through unanimity under a strong king is more than once impressively emphasized.

With respect to the church, too, Shakespeare's attitude did not differ greatly from Hooft's. This problem in fact is intimately connected with the general problem of authority, which contributed not a little, all over Europe, towards the readiness with which the intellectuals ranged themselves behind the secular power. They were fed up with religious strife and with the extremism of the sects as much as with the ambition and intolerance of the old priesthood. These were forces that in the last resort rested on the unreason of the crowd, and in order to keep that under control and protect freedom so that intellectual culture might flourish, they felt the aristocratic organization of society and royal power to be indispensable. No more than Hooft was Shakespeare a fervent Christian (this, too, I indicated in the preceding chapter). The theological controversy cannot have interested him much. He was no doubt satisfied, somewhat indifferently perhaps, with the settlement that had the support of the secular power and that was intended to suppress the extremes of subjection to a foreign papacy and of revolutionary puritanism (the latter, in fact, was not free from foreign attachments either, looking as it did longingly to Geneva).

So much for kinship; but at the same time how striking a difference! This difference was in the first place one of artistic temperament; only in the second place, although no doubt the two were connected, of politics, of opinion.

Shakespeare's attention is first and foremost for events and for human beings; these he wants to bring out individually, in

E.H.   C their own rights. It is not only that the case for Bolingbroke is put with as much force as is that for Richard II; it is especially that the for or against does not hold the stage all the time. We are made to live with both sides; we are interested in the spectacle, in the conflict of passions and personalities. I wrote a moment ago that a moral was emphasized. Was that not putting it too strongly? At any rate, the moral is not (as is the case with Hooft) hammered in, commented upon at length, and illustrated, and in the end triumphantly repeated. Generally it can at most be deduced. Perhaps a strong light will be cast upon it for a passing moment, but always men and events will hold the attention. This peculiarity of Shakespeare's art, a reflection of a leading quality of his nature, has its counterpart in his political views, insofar as it is possible to determine these with any certainty.

Hooft, regarding himself to be above the contest of theological dogmas, was himself a dogmatist. He had complete and finished theories about the relationships in state and society, about authority and freedom, about state and church, and into those he fitted, or forced, life; his history plays show life in those categories.

Take once more the passage in *Geraard van Velzen* from which I quoted before. (It is Aemstel speaking.)

> If the best part of the people [i.e., the States]
> is willing to be oppressed by tyrants,
> Theirs is the judgment. So, if they acquiesce,
> let everybody
> Acquiesce with them, or depart for elsewhere.

I pass by the anachronistic argumentation by which this pronouncement was preceded and in which Aemstel exhorts his friends to leave everything ("after the custom of the ancestors") to the States, that is, to "Nobility and Large Towns, to which the sovereignty has been committed"; at the absolute disposal of this assembly stands the decision between submission or resistance with respect to the Count. This is bodily transferring the seventeenth-century States into the thirteenth-century assembly! But does not so positive a prescription in itself transcend life? Does it not go against life? The play is a rhymed treatise of dogmatic constitutional law, not history.

And indeed where do we find life in it? We heard Aemstel's warning that if the decision is not left unconditionally to "the best part of the people," "the scum of citizens and of peasants," the mob, will be roused and spoil everything. So it happens. The project to deliver up the captured Count to England leads to a commotion in which Velzen stabs him to death. And now there is a great deal of talk about the raging people, of song even about the blind people; the murder is described, though now the furious mob is not even mentioned. The sequence of rioting, too, is dispatched in a chorus; and that is all. Shakespeare, on the contrary—but have I not dealt with the mob scenes in *Henry VI*, in *Julius Caesar*, in *Coriolanus*? It may be said that he did not there maintain his high impartiality, but nevertheless those scenes pulsate with life and testify to his keen psychological and political insight; and above all, these men of the people are brought to the stage for their own sakes as well, with their humour, and in their trades.

Baeto does not in this respect differ from *Geraard van Velzen*. Baeto's submission to his father at the moment when he has the victory in his hands can hardly be called human; it is not, at all events, how one would expect the hero, or the prince, to behave; it is more suited to the saint, or to the martyr. But to Hooft it seems the acme of political wisdom, and in those terms he imagined himself able to give history and drama!

How much freer is Shakespeare's mind in its attitude toward the phenomena of life, how much broader therefore is his outlook, and how much more truly historical and at the same time dramatic his presentation! Richard II is the Lord's anointed. According to Shakespeare's English view he was a more exalted figure than was the medieval Count in Hooft's Holland aristocratic and republican system. The deposition could not, to Shakespeare, be anything but an unlawful act, yet he understands, and makes understandable, that life sometimes demands that the law shall be broken. He realizes that this must have its sequel of commotions; retribution will follow; but Henry IV, who has to atone for the transgression committed when he was still Bolingbroke, is not therefore any the less a true king and a man.

I am not writing about Hooft and his work in its entirety. Most certainly he succeeded in largely overcoming the system-bound rigidity of his historical outlook. When, later on, he undertakes his *Historiën*, it will be in a more truly historical spirit, with a broader and more human feeling for the spectacle as well as for the actors. In fact, if that enormous work still makes an appeal to the modern reader (as it does) and deserves to be numbered among the great achievements in historio-graphy, it is on account of the close attention to the significant as well as colourful detail and of the plastic capacity of its sometimes laboured but always vivid and personal style. What strikes us in the youthful Hooft of the history plays, however, is the *a priori*, the abstractness of the approach. The comparison helps us to discern in Shakespeare's work, glowing with life and gloriously concrete, the historic veracity that cannot exist without those qualities.

SHAKESPEARE'S AIM IN THE ENGLISH HISTORY PLAYS

Hooft wanted to illustrate with his history plays certain political tenets. What was Shakespeare's aim?

Above all, Shakespeare was concerned in his plays about the English kings to picture thrilling events—this is what he repeatedly says himself, in the prefaces to each of the acts of *King Henry V*. To none of his other history plays did he add comments of exactly this nature, but the *poetica* to be found here holds good for all, at least for all those on English subjects. What makes itself heard in these prefaces is the passionate desire to bring to the stage the variety and the fullness, the colour and the life, of history. The poet feels overwhelmed by the rich abundance of history. The small compass of his stage is compared with the realms of England and of France, where the reality had been enacted; the poor trappings, with the grandeur and the luxury; the little company of actors he will show, with the armies that actually engaged

in battle; the couple of hours the performance may take
up, with the period of years embraced by the reign of his
king.

> A kingdom for a stage, princes to act
> And monarchs to behold the swelling scene.
> Then should the war-like Harry, like himself,
> Assume the port of Mars; and at his heels,
> Leash'd in like hounds, should famine, sword, and fire
> Crouch for employment.
> . . . can this cockpit hold
> The vasty fields of France? or may we cram
> Within this wooden O the very casques
> That did affright the air at Agincourt?

The ambition is a superhuman one. Shakespeare is aware
of it and calls on the spectator's imagination to assist him.
"Let us . . . On your imaginary forces work."

> Piece out our imperfections with your thoughts:
> Into a thousand parts divide one man,
> And make imaginary puissance;
> Think when we talk of horses that you see them
> Printing their proud hoofs i' the receiving earth;
> For 'tis your thoughts that now must deck our kings,
> Carry them here and there, jumping o'er times,
> Turning the accomplishment of many years
> Into an hour-glass. . . .

That subject matter, that action, those events, on which the
interest must turn in the English history plays, were to a
certain extent known; they appealed to a vigorous sentiment
that it was possible for the poet to suppose present in his
public, that, in fact, he shared with it. I said something about
this in the preceding part about Shakespeare's ideas on state
and society. Let me again summarize it here, in the words of
an English writer.[17] The points of interest, apart from the
pure spectacle, that would be uppermost in the mind of the

[17] N. W. MacCallum, *Shakespeare's Roman Plays and Their Background*
(1910), p. 76.

average Englishman watching these dramas based on his national history would be mainly these three:

The unity of the country under the strong and orderly government of securely succeeding sovereigns, who should preserve it from the long remembered evils of Civil War;

Its rejection of Papal domination, with which there might be, but more frequently among the play-going classes there was not, associated the desire for a more radical reconstruction of the Church;

The power, safety, and prestige of England, which Englishmen believed to be the inevitable consequence of her unity and independence.

It is not that all this is expounded or argued in the plays. It was the advantage the English playwright had over the Dutch with respect to national subjects taken from the Middle Ages that these considerations were still so alive in people's consciousness that no argument was required. Of course I need hardly recall that Shakespeare went beyond both the spectacle and this touching of the chords of national feeling. He made human beings of his kings, of his noblemen, of all his personages. A few times, for example, in *King Richard II* and *King Richard III*, the figure of the leading character even took on a dominant interest. Yet, speaking generally, the prologues of *King Henry V* can be taken as an indication of Shakespeare's primary aim in the English plays.

In the English plays. For in the Roman plays it is a different matter. There the leading personage, or personages, and the inner conflicts in which they were involved, were always the main thing. More truly than any of the English history plays, these were tragedies. It goes without saying that the poet could not rely there upon comparable familiarity, or upon passionate participation, with the events staged. Yet, just as in the English plays he fashioned human beings and was at times fascinated by the development of a personality or by a purely individual conflict, so in the classical plays he was also interested by the events, by the spectacle. In fact, it was through the minor characters and the scenes outside the main line of the action that he came into the closest contact with history. Not only from the literary point of view of dramatic construction, but from the point of view that has here had my particular attention, that of the dramatic work as historiography, one notices a striking contrast presented in this respect by the classicist drama that was soon to achieve triumphs in France.

THE HISTORIC POWERS OF CORNEILLE AND RACINE

I have attempted to bring out the personality of Shakespeare by comparing him with Hooft. The contrast with the French tragedy writers of the seventeenth century is no less striking and will prove equally helpful in making us realize the unique, the distinctive, qualities of the English poet.

Shakespeare's ambition, which was noted a moment ago, to resuscitate on the stage the whole of life, never occurred to Racine, in whom the French style reached its pinnacle; or rather, Racine rejected it decisively. The feeling of insignificance and impotence which Shakespeare overcame with the aid of the imagination, the Frenchman, in proud self-restraint, denied. One has only to read the preface to *Britannicus*, in which Racine makes front against the activities of a more romantic school and against Corneille, his elder contemporary. Corneille, no doubt, accepted the Aristotelian precepts, and compared with Shakespeare's, even *his* work gives the impression of extreme classicism; yet he still permitted himself liberties that offended Racine's ideal of stark and rectilinear simplicity. What ought I to do—Racine asks scornfully—in order to please my critics?

Instead of a simple action, containing little matter, such as must be an action that runs its course in one single day, an action that, step by step proceeding toward its conclusion, is sustained by nothing but the interests, the sentiments, and the passions of the characters, one would have to fill that same action with a quantity of accidents which could not happen in less than a month, with a large number of stage tricks the more surprising as they would be less probable.

A simple action, then, and perhaps it is even nearer the truth to say, a single action, an action reduced to a single motif, that is the French classicist ideal. It has been said—by a Frenchman, but a Frenchman who has commented on Shakespeare with both subtlety and good sense[18]—that it is this in which the high poetic quality of the French drama appears. According to Aristotle, as we know, the peculiar task of poetry is to express the general, while history remains stuck in the particular. We shall have occasion to observe in passing several things about the poetry of Shakespeare and of others, but in my argument it is history that matters. And this much is certain: history attempts to get to the truth of life in a way that cannot be simple, cannot be "single." *Simplex sigillum veri* is a saying without sense to the historian, he would rather make a thesis of the opposite. And is it not so, indeed, that Shakespeare's dramas owe their effectiveness as history largely to their not being "single," to their action being composite and varied?

This is not all, of course. There are other elements, and among them some that have a profounder significance than the stage technique that Shakespeare found existing in England or the authority of the Aristotelian rules that the French drama so universally accepted at the time of its highest development, a generation or two afterward. No doubt there was an organic connection between these rules and the "classical spirit," but even so, this spirit meant a good deal more than faithfulness to "the Aristotelian unities."

In reading Corneille, it does not matter which play, one notices first of all the logical construction and the cerebral method. Take *Horace*. The subject, typical for Corneille, is a conflict of loyalties; it is shown in five characters, moved by opposing sentiments of duty or affection, finely shaded, and in varying degrees of strength. At one end of the scale there is Horace, a man to whom country and honour are all and who

[18] Stapfer, whose ideas will be more fully discussed below.

considers himself obliged to sacrifice friendship and family relationships to them—and even makes these sacrifices with spontaneity and joy. The other characters all feel themselves more or less torn in different directions. As situations succeed each other, the entire register of their affections comes into play. The element of design is, in the composition and development of a case like this, somewhat disconcertingly obvious, and the execution proceeds in strict accordance with the rules of the analytical intellect. Every new turn in the drama affords its personages an occasion to dilate subtly on their emotions, fears, and hopes, on their opinions and states of mind. As Camille puts it:

Was ever a soul seen more affected in the course of one day
By joy and by sorrow, by hope and by fear?[19]

It would be possible to compose a textbook out of the disquisitions, subdivisions, and conclusions of the characters in this play. Horace senior, for instance, at the moment when the fight between the twice three brothers (his sons for Rome, and Curiace and his brothers for Albe) is already on, delivers a lengthy speech to the two women, his daughter-in-law and daughter, Sabine (wife to Horace junior, sister to Curiace) and Camille (affianced to Curiace, sister to Horace). Both are naturally deeply moved, but Horace, the father too, admits being near to tears. Yet, he says, my interest in the event is less close than yours.

It is not that Albe has by its choice made me hate
    your brothers.
All three are still very dear to me;
But after all, friendship is not of the same rank,
Nor has it the effect of love and blood relationship;
I do not feel for them the sorrow that torments
Sabine the sister or Camille the mistress.[20]

---

[19] Vit on jamais une âme en un jour plus atteinte
    De joie et de douleur, d'espérance et de crainte.
[20] Non qu'Albe par son choix m'ait fait haïr vos frères.
    Tous trois me sont encor des personnes bien chères;

This amazing faculty of self-observation and conscious living is common to all the characters. And indeed what Corneille wants to present to us is, as motive force, a moral conviction becoming will, and, as directive, an intellectual awareness and sense of distinctions, allied to a devotion to duty which can overcome sentiment or passion. *Vertu, honneur, gloire, magnanimité*—these are magic words in his dramas. The personages—and the poet—react to them almost automatically. Pain may force cries from them, or at least, long speeches, but they do not seem to struggle with these behests laid upon them as it were from outside. It is the greatness of Horace's qualities that in the end makes him kill his sister. One would like to see the hollowness and falsity of a *vertu* that leads to such an effect argued, or rather, felt. Nothing would have been more natural for the poet, one thinks, than to have hinted at the question of whether Horace was not in reality betrayed by his vanity, whether his conception of duty to country and family honour did not rest on rickety foundations. But that is not Corneille's way. Unhesitatingly he sticks to the established social precepts and rules. He can dissect them down to a fine point; he can even show them in conflict one with the other. What he cannot do is to throw doubt on them; he is unable to reveal their emptiness or unreality by a lightning shaft of divine or human truth.

Moreover, the denouement of *Horace* supplies another instance—we came across one before this [21]—of how Corneille sacrifices higher moral feeling to social or state convenience. The solution through which Horace is safeguarded against punishment lacks all connection with the inner life, it is imposed by the King's command. With so many words the *raison d'état* is invoked:

Mais enfin l'amitié n'est pas du même rang,
Et n'a point les effets de l'amour et du sang;
Je ne sens point pour eux la douleur qui tourmente
Sabine comme soeur, Camille comme aimante.

[21] See above, p. 10.

Such servants make the strength of kings,
And such, too, are above the law.[22]

How sharp is the contrast with Shakespeare's sense of justice, which is not bounded by any external or conventional taboos! And how little can we expect, after having observed these features of Corneille's mental make-up, that he will tell us anything very profound or novel about historic conditions or historic personalities! Yet his outlook is at least compatible with interest in such conditions and personalities, an interest that is indeed much less pronounced with Racine.

Between Corneille and Racine there are profound differences. It is in the method of their dramatic presentations that they give the clearest sign of their close relationship in classicism. Like Corneille, Racine constructs his plays around a simple conflict that lets itself be unwound like a spool, ever displaying new situations, or new aspects of a given situation. The main characters, three or four at most, are systematically and ingeniously exposed to those changes so that they can show the entire register of moods of which they are capable. In this game, Racine shows himself a greater artist than Corneille, and the basic tone of his work is, moreover, utterly different. Instead of by the social virtues, by will, by a sense of duty or of honour, we see his characters moved by sentiment and passion. And so completely is the poet's attention concentrated thereon that to an even higher degree than is the case with Corneille the play is bared of all adventitious matter; secondary personages, for instance, are mere "confidants," without any strongly marked characteristics of their own that might stand in the light of the central figures.

The most typical of Racine's plays, and from this point of view the foremost achievement of his art, is *Bérénice*. It is a history play. The chief personages are the Emperor Titus and the Palestinian Queen Bérénice. At his accession to the government, Titus, to meet the prejudice of the Roman people, sends Bérénice back to her native country—in spite of the love they

[22] De pareils serviteurs sont les forces des rois
Et de pareils aussi sont au-dessus des lois.

bear each other. Five words from Tacitus—there Racine had his entire plot: *Titus Berenicem dimisit invitus invitam.* The action is resolutely reduced to variations on a single theme, a theme purely of sentiment. The play, in Racine's—for all its seeming monotony—sensitive verse, impresses like a piece of music—chamber music to Shakespeare's symphonies. Of its kind it is a triumph, but when one comes to it fresh from a reading of Shakespeare, how strongly does one feel the artificiality, the thinness, the overbred delicacy of the genre.

And does it need arguing that in such a treatment history cannot come by its due? The case, and its ramifications in the depths of the heart, that is what matters to the poet. He tracks them down without caring very greatly about personalities as such. Why is Titus worth more than Bérénice's unfortunate wooer, Antiochus? He is the Emperor; he has done glorious deeds. But about these we are merely informed, and this, in the usual conventional language. There is nothing distinctive. Nor do we *see* anything. We are not shown Titus acting as Emperor, in his relations to his people, to the army, to the Senate; in such small scenes, in other words, as Shakespeare would have loved to devise, but which could not be allowed into the classical drama because they would have detracted from its "singleness." We see Titus as lover only. But now compare Mark Antony in *Antony and Cleopatra*! Him we come to know as a commander; we hear of the admiration and of the sorrowful impatience of his subordinates. We come to know him as a triumvir, in his relations to the cold, self-controlled Octavius and to the nincompoop Lepidus. And as a lover we see him in the grip of a passion that wrecks him. What a drawing-room lover does Titus seem, with his *larmes*, and his *flamme*, and his *chaînes*, and his *soupirs*. All that there is of true passion in the play is in Bérénice—once or twice, for brief moments; enough for the genre. It is just that which gives one the shock of surprise, the keen sense of beauty: the melodious stream of the alexandrines suddenly, as it were, held up by these very few, brief, vehement utterances.

There is in any case nothing specifically Roman in Titus, nothing Oriental in either Antiochus or Bérénice. And this holds good for the entire *oeuvre* of Racine. Whether it be Romans, or prehistoric Greeks, Asiatics before Christ, or contemporary Turks, it is really always Frenchmen, and even that very special brand of Frenchmen raised in the court of Louis XIV and in the drawing-rooms of the nobility.

Taine, once, in a famous essay, proclaimed Racine as the finest product of that hothouse culture. A good many objections can be raised against his argument; as always with Taine, there is in his constructions a strong element of arbitrariness, of paradox almost, and he carries them to the point where they become impossible. His theory of "l'esprit classique" (of which Racine is made to be the representative par excellence) as the true expression of the French national character, for instance, seems incompatible with his other view of the close connection of that state of mind with the court life under Louis XIV, which was after all no more than an episode in French history. And the way in which Taine pictures that society, stressing its artificial and aristocratic and even bitterly antipopular character, should have made it clear to him that it could not possibly be *the*, the *true*, expression of the French mind. It was a temporary, an ephemeral phenomenon, and nothing is more absurd than to try to shut up French civilization in its entirety, and the intellectual and spiritual potentialities of the French nation, within the narrow bounds of that "esprit classique"—stiflingly narrow indeed as traced by Taine himself.

Moreover, Taine's aesthetic and moral appreciation of that seventeenth-century French civilization does err on the side of enthusiasm. He draws the picture with a master hand, and that there was much that was admirable and delightful can readily be granted. But undiluted enthusiasm hardly seems to accord with the emphasis, the almost exaggerated emphasis, with which he harps on the divorce from nature characteristic of that society. Especially when he compares—and he does so repeatedly, mainly with Shakespeare—he rouses to opposition. Taine feels at home with the courtly, delicate, mild, civilized, sensitive Racine; he shrinks at the touch of the savage, barbaric, unmeasured Shakespeare. He prefers, so he says, having to do with good manners rather than with unbridled passions, with a man raised in a hothouse than with one abandoned in the state of nature. As if the latter parts of these contrasts could be applied to Shakespeare! Taine has not proceeded beyond Voltaire's misapprehension. But more: as if the first parts gave a true image of Racine! For is not the secret of Racine's genius this, that through the veil of that decorous and artificial style which Taine describes so brilliantly—and so mistakenly identifies with the poet's innermost being—we can discern the man, who did not wholly belong to the court of Louis XIV?

The man, the human being, can supply the link needed by the historic sense. Yet that human factor reduced in Racine's way to its most general substance, although clothed in an outward shape so intimately connected with a particular period, does not offer much for our particular purpose. As an instance of what Racine can do as a historian, take the Nero he presents to us in *Britannicus*. Taine himself points out how different a Nero it is from the one portrayed by Tacitus. Racine's Nero is the perfect diplomat, and he could not possibly be more gracefully courteous to Junie; his falseness and wickedness only transpire in glints from behind the mask of the man of the world. In short, the bloodthirsty and insane despot has been transposed into the terms of Racine's own, all-too-narrow sphere of life.

This peculiarity of Racine's, which, with the concentration of his attention on the sentiments and the passions of love, so little fitted him to create a history drama, did not escape his contemporaries. Dryden poked fun at the delicacy of Racine's Hippolyte, who even in order to clear himself did not dare openly mention Phèdre's crime to Thésée. Taine holds Dryden's criticism typical of the rude character of English as compared with French civilization. Though the contrast of "refined" and "rude," which Taine uses repeatedly—and especially to get at the core of Shakespeare—may be one, it is certainly not the most important, aspect of the difference. As to this particular point, Corneille, in France, made similar remarks about Racine. Of *Bajazet* the older writer said—quite rightly—"all the characters of that play have, underneath their

Turkish dress, French sentiments." And he even spoke quite generally—the critical intention is unmistakable—of "the ancient heroes recast to suit our fashion."[23]

Racine's son naturally considered this criticism unfair and maintains that "Mithridates, appearing with all his hatred for Rome, his dissimulation, and his cruel jealousy, showed the poet to be capable of giving to the ancient heroes their full likeness." The verdict cannot be accepted without demur. No doubt Racine made an attempt. Nevertheless, when Mithridate, on entering upon his dissimulation, tells himself that it is unworthy of him, when, in the final scene with Xipharès, his son, and Monime, his wife, from whom he has wrenched the secret of their love, he practically gives them, with his dying breath, his blessing, then one feels that the poet has remained blind to the barbaric—that is, to the really distinctive element on which true historic perception would have fastened.

Returning to Corneille, we must admit that his historic capacity does not after all very much surpass Racine's. I mentioned Corneille's *Horace* before. On close examination its ancient (almost prehistoric) Romans turn out, like Racine's characters, to be nothing but Frenchmen, of the age of Richelieu perhaps, rather than that of Louis XIV (and indeed, Corneille was born in 1606; Racine in 1639; Louis XIV in 1638). The objection that a Frenchman of Corneille's time can hardly be imagined killing his sister for the reason that seemed sufficient to the hero of Corneille's drama might cause a moment of embarrassment; it can, however, be disposed of by marking two points. First, the excesses of the play's action are situated in a line whose direction certainly runs parallel with that of French thinking of the period, and moreover the prolongation of action into the excessive is typical for Corneille: it is his conception of heroism, of *vertu*. Nonetheless—and this is my second point—although it is undeniable that the deed is not in harmony with the general tone of the play, and also, that it met with disapproval on the part of the contemporary public, does not this, it might be argued in Corneille's defence, show how "ancient Roman," that is to say, how historic, it was?

[23] Similar remarks were made by Fontenelle.

Of course Corneille had found the terrible act related in the legend. But his failure both as a poet and as a historian is that he did not succeed in preparing for it. He conceived the whole play as a dialectical treatise in casuistic morals in accordance with the ideas of his own time. His subtle and exact distinctions did not leave him any time or space (supposing that the Aristotelian unities would have permitted him, and his inclination and poetic powers would have run that way) to evoke in concrete incidents the profoundly different sphere of the ancient Roman age. Shakespeare excels in such background painting. Here it is practically absent.

Take *Le Cid*, which is set in eleventh-century Spain. Of a distinctive historic atmosphere, different from that in Corneille's other plays, there is no trace. No doubt the great motive force of the characters is honour, which may suggest Spain, although hardly the eleventh century; and there is much talk about the Moors. Similarly, in *Cinna* and *La Mort de Pompée* (about both of which plays more hereafter) the talk is about liberty, about Rome, about dignity and glory; and, while local colour is not entirely lacking, it is always in the shape of definite facts supplied by the plot: Egypt, Roman conspirators. A different moral or spiritual atmosphere is not thereby constituted.

Of the feudalism, religious wars, barbarousness of the world to which the Cid belonged, nothing will be found in Corneille. Once more, he unfolds before his spectators a highly cultured, and in many respects artificial, society. It is not quite the same as that of Augustus or of Ptolemy, but much less is it the reality of eleventh-century Spain. It is the French court as Corneille knew it. The pugnacious and unruly noblemen have become courtiers; the King, who in reality was engaged in a daily struggle to maintain himself against them, an autocrat raised to an unattainable height. The political maxims are those of Corneille's own age. For instance:

> But this respect is due to absolute power,
> That nothing should be looked into when a king has
>   willed it. . . .

Whatever illustrious or considerable deeds one may do,
A king never owes anything [any gratitude] to his
subject.[24]

With all his veneration for royal authority, Shakespeare,
whose English history plays were so largely intended to
demonstrate the salutariness and the indispensability of the
regal office, would not have overlooked the conflict between
these slavish tenets and the higher moral law. And especially,
he did not, for all his royalism, do violence to history in the way
Corneille did. But indeed, we know already that Shakespeare,
in addition to carrying through a certain general view of
English history, desired to call up the spectacle of the past;
whereas Corneille in *Le Cid* (to a lesser degree in *Cinna;* least
of all in *La Mort de Pompée*, although here too) concentrated
on the love interest and the conflicts of the heart.

It can be confidently affirmed that Corneille, like Racine,
always staged the same sort of characters engaged in the same
sort of inner conflicts (each of the two poets, as we saw, had his
own sort)—in different settings, perhaps, but in settings that
never had any profound connection with the theme. Nor were
these sorts of characters and of conflicts anything like so
universally human as has often been asserted; on the contrary,
they were strictly determined by Corneille's—or Racine's—
own age and culture, so that their appearance in other nations,
surroundings, and periods always resembles fancy-dress parties.

Corneille had, moreover, only one style for all his personages; again, like Racine for his. With inexorable regularity the
alexandrines succeed each other from beginning to end. That
style, steadily flowing, ever logically developed, the style of
highly cultured drawing-room ladies and gentlemen trained
in argument and analysis, remains more purely cerebral in
Corneille's handling than in Racine's. It is a style full of
clichés. Everything that comes up for treatment falls under the

[24] Mais on doit ce respect au pouvoir absolu,
De n'examiner rien quand un roi l'a voulu. . . .
Quoi qu'on fasse d'illustre et de considérable,
Jamais à son sujet un roi n'est redevable.

sway of the current moral code, of conventional or social conceptions of love, duty, honour, country, parental authority. The problems, too (leaving aside *Polyeucte*, which is a religious drama), are, so to speak, given. History supplies the plot and the setting, but it has no independent existence. The dramatic effect must be obtained by means of a love interest, or one of the recognized, duly labelled conflicts. Even Caesar has, in *La Mort de Pompée*, to submit to that law. Corneille's characters are not individualized human beings; they are merely embodiments of the familiar stage types, the lover-hero, the lover-ambitious-politician, or for the women, the lover-dutiful-daughter, the lover-patriot. The conflicts in which these characters get involved, as in a complicated, but well-known and symmetrical, dance, supply them with abundant matter for ratiocination, carried on with amazing subtlety and quickness of wit. And they all raise their voices to the same pitch, and display the same kind of sensitiveness.

Rodrigue, the hero of a hundred battles, sighs and whimpers about the sorrows of his love no less than does Cinna, the Roman conspirator, and Caesar himself would do the same if Cleopatra happened to have been "cruel". That "scourge of the Moors," Rodrigue, living before the year 1100 (in historic reality, by the way, he was not above occasionally making common cause with the Moors), this "Cid", holds forth about his *flamme* and his *âme* like everybody else, and about his despair, and about his having lost his all now that Chimène pursues him with her hatred.

I recall in passing that Shakespeare's heroes of the battle-field are presented to us as heroes of the battlefield indeed. Coriolanus, hard and proud, whose wife hardly counts in his life; Hotspur, loud-voiced and jovial, fond of his Kate no doubt, but easily, and without pretending that she comes before the all-important business of war; Henry V, whose love scenes with the French princess have no other purpose than to make the public laugh about the language problem, except insofar as they illustrate the triumph of the English conqueror. . . . How infinitely more richly shaded is the presenta-

tion of life, and how much better will a mind like Shakespeare's
be able to comprehend the varied multiplicity of history!

'CINNA' AND 'JULIUS CAESAR'—'LA MORT DE POMPÉE' AND 'ANTONY AND CLEOPATRA'

Corneille's most ambitious attempts at history writing are
Cinna and *La Mort de Pompée*.

Cinna, ou la clémence d'Auguste, was obviously written to
glorify that magnanimity mentioned in the title. In Corneille's
play the aristocratic-republican opposition to the establishment
of the monarchy is more articulate than in Shakespeare's
Julius Caesar. But that does not mean that the French poet
shows a more profound understanding of it.

With *Julius Caesar*, Shakespeare ventured out into an
entirely different political sphere from that which he knew in
England. The theme is of a dictator who, leaning on the
people, overthrows the aristocracy, and of the last, convulsive
resistance of that aristocracy. Was the poet, with Plutarch for
a guide, able to find his way through those unfamiliar conditions?

The monologue in which Brutus tries to defend to himself
the murder plan is, it must be admitted, very thin. Suppose
Caesar succeeded in making himself king, how might he
misuse his power! English criticism pointed out more than a
century ago that the argument ill fits the traditional republicanism of the Roman, to whom the royal title was detestable as
such. But apart from that passage it is surprising with how firm
a hand Shakespeare brought out circumstances sharply
different from any in the history of his own country. He is
far from confounding the Roman patricians with the English
feudal nobility, or Caesar's dictatorship, continued by the
triumvirs, then by Octavius alone, with English monarchy.
The Roman conspirators may wear hats and Caesar a
"doublet," but they make a very different appearance indeed
from the great noblemen in the English dramas, with their
estates and their fighting ideals, and from the kings, trusting
to their blood and their divine right. It may be true that

Shakespeare failed to grasp the exact tenor of Brutus's republican theory, so foreign to his own experience of politics. He rejected it no doubt unhesitatingly, and he did put Caesar in the place of an English king to the extent that he saw him as dominating the situation even after his death ("O Julius Caesar! thou art mighty yet!"), and the opposition to him as a vain revolt against the only possible order. But after all, that view had sufficient roots in history to enable Shakespeare to evoke an entire world that gives us an impression of being un-English, and at the same time, authentically Roman. Touches supplied by the other conspirators—Casca's scorn for the mighty Caesar compelled to seek popular acclaim like any play actor; Cassius's devouring envy of the man who is after all no more than a man, and not, for that matter, a better man than he, but who is taken for the only man of the age—such touches, unthinkable in any of the English history plays, do effectively transfer us to ancient Rome.

But the greatest contribution toward that end is the complete sympathy with which Brutus is treated, even though an ingredient may be missing from a purely intellectual comprehension. Shakespeare pictures Brutus as the intractable, unworldly, unpractical idealist, but he has withal made him a human being of unmistakable goodness and greatness. It is that glorious liberty of his mind that makes it possible for him to recognize a good and a great man on a side that is not his. For it is Caesar's spirit that he makes us feel dominates it all. And in spite of the small foibles and pettinesses with which the poet shows him to us in his last days, it is Caesar's spirit that continues to dominate the drama when after the great man's death his power has fallen into the hands of that hardly impressive triumvirate. The little scene in which Shakespeare presents Mark Antony drawing up a proscription list is in itself a brilliant sample of his art. It is taken almost bodily from Plutarch, but in the few lines given it takes on fresh meaning, and we are made to see that bartering of lives in all its repulsiveness. In this, too, we are a long way from English history—not that there was a dearth of horrors there, but they were of a different kind.

Corneille, as I hinted, rendered the republican arguments of his conspirators more correctly than did Shakespeare in the Brutus monologue. But after all, Corneille only followed the Latin sources without probing underneath the words. Shakespeare, on the other hand made of Brutus a living character and of the conspiracy a gripping reality. If this proved to be beyond Corneille's power, it was first of all because he was lacking in that comprehensive sympathy which enabled Shakespeare to approach the losing side, whose defeat he felt was required by the immutable order of things, with understanding, let it be intuitive rather than intellectual understanding. Corneille presents the exposition of the republican ideal, but only in order to dissent from it, to make it appear as nothing compared with Augustus's (calculated) magnanimity. The whole play ends in an apotheosis of the ruler, which was what was intended from the start.

And certainly, the poet here for a moment succeeds in infusing life into his handiwork. In the long speech in which, in the last act, Augustus addresses the discomfited conspirators, revealing his imperial dignity and his contained force—a force which could annihilate did it not let itself be dominated by higher considerations—one feels in contact with a poetic, which is at the same time a historic, reality.

But this in the final reckoning is all. The rest of the play, the secondary characters and preparatory scenes, lack all value. In the poet's mind, or heart, the play had no other significance than that it should contribute to this one leading motif. The consequence is that this conspiracy of Cinna and his comrades remains a thing of purely mechanical dramatics and never becomes true history. All republican tirades cannot make it appear less factitious. Aemilia seems to take the creed seriously, but Aemilia, too, collapses. Cinna and Maximus are stage lovers rather than republicans. This complication of politics with love is purely a matter of stage convention; we have to accept such love as a mere verbal affirmation, for it never communicates itself to us by touching our feeling; and it destroys historic truth. It is as in *La Mort de César*, in which Voltaire (who was still, two or three generations later, a faithful adherent of seventeenth-century poetics) imagined he could improve upon Shakespeare (and upon history!) by making Brutus Caesar's natural son. But in consequence, veracity has fled. In *Cinna* Corneille has devised a plot that gives him an opportunity to let his personages (or puppets) declaim on all the variations of the given theme; but a real conspiracy and real Romans we are never made to see.

La Mort de Pompée is different. Here, more than in any other play, the poet has set out to give history from beginning to end. He is not a little proud of his documentation. In his preface he writes:

> If I were to do here what I have done in my earlier works and give the texts or summaries of the histories from which this play has been derived, . . . I should have to compose an introduction ten times longer than my poem, and entire books of almost all the authors on Roman history would have to be transcribed.

Good documentation does not by itself make a good work of history, much less a good history play. What did Corneille want to use his material for? Was he able, through imagination, to achieve contact with the life of antiquity? The underlying idea may be said to have been historic, albeit, in the proper classicist manner, generalizing and abstract. Corneille wanted to oppose the baseness, cowardice, weakness, and treachery of Egyptian royalty and the grandeur and nobility of the Romans. The ideal figure of the Roman, the dominator of the world, proud of his *vertu*, looking down on other nations and indeed inspired by a higher principle than any within their reach, is here embodied in Caesar; Cornelia, Pompey's widow, although Caesar's enemy, is in this respect his worthy compatriot, living even more completely as one dedicated to the ideal. The figure of Cleopatra is the play's great weakness. She has not been conceived historically, but was construed out of the logic of the poet's scheme. She is a ruler rather than a woman; and she wishes to show herself worthy of Caesar, her lover, by treating Ptolemy, his enemy, magnanimously, in the Roman fashion.

When Charmian, her lady-in-waiting, does not know what to make of this, Cleopatra says, superbly:

> This is what rulers owe to their high birth:
> Their souls take from their blood impressions
> Which subordinate their passions to their virtue.
> Their generosity places everything beneath their glory.[25]

This is not the historic Cleopatra, nor could it be. Such boasting, in one breath, of high birth, *vertu*, generosity, and glory belongs indissolubly to Corneille's own time and nation. Stapfer, while clearly discerning this, wants nevertheless to praise the tragic playwright and his classical manner. "Thus does Corneille, a great poet rather than a great painter, ennoble all that he touches." But this distinction between poet and painter is senseless. It is the poet himself who fails when his imagination will not create a Cleopatra in whom we can believe. And it is the poet in Shakespeare that made him create a Cleopatra who not only *lives*, with all her indestructible charm and insatiable coquetry, but might *really* exist in history. Corneille, in his customary style, has been able to evolve only a puppet, and the result, with all the eloquent phrases and high-sounding words, is no more poetic than Shakespeare's, nor is it any nobler—for what is the good of a nobility that has not come to life?

But Corneille's Caesar, too, misses the tune of both life and history. I hinted before that Corneille does not dispense even Caesar from his rule that the drama depends on love interest. The enamoured Caesar assures Cleopatra that it is in order to possess her that he has conquered the world. His assurance takes forty verses, and then another twenty-four, with a brief addition in conclusion, all in the insufferably repetitive language of convention, which any courtier familiar with the knightly epic of the decadence might have used. In Shakespeare's *Antony and Cleopatra* the love for Cleopatra is pictured

[25] Les princes ont cela de leur haute naissance:
  Leur âme dans leur sang prend des impressions
  Qui dessous leur vertu rangent leurs passions.
  Leur générosité soumet tout à leur gloire.

as a destroying element. Mark Antony, too, was a Roman and a dominator of the world; but because he was at the same time a lover, and a real one—not one only in protestations such as anyone in Corneille's age could reel off—he had to go to pieces. The distance between Corneille and Shakespeare is unmeasurable: as poets no less than in the capacity to get a grip on the past, in historic power. That these two qualities can be closely related, here becomes plain.

Racine's perception of Corneille's shortcomings was as keen as Corneille's perception of his. In the preface to *Britannicus*, from which I previously quoted his confession of faith in the single-motif drama, Racine added, as an instance of the senseless incidents and silly decoration with which others wished him to spoil his work, a caustic reference to this scene in *La Mort de Pompée* showing "a conqueror who would do nothing but descant on love." How could I dare, he exclaims, enter with such speeches as these into the presence of the great men of antiquity—for such he liked to imagine would be his readers and spectators. That his work is incomparably more harmonious than Corneille's, that it penetrates more profoundly into the human heart, and that in its own artificial world it exists triumphantly, everyone who is sensitive to poetry will admit. But in Racine's case it appears that the poetic imagination is not necessarily identical with the historic. Corneille manages occasionally to get hold of history; Racine, whatever he might think, remains divorced from it.[26]

SHAKESPEARE'S HISTORIC ATMOSPHERES, OR BACKGROUNDS

That the history dramas of Corneille and of Racine, albeit in different ways and to different degrees, are largely unhistoric,

[26] I agree, generally speaking, with Lytton Strachey's dictum, in his famous essay on Racine: "If, instead of asking what a writer is without, we try to discover simply what he is, will not our results be more worthy of our trouble?" But I am not writing on Racine; I am writing on Shakespeare; and if I have to apologize to the shade of the great Frenchman, it is only for using him as a foil to bring out more effectively the distinguishing qualities of Shakespeare.

has been recognized long, and on all sides. But on Shakespeare there is, in this respect, much less agreement among the critics. In France especially the theory has been expounded (it was already adumbrated in the passages quoted from Stapfer) that history and poetry cannot really exist together; that the dramatic poet cannot do otherwise than bring to the stage men and conditions of his own time; and that history can only serve him for a poetic haze or by way of decoration. Already Goethe said that Shakespeare had turned both his Romans and his medieval barons into Elizabethans.

Before Stapfer, Taine, in the essay on Racine which I discussed before, had systematized this view:

> Racine has been blamed for having under ancient names portrayed courtiers of Louis XIV; but that is just where he deserves praise: the theatre always represents contemporary morals. Euripides' mythological heroes are lawyers or philosophers like the youthful Athenians of his day. When Shakespeare wanted to paint Caesar, Brutus, Ajax, and Thersites, he made of them men of the sixteenth century. All Victor Hugo's young men are gloomy plebeians in revolt, the sons of René and of Childe Harold. In the last resort, an artist copies only what he sees, and cannot copy anything else; the remoteness and the perspective of history are of use to him only to add poetry to truth.

It is surprising that a theory which on critical analysis turns out to be completely untenable made such an impression on Stapfer. He closely follows Taine. The staging of a drama in the past or in a distant country, he says, has a poetic object: "The poet finds there the elevated generality that suits the inventions of poetry." So far his argument is less offensive than Taine's thesis of poetry (the past) superimposed upon truth (the poet's own civilization). Stapfer continues by saying that the illusion of remoteness in time and space is therefore all that is required, and that the antiquarian exactness of Ben Jonson imprisons the imagination in an inelastic reality. Here, too, I can assent. Ben Jonson, Shakespeare's contemporary, whom many scholars of the time placed above Shakespeare by virtue

of his erudition, cannot base thereon any claim either as a poet
or as a historian; no more than can Corneille on the wide
reading of which he boasts in his preface to *La Mort de
Pompée*. "The Turkey of the Turks," says Stapfer, "the China
of the Chinese, is the object of erudition, not of poetry." I am
not sure that I will agree, but now Stapfer jumps to a conclusion to which I most certainly cannot follow him. "The
Turks, and also the Greeks and the Romans, staged by Racine,
exhibited French and modern sentiments, but what to superficial criticism seemed a ridiculous error is at bottom the very
law of art." Voltaire (it is still Stapfer speaking) was wrong in
wanting to fix forever the particular style and the particular
anachronism of the age of Louis XIV. "But the great poets of
that age of Louis XIV had, in accordance with the law of art
and of the theatre, made their own anachronism: they had put
Greeks and Romans on the stage, and through the mouths of
those Greeks and Romans they had voiced the soul of their
own epoch. They were right."

They were *right*? If this is meant to mean "It does not matter
in Racine's case because, when all is said and done, he has,
in whatever way, created imperishable works of art, perfect of
their kind," I for one shall not demur. But if a "law of art and
of the theatre" is constructed and the historical drama told it
must not be anything but anachronistic, or it will become
unpoetic, then it is time to protest. I readily concede Victor
Hugo to these system builders. Again like Taine, Stapfer
adduces him triumphantly, remarking that he, who laughed
at Racine's "Frenchified Greeks," did not, in *Hernani* and
Ruy Blas, show Spaniards, but only "young men of 1830,
their heads afire by the reading of Chateaubriand and Byron,"
a new anachronism in the place of an old. That may be—but
is it not due to the egocentrism of that romantic school that
nowadays its work sounds so unbearably hollow to our ears?
And in any case, it denotes a curious blindness to put Shakespeare's work on one line with that of French classicist and
romantic poets and to suggest that it, too, owes its beauty to the
observance of that alleged law.

Stapfer admits that there are anachronisms in Racine that

offend (that there are such in Corneille we have seen); such, for instance, are the presentations in the same play of barbaric customs of the past and modern delicate sentiments: in *Iphigénie*, the human sacrifice; in *Andromaque*, the vanquished reduced to slavery. As a matter of fact, it would be possible to extend that objection considerably and to observe in all these plays a lack of harmony between the setting and the temper, or tone. But I shall confine myself to pointing out how far-fetched and how lame is the argument when it is invoked to prove that Shakespeare was saved from offending anachronisms only by the striking resemblance existing between the cruelty of ancient Rome and the rough manners of his England. The remark had already been made by Heine. Goethe and Heine, Voltaire and Taine,[27] and apparently Stapfer too—how little did they know of the England of their own day, let alone Elizabethan England! But one is tempted to add: how little did they understand Shakespeare, when, as against the uniformity of the backgrounds and characters in the French drama, they failed to observe the rich variety in his work; when they overlooked the miracle of his genius manifesting itself in the capacity to present mutually differing civilizations and the characters germane to each, and thus transcending mere observation (and "copying," to use Taine's word!) of the reality of his own day and surroundings.

No, if one reads Shakespeare without preconceived notions of what poetry should do or can do, it will be seen that the imagination opens up the past to him. He was aware of the difference of periods, and of the difference of civilizations. I think that this is the essential feature of his historic powers—which will always remain mysterious up to a point. His plays are not always set in the same stage-world, in what was really—in varying disguises—the poet's own drawing-room. Each play

[27] Even Taine. His *Histoire de la littérature anglaise* is uncommonly brilliant (as is all that he wrote), but as a picture of the English mentality, it is no less uncommonly one-sided and *outré*. And in any case, Taine committed the error of proclaiming all that he observed in his own day (and he observed only what fitted in with his preconceived opinion) as permanently and unalterably fixed in the English character, civilization, and society. Cf. F. C. Roe, *Taine et l'Angleterre* (1923), p. 144.

has its particular background, its own historic ambience. Its history is not just a superimposed decoration; it makes itself felt in all parts, like the key in a piece of music.

Shakespeare's sensitivity to different spheres or states of society and his capacity to suggest each in its peculiarity—one of the great gifts for which the historian should pray—appears in the whole of his work, including the plays that cannot be counted among the history plays. Action never develops in the abstract, nor necessarily in Shakespeare's own English, Elizabethan society. The impression made by the setting cannot always be expressed in historic terms. Sometimes only vaguely sociological terms, or even terms indicative of a mood, will suggest themselves; then one will speak of primitive, or highly-civilized; of fresh and sound, or corrupt; of cheerful, or melancholy; of light, or dark.[28]

How masterly is the evocation, in *Romeo and Juliet*, of the character of the little Italian town torn by a noblemen's feud, and how very specifically historical is this evocation. The very first scene gives a little sketch (I allude to that of the quarrel between Capulet's *bravi* and the adherents of Montague), in itself irresistibly witty and alive; moreover, it "places" the whole drama—and places it outside Shakespeare's own England. The love story, the character of Juliet, the monk, all helps to keep up the Italian atmosphere. No doubt, Mercutio's rousing tirade about Queen Mab is, listened to with this idea in mind, out of tune, for both the fancy and the folklore are thoroughly Germanic and English.[29] But the poet must be allowed his liberty. In some of the comedies such mixing of ingredients has been done systematically. And even so,

[28] A very fine example of this approach is Bradley's characterization of *Macbeth*. See *Shakespearean Tragedy*, pp. 264 ff. The atmosphere of the play, he summarizes, is that of "blackness," but "not that of unrelieved blackness. On the contrary, as compared with *King Lear* and its cold dim gloom, *Macbeth* leaves a decided impression of colour."

[29] This is not, of course, the only instance. Even in the quarrelling scene with which the play opens, typically English and un-Italian traits can be observed. I mention only Sampson's comical anxiety, while challenging the rival party, to keep "the law," on his side. One should not look for exact archaeological faithfulness in Shakespeare.

Shakespeare shows his mastery in the characterization of social atmospheres. This very thing is one of the delights of *A Midsummer Night's Dream:* the Athenian court and the regal air of Theseus and Hippolyta and the two pairs of lovers, contrasted with the lower-middle-class (and frankly English) appearance of Bottom and his companions, and behind or above these two groups the ethereal world of the fairies.

The scene of *Othello* is laid, and laid truly, in a Venetian, a Mediterranean surrounding, and one of a not very distant time. The play's vivid colouring and passionate temper agree with that setting. Against this, *King Lear* is a northerly piece, with grey and gloomy tints; in the storm and on the heath that tonality culminates, and withal there is—from the opening scene on—the distant in time, the primitive. Compare *Hamlet* and *Macbeth*. What a contrast! One will best realize this by trying mentally to transpose a character like Polonius from the one play to the other: he would be completely out of place. But the same is true for Horatio, for Osric and the duel, for the travelling players and their performance at court, and really for every character and for every scene. *Hamlet* may have nothing very typically Danish, but the world in which the action unfolds bears a modern, a sixteenth-century, character; the scene is laid at a highly-cultured Renaissance court. As against that, the world of *Macbeth* is, and not through the witches only, but in all its details, wild, barbaric, remote in time.

Need I remark that this transposing of minor characters from one play to another would not in Racine's dramatic *oeuvre* raise the same difficulty? Make, for instance, Phénice and Zatime exchange places, your only difficulty will be that you cannot picture to yourself either of these personages in any sharply marked delineation. Zatime, the slave woman of Roxane in *Bajazet*, has nothing Turkish but her name; while you will, I trust, take it from me that Phénice is Bérénice's "confidante."

VONDEL'S HISTORICAL DRAMAS

There is another poet whose work will yield interesting points of comparison: Joost van den Vondel (1587-1679), who, between 1620 and 1674, wrote a large number of plays, some of which are among the glories of Dutch literature.

Many of these plays were history plays, and Vondel, more than the French playwrights, more also than Hooft, plainly and principally intended, in several of them at least, to do justice to historic truth—to stage an episode of history, certified by the best authorities. In this respect there is a similarity between Vondel's history plays and Shakespeare's plays about the kings of England. Unfortunately, Vondel saddled himself with one crushing difficulty: the Aristotelian unities, which he obediently accepted, and which could not but hamper and stunt the execution of this task.[30] Local colour had mostly to be supplied in the form of lengthy descriptions, or in relations of events that had happened before, or elsewhere.

This is one explanation of the appalling long-windedness and the deficiency of true dramatic power by which so much of Vondel's work for the stage is characterized. Another is in Vondel's propensity to casuistry, in which he betrays his relationship with the French, and especially, with Corneille. The intellectualism of the seventeenth-century classicist mind, which the personages of Vondel's plays can so tiresomely reveal in their finespun dialectics about moral problems, about the divine law, about social propriety, tends not only to lessen the dramatic tension but to blot the delineation of character. Must I in this connection make mention also of the alexan-

[30] The most striking example of how the compulsion of the unities hampered Vondel in his presentation of history is afforded by his *Maria Stuart*. What a subject! The conflicts with Knox, the murder of Darnley, the murder of Riccio, the flight to England, the imprisonment, the conspiracies against Elizabeth! But Vondel stages for us only the last day of the martyred Queen's life. The Catholic propagandist conception of the drama ruled out, in any case, the possibility of its imparting any truly historical impression.

drine? The alexandrine was perhaps a disaster for French poetry and the French drama; that it was a disaster for Dutch poetry and the Dutch drama seems to me undeniable. The Dutch alexandrine, lacking the rapidity and the suppleness that the French still managed to impart to the cumbrous metre, was like a heavy cloak thrown round each of the characters in the drama, impeding natural movements with its stiff folds. Quick, witty, passionate, subtle touches could hardly be attempted; they would in any case be stifled under that oppressive decking. Shakespeare's pentameter, especially as he developed it in the course of time, eliminating rhyme altogether and freely using enjambments, afforded incomparably greater facilities for adaptation to various characters and to dramatic situations. And Shakespeare, moreover, did not scruple to drop into prose when he thought fit.

However, the purely historic intention can be observed in Vondel. It is even predominant, to such a degree that several of his plays are no more than dramatized historic events. True dramatic conception is lacking; there is no denouement, at least no tragic one, none that might shed significance on what the spectator had witnessed on the stage, that in his perception might elevate or ennoble the hero.

Take *Jozef in Dothan.* In the last act Joseph is sold into slavery by his brothers; the entire play before that consisted of their deliberations and of their disputes with the one among them who attempted to prevent the crime. At first they had intended to kill Joseph; the kindly brother had indeed thought, for an instant, that Joseph had been killed. This brother is enlightened, yet the play ends on a misunderstanding: the plotters trick their aged father, Jacob (whose preference for Joseph was the source of their hatred), to believe, by means of a coat dipped in goat's blood, that Joseph has been devoured by an evil beast. Since Jacob could not be shown on an Aristotelian stage, the kindly brother has perforce to portray his despair for the benefit of the audience. That Joseph still had a future, the spectator knew because he was familiar with the Bible, but Vondel could not realize this fact dramatically. The incident alone was what the poet sought. And, indeed,

Vondel followed the play with another about an incident in Joseph's life, his involvement with Potiphar's wife. *Jozef in Egypte* ends equally undramatically, with Joseph's imprisonment. The guilt of the lying temptress remains hidden, and once again the perilous situation in which the hero is left is not in reality the last chapter of his life.

Nevertheless Vondel has most certainly in *Jozef in Dothan* at least (for *Jozef in Egypte* is a much weaker play), caught something of the flavour of the Old Testament world. How heavy a handicap he imposed upon himself by submitting to the Aristotelian rules is most strikingly apparent in Jacob's absence from the stage. We are only told about him. The motif of the patriarch and his sons is, after all, the most characteristic, and the most historically as well as dramatically significant theme of the story—we would like to have *seen* it. Shakespeare, with the so much greater latitude afforded him by his dramatic style, would never have allowed it to escape him. But at any rate, Vondel, if only in the circumstantial accounts given by the conspiring and quarrelling brothers, proves, not only that he has understood something of the relationships of their patriarchal society, but that it has moved him and that he has sought to communicate his interest. The play has more colour and more historic background than the average French tragedy.

At times Vondel has been completely successful in such milieu painting, in such placing of a drama in a particular past.

Will it be permissible in this connection to mention *Lucifer* and *Adam in Ballingschap* ("Adam in Exile")? In any case, the beauty of these—the greatest of his plays—is to be found largely in the grandiose experience they have in store for us, the suggestion of actions occurring not simply on our everyday earth, not simply among human beings, but among angels and archangels, and between the first created couple and God. In characterization Vondel is never strong, but it is not only symbolism or theology with which his mind is occupied: he is an imaginative poet; his work has a strong plastic quality.

For purely historic presentation or description we must, of

course, turn to other plays. The finest instance, truly poetic, that I know in the whole of Vondel, is the first act of *De Gebroeders* (*The Brethren*). The play itself, which in Vondel's *oeuvre* immediately precedes *Jozef in Dothan*, is not without dramatic power. The theme of the killing of Saul's seven sons by the reluctant King David, at the bidding of a divine oracle and under popular pressure—a placatory sacrifice in the face of the destructive drought with which God is visiting Israel—that gruesome theme lends itself to dramatic treatment. It is true that Vondel gives free rein to all those peculiarities that so easily chill us: the case is *argued* with the greatest intellectual refinement; the tragic mother's despair is presented movingly enough, yet always conventionally as a tragic mother's despair, without any of those lightning or abysmal phrases that might make us feel in the presence of a human being struggling with the eternal mystery, or with fate; moreover, she proves herself, in a pages-long stichomythia, to be possessed of a dialectical readiness of wit that is indeed highly untragic. As for the seven unfortunate brothers, they remain completely devoid of individual features, and throughout they are made to speak in chorus.

However this may be, the first act is a splendid piece of poetic evocation. It portrays no more than the meeting between the High Priest of Geba, accompanied by his attending priests, and David, with his train of Levites. The misery caused by the drought is related, and it is decided to go and pray for God's counsel. The broad swell of the alexandrines, interrupted by some single lines at the moment of salutation, and concluded by a chorus, flows along with the action: Abiathar and his priests descending from the mountain, David and his followers coming up, their meeting, their going off together. The exalted status of the priesthood, and the majesty of the kingly office are expressed in that powerful rhythm. And meanwhile, from the exchange of speeches there has risen the spectacle of the parched land, of the desperate people, of the priest in his symbolically meaningful garnish, of the pious David chosen by God himself to take the place of the idolatrous Saul—and we feel that we are not in Amsterdam or in Holland, nor in

the year 1639, but in the distant, foreign world of the Old
Testament.

As a matter of fact, this Old Testament world lived particularly insistently in Vondel's imagination.[31] He has most
convincingly succeeded in giving shape to it in *De Gebroeders*,
but it may be said that generally, in all the plays dealing with
this kind of subject, it makes itself felt to some extent. He was
less successful with the earlier history of his own country.

Gijsbreght van Aemstel? It is obvious indeed that the poet set
out in that play to sketch a society different from that of his
own day. His loving treatment of Romish features was one
contribution to that end (he was, indeed, soon to become a
convert to Catholicism). The turmoil of war, too, must have
given the quiet citizens who saw the play performed the feeling
that they were transferred to older times. But in the play's
characters there is nothing, either in behaviour or in outlook,
that is specifically medieval.

No doubt the poet has done his best, and he treats us to a
good many historical particulars. These, however, strike us as
interesting bits of knowledge and as evidence of erudition
rather than as indispensable elements that set the play's
historical atmosphere. This is partly due to the technique to
which I alluded before: lengthy narrative speeches instead of
action; characters who argue and deliver dissertations instead
of speaking from the heart or just simply living in their own
different ways. There are moments when we seem near to
getting scenes such as those through which Shakespeare makes
us breathe the historic atmosphere of a play, scenes that would
be unthinkable in a French tragedy: when, for instance, the
soldiers violently break into the monastery. Nobody will want
a period piece, correct in all details, so long as life has been
surprised in one of its universal manifestations. Yet, although
there is the attempt, Vondel's strength does not lie here. One
could more easily imagine that the great comic playwright
Bredero (1585-1618) might have equalled Shakespeare in the

---

[31] I recall here Racine's *Athalie*, which also owes its Old Testament
setting to an atmosphere definitely distinct from that prevailing in the
poet's other plays.

achievement of this kind of effect, if only the classicist fashion had not made so rigid a separation between tragedy and comedy as to leave little more than the lower forms of life to the latter.

No play is so exclusively a piece of staged national history as *Batavische Gebroeders, of Onderdrukte Vrijheid (Batavian Brothers, or Freedom Oppressed)*. One cannot without a certain hesitation undertake to test it on its poetic and historic value: it was a work of Vondel's extreme old age. Yet *Adam in Ballingschap* was still to come. Was not the weakness of *Batavische Gebroeders* the result of the impotence of Vondel's imagination in the face of this kind of subject matter, and does the play not therefore demand a relentless examination?

What strikes us in the first place, then, is the utterly undramatic character of *Batavische Gebroeders*. There is no action, there is no conflict, there are no living persons; the historic atmosphere is only related (and with the most startling anachronisms), it is never made visible.

One would expect any poet who intends to show us Claudius Civilis in opposition to Roman dominion in the country of the Batavians to place him, as the great leader of the revolt, squarely in the centre. But when one has finished reading the *Batavian Brothers*, the revolt is still only in prospect. Vondel chose as his theme the oppression that went before (and he plainly expressed this in his subtitle). The unity of time, the compulsive prescription of the one day, which did not hinder Racine in the development of his purely inner conflicts, was a serious stumbling block for Vondel. He could not treat together both oppression and revolt—in this he was less fortunate than Shakespeare, who would not have scrupled to cover a period of years if this was necessary for the purpose of making history live. Historically speaking, Claudius Civilis had not been the indisputable leader during the oppression, for he had shared that position with his brother; together they were arrested, and it was the brother who was put to death. What matters to Vondel is to display their innocence. This lends to their appearance something of timidity. The chorus and even their sister, who in the first act come to incite them to action, obtain nothing but dilatory and pacifying words.

The brothers are, nevertheless, arrested, and sentenced—unjustly. Again, the brothers merely proclaim their innocence, and subsequently, stage a contest of magnanimity to determine which of them shall bear the (undeserved) blame. Martyrs, much more than heroes, are these two.

Typically Vondel? Indeed, even of Lucifer he—differing from Milton!—was not able to make a true rebel. But it is typical, too, of the spirit of a century in which there was a widespread feeling that submission to the established powers was the highest virtue. It is typical, moreover, of the then current historical view of the Batavians. In them and in their "constitution" Dutch intellectuals recognized (no less a person than Grotius had set the fashion) the prototypes of themselves and of their own constitution, and moreover, they idealized themselves and that constitution as the embodiment of the pattern of liberty consonant with order and respect for authority.

The observation I made with regard to Hooft can here be applied to Vondel as well. The poet's object is rather to offer a lesson or treatise on constitutional law than to evoke an image of the past; and the drama suffers. When the mother of the two brothers exhorts them to fight to the death, it is for "the country's liberty" and for "the holy right of the States" (meaning the sovereign assembly of the province of Holland, which was, of course, far to seek in the days of the Romans). Claudius Civilis and his brother (who is called Nicolaas Burgerhart in Vondel's play) are therefore pictured as patrician gentlemen, averse to precipitate action and popular passion, fond of liberty no doubt, but above all dedicated to order and the rule of law.

This makes it understandable—although it does not make it any the less undramatic—that Vondel has neglected that splendid detail offered him by Tacitus, namely, that Civilis used to compare himself with Hannibal and Sertorius, both one-eyed like himself. In the play, Fonteius, the Roman governor, does mention those two dangerous enemies of Rome —in order to compare *both* the brothers to them. We are meant to note the injustice done to the brothers, who were—we are not allowed to forget it—loyal, and men of order; but meanwhile all difference between the two is obliterated, and there is not a word about that thrilling bodily defect of Civilis. The fire of opposition to an alien rule is expressed only at the very end of the play, in an explosive speech by Burgerhart. Five acts had apparently been needed to justify Burgerhart's outburst for Vondel's tender sense of legality.

And how much prolix argumentation has been involved. The play as a whole is almost intolerably wordy. The endless stichomythias are not more exhausting than are the lengthy speeches made by each character in turn. A feeble attempt has been made to characterize Fronto, the Roman director of the press gang: he is the lawless oppressor, the exponent of tyranny. But he is no less given to long speeches. When he has managed, for instance, with great difficulty, to load a number of Batavians aboard a ship, he describes the scene of woe thus:

> . . . all the river's bank was wet with the tears
> Of grandmother, mother, niece, daughter-in-law,
>   sister, aunts.

No parody could surpass this!

As regards the historic background, Vondel, although he had Tacitus's *Germania* before him, was not even remotely successful in visualizing that primitive society. When Fonteius describes the defeat of the Chatti (of course, the rules prevented this being shown on the stage), for a fleeting moment we seem to be getting nearer; elsewhere, too, we hear of holy oaks and orgies in dark forests. But *mentioning*—and there is nothing else, never more than narration—will not do the trick. Besides, the characters talk just as fluently about streets and towngates, and about milkmaids with shining copper pails. And what is the important thing: these sentimental, tearful, softhearted Batavians, forever holding forth about their rights, resemble in nothing the Batavians as they were in reality, do not even resemble the idealized Germans Tacitus had sketched.

A moment ago, to explain Vondel's presentation I referred to the spirit of the time. Genius, of course, does not let itself be curbed by such a master. In Shakespeare's time the horror of rebellion was already making headway, and Shakespeare had his share of it. But that did not prevent him from understanding the great rebels and bringing them to life. The comparison that here thrusts itself upon one is, however, with Rembrandt. Just before Vondel wrote his *Batavian Brothers*, Rembrandt had been commissioned to paint the "Conspiracy of Claudius Civilis" for one of the walls of the Amsterdam town hall. All that is lacking in Vondel's play is to be found in Rembrandt. The barbaric, the savage, the vigorous, the passionate—in the countenances and in the attitudes of the plotters who crowd about the table lighted up by torches in the vast dark room—it has all been grippingly evoked, and the effect is embodied in the mighty one-eyed figure, who, sturdily and fatefully seated, holds his sword aloft, while the others touch it with theirs. That blunt presentation of the first Dutch warrior for freedom apparently offended the chastened convention soon to be enshrined afresh by Vondel. At any rate, the burgomasters of Amsterdam refused Rembrandt's largest historical painting. Today only the central fragment survives— in the museum at Stockholm![32]

Modern historic, no less than artistic, awareness will unhesitatingly recognize the veracity of Rembrandt's fantasy as against the nerveless invention of Vondel. What does it matter that the oaths were taken in a forest rather than, as the painter saw it, in a room; or that not everything is accurate about the costumes and the swords of these Germanic warriors; or that Civilis wears a turban! Rembrandt knew how to render the primitive and the savage. Everyone can see at once that his are the authentically desperate conspirators and that they were moved by very different motives and acted under

[32] The contrast between *Batavian Brothers* and Rembrandt's "Conspiracy of Claudius Civilis" was indicated by Schmidt Degener, *De Gids*, 1919 (reprinted in *Phoenix*, 1942, pp. 142 ff.) As for the reasons underlying the rejection of the picture, stress is usually laid on the offence given by its baroque style to the still dominant classicist tradition. The whole question remains debatable. See Seymour Slive, *Rembrandt and His Critics* (The Hague, 1953), p. 78, where, however, the point made by me, and before me by Degener, of the departure from the legendary representation of Claudius Civilis the Liberator, is not even mentioned.

the stimulus of very different passions from those the poet or the painter might have observed around him in the erudite and decent burghers of Amsterdam, familiar with the pen and the account book and the law court.

As an illustration accompanying the *Batavian Brothers*, Rembrandt's "conspiracy" would be absurd. But Macbeth's banquet, at which Banquo's ghost horrifies Macbeth and Macbeth's terror disconcerts his guests, might have been painted by that same hand.

(*Cetera desunt.*)   (1947)

II

HISTORIANS RECONSIDERED

1. Motley and his "Rise of the Dutch Republic"

A hundred years ago John Lothrop Motley published his famous history of the revolt of the Netherlands against Spanish rule. Generations of English and American readers since have gathered from its pages all their notions of that famous episode and even of Dutch history.

A work that conquered the world in the way *The Rise of the Dutch Republic* did must have qualities. They are not the qualities that appeal to professional historians, and some reserve was apparent in the reception the work received in their circles, especially in Holland. Indeed it was a little hard on the small band of devoted workers in the field of history, men whose names are still honoured in Holland among scholars, and are not unknown to the general public (let me mention only Fruin); it was a little hard on them that, while they were laying the foundations for a truer understanding of the great events of the second half of the sixteenth century, along came this unknown American from Boston and set the world (including the Dutch public) reading about the wicked Philip II and the noble William the Silent, about the struggle between the tiny Netherlands and the mighty empire of Spain.

Fruin, in a review expanded into an essay of two hundred pages, in effect rewrote all Motley's chapters on the preliminaries of the revolt, down to the arrival of the Duke of Alva in 1567, and, while he never departed from the tone of courtesy and respect, the impression Fruin left with the reader was that Motley had not really understood the events about which he wrote with such fervour and in such glowing colours; that he had used all his art to heighten the effects of the drama by representing one side as villains or fools and the other as Virtue, Wisdom, and Heroism personified; that he had not probed behind the appearance of events. The truth, as shown by Fruin, was less dramatic; the rights and the wrongs, the virtues and the vices, were more equally divided. The actors prominent on the stage of events were not the masters of the action either; history was not decided by their personal aims and qualities so much as by large tendencies, general European developments of which they were the exponents.

Fruin's work could never attain the popularity that Motley enjoyed for so long, but it has stood the test of time infinitely better. His interpretation has been found to be faulty in more than one respect, but it is still a matter of debate among historians. No historian, however, can take Motley's interpretation seriously any longer, and scholars carry out their investigations and conduct their discussions without referring to him or to his views.

Nevertheless, when, after I don't know how many years, I read *The Rise of the Dutch Republic* again, I could understand how it came to make such an impression. It is admirably told. The characters are sketched in bold outline. There are about the book a vigour and a conviction that sweep the reader along. One is not invited to pause and consider subtleties or contradictions. A sense of drama is conveyed by clear-cut contrasts, and the plot and the solutions all seem perfectly obvious.

Yet even the general reader of today—more than the general reader of the nineteenth century—will instinctively doubt whether life can have been as dramatic, and especially, as clear, as all that. The positiveness, the absence of half-shades, will arouse his distrust. As for the historian, who comes to the book with some independent knowledge, what amazes him is how it has been possible to miss the realities to such an extent and yet to create an illusion of pulsating life.

To Motley—and this explains both the weakness of his history and the fascination it exercised over readers of the Age of Liberalism—the story of the revolt was an epic in the eternal struggle waged by Liberty and Enlightenment with Despotism and Darkness.

Motley sees Philip and his servants (above all, that unspeakable man of blood, the Duke of Alva) as the forces of Evil. He admits no redeeming features. He cannot accept that they honestly believed themselves to be doing their duty, and instead of explaining their harsh policy as conditioned by the prevailing sentiments of their time, or as the outcome of all-too human shortsightedness or stupidity, he can see nothing but the crimes of cruelty or of sycophancy. It is not only Philip who is to him the Prince of Wickedness: from Charlemagne on, that is how he regards all emperors and kings. In the Netherlands he sees the rulers, throughout the centuries preceding the revolt, trying to fasten lawless domination and oppression upon a brave, innocent, and liberty-loving people, a people as brave, innocent, and liberty-loving as were the English who rose against the Stuarts, and the Americans who rose against George III and his ministry. This, to him, is the true meaning of history: the struggle between Despotism and Liberty resulting in the glorious victory of the latter. The Netherlands and the English revolts had been important contributions to this victory, until it was finally consummated in the American Revolution.

I hold no brief for despotism, nor do I wish to decry liberty. But the simplistic view of Motley is a denial of history. History is not made up of struggles between God and the Devil. The Good Cause is inevitably and treacherously attended by tendencies less good. The Bad Cause has its connections with what is wholesome and indispensable. Fallible man, on whichever side of the struggle he is engaged, is not sanctified, nor is he entirely given over to evil. The absolute rulers of the sixteenth century, and indeed their predecessors, tyrannical as they were at times do represent a beneficent principle; they were the builders of states in which order prevailed; order, not of subjection only, but of law.

On the other hand, the cry of "liberty" covered a multitude of selfish interests, local narrowness, class privilege. In the Netherlands especially, the national unity that was to shake off the alien monarchy so dramatically had had the way prepared for it by the centuries-long action of this same power acquiring

or conquering one after another of the separate counties and
duchies that were to become the seventeen provinces. The
republic born from the violent reaction against the authoritarian tendencies of the monarchy is unreservedly hailed by
Motley as a great achievement of wisdom and true statesman-
ship, and no doubt it did make a striking appearance in a
Europe in which absolutism continued to prevail for another
two centuries and more. The principle of liberty proved a
fruitful one in many areas of life. The seventeenth century
became Holland's golden age in power, in art, and in literature.
That burgher society teemed with energy.

But it was a major disaster in Netherlands history that in
the process north and south were disrupted. The Dutch
Republic consisted of only seven of the seventeen provinces.
Moreover, interprovincial relations were regulated by the
Union of Utrecht on the basis of provincial sovereignty. The
problem of unity, in other words, remained unsolved, and this
was a constant source of weakness and of trouble, to which in
the end the Republic succumbed. Another revolution, under
the aegis of the great French Revolution this time, was needed
to bring about that national state to which Netherlands history
had been tending—but this state was achieved only on the
basis of the seven provinces, all situated north of the river
barrier, that had been able to hold out against the Duke of
Parma's campaigns of reconquest. In the later stages of the
protracted war (the Eighty Years' War!), some forty or fifty
years after the southern provinces had been reduced to
obedience and at the same time purged of Protestantism, the
northern Republic (as it now was) had been able to launch out
south of the rivers and occupy portions of the provinces of
Flanders and Brabant, which, completely re-Catholicized as
they were, were held as "Generality Lands."

There are questions involved here which belong to the very
heart of the story and to which Motley gave only scant
attention—questions, one may say, which he never understood.
The most fundamental problem, the problem of Protestantism
and of its role in the opposition and the revolt, was entirely
beyond him. In Motley's account the fight for liberty and the

fight for Protestantism seem one. In reality the two were not only distinct, but, although in some ways and at some moments they coincided and reinforced each other, they were also liable to lock in disastrous conflict.

"All this we do for liberty," or "all this we do for religion": these tags formulated two opposing views of the aims of the rebellion. The first: to put a stop to the centralizing policy and its highhanded methods; to safeguard the old liberties and privileges of towns, provinces, and classes: to ward off the arbitrary interference of an alien ruler served by alien ministers and soldiers. The second: to break the monopoly of the Roman Catholic Church and to make the country into a preserve for the elect, a temple for the true word of God, cleansed from superstition and priestly tricks; in short, something entirely different. The first programme may be described as the national one. Insofar as the revolt was dominated by it, the parallel, on which Motley insists so much, with the English Revolution of 1688 and the American Revolution of 1775, is justified. But the second, the programme of the Calvinists, which appealed to no more than a minority, a tiny minority even, of the nation, introduced into the situation a more violently revolutionary element.

What Motley never seems to realize clearly is that the Protestants *were* but a minority—and the Calvinists were but a section of the Protestants. The Calvinists, naturally, pricked up their ears when the nobility began to oppose the King, and they became the most energetic and determined supporters of the struggle when it developed into a rebellion. But from the first their coming out into the open tended to frighten Catholics back into the royal fold. I am thinking now of what happened in 1566, as a result of the famous outbreak known as the "Breaking of the Images."

Radical minorities, no doubt, often manage to impose themselves in revolutions. That they could do so in Holland, however, they owed entirely to geographical circumstances and even to help from outside. In the first real act of rebellion, in 1572, when the two seaboard provinces of Holland and Zeeland declared for the Prince of Orange, their stadholder, now in exile, the determining factor had come from overseas. It was the Sea Beggars—the Calvinist exiles of 1567, drawn from all the provinces, who had taken to the seas, forming an irregular fighting force for the displaced Prince—it was they who now invaded the two coastal provinces and by their unforeseen intervention brought their co-religionists into positions of power.

This is how Motley opens his chapter on this really crucial moment in the revolt: "The example thus set by Brill was rapidly followed." But look a little more closely and it will be seen that Brill, the little seaport where the Beggar fleet first put in an appearance, did not do anything so active as setting an example. The magistrates fled in fear of their lives, followed by most of the inhabitants. It was an almost empty town in which the Beggar chief effected a landing. Motley, however, goes on to describe the subsequent events in the province as "a spontaneous movement": "With one fierce bound of enthusiasm the nation shook off its chains."

Again, how different was the reality! With one single and still somewhat doubtful exception, not a town declared for the Prince of its own accord. All waited until a Beggar chief with his armed band appeared before the gates. Generally he was only reluctantly admitted, after a long parley, and after articles of capitulation had been agreed upon. Chief among these there was always a stipulation that the exercise of the Catholic religion and the persons and goods of the clergy should be left undisturbed. Hardly were the Beggars inside when, in most cases, returning exiles, with the help of secret sympathizers in the town and backed by the presence of the armed invaders, made themselves masters of the town hall, reconstituted the town government, and seized one or more churches for the Protestant service.

Once matters had come to that pass, there was no holding them. The States of Holland, representing the revolutionized town magistracies, which began by proclaiming the Prince of Orange, soon forbade the exercise of the Catholic religion. And when the Spanish army, which had easily overawed the provinces south and east, entered Holland and Zeeland to put down the rebellion, it found an established government, headed now by William the Silent and provided with a fighting force determined to stick it out. It was this that stiffened the resistance of Holland and Zeeland through those heroic years from 1572 to 1576. And when, in the latter year, by the Pacification of Ghent, the other provinces joined in, spontaneously this time, under their traditional and unchanged magistrates and assemblies, it was still the fixed point acquired by Calvinism in 1572 in Holland and Zeeland which determined the course of events in the Netherlands as a whole—which determined, in particular, that the rebellion was to be wedded indissolubly to Calvinism. Note that the part played by the two provinces was due, not to the exceptional enterprise of their populations or to any more than average inclination towards the new religion, but to the descent, at an opportune moment, of the Sea Beggar forces, which were drawn from the more radical elements of all the provinces.

It is at first sight extraordinary that Motley praised the revolt as a triumph of Liberalism, of Enlightenment, of Democracy. That it was carried through by a minority dictatorship, using the customary methods of violence and suppression, seems to have escaped his attention. Revolutions do not work by the rules of liberalism; enlightenment and democracy do not fare well by them. We of our generation have had our memory refreshed on that score. At the same time it is also true that one must not paint all revolutions with the same brush. In the case of the Netherlands revolt the excesses of minority dictatorship were soon mitigated by the new regent class, which, while dutifully conforming to the new dominant church, was in truth more concerned about freedom than about religion. Its members were, in fact, regents before they were Calvinists, and they were very determined not to allow themselves to be dictated to by the Calvinist ministers. The Dutch Republic was certainly very far from being a model of either a liberal or a democratic state, yet it was much more liberal and democratic than its origins would lead one to expect.

This no doubt was one of the factors that led Motley into

his interpretation of the revolt. And he was, in fact, far from being singular. Among Dutch historians, too, the myth that suited the interests of the newly dominant group of Protestants has long ruled supreme. Today one will not look in Motley's work for a faithful presentation of sixteenth-century men and conditions. But one can still enjoy it as an eloquent and sincere testimony of nineteenth-century liberal idealism.

(1956)

2. French Historians For and Against the Revolution

Is the French Revolution still worth talking about? Is it more than a subject with which historical erudition will no doubt go on playing its sterile game, but which can hardly affect us in our actual problems, in our thinking about the world as it is today?

If I ask these questions, it is not because there are any doubts in my mind. But there is a school of thought in our Western countries, nowadays, vocal, animated by the consciousness of having a significant message to impart, according to which this preoccupation with strictly European subjects denotes our blindness to the changes the world has gone through.

Professor Barraclough, for instance, tells us that we should "disabuse our minds of the illusion that there is any special relevance, from the point of view of contemporary affairs, in studying those neolithic figures"—he means: Louis XIV, Napoleon, Bismarck! Dr. Toynbee has made the word "parochial" a familiar one in this connection. One of our Dutch historians (Professor Presser) gave it as his opinion, a couple of years ago, that compared with the Russian and Chinese Revolutions the French Revolution was but a provincial affair; others in Holland exhort us to take a "universalist" view of history and denounce "the Eurocentric" attitude.

I shall not enter into a discussion of these views. But I want to state, somewhat apodictically, that such views seem to me to lead dangerously close to a denial of history. Is not western Europe, much as it may have lost in power, the same western Europe? And is it not our own past that is so cavalierly pushed aside? Do our traditions and ingrained beliefs no longer count because we have lost our grip on Asia and on Africa?

The inspiration of our universalists often seems to be what I regard as a detestable defeatism with respect to the vitality and prospects of Western society and civilization. They are obsessed with the idea of change to the extent of not caring any longer to preserve our heritage. Their outlook is akin to that truly revolutionary mentality which Croce, twenty-five years ago, described under the name of "anti-historism"— "that feeling," as Croce defined it, "that true history is only about to begin, and that we are at last escaping from the bonds of false history and struggling into freedom and space." What strikes me as being a little pathetic is that the advocates of a universalist revision have not even the satisfaction, and the excitement, and the pride, that can go with making your revolution yourself. But in the meantime, the illusion of anti-historism, as Croce, faced by the new barbarisms of Fascism and National Socialism, pointed out, entails a frightful wastage of cultural riches. True history, by ensuring, not immobility, but continuity, is indispensable for the preservation of civilization.

If there is one subject that can enlighten us on this score, it is the French Revolution, in which the anti-historical mentality was so prominent. In itself a fascinating spectacle! But it is not less fascinating, and certainly not less instructive, to watch the gradual disillusionment when reality did not so readily and completely as the enthusiasts and the fanatics had hoped, yield to theorizing divorced from history and tradition.

In referring, then, to the French Revolution, what I mean is the action and the reaction, the reforming zeal and the stubborn resistance. Neither the one nor the other tendency is to be wholly accepted, nor is either to be wholly rejected. Revolutions, for all their being necessarily destructive and but a clumsy and costly means of achieving a sometimes scanty result, belong to the forms of the life of mankind which historians cannot simply condemn. To us at any rate, the French Revolution will always be, in its entirety, of the most immediate interest, for it can be said that our modern Western world is largely shaped by it. But it is shaped by the negation as well as by the assertion, by the example of the daring attempt, and also by the warning implied in the partial failure, by the striving and by the recognition of the bounds calling a halt to it; it is shaped not by the revolutionary doctrine so much as by the protracted struggle to which it gave rise, not by orthodox acceptance, but by the debate.

A debate that was carried on through several generations! The French Revolution, when viewed in this way, did not end in 1794, with the fall of Robespierre—as Michelet thought it did; nor in 1795, when Bonaparte dispersed the Paris mob by "a whiff of grapeshot"—with which Carlyle concludes his history; nor in 1799, when Bonaparte constituted himself a dictator—where Madelin and a host of others write *finis;* not even in 1814 and 1815, when the Bourbon monarchy was restored. The contrasts had not been resolved. France was to be shaken by one violent change of regime after another. If at last a conclusion has been reached (and can we say it has been, even now?), it is one of compromise, of equilibrium, of synthesis.

I propose, in this essay, to trace developments since the Bourbon restoration, especially as they were reflected in the ever-changing historical interpretation of the great initial crisis. I shall limit my observation to France, because nowhere else was the great clash of ideas more continuous and more vehement, and nowhere else did it centre to the same extent round the issue of the acceptance or rejection of the principles and the doings of the men of 1789 and 1793. Moreover, just as the exceptionally profound social contrasts and the economic maladjustment in France had caused the outbreak to occur there, so the resentments and hatreds left behind by the upheaval—resentments and hatreds that hindered developments after the Restoration from taking a smooth course—were more implacable there than elsewhere. Extreme still stood against extreme. The Revolution was not really overcome.

I

Mme de Staël

Stability would be possible in France only if the government took seriously the *Charte*, which had been granted by Louis XVIII shortly after his return. This was the view presented by Mme de Staël in the book she left upon her death in 1817, *Considérations sur la Révolution française*. And her conclusion was based on a reading of the history of the Revolution.

"Not to be wholly accepted, nor to be wholly rejected"—this is indeed what had been said at once by those reacting from the extreme course of the Terror,[1] and it was repeated on innumerable occasions by their successors, by Napoleon himself. The idea that the Revolution must be terminated, and that it could be terminated only by a compromise safeguarding its beneficent achievements, had been a commonplace of French political thinking ever since the fall of Robespierre. Only, the compromises attempted had not worked. What *were* its beneficent achievements? What were its unfulfilled aspirations worth reviving? Those questions admitted of widely differing answers.

Equality was a principle commanding wide assent, but in practice no advance had been made beyond an equality restricted to legal or civil rights, an equality that did not hamper the propertied classes in enjoying their property, and adding to it. The aspirations towards social reform stirring wildly and blindly in 1793 and 1794 had been defeated, but they had not been really disposed of. The time was to come when this antinomy between bourgeois complacency about civil equality and the economic and social inequality that in fact it favoured was once more to cause the most dangerous discontent.

---

[1] For instance, Benjamin Constant in 1797; see Stanley Mellon, *The Political Uses of History: A Study of Historians in the French Restoration* (1958), p. 27. The book was reviewed by me in *The Annals of the American Academy of Political and Social Science*.

Yet this was not at first the chief difficulty. For a generation after the defeat of the sans-culottes the most acute tensions were created by purely political problems, all coming under the head of distribution or implementation of power. The decentralization and the division of power that had marked the constitution of the year III (1795), the constitution of the Directorate—a reaction against the frightful despotism of the *Comité de salut public*—had resulted in the most hopeless confusion, accompanied by shocking dilapidation and corruption; the strong government soon afterwards established by Bonaparte had resulted, on the contrary, in enslavement to the will and to the ambitions of a master.

The lesson that Mme de Staël, true to her lifelong faith, now extracted from history, was that of liberalism. She writes enthusiastically about the beginning, about 1789. The *ancien régime*, the monarchy, had made the Revolution inevitable by misgovernment, by the arbitrary use of power. Liberty had the older rights; it was despotism that had been the disturbing innovation.

In sounding that note, which was eagerly caught up by liberal writers—of historians I mention only Thierry and Guizot—Mme de Staël may seem to have merely revived the tradition of the appeals to history made by clergy, nobility, and *parlements* in their opposition to royal policy in the days of Louis XV and XVI. These representatives of the privileged classes had been accustomed to decorate their captious protests against attempts to make them submit to taxation or to the needs of unified administration with references to Louis IX or even to Charlemagne and his March Fields. In fact they had contributed not a little to the creation of the revolutionary atmosphere; but as soon as—even in the preparation of the election of the States-General in 1788 and 1789—liberty was made to mean liberty for the people, or for the bourgeoisie, the vocal leaders of the anti-absolutist movement were disconcerted; put on the defensive, they were finally swept into perdition as the Revolution took its course. But as a matter of fact, Mme de Staël's interpretation of liberty in French history and of liberty as the goal now to be striven for had a wider scope. And as she read the events of 1789, too, these, and the States-General turned National Assembly, had offered the golden promise of liberty securely based on reason.

All the more horrifying had been the spectacle of the Terror and of the sanguinary reign of the small band of Jacobins who suddenly usurped the power that was to have been invested in the enlightened people, in the people as far as they were enlightened. Political fanaticism proved to be as reckless and inhuman as religious fanaticism had ever been. Bonaparte, who had been hailed as the restorer of order and moderation, soon abused power in a less barbarous, but no less insufferable and disastrous manner.

Parliamentary government, therefore, was Mme de Staël's prescription, but always allied to respect for enlightenment and for property, and guarded by a wise monarchy accepting the limitations set by the constitution.

In actual fact constitutional monarchy and parliamentary government did not work any more than had the other compromises. Because, Mme de Staël maintained, the government did not keep faith with the *Charte*. She was quite prepared to accept a monarch of the ancient line and praised Louis XVIII's good intentions. But in practice the tone was set by the reactionary temper of his faithful adherents. And it was not very likely that they should take to heart the admonitions of this bluestocking who lauded the mischief-makers of 1789 to the skies and was, moreover, always holding up the example of the English constitution to her French public. Her constant reminders that "they order these things better in England" could only rouse their impatience. "Anglomania" had long been, and was to be throughout the nineteenth century, the term of reproach with which the sermonizing of French liberals was met by their counter-revolutionary compatriots. In fact the reproach rose as readily to the lips of full-blooded revolutionaries, of those to whom the *Contrat social* was gospel and the years 1793 and 1794 the culminating point of the glorious liberating movement. But these voices were hardly heard in the first years after the restoration of the monarchy.

The danger that Mme de Staël saw as immediately threatening was that of a reaction against the great principles of 1789 under the shelter of absolutism.

The air resounded with the clamours of the ultraroyalists. To these men, to take a detached view of the upheaval from which they or their fathers had suffered so cruelly, seemed little less than treason. Benjamin Constant (and I quote him from among many who continued in the same strain when the voice of the great prophet of liberalism was silenced) asked them not to confuse the Terror with what was admirable in the Revolution.[2] But in their view the Terror *was* the Revolution, and the Restoration ought to be a restoration in the full sense of the word. As an instinctive reaction this mood was natural enough, but it also found expression in the works of a few great theorists. One might say that it was rationalized by them, however incongruous the word may sound in connection with these despisers of reason. For distrust of reason as a guide in human affairs was a prominent feature of all these counter-revolutionary theories.

De Maistre and De Bonald

Of the writers, De Maistre and De Bonald were already past middle age and had testified to their detestation of the Revolution and all its works long before, while in exile. The Abbé Lamennais was a younger man, and with him the religious sentiment, which now made him reject the Revolution, was so much the dominant motive that it soon led him into conflict with a church relying on the restored State, to the detriment, as he saw it, of the Church's spiritual freedom. De Maistre, too, made Catholicism the centre of his system, but it was a Catholicism of a very different quality. One cannot help feeling that to him the primary motive was a horror of the insecurity and change threatening the social order, a fear that made him exalt authority; and while he duly honoured the monarchy, the highest authority that he could think of, and from which the

[2] Quoted by Mellon, op. cit., p. 23.

monarchy, too, should therefore derive its power to do good,
was that of the Pope.

As for trusting to reason, or to liberty, De Maistre derided
the notion in a famous passage:

> We have seen a great and powerful nation making the most
> tremendous effort toward liberty that has ever been made
> in the world's history; and what has it attained? It has
> covered itself with ridicule and shame in order to place
> upon the throne an italic *b* [a Bonaparte] where there had
> been a capital B [a Bourbon king]; and for the people it has
> substituted servitude for obedience.

So much for the achievements of the Revolution! And
indeed, how could there be any constructive achievements,
since the Revolution, according to De Maistre, proceeded
from "a satanic principle"!

But did not the reality patently contradict this negative
valuation?

The Revolution and the "italic *b*," who had consolidated so
many of its novelties in a more respectable manner, left behind
them reforms that the royal regime did not dream of touching:
the centralized administration, for instance, which was, as a
matter of fact, no more than the completion of what had been
prepared under the monarchy; the Concordat also, which
incorporated much of the old Gallican tendencies. Above all
they left behind them a personnel of Bonapartist high officials
and dignitaries co-operating quite smoothly with the restored
monarchy—a token of the hidden but profound solidarity
between some of the tendencies of the Revolution and the
interests of that monarchy. And was not even the Church
caught in a similar ambivalence? The bishops were not likely
to welcome De Maistre's extreme ultramontanism—let alone
Lamennais's ecclesiastical libertarianism. They were quite
happy with the Concordat, to which, moreover, Rome itself continued to adhere. They might agree as to the satanic character
of the Revolution, but they found it only in certain tendencies
of the Revolution. They had compacted, and so had Rome,
with the Revolution as regards other tendencies. They were

now ready to preach obedience to the King, as they had until lately preached obedience to the Emperor. One is a little startled by the fervent servility toward the Bourbon king displayed by the Bishop of Troyes in a pastoral letter in which he exhorted the faithful to imitate this, and one is especially shocked when one learns that he had been Napoleon's great-almoner. But indeed, as Mme de Staël remarks with scathing sarcasm, he had learned how to bow in a good school.

The Revolution could not be so easily wiped out. Of the counter-revolutionary theorists, it was De Bonald who made the most genuine attempt to think historically; he has the most affinity with Burke. But in practice his view of the Revolution as a mere interruption of the historical process could not but land him in insuperable difficulties. How was one to link up the restored monarchy with the state of affairs prevailing before 1789? De Bonald became a member of the Chamber; he took an oath on the *Charte*—it is true that he accepted it as having been freely granted by the King, not as a compact. Yet in fact he became a party to the Restoration compromise.

These ultraroyalists had a particular aversion to the well-to-do middle-class upon which the regime actually came to rest. De Bonald and many of his friends wanted to have the suffrage extended, for the primary assemblies at least, to a numerous class of small taxpayers. The majority of the members of the Chamber clung to their narrow *pays légal*—ninety thousand voters out of twenty-five million. But the aristocrats who listened to De Bonald still believed in the ability of their own class to lead. They still believed that their prestige, that gratitude or fear, that religion and the assistance of the priests, could win them the support of the farmers and of the lower middle-class. The ideal, in short, of Disraeli's Young England. But in France this ideal was vastly more remote from the possibilities of reality. When Mme de Staël, with all her respect for property, described the suffrage clause as the principal blot on the *Charte*, she was not thinking of a submissive class led by noblemen and parish priests and to which the suffrage ought to be extended. Was such a class still in being? For a long time before the Revolution the French aristocracy had neglected its task of leadership in local affairs. The Revolution itself had created a gulf between it and the people, and had left behind unappeasable resentments and distrust on both sides.

Courier

If one wishes to get an idea of the bitterness animating the class of small men, especially small farmers, against the leading class clustering round the government, there is no better way than to read the pamphlets of Paul Louis Courier. One must not expect in them any comprehensive views of the significance of the Revolution or of the problems raised by the Restoration. But they are a startling revelation—even if the concentrated venom of these witty productions is very much the writer's own—of the suspicion tinged with hatred with which the inhabitants of his village in Touraine regarded noblemen and priests, and above all, the arbitrary and grasping Paris government and its instruments, the police, the judges, the *maire*, and all the government's officials. Reminiscences of the time when a nobleman could kill a villein for a fine of five sous lead Courier to the reflection that nowadays a *maire* had to spend seven and a half sous for a sealed paper to have a man arrested; the judge would see to the rest. Once upon a time, Courier observed, *corvéable, taillable et tuable à merci;* now only *incarcérable:*[3] we progress; this is what five or six centuries have produced—who knows but what in another five or six centuries it will be possible to sue the *maire* for money if he owes it to us, without being thrown into prison for our pains. Even the royal family was not safe from Courier's barbed witticisms, and when he was tried for libel, he had a gorgeous time describing the trial and making fun—always mordant and with undertones of subversive intent—at the expense of the public prosecutor.

The Revolution was never far from people's thoughts. In the political discussion liberals and royalists were constantly

[3] Liable to be subjected at pleasure to forced labour, to taxation, to death; now only to imprisonment.

belabouring each other with interpretations of that great episode or of the causes that had led to it, with diametrically opposed arguments suited to each side's particular case. The Revolution, a wicked break with a beneficent past; or the Revolution, the culmination of an age-long striving after liberty which the monarchy had tried, to its own undoing, to impede.[4]

But the history of the crucial years from 1789 on was not at first examined at all closely. The politicians and the journalists dealt mostly in generalities, while the historians participating in the debate dwelt on earlier periods to bring out the trends that seemed to prove either the one or the other of the two opposing theses. The conservative or reactionary writers I discussed above took their views, so to speak, for granted and went on to elaborate their theoretical conclusions. If Mme de Staël's book created a sensation it was not only because it discussed events of the revolutionary period sympathetically—as far, at least, as the first phase went—but because it discussed them at all and in some detail. Under Napoleon silence had been the order of the day. The revolutionary tradition had lingered on, almost inarticulately, among the generation that had been active in the crisis. The younger generation was raised in the tradition of abhorrence. But just when, after the assassination of the Duc de Berry in 1820, ultraroyalism as well as ultra-Catholicism became more aggressive and opposition to the regime consequently more determined and more vocal, there appeared, in 1823 and 1824, the first two real histories: the first volume of the many that were to compose Thiers's *History*, and Mignet's two small volumes.

II

Thiers and Mignet

It is with Thiers and Mignet that the historiography of the Revolution really begins, and it is worth noting that it begins with authors who had very definite political aims.

[4] It is this controversy that forms the subject of the book by Stanley Mellon cited above.

Thiers and Mignet, young men, were intimate friends, both hailing from Provence. They intended their accounts of the Revolution to be contributions to the opposition against the absolutist and clerical tendencies of the Bourbon regime. In essentials they followed the line traced by Mme de Staël. They, too, were liberals; they shared the ideal, so characteristically middle class and intellectual, of liberty through enlightenment and a parliamentary monarchy.

It is perfectly natural, then, that they explain the Revolution by the abuses of the *ancien régime* and by the errors committed by the monarchy before and during the crisis, and that they wholeheartedly accept the early phase, the phase of the National Assembly, and even, a little less wholeheartedly, the phase of the Legislative Assembly. It is also natural that they, like Mme de Staël, deplore the dictatorship of the *Comité de salut public* and the excesses of the Terror. And yet here one notices a marked difference. There is in their comments nothing like that profound moral distress into which these developments threw Mme de Staël; nothing like her straightforward condemnation. They deplore; but in the end they condone.

In order to show their style of treatment in some particular instances, let me confine myself to Mignet, whose rapid sketch brings out the main points with such admirable lucidity.

The sale of the church lands, while antagonizing the clergy, was, so Mignet argues, necessary to save the Revolution. The *constitution civile* may have been an injudicious measure, for it served the clergy as a "plausible pretext" to indulge in hostility to the Revolution, but, Mignet insists, the Revolution was not opposed to religion. The anticlerical tone can be heard throughout his book. Anticlericalism constitutes a major strand in the bond by which he (and the same is true for Thiers) feels himself united to the triumphant majority of the National Assembly.

The constitution of 1791 is to him the zenith of political wisdom. If it failed, it was not the fault of the Assembly, but of the factions: "attacked by the aristocracy, invaded by the multitude," the Assembly was thrown off its course.

The middle position of the bourgeois becomes very clear.

Mignet does not waste a word about the census clause in that constitution he admires so much. The curious arrangement by which members of the Assembly were debarred from becoming ministers to the King; the folly of vesting executive power in a King who was only too patently out of tune with the Revolution—he passes all that by in silence. But the ever-more-violent action of the clubs, the terrible schemes of the Commune of Paris—this he notes with disapproval. The Girondins are the men after his heart, and their extermination is in his eyes a disaster.

He does, it is true, shake his head over the bellicose speeches delivered by some of the leading Girondin spokesmen in the Legislative Assembly, which contributed so much to the outbreak of the war in 1792. And the war, he does admit, opened "the dictatorial and arbitrary phase of the Revolution. . . . The energy roused by the war made the dominance of the lower class restless, oppressive, and cruel." But—and now there follows the twist in the argument which enabled Mignet, and has since enabled countless French historians and politicians, writers and orators, to accept without further qualms the *Comité de salut public* and its sanguinary exploits as part of the glorious tradition of the Revolution—*but*:

> The issue was no longer liberty, it was *salut public*. The Revolution became absorbed in a protracted struggle against Europe and against the parties. Was anything else possible?

To answer this question Mignet quotes an extraordinary passage from a book written as long ago as 1796, by De Maistre, the prophet of legitimacy and of ultramontanism. De Maistre was at that time already an implacable opponent of the Revolution, and his book had been published outside France.

> The Revolution once established [so he had written], France and the monarchy could not be saved but by Jacobinism. . . . Our descendants, who will care very little for our sufferings and who will dance on our graves, will laugh at our present lack of perspicacity; they will easily console themselves over

the excesses that we have witnessed and that will prove to have preserved the integrity of the finest kingdom on earth.

The passage contains several points of interest. But let us only ask ourselves why Mignet thought it worth his while to quote. The answer is indeed obvious. What good fortune for the apologist of the Revolution to be able to extract this reflection from the writings of the royalist, for it clearly implied the simple statement: The dictatorship and the Terror were necessary to preserve the integrity of the French state. Mignet, of course, adds: "and to save the Revolution." Also: "it could not have gone otherwise."

The addiction of Mignet—and for that matter also of Thiers, for the two are remarkably like in these fundamental respects—the addiction to the doctrine of the inevitability, of the fatality, of the course of history has often been remarked upon. I do not know whether it has been sufficiently observed that this doctrine served the very useful purpose of glossing over the less sightly aspects of the Revolution and of French policy in those terrible years.

A host of questions seem to clamour for answers. To what extent was the bellicose policy of Brissot and Isnard—of the Girondins—responsible for the war? If to some extent it was, can the war be used as a sufficient excuse for the excesses that followed? Did not the Revolution carry within itself the principle that made both the war and the excesses difficult to avert? And when a man strove to avert both by preaching moderation, is it right to reproach him (as Mignet does Lafayette, although on the whole he had the greatest respect for Lafayette) with overlooking the extraordinary circumstances in which France found herself? For here another question arises, one that ought not to be evaded: is it so certain that the Revolution could only be saved by the war, and the war won only by the dictatorship? More, *was* it saved by the war and by the dictatorship? Was it not, on the contrary, ruined or frustrated by these wild courses?

For the advocate of the revolutionary tradition, and also for the French patriot to whom France must always have been in the right, the most convenient way of putting an end to a somewhat uncomfortable discussion is to say: It had to be so.

It would be difficult to determine which was, in the case of Mignet or of Thiers, the strongest incentive, the desire to whitewash the Revolution, or the desire to whitewash France. It is a difficulty that will repeatedly recur when one reads later French historians, indeed, down to the present day. For Mignet's method had a long career before it, and the blending together of worship of the Revolution and worship of the French fatherland became an enduring feature of French thinking. It should not, indeed, be forgotten that at the height of the crisis in the seventeen-nineties this double cult had already obliterated the original devotion to mankind. The combination of revolutionary and of patriotic ardour was, therefore, itself a legacy of the heroic years of the Revolution.

Mignet, to be fair to him, was perhaps too balanced, at times too critical and willing to make reservations, for the words *worship* and *cult* to fit his work. But he and Thiers pointed a way that was soon crowded by a rush of writers, neither balanced nor critical, but gifted in other ways, fervently preaching the revolutionary tradition as the true national religion. The two friends had had the satisfaction, almost immediately, of seeing the regime against which they had helped to mobilize the Revolution topple, making room for one that they could hail as being more in agreement with the revolutionary principles, with those worth retaining at least, with the principles of 1789. But they lived on, for something like half a century, to see the legend they had created flourishing almost too luxuriously and indeed bearing fruit that was not always to their taste.

Before long the bourgeois monarchy of Louis Philippe, too, ran into troubled waters. The working class began to make its voice heard. As a matter of fact, it had contributed not a little to the turn of affairs in 1830, only it had been the middle class that had benefited. Soon afterward, however, the restricted suffrage for the Chamber became a burning grievance. At the same time the Church attempted to regain its hold over education. Many bourgeois, Voltaireans as they might be, or "enlightened" as they would describe themselves, were prepared to accept the help of the Church in keeping the people submissive and preserving the social order. But others were roused to fierce resentment, especially by the activities of the Jesuits. The compromise of 1830 was not to be the end of the journey. In the late forties revolution was again in the air—not in France only, it is well to remember, but in France that mood again fed on recollections of the events of fifty years earlier.

Buchez

The discussion now had more material to go upon, owing not only to the circumstantial accounts of Mignet and Thiers, but to the labours of Buchez and his associate Roux, who had between 1834 and 1838 published, in forty volumes of some four hundred and fifty pages each, that invaluable collection of extracts from the debates in the revolutionary assemblies, from pamphlets, newspapers, memoirs, decrees, treaties, the *Histoire parlementaire de la Révolution française.* That this enormous series could be let loose on the public in so short a space of time and prove an immense publishing success shows the avid interest that the Revolution now evoked.

Buchez's prefaces are in themselves absorbingly interesting. Nearly every one of the forty volumes opens with a lively disquisition of a few pages in which he often takes issue with reviewers. The very first sentence of the first preface strikes the note that was to dominate all the rest of them; it is a note well suited to rouse the attention:

> The French Revolution is the last and most advanced consequence of modern civilization, and modern civilization has in its entirety sprung from the Gospel.

Liberty, equality, fraternity: these words summarize the aim of the Revolution. And what can be more in keeping with the teaching of Jesus?

We see at once how different is the state of mind in which Buchez will judge the Revolution from that which we observed in the liberal school of Mme de Staël. Buchez speaks for the people, which Mignet regarded with so much distrust: the Assembly, whose moderation and wisdom were extolled by the liberals, can find no grace in the eyes of a "Christian Socialist" like Buchez.

According to him there was unanimity in France, before the meeting of the States-General. The *cahiers* prove it, all breathing the spirit of Rousseau. The Revolution's high design to realize Christian principles was the outcome of fourteen centuries of French history. Buchez reviews that period in a lengthy introduction, bringing out the great historic task of France, France the champion of European civilization.

> The entire past of Europe can be comprised in two words: France and the Church. All the temporal work was, in the Christian era, done by the French; the spiritual achievement was the Church's.

Unfortunately, by the end of the eighteenth century, the rich, the nobility, part of the intelligentsia, had been fashioned by the exclusively critical spirit of Voltaire rather than by Rousseau, and immediately after the Fourteenth of July the bourgeoisie made themselves masters of the Assembly. The Declaration of Rights, instead of reorganizing society, asserted only the rights of property and other individual rights. If disturbances occurred, it was due to the fact that the new order, like the old, neglected its duty. The National Assembly was responsible for the insurrections that marked the course of the Revolution. "When men are blind, or prejudiced, or interested, must society therefore halt in the conquest of its aim?"

For the Revolution *had* an aim, and if in its own day so many of its leaders did not discern it, he, Buchez, knew: it was to cast out individualism and to realize the fraternity and sovereignty of the people.

Faced with the September massacre (1792), the Christian thinker does not falter. Other apologists of the Revolution, when Catholic writers denounced that horror, were to cast the

memory of the Massacre of St. Bartholomew in their teeth.
But Buchez boldly justifies both. The victims of September
were to be commiserated, but they were guilty. Like the
victims of St. Bartholomew's Day, they had conspired with
the enemy and were attempting to "federalize" France.[5] It was
to be regretted that they were not put through a regular trial,
but even so, it should be remembered that it was the Assembly
that by its culpable moderation, or rather inaction, had thrust
the Revolution into the fatal sequence of disorder. As for the
murders in themselves, they, like the murders of St. Bartholomew's Day, should be regarded as: "une mesure de salut
public."

There is a strong element of monomania in this reasoning.
Buchez was impervious to the evidence of the facts he so
industriously collected. Instead of deducing from careful
observation what this extraordinarily complicated phenomenon, the Revolution, really was, he began by dogmatically
equating it with Christianity in action. He sees history ruled
by purpose: "A nation is an association of men united to
practise and to act for the same purpose." And he admits of
no doubt as to what was the purpose of the Revolution. France
was chosen, and had been prepared by the centuries, to
accomplish the great task of leading Europe on the way of social
reorganization in accordance with the principles of the Gospel.
And after having exulted in the unanimity displayed at the
start of that great undertaking, Buchez proceeds to quarrel
with the actual doings of the men elected to carry it out, explaining their mistakes as the result of private interest and
faulty philosophy—Voltairean, and also Protestant, a term that
is to Buchez as opprobrious an epithet for individualism and
selfish egoism as it had been to De Maistre. If it went badly
with many of the obstructionists and the bunglers, their fate
was not to be judged by any other consideration than that of
the public interest as it had been revealed to him, Buchez.
And in the end, after all his philosophizing, surveying the
scene of the France of his own day encumbered with the

[5] That is to say, to break up the unity of the state for the benefit of
provincial self-government.

remains of old abuses, he still exhorts his compatriots to complete the great work of the Revolution and to reconstruct French society, and at the same time to resume the leadership of Europe, by placing themselves on the firm ground of Catholicism. Thus will society realize the morality of Jesus Christ.

The importance of Buchez's forty volumes lies, of course, in the material they made available.[6] His prefaces will not find many readers nowadays. At the time of their publication they were already received with head-shakes—if not with ridicule— more often than with approval. And yet they were more than the lucubrations of a solitary eccentric. The absolutist thinking of Rousseau and his disciples, the Terrorists of 1794, was closely allied to certain religious states of mind, although, normally, Catholics and Protestants alike, even if they recognize the affinity, will abhor its manifestations as perversions of true religiosity. At any rate, we shall see in a moment that even this most surprising aspect of Buchez's interpretation of the Revolution—his regarding it as the culmination of Christianity—was eagerly fastened upon by Lamartine, a writer of infinitely greater literary power, who enjoyed, as a matter of fact, a great popular success by his presentation of it.

It was much less singular and farfetched, of course, to represent the socialistic proclivities that dominated the scene in the violent years from 1792 to 1794 as constituting the real significance of the Revolution. Mignet, and indeed Mme de Staël, had already made this distinction between the early bourgeois phase of the Revolution and the later rise of proletarian influence. Their sympathies, however, had been with the Assembly and its respect for property; and the invasion of the scene by the hungry and impatient populace had seemed to them an unmitigated disaster. It was only natural—and from the point of view of the strictly historical discussion, it was useful—that the roles of the villains and the heroes should for

[6] One of the first writers to make use of it was Carlyle, in whose *French Revolution* (1837) one will find frequent references to it.

a change be reversed. The time, moreover, as I already hinted, was propitious for this particular view. And so, here again, the suggestions contained in Buchez's prefaces were to be elaborated by an abler writer. The work of Louis Blanc, a bitter enemy of the triumphant bourgeoisie, although lacking in the romantic and poetic appeal exercised by Lamartine's immensely more popular *Histoire des Girondins* (which appeared about the same time as Blanc's first volume), did demonstrate some grasp of the reality of history.

Christianity, Socialism—but apart from any particular ideology or political conviction, Buchez represented a method of thinking that strongly appealed to the men of his generation. Its effect on the historiography of the Revolution was to survive him. To approach the confusion and multiplicity of reality with the presumptuous claim of knowing the one and only answer to its riddles, of knowing what History or Fate or Providence intended—how tempting it must be! Buchez's method allows one to walk in the light of an infallible revelation, ignoring or explaining away inconvenient features of the past; more than that, to feel able to censure or indict the men who had actually struggled with the problems as they arose; to censure or indict them for being unaware of the true significance of the events and consequently of their duty, and in the face of their insufficiency, of their gropings and fumblings, to maintain intact one's own preconceived idea of the Revolution and its predestined course.

Buchez's principal disciple in this devotion to an idealized Revolution was, as we shall see, Lamartine. But Michelet, too, the greatest of the three writers (Louis Blanc being the third) who undertook large-scale histories of the Revolution just before the Orleans regime was overthrown in 1848, Michelet, although neither a Christian nor a Socialist, proved himself a kindred spirit.

III

In the late forties revolution was again in the air. In 1844, Michelet and his friend Quinet, both professors at the *Collège de France*, lectured to excited crowds of students on the iniquities of the Jesuits and on the noble and eternal principles of the Revolution. They were dismissed by the government, but the atmosphere of Paris remained thick with forebodings and with hope. The young men in Flaubert's *Éducation sentimentale* (the novel appeared in 1874, but these scenes are laid in the years immediately preceding the Revolution of February 1848) dream of that glorious time, when "people *lived*, when they could assert themselves, prove their force." One modelled himself, or his future self, on Saint-Just, another on Danton, or on Marat, or Robespierre. And they loved to hear Barthélemy's poem recited: "Elle reparaîtra, la terrible Assemblée. . . ."

All three of the great histories that appeared, or began to appear, in 1847 were affected by that spirit. Widely as they differed among themselves in their interpretation of the action or of the actors on the stage of the great Revolution, their authors (and this, of course, can be said for Buchez as well) had in common a far more radical temper than had animated Thiers and Mignet. The influence of Mme de Staël seemed for the moment to have lost its power. That the Revolution and monarchy, albeit constitutional monarchy, were compatible seemed an outworn creed to all; some, as we saw, broke decisively with the bourgeois tradition in its entirety. And each, in exploring the inexhaustible story of the Revolution, brought out the aspects and the meanings that seemed to point his own particular moral.

Lamartine

Everybody agrees that Lamartine's *Histoire des Girondins* has no value as history. Particularly scathing was Tocqueville, who says (in his *Souvenirs*) that Lamartine not only made light with historical truth, but had no idea of what truth meant. It was, in fact, as a poet that he had suddenly, more than twenty-five years before, achieved fame. I do not mean to imply that the poet "has no idea of what truth means"; but Lamartine was a typically romantic poet, who could not imagine truth but in the unsubstantial and otherworldly regions of the imagination. As a politician, too (he had become a member of the Chamber after 1830), he only dealt in vague nobilities, in well-meaning generalities of a somewhat indeterminately democratic trend. If his historical work deserves our attention, it is because of the enormous influence it had at the time of its appearance—an influence that, in spite of the work's underlying chauvinism, was not confined to France.

Lamartine's is purely legendary, almost fictional, history. The spirit animating it is that of the growing opposition to the uninspired bourgeois conservatism of the Guizot regime, although Lamartine does not as directly and consistently preach socialism as did Buchez. He is nevertheless obviously inspired by Buchez's prefaces when, in his Introduction, he derives the Revolution from Christianity. Christianity had prepared men's minds for fraternity and equality, and French eighteenth-century philosophy had helped to carry them to that further stage where the Revolution could realize the application of these principles. A gospel of social rights and duties (it was Buchez's grievance against the Declaration of Rights that it had failed to state any duties); a charter of humanity—and France the apostle of this creed. "When Providence desires that an idea shall enflame the world, it kindles it in the soul of a Frenchman."

Again we see French chauvinism and revolutionary messianism walking hand in hand—as indeed they did in the great years of the Revolution itself. We noticed this self-intoxication in Buchez; we shall notice it in others. As a matter of fact, something very like it was already observable in Mignet and Thiers, although their general attitude was more sober, and in this particular aspect, more plainly and simply nationalistic.

When he comes to tell his story, Lamartine, every now and again, represents the Revolution as a living thing, with a character and aims of its own, independent almost of men and of events. It is the reversal—and we noticed it already in Buchez—of the truly historical approach. A subordination of the entire historical process to an abstract ideal, to a subjective a-priori. He writes, for instance: "The Revolution was not at first understood, except perhaps by Robespierre. All were blind, except the Revolution itself."

One is reminded of Hegel. The Idea compelling men to realize it in spite of themselves. Lamartine is even more extreme in practising this personification than was Buchez, although the absurdity of his system occasionally led him to inconsistencies—by which he does not seem in the least troubled. What made him cling to these grandiloquent and philosophical-sounding pronouncements about the Revolution living its own life apart from the struggles of men was that they supplied a subtle way of apologizing for the Terror. Indeed, this and the other concepts with which he worked—the sophisms, or tricks, one might say—suited the public temper and certain idiosyncrasies of the French admirably well and helped to make the memory of the Revolution into an even more potent force in the politics of the present. "The shocks and the crimes," Lamartine says explicitly, "do not detract from the holiness of the Revolution: they were due to the imperfections of men. The holiest, most just and virtuous thought, when it passes through the medium of imperfect humanity, comes out in rags and blood."

Lamartine is full of admiration for the National Assembly—in which, of course, he sharply differs from Buchez and betrays a lingering kinship with Mignet and the bourgeois liberals. His exaltation in praising it, however, is peculiarly his own: "It was the most impressive body of men that had ever represented, not only France, but the human race. . . . Its members were not Frenchmen, but universal men. . . . They were the workmen of God."

This wonderful Assembly wanted peace. If war came, it was the doing of the party men and the ambitious. Lamartine even admits—it is one of those moments when he slips into forgetting his own system—that the Revolution had degenerated. He then proceeds as if nothing had happened and uses all the superlatives at his command to laud the Girondins, those great souls, whose delight in the triumphant moment of the deposition of Louis XVI he shares unconditionally—parting company with Mignet again, to whom the establishment of the Republic ushered in the "arbitrary and dictatorial" phase of the Revolution.

It is more surprising that when the dictatorship of the extremists comes along and the Girondins, his heroes, are the first to suffer, Lamartine, who had firmly rejected all palliation of the September massacres (differing this time from Buchez), submits. He admits necessity—Christianity and high morality now seem to be forgotten—and his explanations become as frankly realistic as were those of Mignet and Thiers. The *raison d'état* is invoked. The revered Girondins failed because they proved to be insufficiently energetic. The Revolution could not but rise against them and escape from their control.

> Did the people act illegally? It believed that in acting as it did it made use of its supreme right, the right of survival. . . . In times of extremity, authority [*le gouvernement*] is, not legally but actually, wherever it can be made good. The centralization in Paris was necessary. The law had been violated too frequently already. And after all: the law was the Revolution itself. . . . The law was the instinct of self-preservation of a great nation.

Later on, he is horrified at the Terror, as he had been at the September murders. But in fact he had, by condoning everything beforehand, placed it beyond the reach of moral reproval —witness the passage I quoted. So, again, he is free to picture the Revolution as an all-powerful, suprahuman, indeed divine, being: "The social laws of the Committee of Public Safety emanated from its dogma; the Terror from its wrath."

Nevertheless, once more Lamartine presumes to blame the Revolution. It had become untrue to itself. The demolition of Lyons, for instance, was "a crime against the nation." But we also find him speaking as follows: "The anger of the Revolution had attained the power of a divine scourge." Thus he magnifies and embellishes the excesses of that gruesome band of maniacs thrust into their short-lived position of power through the demented fight of the factions. Lamartine's favourite method, however, is to talk of *necessity*. In the execution of Danton, for instance, he sees "the cruel necessity of politics."

Like Buchez, Lamartine intended his book as an exhortation to the French public to prepare for a new revolution, but at the same time "to purify the doctrine, so that next time the Girondin spirit will not be assailed by Jacobin excesses." His recognition of these excesses did not, however, prevent him from extending in his conclusion a general pardon to the chief actors in the drama. After attaching to each the word indicating his characteristic quality—*liberty*, *energy*, etc., and also *crime*—Lamartine continues: "All [and Robespierre was among them] deserve the funereal inscription: *Died for the future, and workman of mankind.* Everything, the whole story, means imperishable glory for France."

Let me note, in fairness to the eloquent rhetor, that a number of years later he admitted, in an appendix to a new edition of his book (published in 1861), the falseness of this kind of argument. The disappointments of 1848 and the following years had created a different climate of opinion from what had prevailed before the crisis; we shall see this when we come to Tocqueville, Lanfrey, Quinet, Renan, Flaubert. To Lamartine personally, too, the experience of revolution in action had brought some unpleasant shocks. So now he rejects emphatically "the detestable theory" that the Terror had saved *la patrie*, and he blames himself for having written as if that were so. The indulgence and justification implied in the passage just quoted from the conclusion of the work of 1846 he now repudiates. The passage, he says, sounds "more like an ode than like a verdict."

> It seems to hover over the entire scene of action like a glorious amnesty and to justify deeds and doers alike by casting a halo round them. . . . I was angry with myself when this morning I reread that lyrical last page of *Les Girondins*.

This is very fine as far as it goes. But even here, Lamartine's critical judgment is in default: he rejects only a few all-too-blatant passages, but the whole of his *Histoire des Girondins* is permeated with these sentiments.

Blanc

Louis Blanc's twelve volumes appeared for the most part after he had had to flee to England in 1848, when the reaction to the revolutionary spirit that had triumphed in February 1848 had set in in earnest. The change in the political atmosphere in France did not, however, affect his outlook, and his residence in England seems to have influenced his work only in that it enabled him to make use of the large collection of pamphlets that Croker left to the British Museum. Blanc differs from both Lamartine and the Buchez of the prefaces in that documents and facts did mean something to him; he could make, therefore, a more serious contribution to the socialistic interpretation of the Revolution than Buchez had done. For it was as a convinced socialist that Blanc came to the problem. But he did not, as had Buchez, identify socialism and the Revolution with Christianity. Indeed he was a Voltairean, anticlerical, even sceptical about religion.

Like Mignet, Blanc made a distinction between the Revolution of 1789 and the Revolution of 1792, 1793, and 1794. But while Mignet was wholly satisfied with the bourgeois Revolution, Blanc associated himself completely with the Revolution's second phase. Mignet was not interested in the social aims that were then voiced; he accepted the second Revolution only because he assumed it was necessary in order to save French territory (and also the initial achievements of the Revolution) from the assault of foreign invaders. When it collapsed in 1794, it had, in his view, done its service. Nothing came of its social aims, and so little does Mignet regret this that he acclaims the typically bourgeois constitution of 1795 as the best constitution France had ever had. To Blanc 1794 meant the end of the true Revolution and the disappointment (for the time being) of the hopes of humanity.

Blanc starts off with a bold survey of world history, which

he sees developing in three movements, each of which is
defined by one dominant characteristic. (The method is
strongly reminiscent of that of Comte.)

The Middle Ages, the period when Catholicism reigned
supreme, was the period of *Authority*. The Protestant Reformation introduced the principle of *Individualism*, which was
extended by the Enlightenment. Both De Maistre and Mme
de Staël likewise connected Reformation and Enlightenment
in this, in itself debatable, way, De Maistre using "individualism" to damn both movements, Mme de Staël to applaud
both. Louis Blanc, however, proceeds to subordinate these
imperfect and inadequate efforts of the spirit, Authority and
Individualism to the final stage toward which he saw them
tending: *Fraternity*.

And this is how he applies the vision of fraternity to the
Revolution:

> There are contained in what it is customary to call the
> French Revolution, two revolutions, entirely distinct,
> although both directed against the ancient principle of
> *Authority*. One was carried out in favour of individualism;
> it can be dated 1789. The other was only attempted in a
> tumultuous manner, in the name of fraternity; it came to
> grief on the ninth of Thermidor (1794). . . . Montesquieu,
> Voltaire, Turgot, were the pioneers of *Individualism*;
> Rousseau at the same time prepared men's minds for
> *Fraternity*.

His heart being so much set on "the second Revolution,"
Blanc naturally is given, no less than was Buchez, to extenuating its excesses. The first test case is, of course, the September
massacres. Nobody will be surprised when Blanc, too, recalls
St. Bartholomew's Day, but while Buchez considered the
victims in both cases equally guilty, Blanc uses the parallel
simply to level a *tu quoque* at the Catholics, who raised their
hands in horror at the second outrage only. "Souviens-toi de
la Barthélemy!"

Robespierre, Blanc defends even more wholeheartedly than
did Buchez. A tyrant? "A strange tyrant indeed, this man who

never disposed of either treasure or soldiery, and who for his alleged tyrannizing had to rely on the effect produced by his eloquence allied to the belief he had established in his virtue."

The most general defence of the Terror, and indeed the most obvious—down to the present day it has been resorted to in various ways by all historians favourable to the Revolution— is the following:

> Whose fault was it if the Revolution in the end flew into a rage? It was what the Counter-revolution had been asking for. This was the answer it got.

In his last volume Blanc describes the *Terreur blanche* of 1814, and the comparison with 1793 and 1794 is entirely to the advantage of the earlier episode.

> There had at least been judges on that occasion. The promoters of the Red Terror were men of ferocious convictions, fanatics of the public weal, violent souls and grim; but at least they spoke the language fitting their actions. They did not offer the spectacle of trying to impersonate humanity while clasping a bloodstained knife and mounted on a pile of dead bodies; they were not seen daubing themselves with perfume and paint before entering the slaughter-house.

But there is more in Blanc's book than mere rhetoric and special pleading. His point of view led him to direct his attention to problems that had thus far, as he put it himself, been "ignored to an unbelievable extent." The lower-class revolt against the exclusive bourgeois regime instituted in 1789 was reflected in certain measures taken by the Committee of Public Safety. There was, for instance, the attempt to control prices.

> Until today the historians of the Revolution [so Blanc writes] have failed—and the neglect is hardly conceivable— to write the history of *le maximum*. I shall attempt to fill that gap. . . . The subject is undoubtedly one of the most inter-

esting as well as the most comprehensive on which the thoughts of the philosopher or of the statesman can be focused.

The execution that followed was less important than was this posing of the problem. By it Blanc pointed into the future, to Jaurès and Mathiez and later specialists by whom the social-economic history of the period of the Commune and the Committee of Public Safety was to be examined very closely.

Blanc had another brain-wave when he noticed another omission—"a strange gap," as he says himself—in all the histories of the Revolution: "One would think that the historians, dazzled and fascinated by the spectacle of this France in transformation, never saw, never knew, anything of what went on around her."

Indeed, take Mignet and Thiers, Buchez and Lamartine, Michelet—international relations are disposed of very lightly and irresponsibly by all of them. The outbreak of the war in 1792, the declaration of Pillnitz, the bellicose speeches of the Girondin leaders, are all left without any background and judged from a narrow national or partisan point of view. The first historian to try to penetrate the secret of the relations between revolutionary France and the rest of Europe was Sybel, a German, writing in the fifties; Albert Sorel's classic work was not to appear until a generation later.

As for Blanc, the brain-wave was all. His state of mind was hardly such as to fit him for the required task of scholarly investigation. He, too, was subject to the usual chauvinistic and messianic temper, which made him regard France as chosen among nations to be the agent of progress, and to suffer for it.

If France is tormented by a perpetual changeability, if her life is made up of the alternation of successes and reverses, if she is fated to astonish the world by so many different and unexpected vicissitudes, it is because the initiative of moral progress resides in her, because she runs an adventurous course for the benefit of the entire human race.

There is a torch in the light of which all peoples march

toward justice, with unequal steps it is true, and since it is
carried through storms, we should not be surprised to see
it flutter occasionally and be near to extinction. It is France
who carries it, that torch.

Michelet

But Michelet, the greatest writer of them all, and in spite of
his unbridled emotionalism, the greatest historian, is the one
who, in the long run, exercised the most profound influence
and the only one who is still read today.

Michelet, who was born in 1798, had in his youth adhered
to Catholicism.[7] His father, a Paris printer, had taken his
small part in the Revolution, but the family tradition was
dormant. The revolution of 1830 had made a tremendous
impression on Michelet, but it was not until the forties that,
under the influence of the rising excitement all around him,
he was converted to the full doctrine. He did nothing by halves.
He abjured the work he had written on the Middle Ages. He
now saw that Christianity, preaching original sin, sacrificial
death, and grace, meant arbitrariness; only the Revolution
meant justice. No compromise between the two was possible:
the Revolution must conquer. How different from Buchez!
Henceforth the spirit of the Revolution was to be Michelet's
teacher. "It knows, and the others do not know. *It* possesses
the secret of all the preceding ages." The epic of the liberation
of the French people, nay of the human mind, that was what
his history of the Revolution was to be. Michelet's first volume
appeared in 1847.

The past was forgotten in the dazzling light of a new day.
Forgotten, denied, abolished. One is again irresistibly
reminded of Croce's description of anti-historism. But no less
remarkable is Michelet's terminology—*the Revolution, the spirit
of the Revolution*—and in its absolutism and simplism no less
unhistorical. To distinguish between phases when the Revolution was on the right track and when it went astray, and

[7] I have dealt with Michelet at greater length in an essay included
in *Debates with Historians* (1955); re-issued in Fontana Books, 1962.

between beneficent and harmful tendencies; to accept and to reject—Michelet considered all that to be no better than juggling with truth. Truth was: there was but one Revolution. It came to a tragic collapse in 1794, with Thermidor, with the downfall of the *Comité de salut public* and the death of Robespierre. Our salvation can only be in the resuscitation of the great enthusiasm and faith of those unique five years, handed down to us by an unbroken chain of fidelity and hope.

Was Michelet, then, a worshipper of Robespierre and of the Jacobins? No: he was less of a partisan than were Buchez and Louis Blanc. To Michelet the first Assembly, the Girondins and the Jacobins, were all admirable, because in any case the true hero of the story was the French people. It is the French people he reveres, whose soul is all goodness, and who thirst after justice; their immense labours and sufferings in the heroic years of the Revolution were their sacrifice on the altar of the love of mankind.

It must be difficult, one cannot help reflecting, to write that terrible story and to retain this faith untouched. How could a man who admitted that the September massacres were "a crime," and who described (with shuddering emotion even) the Terror and Robespierre without extenuating its horrors and the man's insane egotism—how could this man lament the break-up of that system and the elimination of that agent as a catastrophe for Justice, Liberty, Democracy, Humanity? But moreover—and this, one should think, is a question, not of morality but of fact—*was* the Revolution in all its stages the work of the people? What, then, about the resisters? What about the civil war? What about the undeniable fact that the Revolution, after a while, fell into the hands of the Jacobin minority, an exiguous minority, but well organized, and ruling ruthlessly and dictatorially?

It all turns on the meaning attached to the term *the people*. Michelet excludes from the people all those who opposed the Revolution. The nobility, the priests, the Anglomane liberals, to begin with. But also the multitude of ignorant, simple souls who were led astray by them. The crimes, too, were committed not by the people, but by ruffians—or under the unbearable provocation of the foreign enemy, of Austria, of England, the personification of evil. The war, too. You say that the Belgians were plundered and oppressed by their French conquerors? That was no more than they deserved for being so blind as not to see that these conquerors were fighting a life-and-death struggle to make them happy, and indeed to spread liberty and democracy over all Europe and the world. The French people were good, the Revolution was beneficent. How can bad spring from the good and the beneficent? If the bad was there, it must have been in spite of the French people and in spite of the Revolution.

More than any of the writers discussed earlier, Michelet had made his own the spirit that had come to reign at the height of the Revolution. The others, as we saw, were all much affected by it, but each of them had a marked preference for one tendency, or was devoted to one rigid ideal of his own, to which he attempted to make the history of the fascinating episode conform, not scrupling to express disapproval when it too patently departed from the pet doctrine—be it liberalism, or Christianity, or socialism. Michelet wanted the Revolution itself to be his one and only guide. The philosophers' transposition of the Christian ideal of a Heavenly City [8] into secular terms, and from the indeterminate future to the immediate moment, was what had inspired both the courage and the follies of the enthusiasts and extremists. To Michelet this was the unique and elevating quality of the ever memorable spectacle. To justify their high-handed actions nothing had been more useful to the men of the Revolution than Rousseau's doctrine of the *Volonté générale*, that is, the well-informed wish of the people for its own well-being. The well-informed wish, the ideal wish, is a mystic and unchangeable entity, and if the majority do not understand their own interest, it may be carried through, it *must* be carried through, by the minority of well-thinking men. For our generation, this kind of reasoning has a familiar ring. It is in this way that the modern

[8] Carl Becker's phrase: *The Heavenly City of Eighteenth-Century Philosophers* (1932).

minority dictatorships justify themselves. They may not know the *Contrat social*, but they have their own prophets who knew it. And Michelet had drunk from the source.

What dominates his work more completely than it does that of his contemporaries, is this conception; or let me rather say, this state of mind. I called it absolutistic, simplistic. It is a state of mind that is impervious to criticism or to argument, that triumphs over contradiction and confusion, and over the contradiction and confusion of the facts themselves, by an act of will, by a faith. It enabled Michelet to glorify the Revolution and the French people with unshaken ardour, yearning for the new revolution, or rather for the resurrection of the old.

One can imagine Michelet's exultation when the Orléans dynasty was overthrown and the Second Republic founded. But how grievous, once more, his sorrow when the new revolution, too, was soon seen not to have introduced the reign of Justice and Universal Happiness! Liberty and democracy had appeared on the scene only to be tragically and ignominiously defeated, and in 1851 the dictatorship of Louis Napoleon began. Was, then, the Bonapartist tradition all that was to survive of the Revolution? Michelet sorrowed, but he did not despair. His volume on the Terror, in which he testified to his faith as ardently as ever, was written when the enchanting prospects of February 1848 had already been hopelessly compromised.

IV

And indeed, although the enthusiasm of 1848 (the "folly" of 1848, as others termed it) led to a staggering anticlimax when, once more, the well-to-do middle-class, sheltering behind the dictatorship of a Bonaparte, roped in the gains, it was more than the outburst of a moment. The messianic illusion—a mixture of idealism and national conceit—the feeling that the Heavenly City was round the corner and that it was the high mission of the French nation to lead mankind towards it, had been roused to a pitch by these eloquent revivers of the revolutionary legend, and although cast down by unforeseen developments, it continued to lie ready in the depths of the French mind.

It found encouragement, on the one hand, in the confident positivism of Auguste Comte, in the doctrine that by means of his reasoning powers man could shape his own future. Comte's voluminous and often obscure writings were made accessible to a large public by that many-sided scholar, Littré, the "Apostle of Positivism," as he came to be called. His *Conservation, Révolution, Positivisme,* published in 1852, enjoyed an enormous vogue. In it the Revolution was described as a national movement that would infallibly lead to a final stabilization of society.

On the other hand there was the romantic temper of the time. At first sight this would seem almost incompatible with the solemn asseveration of the omnipotence of science which was the message of positivism, but as a matter of fact the exorbitance of the scientific pretension was not itself free from the romantic impulse. As an instance of how unadulterated romanticism could act as a lasting influence, even while the political situation was adverse, take Victor Hugo. Hugo had long venerated Napoleon the Great as the chosen instrument to propagate the revolutionary gospel in the world—this, too, was a much more than individual variety of the messianic faith—but Hugo became, during his exile after 1851, the high priest of a more popular cult. In his famous diatribe against "Napoléon le Petit," who had overthrown democracy in France, Hugo professed his unshaken confidence in the glorious future, and the great role that France was to play in its consummation. "This century," he wrote, "proclaims the sovereignty of the citizen and the inviolability of life; it crowns the people and it hallows man." The ideas were at hand; the actual liberation was about to be realized. "The Chinese Wall around thought is crumbling. The fanaticisms are dying, oppression has become impossible," etc. As for France, in her present state of humiliation, brought about by a contemptible adventurer, "not a word against France. . . . It is the nineteenth century itself which is lying there prostrate with France." But do you believe that God will halt in his march before this ludicrous plebiscite?

And certainly the Bonapartist dictatorship was not to be the last word. Already in 1848 the clash between the middle class and the proletariat, following hard upon the successful *coup* of February, had been far more violent than in 1830. The proletariat had again been frustrated. Louis Napoleon reigned as a result of universal suffrage plebiscites. It was the groups that were frightened at the prospect of a real revolution which had rallied round the heaven-sent preserver of the social order and made these plebiscites possible: the bourgeoisie, the farmers, the Church. Whether that made the plebiscites "ludicrous," as Hugo said, is another matter. The essential thing is that among the urban masses the revolutionary tradition could at any moment spring to vigorous life again. When bourgeois and intellectual opposition became bolder, as it did in Napoleon III's later years, the revolutionary spectre, too, reared its head.

Was French history, then, doomed endlessly to repeat itself? Was the Revolution, violent as ever, and this time more decidedly proletarian, again to be the answer to despotism and social privilege?

The historians of the French Revolution I have so far mentioned were all sympathizers. As a matter of fact, the Counter-revolution produced theories and systems, but in the first half of the nineteenth century it founded no important school of Revolution history-writing. This was to be different now. At least, attempts were to be made to question the historical legend that had been growing up and that seemed to many, by no means exclusively Catholics, royalists, or Bonapart-ists, a danger to the sanity and stability of French public life.

This will be discussed now, but later on the vitality and per-sistence of the legend will still form part of my theme.

The legend of the Revolution had been cast in historical form by Mignet and Thiers. A succeeding generation of historical writers had transposed it into a higher key of enthusiasm and radicalism; and among these writers it was Michelet who presented it most brilliantly and probably did most, even after the discomfiture of the radicals in 1848, to impress it upon the public mind. But simultaneously a reaction was setting in. The well-to-do classes had had a bad fright. The disappointment of fervent expectations had shaken many of the revolutionaries.

Tocqueville

Of the historical works that reflect the change in the public atmosphere the first that I shall consider is the Vicomte de Tocqueville's *L'Ancien Régime et la Révolution*, which appeared in 1856.

Although its incentive was undoubtedly Tocqueville's deep concern over the present state of affairs in his country, *L'Ancien Régime* was first and foremost a work of scholarship, based on patient research,[9] and one of the world's great masterpieces of historical interpretation.

The first thesis of this single volume (Tocqueville's death in 1859 prevented the work from being completed as planned) was that the Revolution had been long prepared by the monarchy—by its reforms, which left the feudal system an empty shell, and also by its failure to evolve a coherent and workable system to replace it. "The Revolution was no fortuitous event. It was but the completion of a long effort, the sudden and violent termination of a task on which generations had been engaged." And in which, in the end, the monarchy had failed to provide a consistent or effective lead.

It will be seen at once that Tocqueville was far from being actuated by counter-revolutionary motives. He knew that no return to the past was possible and also that the past was not worth returning to. But at the same time, in the place of the exaltation of the Revolution as an entirely new departure, as the beginning of a new era owing nothing to a past entirely evil, we receive a view in which it appears merely as the outcome of

[9] Michelet and Louis Blanc, it should be remembered, had been no less industrious in this way than Tocqueville.

that past—of its shortcomings, but also of its constructive powers.

In his second thesis, too, when he attempts to evaluate the achievement of the Revolution, Tocqueville speaks neither in counter-revolutionary nor in revolutionary terms. The Revolution's original aspirations were, he says, towards liberty, but they were largely frustrated. One explanation he finds in the large part played by men of letters in the elaboration of political schemes and systems, a phenomenon due really to the fact that the monarchical regime had left no room for the development of responsibility on either a national or a local scale. Without a competent aristocracy, or effective leadership at various levels of society, there can be, according to Tocqueville, no liberty securely grounded in reality. A further explanation was the growing anarchy consequent upon wild popular outbursts. For these, too, the royal government was to some extent accountable. Promises had been made, and never executed (Tocqueville quotes the proclamation in which Turgot, then the King's minister, had spoken of the right to employment); they amounted to a "revolutionary education" of the people.

And so, in its dire need, the Revolution borrowed or copied from the regime it had displaced its pernicious tendencies toward despotism and arbitrariness; indeed, in the person of Napoleon, the Revolution, anxious as it was only to safeguard the equality for which it had also found the preparatory conditions laid down and which now had only to be developed and consolidated, practically restored the monarchy.

Tocqueville's conclusion is a gloomy one. As a result of that extraordinary episode, the desire for liberty, although by fits and starts manifesting itself, is, to his view, still weak in France. It is stifled by the strong tradition of *raison d'état*, by the cult of unity, and by the mania for equality.

Neither revolutionary nor counter-revolutionary, but not therefore free from bias, Tocqueville was a liberal and a professing Catholic, too. He had studied democracy in the United States and been struck by its levelling and illiberal tendencies. He had witnessed the revolution of 1848, and after shuddering at the vulgarity and harebrained optimism (so it had seemed to him) of its short-lived first period, had served the Second Republic as minister of foreign affairs. He was, after these experiences, oppressed by one great fear, that of the rise of the masses. He knew it was impossible to check this rise, and moreover, he accepted it and was willing to try to direct it into safe channels; nevertheless he saw in it a danger to the highest values of civilization. Let me add that he would never stoop to encourage despotism as a curb upon that tendency, nor did he indulge in contempt for the human species. On the contrary, he held fast to the hope that men would prove amenable to reason.[10]

So much for Tocqueville's bias. When we remember that pure, objective, historical truth is hardly within the reach of man, we shall marvel at the serenity of vision manifested in a book on the Revolution written in the disturbed and feverish atmosphere of France. If anything could break through, or bypass, the fatal conflict between revolutionary and counter-revolutionary, this lucid and dispassionate treatise should have succeeded. Fustel de Coulanges must have, for a moment, forgotten Tocqueville when later, in the eighties, he wrote:

> For the last fifty years our historians have been party men. However sincere they may have been, however impartial they thought they were, they were subject to one of the political opinions that keep us divided. . . . The writing of history was one way of working for a party or assailing an adversary.[11]

Fustel's comment might indeed serve as an epitome of the story that I have been telling—up until the moment that Tocqueville appeared in it. Moreover, Fustel's words may be taken as evidence that Tocqueville's intervention did not really

[10] See, for example, *Correspondance entre Alexis de Tocqueville et Arthur de Gobineau* (Schemann, 1858), pp. 311-12, 333.

[11] "De la manière d'écrire l'histoire en France et en Allemagne," in *Questions historiques* (1893—published posthumously: Fustel de Coulanges died in 1889).

change the state of affairs. Not that Tocqueville's book did not influence, and deeply—at once and to this day—the historical treatment of the Revolution. Yet it will be curious to see how, on both sides, passion now ignored and then for its own purposes distorted Tocqueville's argument.

Lanfrey

The influence of Tocqueville is patent in an essay published in 1857 (the year after the appearance of *L'Ancien Régime*) by Pierre Lanfrey, a journalist of liberal principles, and a determined opponent of the empire. Later, Lanfrey was to strike the empire a keen blow by his *Histoire de Napoléon Ier*, in which he tried, often with great ingenuity, to expose as a disastrous fraud the great career from which Napoleon III derived his own.[12] In his essay on the Revolution, however, Lanfrey shows a closer attachment to its principles and slogans— always of the first phase—than does Tocqueville. Lanfrey's line is really that of Mme de Staël and Mignet; he attacks Louis Blanc (who was still, in his London exile, continuing his *History*, extolling Robespierre, and writing off the Girondins). But typically Tocqueville is Lanfrey's preoccupation with the contrast that had somehow grown up between the desire for liberty and the desire for equality. He duly reveres Rousseau, but he abhors the doctrine of the *Contrat social*, which seems bound to lead to the complete extinction of the individual and the individual's rights in the community. "Absolute democracy, as conceived by Rousseau, amounts to the most unlimited despotism." And it was that doctrine that triumphed under Robespierre, after whom the despotism of the multitude was countered only by the dictatorship of an adventurer. That is the depressing dilemma into which, more than sixty years before Lanfrey wrote, the derailment of the Revolution seemed to have landed France.

Many French intellectuals, while chafing at the restraints put upon French life by the thinly veiled dictatorship of the Second Empire, were depressed by the thought of the

[12] See my *Napoleon For and Against*, pp. 86-105.

alternative that the future might hold in store. Lanfrey was more alive than Mignet had been to the inconsistency with the principles of the Revolution offered by the limitation of the suffrage in the constitution of 1791. He tried to defend the bourgeois revolutionaries of that time against the charge that they had pursued a mere policy of abstention from interference with the social and economic process. But if the imperial regime, which for its part did its best to win the masses by material benefits, was overthrown, would the passion for equality again lead to another, and a worse, despotism?

Renan

Reflections like these passed through the mind of Ernest Renan, and they led him to a much more resolute rejection of the revolutionary tradition than was suggested by Lanfrey, or even by Tocqueville. In 1859 Renan added to his *Essais de critique et de morale* a preface, which struck a note then startlingly novel, coming as it did from a man who had renounced Catholicism, whose God was science, and who even now extolled liberalism as the "formula of the highest development of humanity."

"At the beginning of 1851," so Renan confesses, "I still had, with respect to the Revolution and the form of society which issued from it, the prejudices current in France." He had believed that the Revolution was synonymous with liberalism. He now saw that it contained:

a hidden virus: violence, a wholly materialistic conception of property, contempt for personal rights, attention for the individual only, and the individual considered as a being unconnected with yesterday or tomorrow and without any moral ties. If this is what the principles of 1789 mean, as they have too often meant in practice, let us renounce them. Nothing is more fatal to a nation than this fetishism, which makes it place its pride in certain words, with which one has only to cover oneself in order to lead it to the last limits of servitude and abasement.

What we can gather indirectly from this passage is that the strength of the legend of the Revolution was unbroken. The situation was indeed full of complications and contradictions. The Bonapartist regime was, after not very many years, to be swept away by a movement of opinion covering itself (to use Renan's phrase) with the great revolutionary words and indeed glowing with revolutionary ardour. All the time, however, Bonapartism had felt its own position to be grounded in the same legend, a legend it had therefore never been able whole-heartedly to oppose.

Another writer testified a little later, in 1865, to his disillusionment: no other than Quinet, who had in the turbulent forties been the comrade in arms of Michelet against the Jesuits and in defence of the Revolution, the champion of the eternal principles of liberty and democracy. He now, as he put it himself in a letter to a friend, "dared to break the holy seals of the book of the Revolution in order to put it to the test of the spirit of criticism." "Liberty," he wrote in his book, "is to be found at no epoch of our history. Do not let us look back for it."

Renan, meanwhile, was on a track much more definitely hostile to the Revolution, and events were to push him to its extreme limit.

In the late sixties, the position of the imperial regime was shaken. Its weakened prestige, resulting from setbacks to the Emperor's foreign policy, encouraged opposition on the home front. The newly founded First International had its branch in Paris and was agitating among the working population. The close alliance between the Church and the government and the Church's zealous concern for the social order, that is to say, for the socially privileged, roused the latent but ever-present anticlericalism to renewed activity. "Be atheists first, you will be revolutionists next," said an orator at one of the innumerable meetings that were now being held in the less fashionable quarters of the great city.[13] The memory of the Revolution, and especially of the great years of the sans-culottes, 1792 and 1793, was constantly invoked. When in a

[13] De la Gorce, *Histoire du Second Empire*, v.

discussion a speaker ventured to express his horror at the September massacres, the chairman interrupted him: "I shall not permit any of our great revolutionary dates to be insulted." The unrest was not confined to the popular masses. Nor were only isolated intellectuals affected by it. Freemasonry provided an organization, especially for the anticlerical tendencies of the movement. A regular opposition of journalists, lawyers, politicians was clamouring for the attention of the public, seemingly confident that its hour was soon to strike.

The Emperor himself was no longer spared. Hugo's *Châtiments*, those great poems of invective and moral indignation, were declaimed at students' meetings. In leaflets and obscure little periodicals Badinguet (the nickname by which his adversaries called the Emperor) was assailed; even a great boulevard paper allowed Rochefort to ridicule him in articles cleverly designed to evade the censorship, and for that, all the more intriguing and amusing. In 1868 a demonstration was organized, by men of extreme views who knew very well what they were doing (Delescluze was one of them), to honour the memory of one of the victims of the *coup d'état* of 1851—a painful date from the official point of view, but one that was now suddenly exposed to the glare of what almost seemed like concerted publicity. The organizers of the demonstration were prosecuted, but their views could not have received more sensational support than they found, at the trial, in the powerful speech made by Gambetta, a young, and till then unknown lawyer, but who now suddenly sprang to fame. Delivering a scathing denunciation of the man who, with his crew of fortune hunters and adventurers, had made himself master of France by brute force and unscrupulous deceit, Gambetta extolled Delescluze for having "throughout his life striven to have the French Revolution radically carried into effect."

This is the background against which an article of Renan, published in 1869, should be read.[14]

The situation, Renan affirms, is dominated by the Revolution. France was the prime mover of that world event: it was

[14] "La Monarchie constitutionnelle en France"; reprinted in his book, *La Réforme intellectuelle et morale* (1871).

her glory, an epic unsurpassed in history. But that is what now counts against her. Just as Israel had to pay for messianism with extinction as a national state, so France is now torn asunder. (The parallel occurred quite naturally to the man who was later to write the *Histoire du peuple d'Israël*, but we have seen that the idea of France suffering for what she had done for mankind was a commonplace.) Only a liberalized empire (so Renan continues) can ward off the dual menace of despotism and anarchy.

In advocating the liberalization of the regime, Renan was not indulging in opposition, for he was, in his fashion, supporting a policy that Napoleon III had just adopted. Only, what did Renan mean by liberalism?

Equality, the abstraction of the Revolution, which, instead of allowing itself to be carried away by abstractions, ought to have set to work historically, he now resolutely attacked. "Society is a great providential fact." It cannot exist—civilization, humanity, cannot exist—"unless it is admitted that entire classes must live on the glory and the felicity of other classes." So it had been in the old days.

> When Gubbio or Assisi saw their young lord careering by in his splendour, nobody was jealous. At that time all participated in the life of all. The poor man took delight in the wealth of the wealthy, the monk in the joys of the worldling, the worldling in the prayers of the monk. For all, there was art, there was poetry, there was religion. . . . Nature wills that the life of mankind shall be conducted on several planes. The rawness of many makes the education of one. The sweat of many makes possible the noble life of a small number.

It is clear that Renan has come to espouse a frankly counter-revolutionary position. The picture that he sketches of the *ancien régime* cannot be surpassed for idyllic loveliness. It is true that he does not advocate a restoration of the Bourbons: that tradition, so recklessly uprooted by the Revolution, cannot be revived. Rather, a liberalized empire and "a policy of contrition." Hardly an inspiring programme! "Our task is not to continue the Revolution, but to criticize it and to repair the errors it has committed."

But what about the ticklish problem of religion? It is painful to see the famous philosopher and advocate of free thought hedging on this point. He blames the Revolution for having been irreligious and atheistic. Religion has a purpose to serve in society—not for him, Renan, but "to explain to those who are sacrificed to social necessities on earth the mysteries of the divine dispensation that holds out to them abundant consolation in an ideal world."

During the following year, 1870, the liberal empire was confirmed by an overwhelming vote of confidence (in Paris and all the large towns, however, the noes were in a considerable majority); almost immediately afterwards, it was overtaken by the catastrophe of war and defeat, and collapsed.

It was the old story all over again. In Paris the spirit of the Revolution rose exultingly. The provinces showed a much more conservative temper. The great wish of all quiet men and of all who had any property to lose was to have an immediate end to the war, even at a price, and they frowned upon Gambetta, who, flaming with patriotic and republican zeal, tried, while Paris was desperately resisting its besiegers, to organize a *levée en masse*—the magic words of 1792 and 1793. The attempt was bound to fail. Paris had to capitulate. An armistice was concluded in January 1871 and a national assembly elected, which met at Bordeaux. It was dominated by conservatives, royalists numerous among them. Thiers, an old man now, had already, as head of the provisional government, negotiated a treaty by which Alsace and Lorraine were to be ceded. The treaty was laid before the Assembly for its approval. Both Louis Blanc and Victor Hugo, two more old men, back from exile, made speeches against peace on such conditions— speeches, it must be said, revealing two very different revolutionary temperaments, the one as bitter and dogmatic as the other was pathetic, prophetic, and high-flown; they spoke of the example of the Convention, of the undying glory of the Revolution, of the part that it behooved France still to play for the liberation and fraternization of the world. The Assembly refused to listen to them and voted overwhelmingly in favour of the treaty.

Paris now rose in revolt. The Commune—another word handed down from the heroic years—established itself. Among its leading members was Delescluze; most of the others were obscure men, working men, professional agitators. A *Comité de salut public* was instituted. It was to be 1793 all over again. The army of the Assembly forced its way into Paris. Terrible revenge was taken. Shootings, deportations. The red revolution had again been quashed.

The majority of the Assembly now wanted to restore the monarchy. It was only as a result of the refusal of the two rival monarchist parties, the adherents of Bourbon and those of Orleans, to give way one to the other, that in the end the Third Republic emerged. By then the public temper had changed. Royalism, closely allied to clericalism, no longer commanded a majority. Republicanism, strongly tinged with anticlericalism, could stand on its own feet. And again it had sucked strength from the revolutionary tradition, which it now cultivated with jealous gratitude as the ideology indispensable to the safety of the Republic and the greatness of France.

But before I come to that, I must say more about the reaction against the legend of the Revolution which we saw in full spate before 1870, and which of course received a further impetus from the events of that year and especially from the terrifying episode of the Commune in 1871.

In that same year, 1871, Renan published another essay,[15] "La Réforme intellectuelle et morale de la France." It is, in the main, a repetition of the argument of the earlier essay from which I quoted. Only, the contempt for the people, and the impotent despair of the intellectual at the way things have been going and are likely to continue going, is expressed even more crudely. "France beheaded herself when Louis XVI was

[15] Published, together with the one of 1869 and several others, in the volume cited in note 14, above.

executed." Leadership should again be based on birth: "The risk of birth as a criterion is less than the risk of the ballot box." "The people is much less capable than are the higher or enlightened classes of resisting the easy pleasures." (When I remember the wretched conditions in which the working classes had to live, this strikes me as a particularly heartless remark.) "It is well that the superior races should rule the lower." "The origin of property is conquest. Let the love of adventure and war, characteristic of the European, be used for colonial expeditions, and the Negro will work for a master as he was born to do."

Prussia, victorious Prussia, is now the example that Renan holds up for France.[16] "There, the *ancien régime* is continued in a corrected form. There, respect for property and subordination rule, and while France and England are, like America, worshipping the false gods of material prosperity, Prussia cultivates the military virtues."

He puts forward a plan for conservative reform. Almost comical in its mixture of cynicism and lack of a sense of the practicable is the proposal he makes to the Roman Catholic Church:

> At a certain degree of rational culture a belief in the supernatural becomes for many impossible. Don't compel us to wear a coat of lead. Don't interfere with what we teach or write, and we shall not grudge you the people; leave us in possession of the University, of the Academy; and we shall abandon to you the village schools in their entirety.

More extraordinary than the whole of this extraordinary production (which gives one but a low opinion of Renan's character) is that, for all his defiant gestures, Renan has not succeeded in really freeing his mind from the fascination of the Revolution. The preface is here and there in complete contradiction to the book. He who proclaimed conquest to be the

---

[16] There is indeed a striking resemblance between the views quoted from Renan and those that Treitschke developed about the same time on more than one occasion. See, for instance, A. Dorpalen, *Heinrich von Treitschke* (1957), pp. 199-200.

basis of property complains that Germany, in retaining Alsace and Lorraine, is abusing the right of the strongest. With all her great qualities, "Germany is incapable of disinterested actions for the rest of the world." German philosophy has nobility, certainly; "but the rights of man are also worth something. It is our eighteenth-century philosophy, it is our Revolution that has established them." Has Germany a poet like Hugo, a prose writer like Madame Sand, a man of the imagination of Michelet? It is a little surprising to find these names included in Renan's list of honour. And now he returns to his idea that the great creative acts of history are visited on the peoples who performed them: Greece, Israel, the Italy of the Renaissance, the Germany of the Reformation—and so France now atones for the Revolution.

It may be a tragic greatness, but greatness is after all what France owes to the Revolution, in the estimation of Renan as of Michelet; or should I say, the Revolution is evidence of the greatness of France? Renan had a very similar passage in the concluding part of his essay of 1869, and it is, again, curious to note that, while his exhortations all wear an air of disenchantment and lassitude, he seeks comfort in a reflection, from which De Gaulle, too, in our own day, draws inspiration (for a very different policy): "La France peut tout, excepte être médiocre."[17]

Flaubert

But, after all, the indictment of the basic principles of the Revolution remains the significance of Renan's message. Many minds were long prepared to accept it. Flaubert, for instance, who had described with caustic scepticism the romantic young revolutionaries of the forties (I quoted from the passage above), expressed in 1871, in a letter to George Sand, his fervent agreement with Renan.

The people, so he wrote, is an eternal minor, and in the hierarchy of social elements it will always occupy the lowest

[17] Compare to this the opening paragraph of De Gaulle's *Mémoires de guerre*, I.

rank. It is numbers, mass, the unlimited. What does it matter if many peasants are able to read and no longer listen to their parish priests? But it matters a great deal that men like Renan and Littré shall live and be listened to. [Note how variously the political lesson of positivism could be interpreted!] The French Revolution should cease being a dogma and submit to scientific examination. If people had really *known* history, we should have been spared Gambetta, and the Prussian occupation, and the Commune. "The Catholics did nothing but cross themselves" (for Flaubert was as bitterly anti-Catholic as he was anti-Revolution), "while the progressives cried *Vive la République*, evoked the men of 1792, and wanted to rush off to the Argonne—not that the Prussians were there now, but such is the tradition. They imagined that they could stop a modern army by fabricating *piques.*"

"The crowd, the herd," reflected Flaubert in a more general strain, "will always be hateful. Let us be ruled by mandarins, by the *Académie des Sciences*. Universal suffrage is a disgrace to the human mind. So, actually, we plod in the aftermath of the Revolution, which has been an abortion, a dismal failure. . . ." The Commune attempting to regulate rents infuriates him. A throwback to the Middle Ages is what it seems to him. The government interfering with contracts between private persons, folly! ineptitude! . . . The idea of equality, which is the whole of modern democracy, proceeds from Christianity and is opposed to justice.[18]

(Michelet, it will be remembered, loved the Revolution because it promoted justice, while the essence of Christianity was arbitrariness. Buchez, like Flaubert, admitted the affinity of the two creeds, but drew a conclusion opposite to his. Similarly, two generations later, Péguy revered both Joan of Arc and the Revolution as the highest expression of the spiritual life of France. But this in passing.)

What strikes me particularly about these utterances of Renan

[18] George Sand's reply to these outbursts is very moving. See *Correspondance entre George Sand et Gustave Flaubert;* Flaubert's letters of March 31, of early May, and of September 8; George Sand's of September 14, 1871.

and Flaubert is the hatred and contempt with which they regarded the people, the multitude. The problem of the masses and their rising importance was one that oppressed the minds of many of the great liberal intellectuals of the middle and second half of the nineteenth century. This was, as we say, the case with Tocqueville. John Stuart Mill, too, his correspondent and friend, struggled to find a solution for the conflict, which filled him with misgivings, between a mass society and civilization, between the new democracy and liberty. Burckhardt took a gloomy view of the future on this account. But not one of these allowed his feelings to be poisoned by fear as did Renan and Flaubert, and as did a third Frenchman, to whom I am now coming, Taine.[19]

Taine

Hippolyte Taine's *Origines de la France contemporaine* began to appear in 1871 with a volume on *L'Ancien Régime*; in 1878, 1881, and 1884, there followed three volumes on the Revolution; Taine died in 1892 after having completed only one volume (dealing with Napoleon) of *Le Régime moderne.*

As much as any of the works so far discussed, the volumes of the *Origines* owed their inception as well as their tone and spirit directly to the impression made on the author by his contemporary political environment. The war, and even more so the Commune, had been shocks from which Taine never recovered. He had not until then done any historical work in the strict sense of the word. He had made a name—and a great name—as a philosopher and a historian of art and literature. His brilliant books were all marked by an excessive inclination towards systematizing and generalizing. He was a positivist, proud of having his mind freed from the shackles of religion. Science was his idol, as it was Renan's. In the preface to his *Littérature anglaise* he had developed his theory that moral facts should not, any more than physical facts, move the historian either to sympathy or to disgust, for like physical

[19] Treitschke, indeed (see note 16, above), was equally virulent. He, too, of course, had started as a liberal.

facts, they are determined by causes that it is the historian's task simply to establish. "Le vice et la vertu sont des produits comme le vitriol et le sucre."[20] A primary cause, in Taine's view, was race: all the English writers, though differing among themselves and seemingly highly individual in their qualities, he explained by that dubious agency, about which he, however, never had any doubts.

As for his political opinions, his career had suffered, at its outset, from his refusal, however tactfully presented, to give an explicit approval to the *coup d'état* of 1851; next (as long as the *Université* was ruled by the clerical Fortoul), from his positivism. In 1863 the Bishop of Orléans, Dupanloup, had in a solemn "Warning to Young People and Their Fathers Concerning the Attacks Against Religion by Certain Writers of the Present Day" bracketed Taine with Renan and Littré as a particularly dangerous influence.

Indeed all this time Taine accepted the view of the Revolution current in France since the twenties—"the wilful illusion in which we live since the book of M. Thiers," as he put it much later[21] (and he might have added the name of Mignet). As late as 1864, when, as we saw, Renan was already in open revolt, Taine still vigorously defended the current view against Carlyle's presentation of the Revolution as nothing but an outburst of destructive fury.

> You should [he addresses Carlyle] not overlook the good beside the evil, nor the virtues beside the vices. Those sceptics believed in proved truth and wanted no other master. Those logicians founded society on justice only and risked their lives rather than renounce an established theory. Those Epicureans [all these terms of opprobrium, of course, had been used by Carlyle] embraced within their sympathies the whole of mankind. Those raging lunatics, those workingmen, those needy and naked beggars, fought at the frontiers for humanitarian interests and abstract principles. [Taine then attributed to the men of the Revolu-

[20] "Vice and virtue are products, like vitriol and sugar."
[21] *Correspondance*, IV, 30; letter of 1877.

tion qualities equivalent to those Carlyle admired in the Puritans, but moreover:] Their heroism transformed Europe while yours served only yourselves.[22]

Looking more closely at Taine's political opinions, however, it will be seen that this "liberalism" was of a kind with that of Renan and Flaubert. It was heavily laden with bourgeois class-consciousness. The socialist tendencies that came to the fore in the popular commotions of 1848 he regarded with detestation. To him "the right to property is an absolute one." The democrats seemed to him thieves organizing civil war in order to be able to lay their hands on the possessions of the rich. If he still accepted the revolutionary legend, it was because the semidictatorial rule of the Emperor, which in itself he did not like, had relegated the immediate danger to the background. When the shocking outburst of the Commune revived his fears, not only did his views of the politics needed for the present acquire a sharper edge—"what matters is that the enlightened and well-to-do classes should govern the ignorant and those who live from hand to mouth"; "speaking generally, it is wrong for the State to go beyond seeing to the safety of persons and of property"—but he woke up to the dangers inherent in those doctrines he had until then accepted because they seemed to form part of the glorious heritage of his country.

From now on he is out to demolish that "wilful illusion" about the true significance of the Revolution, which he has come to see lies at the root of all the evils from which France is suffering. It takes one's breath away to see him repeating in his preface all the cant about science and to read that he will approach his subject as dispassionately as the naturalist watches the metamorphosis of an insect. One has only to look at his letters written in 1871 to see how he was driven into the camp of the conservatives and reactionaries by fear, fear

[22] This is a passage that Mathiez has missed in his penetrating article "Taine historien," in *Revue d'histoire moderne et contemporaine,* VIII (1906-7), an article to which I owe something for the following paragraph.

mingled with rage and contempt, fear of the mob broken loose, which could be contained only by strong government.

These letters do not make pleasant reading. As early as November 1870 Taine had seen no salvation other than in peace. If only Paris will not spoil chance of it and show some common sense! In January he admits that the resistance of Paris has saved the honour of France; in March, when the Commune has been proclaimed, he takes back even that praise: the resistance had "*appeared* heroic." The Commune is to him a shattering spectacle. "Fanatics, foreigners, and rogues planning a universal *jacquerie*." He sees "the reds" dominating the councils of Lyon and other towns, "fools and tub thumpers who have inherited the style, the violence, and the stupidity of the old Jacobins." "Away with universal suffrage, the lair of the demagogic monster," he says. I am not an admirer either of the old Jacobins or of the Commune, but what one sadly misses in Taine's letters is one word of sympathy with the people in their amazement and confusion, in their distress, infinitely worse than the difficulties of the comfortable bourgeois.

Yet that is the mood in which Taine now sets to work on the history of the Revolution. "The harm the Revolution has done France is that it has left no medium between despotism and anarchy." For despotism is not what Taine wants, even now; he still calls himself "a liberal". This, of course, is pure Tocqueville; or rather, it is Tocqueville carried one stage further towards absolute despair; it is Tocqueville without his moderation, without his love of the human species.

Taine does not idealize the *ancien régime* (except at moments when he forgets what he has written elsewhere, for his work is not without contradictions). He has indeed read Tocqueville and follows him in this most important of that clear-sighted man's perceptions: that the Revolution was not a fortuitous outburst, that it was not occasioned by immediate grievances or by sufferings either, but that the entire trend of the old monarchical government, including its reforming tendencies, had created the situation and the spirit from which the Revolution naturally proceeded. Unfortunately, Taine concentrates on one of the suggestions thrown out by Tocqueville and gives to it a prominence that throws the whole picture out of balance. It will be remembered what Tocqueville said about the part played in French political thinking by men of letters. Taine was a man of letters himself. He eagerly took hold of Tocqueville's idea and made of this factor the centre of his interpretation.

The real cause of the overthrow of the old order, with all its terrible consequences, was a way of thinking: it was the philosophy of the French eighteenth century, the supremacy accorded to the *raison raisonnante*, a fashion to which the privileged classes succumbed; it was what Taine called *l'esprit classique* (a most confusing phrase really).

A society, a state (so Taine says), in order to exist or to survive, needs a submission and a loyalty that reason cannot supply. French philosophy, by calling everything into question, had ended by destroying everything. "En fait d'histoire, il vaut mieux continuer que recommencer,"[23] a phrase that might have been translated from Burke. For the old order, philosophy had substituted one principle, that of popular sovereignty. Rousseau was the architect of the doctrine that inevitably, through 1789 to 1793 and on to 1799, led the French nation from disaster to disaster: anarchy, despotism of the fanatics, anarchy again, despotism of the military adventurer.

When Taine represents the men of 1789 as impregnated with the dogma of the *Volonté générale* as taught by the *Contrat social*, he neglects differences of undeniable historic significance. His disposal of the Assembly as a crowd of mere theorists blind to reality cannot be justified.[24] As he describes

[23] *L'Ancien Régime*, p. 35.

[24] See, for instance, Daniel Mornet, *Les Origines intellectuelles de la Révolution française* (1938), p. 474. Georges Lefebvre, *Peuples et civilisations* (1938), XIII, 50, summarizes the story of the Assembly as follows: "Infléchir les principes ou les contredire, tantôt pour combattre l'aristocratie, tantôt pour contenir le peuple, tantôt pour se le concilier, ce n'est point faire oeuvre abstraite, mais réaliste." The name of Taine is not mentioned, but the polemical *pointe* is unmistakably directed against him.

it, the situation during the early years of the Revolution was one of complete anarchy. Here the objection is not so much that he changes the picture. On the contrary these chapters on "the spontaneous anarchy" are a most useful corrective of the rosy and unrealistic accounts current in the pro-Revolution literature of his predecessors. A historian of a later generation, Albert Mathiez, who was as firmly pro- as Taine was anti-Revolution, accepted that description. Only, Mathiez asks, Why this disorder? and he goes on to lay the blame on the bourgeois Assembly, which did nothing to meet the crying needs of the people. To Mathiez (as to Louis Blanc) the real Revolution was only the second phase, the social Revolution. One may well doubt whether indeed the aspirations of the second team of revolutionists are fully covered by that word "social", and especially whether everything these revolutionists did is thereby justified. But certainly Taine is a good deal more simplistic and unrealistic when he offers as the only explanation, hammering it in at every turn of the story, the state of mind brought about by the generalities of the philosophers, by the *Contrat social*.

Two large sections of the third of Taine's volumes on the Revolution are devoted to an analysis and characterization of the men who dominated the culminating years of that horror, the Jacobins, programme and personnel. One may on good grounds object to the method of fixing into set lines a mentality so composite and so continually exposed to the multiple influence of events. Yet here the picture undoubtedly has an awful reality, and so has Taine's last volume, in which he considers the dictatorial regime of Napoleon.

Taking it altogether, the *Origines* remains impressive. It has the logic of Taine's particular nightmare.

> Our society has been rebuilt upon a false principle, in a narrow and superficial spirit, *l'esprit classique*. And from the first to the last sentence of my book, that spirit is my only and principal subject.

So he wrote to a friend.[25] The old order broken up, that is,

[25] *Correspondance*, IV; letter to Monod, July 6, 1881.

society and civilization, protected by age-long custom and traditional authority, menaced, crippled, destroyed; that is, the lower orders, with their savage and barbaric instincts, set free to do their worst; that is, the fanatics coming into power and doing worse still. Taine revels in relating disturbances, violent incidents, murders, massacres, and the follies and downright crimes of the extremists. All caused by the inexorable working out of the primary principle. As a reader of Shakespeare he might have remembered Jack Cade and his followers, behaving exactly like French Jacobins. But indeed, he seems to have cleared his mind of all recollection of popular outbursts in centuries that knew not Rousseau. All follows from the *Contrat social*, until at last, in the preface to the volume on the Terror, he reveals the secret of the inner sanctum of the temple and shows the Revolution worshipping a Crocodile. The generous elation of the first phase moves him to scorn—"to pity," he says in the letter from which I quoted a moment ago; but there is not really any pity in his work, or at least, he reserves it for what in one place he calls "l'élite aimable et confiante." At any rate, it was all a huge mistake, for from the beginning, the vaunted principles of 1789 bore the poison within them.

I said "impressive." Yet I confess that I do not always find Taine's famous work easy to read, and this in spite of its ever-vivid and colourful style. The cumulation of incidents ("petits faits significatifs," as Taine used to say), the endless repetition of comments of vituperation and loathing for "the gorilla, the immense brute, the human herd, the exasperated brute, *l'animal primitif, le signe grimaçant, sanguinaire et lubrique,*" unchained by the *Contrat social*—this sort of thing does not, quite apart from any independent knowledge that we may bring to the text, seem true to life. The bias is too obtrusive. But the work *has* enormous power, and French opinion in the eighties, and for decades afterwards, reacted strongly. The *Origines* was greeted with delight by the Catholics, who now preferred to have Monseigneur Dupanloup's denunciation of 1863 forgotten; it also excited the indignation of staunch upholders of the tradition of the Revolution.

V

The latter were, as I hinted before, by no means driven from the field. On the contrary, in the actual course of French politics, the protracted attempt of the royalists after 1871 to bring about a restoration had caused the republicans to hoist the colours of the Revolution more defiantly than ever, and when the Third Republic was definitely established, it was they who controlled education. Anticlericalism allied with veneration of the sacred principles of 1789, or even of the Revolution in its entirety, seemed to them a requisite for reliable citizenship.

In the early nineties the Pope, Leo XIII, encouraged among French Catholics a movement of reconciliation with the Republic. Léon Bourgeois, a leading politician on the left and by no means an extremist, said in a speech—pretending to address the Catholics of the *ralliement* (as the movement was called): "You accept the Republic? Well and good. But do you accept the Revolution?"

In 1897 a play of Sardou's, entitled *Thermidor*, was performed at the *Comédie française* It was not anti-Revolution, at least the principles of 1789 received a respectful tribute. But it was anti-Terror, anti-*Comité de salut public*, anti-Robespierre. One performance after another became the occasion for demonstrations and counter-demonstrations. An interpellation in the Chamber followed: the *Comédie française* is, after all, a state institution. In the heated debate, Clemenceau, who in his younger years had belonged to the small group in the Bordeaux Assembly of protesters against the cession of Alsace-Lorraine, spoke the memorable words: "La Révolution est un bloc, dont on ne peut rien distraire."[26] His conclusion is no less worth noticing. Why all this excitement? he asks.

It is because that revolution is still going on, it is because always the same men are facing the same enemies. Yes, *you* [addressing the right] have remained the same, nor have

[26] "The Revolution is a block, from which no parts can be detached."

we changed. The struggle will continue until one of the two parties is victorious.

In 1899, when the Dreyfus affair had exacerbated the (already sufficiently bitter) conflict, Ranc, a friend of Gambetta (who had died years before), wrote: "La France? . . . Oui, la France grande et la République forte, mais la France de la Révolution, et la République représentant dans le monde le Droit et la Justice."[27]

By then Charles Maurras had risen to notoriety on the right, a man who with his *Action française* was to do what he could to inflame feeling still more. He commented, sarcastically: "La France mais . . . La France si . . . La France à condition que. . . ." And he exclaimed: "Français avant tout, et sans conditions."[28] But one of his friends, the highly cultivated literary critic Jules Lemaître, who had after long hesitations entered the ranks of the *Action française*, once wrote to him from a holiday in Switzerland: "I hate much more cordially a certain number of my compatriots than any group of foreigners." And this was really truer for Maurras, too, and for the whole of his movement, than was his own virtuous rejoinder to Ranc.

The above has been no more than a glimpse of the political background that illuminates the significance of the appointment, as early as 1885, of Alphonse Aulard to the newly established chair of Revolution History (endowed by the municipality of Paris) at the Sorbonne.

Aulard

Alphonse Aulard was to study the history of the Revolution, but he was to study it in the right spirit. And this he did in a long and active scholarly life. His influence in the all-embracing

[27] "France? . . . Yes, but a great France, a strong Republic, the France of the Revolution, and the Republic that represents in the world Right and Justice."

[28] " France, but . . . France, if . . . France, on condition that . . . No! Frenchmen before everything and unconditionally."

Université was immense. In spite of the acrimonious dispute in which he was later involved with his disciple, then rival, Mathiez, and although many scholars followed Mathiez's line rather than his, it may be said that it was Aulard who inspired a new school of Revolution historiography, closely related in spirit to the pre-1848 phase. The grandeur of the Revolution was to him an article of faith. However far removed from Michelet in his style and general address—characterized by academic dullness and pomposity—in his wholesale acceptance of the Revolution he was nearer to him than to any other of the earlier writers. Danton was his hero. Indeed, his difference of opinion with Mathiez was brought to a head when the latter, whose hero was Robespierre, exposed Danton as an unprincipled and corrupt opportunist.

There was, of course, much more involved than a dispute about persons. The approach of Aulard was primarily political, while Mathiez, under the influence of Jaurès, whose voluminous *Histoire socialiste de la Révolution française* appeared in the opening years of the twentieth century, and Louis Blanc, who stood behind both, came more and more to look for social and economic aims and factors—with results, it should be added, that have proved illuminating even for those who discerned, and balked at, his bias.

But I cannot go into any detail about the complications and refinements of modern scholarship. From the point of view that I am taking, the broad interpretation of the Revolution and the conflict between acceptance and rejection is what matters. In that connection Aulard's famous attack on Taine and its sequel must now claim our attention.

Aulard's *Taine: Historien de la Révolution française* appeared in 1907, fourteen years after Taine's death. In it Aulard questioned Taine's documentation, method, premises, conclusions—everything. It had, as might be expected, a very mixed reception. It is not an engaging book, and reviewers— I am thinking now particularly of two Dutch historians, leading men in their time[29]—were apt to say that it was a miserable spectacle to see a small mind carping at a great one. There is

[29] Bussemaker and Colenbrander.

something in that. Aulard meant to destroy Taine once and for all. He even said that a candidate for a history degree at the Sorbonne would not make a good impression if he quoted Taine as an authority.

To destroy Taine, of course, was more than Aulard could do. The animosity he displays, the deadly seriousness with which he accumulates the charges of inaccuracy, of incompleteness of documentation, elicited a reaction of sympathy. Even Mathiez, who had written about Taine with infinitely greater comprehension, for all that he, too, detested the great man's reactionary mentality, ended a very damaging review of Aulard's book[30] with a sarcastic warning to "naïve readers" that they should not imagine one is a great historian simply because one never makes a mistake about references to archival files.

One important point Aulard no doubt does make, but indeed it had been made by many others before him, by Seignobos, a colleague and fellow radical, even by Albert Sorel, a man with an unmistakably conservative type of mind and an admirer of Taine, but one who could not for all that accept a purely negative view of the Revolution—one important point, namely, that Taine, in explaining the developments taking place during the years from 1794 to 1799 as the natural consequence of a mistaken philosophy, as the progress of a mental malady, isolates purely psychological or spiritual aspects in a truly unhistorical manner. The leading idea of Sorel's great work was related to that of Tocqueville's. Rejecting the view of the enthusiasts of the Revolution as an entirely new beginning, he brought out, on the contrary, the continuity of the Revolution's foreign policy—as Tocqueville had done for its domestic reforms—with that of the monarchy; a sobering view, but one that could imperceptibly change into apology. In any case, both Aulard and Sorel agreed that external circumstances—the resistance, the court intrigues, the plotting of the *émigrés*, the threats, and at last, the interference of foreign rulers—cannot be overlooked as Taine had overlooked them.

[30] *Annales révolutionnaires,* 1908 (first year), pp. 340-57.

Aulard, however, is inclined unduly to emphasize the factor of external circumstances, to present it as the all-sufficient explanation, and at the same time justification, of the September massacres, of the overthrow and extermination of the Girondins by the Jacobins, of the dictatorial rule of the *Comité de salut public*, of all the excesses of the Revolution. It was always the court, and the *émigrés*, and the foreign powers. Aulard was here in the tradition set by Mignet, and followed by countless others. But Aulard was the first, in his great *Histoire politique de la Révolution française* (1901), to erect this argument into an imposing system based on the statements and apologies of the revolutionary leaders and bodies themselves: Assemblies, Committees, Paris Commune, etc. One will find in his book against Taine lucid and uncompromising summaries of the system as set out in his larger work, summaries that are very helpful for anyone wishing to understand his "philosophy of the Revolution" (to use a phrase that he would have indignantly rejected). It is in this "philosophy" that Aulard laid himself open to counter-attack.

Cochin

In 1909 an essay, "La crise de l'histoire révolutionnaire," written by a young Catholic historian Augustin Cochin,[31] provided a formidable counter-attack to M. Aulard, whose history, says Cochin, is but the history of the professions made by the revolutionaries themselves. As a result his *Histoire politique de la Révolution française* is impeccably orthodox; it is the legend in its pure form. But *la thèse des circonstances* will not do; no more than *la thèse du complot*, by which more moderate revolutionaries had tried to establish their alibi, imputing the crimes and the horrors of the Revolution to the deliberate and conspiratory actions of a small number of evil-minded men.

Taine, so Cochin continues, whose book Aulard imagined that he had disposed of, brought out realities that the legend

[31] A few years later, in 1916, Cochin was killed in the first world war—undoubtedly a loss to scholarship.

had obscured. First, he enabled us to see that the Revolution meant progressive, and more and more oppressive, subjection of the people by the self-styled right-minded people, of the real people by the revolutionary minority, of *la grande cité* by *la petite cité*. Second, by going outside the official circles and their high-sounding and often exculpatory statements, he reminded us of the ordinary men and of what actually happened in the street; not the phrases, not the idealization and the apology, but the stark reality. Third, he showed the connection of all this, or at least that there was a connection, with the revolutionary ideology, which had dissolving and demoralizing, at least as much as it had constructive, effects.

So far, I think Cochin's comments are most illuminating. When he uses the last point to bring out the insufficiency of the thesis of a plot, I can still applaud. Now, however, he goes on to argue that the process revealed by Taine was an automatic process, governed by a social law discovered quite recently by the great sociologist Durkheim, a law that offers "the solution," while Taine, for all his clear-sightedness was prevented by his individualistic psychological method (and he should not be blamed, for he had not yet been able to read Durkheim) from giving a satisfactory "explanation."

The idea is certainly one to stimulate thought, but developed in this way it may lead to a dangerously simplistic doctrinairism. The "law" is the law of mechanical selection and acceleration ("entraînement"), which operates quite independently of "intention" or individual wickedness (no "plot" therefore), and brings, when the dogma of direct sovereignty has once been launched, ever-more-extreme elements to the fore and makes ever-more-fanatical methods prevail, *automatically*.[32]

---

[32] Crane Brinton, in the "Bibliographical Essay" with which he concludes his brilliant volume *A Decade of Revolution: 1789-1799* (the "Rise of Modern Europe" series, New York, 1934), p. 298, has not, I think satisfactorily unravelled Cochin's somewhat involved argument. In stating that Cochin adhered to *le thèse du complot* he is certainly mistaken.

Twentieth-century French Historians of the Revolution

Taine, as I said, was not destroyed by Aulard. His influence continued to be considerable, but it made itself felt almost exclusively outside the *Université*.

Indirectly, no doubt, the work affected even those who were antagonistic to its general tendency by turning their attention to those realities that Taine had dealt with, in a partisan spirit no doubt, but that he had at any rate dragged into the light of day. Not, of course, that French scholarship was not already trying to free itself from the generalities and emotional engagements that characterized so much of the earlier work. I spoke of the new school to which Aulard's appointment in 1885 gave rise. The work on divers aspects of the Revolution produced by scholars formed in the *Université* assumed ever larger proportions. To mention a few names—only of those who wrote more comprehensive accounts—there was Seigno-bos, born in 1854, who was only a few years younger than Aulard; there were Sagnac and Pariset, who supplied the first volumes to the large *Histoire de la France contemporaine* published shortly after the first world war under the editorship of the great Lavisse, who was seven years older than Aulard; and of course, there was Mathiez, whose short history of the Revolution appeared in 1922. Among the scholars he influenced there stands pre-eminently Georges Lefebvre.[33] These men did not all think alike. The clash between Aulard and Mathiez is an extreme instance of what may be regarded as a normal and healthy phenomenon: differences of opinion, which helped to elucidate what had really happened, and what it signified.

Nevertheless practically all of them started from an assumption that they did not even recognize as such: it seemed to them as self-evident as the fact that they were Frenchmen. They began by accepting the revolutionary epoch as the formative period of the republican regime under which they lived. The concomitants of this acceptance were that national

[33] Lefebvre (who died in 1959), though born in the same year as Mathiez (1874) survived him by nearly thirty.

pride in the Revolution, that impatience with opponents whether at home or abroad, and an addiction to those various methods of apology for the excesses of the Terror, which we observed in Mignet (even in De Maistre!) and in Michelet. The signs of it will every now and again emerge to strike the attentive reader from beneath the smooth surface of the well-documented accounts composed by the men I have mentioned, and by other modern professional historians.

I cannot try to show this in any detail by a systematic examination of twentieth-century work. I shall give one single instance of the sort of thing I have in mind.

I take it from Georges Lefebvre's volume on the Revolution in the well-known *Peuples et civilisations* series. Lefebvre's repute as a scholar is richly deserved. His critical powers are unmistakable, his tone is restrained and balanced, in several monographs he made a large contribution to the better understanding of the period. I was surprised, some years ago, on reading his *Notions d'historiographie moderne*,[34] to see how he extolled Michelet as "our greatest national historian," and this on the strength of the volumes on the Revolution and without apparently being put out by Michelet's worship of the Revolution, by his emotionalism and chauvinism. But now this is what Lefebvre himself has to say about the Terror,[35] and it will be enough to show that he did indeed follow the tradition of what Renan termed "the prejudices current in France," and Taine, "the wilful illusion in which we live since the book of M. Thiers." After noting that the Committee of Public Safety at one moment tried to limit the scope of the Terror, he goes on:

Do without it, however, the Committee could not, for it was indispensable for breaking down passive resistance, silencing personal interests, and crushing particularism. The majority of Frenchmen no doubt were devoted to the Revolution

[34] A stencilled volume in *Les Cours de Sorbonne*. The date of publication is not given. I believe it was 1953, although there is internal evidence that the lectures were composed before the second world war.

[35] Op. cit., p. 250 (edition of 1938).

and detested the foreign intervention, but they were lacking in a "civic culture" sufficiently comprehensive to enable them to submit to discipline voluntarily. The Terror compelled them to do so and thus contributed mightily toward developing the habit of, and consequently the feeling for, national solidarity.

The counter-revolutionary tradition, which had been given such an impetus by Taine's work, was not, meanwhile, brought to a halt. It continued on its course, crying defiance to the Revolution, to the modern age, to the Republic itself, but, as I said, outside the *Université*. The influence of Taine's book was reinforced by the spirit of the *Action française*, which, although it never managed to come into actual power, in the early decades of the twentieth century obtained a remarkable hold over the French intellect.

Maurras was far from being a disciple of Taine. Instead of denouncing *l'esprit classique* as the source of the Revolution and of all France's troubles, he held up a return to the classic spirit as the only way to salvation. It is true that the two men used the phrase in entirely different senses. I hinted already that Taine's use of it was very arbitrary and confusing. By *l'esprit classique* he meant the passion for arguing in the abstract, *la raison raisonnante*, indifferent to the realities of history and of life. The classicism that Maurras preached was the spirit of order, of subordination to, or respect for, the conventions and the proprieties; order as it had reigned in the seventeenth century, *le grand siècle*, under Louis XIV, *le grand roi*. National unity and strength. "La France seule!" Renouncing all her history before 1789 would not make France strong; on the contrary. The enemies to Maurras were Romanticism, Individualism, Protestantism, Judaism; these it were that had triumphed in the Revolution. We seem to be nearer here to De Maistre or to De Bonald than to Taine. Yet Taine's denunciations of the Revolution and all its works were grist to the mill of the *Action française*.

One of the ablest books produced by the movement was *Le Romantisme français* (1907), by Pierre Lasserre. It opens with a merciless attack on Rousseau and later on disposes of Michelet and his messianism as baneful products of Romanticism. Presented as a thesis for the doctor's degree at the Sorbonne, it gave rise to an acrimonious discussion between the candidate and Professor Aulard.

A few years later, in 1912, Lasserre published a book in which he boldly challenged the *Université* as a whole: *La doctrine officielle de l'Université*.

The state's educational policy was a hotly debated issue in those years. The radical Combes government, emerging victoriously from the Dreyfus affair, had ruthlessly declericalized the elementary schools (it will be remembered that Renan had offered to leave these to the priests, if only they would not meddle with higher education; a very different climate had come to prevail since). In secondary education the clergy still maintained a position, but in the state secondary schools the programme had been revised in 1902 to the detriment of the traditional classical humanities. This gave rise to protracted and bitter debates, and it was the immediate occasion for Lasserre's book.

Lasserre charged the *Université* with being a fighting machine and attacked the leading men of the Sorbonne, especially Lavisse, Seignobos, and the historian of literature Lanson, for making education serve political ends. What is behind the dead set made against the humanities? They are looked upon as an obstacle to the desired equality. They belong, so Lavisse said, to a stage of society when "the family, the corporation, the order, surrounded and classed the individual." All the more reason to preserve them, Lasserre exclaims. And history, too, he notes, is being badly treated by the men of the regime, treated so as to bring into contempt the "stupid" religiosity of the Middle Ages or to cry down the glorious seventeenth century: Lavisse's (famous!) volumes on the age of Louis XIV amount to a systematic detraction of the great king; Seignobos, in a textbook for schools, characterizes the policy of the Church by an illustration showing a heretic at the stake, and the *ancien régime* by one of a peasant on the gallows.

A special chapter on history as taught and written in the Sorbonne was contributed to Lasserre's book by a young man, René de Marans. He shows us Seignobos priding himself on the share he had taken in the reform of 1902 and from the height of his position in the Sorbonne telling the secondary-school teachers how to carry out their task: "Our pupils will be electors. It is the duty of the history masters to look after the political instruction of future citizens." They must, comments De Marans, fashion electors who will vote Radical Socialist. Less attention, according to Seignobos, should be given to periods of stability (as, for instance, the seventeenth century!); the critical periods, on the contrary, the periods of change, should be placed in the forefront. The concept of change itself, of evolution, should be impressed on the minds of these budding members of our democracy; and from that point of view the eighteenth and nineteenth centuries, "the period in the history of mankind when evolution has been fastest," are the most interesting.

I have been familiar for many years with the work of Lavisse, of Seignobos, of Lanson, and the affectionate regard I have for them can withstand these attacks. Lasserre's book is, moreover, disfigured in places (this does not apply to the part due to De Marans) by the reactionary idiosyncrasies and fanaticism of the *Action française*. I was nevertheless impressed by his book when I got hold of a copy a few years ago (it is so little known that not one of the university libraries in Holland, or the Royal Library either, possessed it). The political preoccupations of the French historians of the period are indeed made unmistakably clear.

The insistence of Seignobos and Langlois in their well-known *Introduction aux études historiques* on the most depersonalized scientific method is shown by De Marans not in the least to provide a remedy against the fashionable partiality. Indeed this talk of objectivity and of sticking to the documents, in which especially Langlois indulges (I used the book in question in my undergraduate days, and my recollection of Langlois is not an "affectionate" one), seems only to serve as an excuse for the most outrageously unhistoric

pronouncements: "en marge de ses travaux scientifiques."[36]
De Marans remarks acutely that once the connection between
the fact-finding and the historic judgment gets lost, opinions
proceeding straight from present-day preoccupations will
obtain a free rein. To look in the past for nothing but what led
up to the Revolution and the actual republican regime that
issued from the Revolution is debasing history. The invaluable
importance of history for our civilization lies in the fact that
history maintains a disinterested understanding of the past,
remote and "stable" periods included.[37]

I have, then, found it instructive to listen to the criticism
levelled at the "official" historians by the conservatives. (Let
me remark in passing that I know of no later work by De
Marans, who I suppose was killed in the first world war, as
was Cochin; and that Lasserre later on seceded from the *Action
française*, a convert to liberalism.) The historical work produced
by the conservatives themselves, however, for the most part
sinned from bias as badly or worse.

One of the most popular of modern brief histories of the
Revolution was Louis Madelin's volume, which appeared in
1911 ("ouvrage couronné par l'Académie française"), in the
Histoire de France racontée à tous. Extreme bias is not the
reproach one can level against this book. *Was* the writer a
conservative? In the sense of viewing things from a bourgeois

[36] "Side by side with, and independent from, the 'scientific' labour."
Cf. my little essay on Professor Butterfield, p. 256, below.
[37] Langlois thought (or said) that history serves only to satisfy
curiosity; Seignobos, to form democratic citizens. Against them De
Marans quotes a passage from Fustel de Coulanges. I gave part of this
passage above (p. 152); the following is also, I think, worth reproducing:
"L'histoire imparfaitement observeé nous divise, c'est par l'histoire
mieux connue que l'oeuvre de conciliation doit commencer." And elsewhere: "La connaissance du moyen âge, mais la connaissance exacte,
sincère et sans parti pris, est pour notre société un intérêt de premier
ordre. . . . Pour remettre le calme dans le présent, il n'est pas inutile de
détruire d'abord les préjugés et les erreurs sur le passé." Comte and the
positivists attributed to history a leading task in the work of ordering
and controlling society. One can see a connection between Fustel de
Coulanges's insistence on history's beneficent influence and the
positivist dogmatism and arrogance in his outlook.

and chauvinistic point of view, yes; but not in the sense of rejecting the Revolution *in toto*. He says expressly that he does not want to range himself among either the Guelphs or the Ghibellines. He is only a Frenchman, "adoring" his country "under whichever flag it may triumph or succumb." In fact, of course, he was deluding himself when he thought this pronouncement was a guarantee that his appreciation of events would not be governed by any definite political philosophy.

The Revolution was, Madelin considers, inevitable. But the reforms that "the nation" wanted were all comprised in the *cahiers* of 1789. In other words, Madelin regards the second Revolution, of 1792 to 1794—the real Revolution in the eyes of Mathiez—as an aberration that could not lead to enduring results. What enables Madelin to approach even the extremists without the detestation that might go with this position is his chauvinism: they were Frenchmen engaged in a life-and-death struggle with the foreigner. It is also the conviction he expresses in one place that the Revolution was "the explosion and the assertion [*revanche*] of the noblest sentiment that, to my view, distinguishes man: I mean *Energy*." A conviction on so different a plane from all ideology or moral sentiment that it not only guards the man who holds it against giving way to blinding indignation, but also debars him from profound understanding.

Madelin devoted the rest of his life to a many-volumed work on Napoleon[38]—the admirer of "Energy" had found his subject. He may be regarded as a professional historian, although with him we are not really, any more than with Lasserre and De Marans, in the sphere of the *Université*.

Of more definitely counter-revolutionary writers, I mention Bainville and Gaxotte, both members of the *Action française*, both elected into the *Académie française*, as indeed was Maurras himself. In my *Napoleon For and Against* I drew attention to the contrast between the conservative *Académie* being for, and the radical *Université* against the dictator. With respect to the

[38] I mentioned that Madelin's book on the Revolution was awarded a prize by the *Académie*. On the strength of his Napoleon book he was later elected a member.

Revolution it was the reverse: the *Université* was for, the *Académie* against.[39]

One quotation from Gaxotte's book, which appeared in 1928 and went through innumerable editions, must serve to indicate the sort of French nationalism that went down with the public, as well as the incredible, almost childish simplification of history that did not prevent the "Immortals" from voting for a "well-thinking" candidate.

> The seventeenth century had been, for the French genius, an epoch full of efflorescence. The Frenchman, such as one loves to picture him then, is a being conscious and reflective, capable of silencing his instincts and his passions in order to submit himself to a superior rule of order and harmony. He is on his guard against individual fantasies.

> In the early eighteenth century, Gaxotte goes on, slight movements of impatience may be observed. But the imposing good sense of the admirable Louis XIV easily had the better of them. The Germans, always individualistic (did not the Reformation have its origin in Germany?), the English, given to rebellion against their kings, go on indulging in the most reckless speculations. In France there were at most little sparks, here and there, which did not kindle any fire. Until? . . .

> Until Montesquieu and Voltaire went to stay in England for a while. Then, and this time in real earnest, the individualistic and revolutionary preaching was revived.

VI

I must try to come to a conclusion. Or *is* there no conclusion? Is the story that I have been telling just going on endlessly repeating itself?

I cannot help recalling a personal experience here, one that is not of any importance in itself, but that has stuck in my mind because I found it so revealing on this very point.

It happened in 1948, when I attended the last sitting—only

[39] See my *Napoleon For and Against*, pp. 390-402.

the last—of the great international congress held in Paris and
devoted to the history of the revolutions of 1848. Professor
Labrousse delivered the final lecture. Then, in the discussion,
up rose from a back row an old gentleman, bearded all over
his face and rather shabbily dressed, who sounded a note that
apparently, after a full week of talk, impressed the assembled
members as altogether novel. He said that what had struck
him in the proceedings was that everybody seemed to have
started from the assumption that revolution was "a good thing."
As for him, he ventured to question this and to urge his hearers
to ask themselves whether really revolution was the best
method for promoting reform and progress, whether it was
not on the contrary an extraordinarily wasteful and risky
method, a method always leading to unforeseeable complications and unhappy after-effects. *"Taine,"* he said, and at that
name the audience of distinguished French historians, which
had turned round to look at the speaker with slightly bored
amusement, positively broke into a ripple of laughter. Imagine
mentioning Taine, who was a mere interloper, and to mention
whom seriously (as Aulard had actually written) would almost
cause a candidate for a history degree to be ploughed! I
particularly noticed the broad smile and the expressive shrug
of the excellent and deservedly famous old Professor Lefebvre.

The speaker was Daniel Halévy, and I confess that my
sympathy at that moment was with him. Later on I read his
Histoire d'une histoire (1939), an essay in which he made his
contribution to the one hundred and fiftieth anniversary of 1789
by attacking the cult of the revolutionary tradition as he saw it
observed in the official world of French historians (exactly
as Lasserre and De Marans had seen it twenty-seven years
earlier), and I found the little work very stimulating and
instructive. At the same time, how one-sided was the view
taken by this same M. Halévy. How blindly he revered, not
either Danton or Robespierre, not Mignet or Michelet, but
Renan and Taine. And still later on I discovered that M.
Halévy had, during the war, been an ardent supporter of
Marshal Pétain.

Isn't it clear, not only that the Revolution still is an issue in present-day French politics, but also that the attitude of French historians towards it is still connected with their political convictions? I believe that this is indeed so, but at the same time I see plenty of evidence for the statement that, compared with the situation in the nineteenth century, the tension has slackened.

This is partly due to the passage of time. So much has happened since the end of the eighteenth century! And while 1848 and even 1871 could still with some show of reason be connected with the great Revolution, there have since been shattering events of a tendency and an origin patently different. The effect has been to draw dividing lines right across the traditional one separating radicals upholding the revolutionary legend from conservatives rejecting it. Take the Communists. How embarrassing must it be to some of the older devotees to see them posing as the true and only heirs of Robespierre's greatness and ideals![40]

But men of a different type altogether on occasion invoke the glorious epic, thereby upsetting the original pattern of for and against. In 1956, for instance, Jean Dutourd, exasperated by the slackness and lack of spirit that were responsible for the collapse of French military resistance in 1940, and even more by the complacency with which the humiliation of that terrible episode was now on all sides glossed over or forgotten, and wanting to goad his fellow countrymen to a proper appreciation of their plight and to the courage required to overcome it,

[40] A situation full of irony resulted in 1957 when the committee of party chairmen in the Chamber in an unguarded moment decided to request the government to organize a national commemoration of the bicentenary of Robespierre's birth. On second thoughts, when Pinay and Bidault had issued resounding protests, several of the gentlemen were seen to waver. *L'Humanité*, the Communist newspaper, poured scorn especially on the Socialists who were trying to explain away the great man's inhumanities. As if any apologies were needed for the Incorruptible! These lackeys of the bourgeoisie were only trying to decorate their miserable cause with the name of a man of whom they would be mortally afraid if he were not safely dead! . . .
Insofar as the memory of the Revolution still does have an immediate impact on French politics, the Communists have found it a useful asset.

wrote in that bitter book, *Les Taxis de la Marne:* "The
Revolution of 1789 and the Terror convey a solemn warning"
—to the Republic, which, according to the writer, had sunk
almost to the degree of stupidity at which the old monarchy
had been overtaken by disaster. "It was not so much the
aristocrats as stupidity which then [in 1793 and 1794] had its
head cut off."[41]

But the passage of time and the intrusion of extraneous
events is not all. Modern historical scholarship has undoubtedly
made a contribution of its own towards softening the all-too-
rigid contrast. In the foregoing I have mainly brought out the
weaknesses of the application of it by the French in dealing
with their great Revolution. I have shown that the historians
on both sides of the traditional controversy had in many cases
succeeded but imperfectly in freeing their minds from the
domination of the legend—of the legend of either for or against.
To bring out the positive effects resulting from indefatigable
research and from incessant questioning and trying out new
approaches, I should have had to review dozens of writers and
to enter into subtle and complicated arguments. By avoiding
doing so, I am afraid I must have created an impression that
does not do full justice to French historiography.

Let me now state emphatically, however generally, that
modern historical scholarship in France, taking it as a whole,
has helped to free men's minds from easy generalizations and
from tendentious exaggerations. Modern historical scholarship
is from its very nature inimical to simplistic views like the
Revolution being "a block," to be religiously accepted or to
be rejected *in toto*.[42] It tends to complicate the image of the
past to such an extent that the legend, and for that matter the
counterlegend, more and more comes to wear an air of

[41] That was in 1956—before the coming into power of De Gaulle.
And what seems finally to confuse the picture is the fact that General
Massu, the instigator of the military *coup* in Algeria by which the Fourth
Republic was, in May 1958, overthrown, organized his adherents in a
Comité de salut Public!

[42] Clemenceau's phrase, see p. 170. This "block" theory was expressly
refuted many times, very strikingly by Vandal, quoted with approval
by Madelin.

unreality. This, as Fustel de Coulanges realized with such clarity of vision, is the great service that the study of history, if rightly practised, can render to the community. And to some extent undoubtedly French historiography, in spite of the shortcomings that it is easier for the foreigner to detect than for the Frenchman to avoid, has succeeded in doing so.

(1956)

3. *Huizinga as Accuser of his Age*[1]

Huizinga[2] was a notable figure in the Dutch, and even in the wider Western, life of his time. None of our Dutch historians has been so much read and so much admired. At the same time he irritated many and was sharply attacked. His fascination is by no means spent. Even now one can surrender with delight to the pictures he creates, one can both learn from and enjoy the sparkling of his intellect; then again one feels repelled by his prejudice or wonders how it could dominate this subtle mind to that extent. An uncommon and an important personality he remains.

I say this at the outset so emphatically because I am going to approach him from the side that rouses me to opposition. Those charges against our time in which he indulged especially in the years of crisis before and during the Second World War, and which procured him an entirely novel reputation with the public at large, seemed to me at the time already to be missing their mark, inspired as they were by personal feelings of unease, historically and politically unwarranted. A thorough rereading has confirmed me in this opinion, and it will be the starting point of this paper. Next I shall ask myself how these prejudices and these personal sentiments are to be explained. In looking back on his earlier work we shall find that they were present in his mind from the beginning; in which peculiarities, in which general attitude toward life and society

[1] This essay appeared originally in Dutch, *Huizinga als aanklager van zijn tijd* (Amsterdam: Akademie van Wetenschappen, 1961). With the omission of *Appendix to Section 1* it was published in *History and Theory*, Harvard, 1963.

[2] Johan Huizinga, 1872-1945, Professor of History at the University of Groningen 1905-1915, at the University of Leyden from 1915.

did they have their roots? A further analysis of his general
outlook—at first more particularly in connection with the
severe criticisms levelled against him from three sides in 1930—
will then occupy the two concluding sections.

I

In 1935 there appeared *In de schaduwen van morgen* (*In the
Shadows of Tomorrow*). Our world was living under the double
menace of Communism, which professed world revolution as
its great aim, and of National-Socialism, which had just come
into power in Germany and whose unbridled dynamism
seemed to constitute an even more immediate danger, at any
rate one closer by. And now here appeared the famous historian—the scholar, or at times it seemed more like the aesthete,
the man playing with beautiful forms and subtle ideas—and
threw this book into the fearful tension of the moment like
a loud cry of anguish.

"A diagnosis of the spiritual distemper of our age," so ran
the subtitle. The book drew an enormous amount of attention.
The first edition was sold out almost at once; in 1938 appeared
the seventh, and by then translations into nine languages
were spread over Europe.

The book has indeed uncommon qualities. It is written
vividly. The anxieties of the present are taken up in a broad
argument, which could not but impress by the inexhaustible
erudition of the author, not a mere expert in his particular
branch of study, but apparently at home in all fields of the
mind. What a power of observation, what an ever ready
adequacy of expression, and how did he not seem, with quiet
authority, to reveal undreamt of depths! And at the same time
there rose from the book a profounder tone of true concern
and sacred conviction. The scholar as warning prophet and
guide towards salvation. It is small wonder that he was avidly
read by countless disquieted and bewildered readers.

Huizinga envisaged the crisis through which the world was
going as an exclusively cultural crisis. It was culture, our own,
our Western culture, which had lost its bearings and seemed to

be making for disaster. And to avert that happening? Yes, for that, too, there was nothing but that we should reform ourselves, our attitude of mind, our spiritual life.

Was the diagnosis correct? Would the cure he indicated prove effective, was it even practicable?

Banning,[3] whose own view of the book was critical, spoke at the time of "the uncritical veneration and the disgusting yapping" with which it had been received. The profoundest word came from Verwey." In his last published article the great poet and critic wrote in the monthly journal *Het Kouter* of 1936 that "Being Distempered with the Age"—this was the title of the article, in which Huizinga is not mentioned by name—"with some of our contemporaries, and not the least, takes on forms which seem to me regrettable." They lament "the decline of what they regard as culture." Verwey then dismisses the indulging in thoughts of ruin, melancholy cogitations, and discouragements, as poisonous weeds. And he says: "I esteem of importance only those minds—they need by no means be great minds—who resist these sorrowings and unconditionally believe and confide in the powers, first defensive then creative, of the human mind." A confidence, it is true, which is not presented to us as the result of scholarly investigation; an unconditional *belief*. But will not critical reason admit that it constituted an element of culture of greater constructive capacity than did the equally preconceived pessimism of which Huizinga made himself the spokesman?

They were indeed terrible years, the years in which our lives were then cast. But one should remember (so it looks from the vantage point of the present, and so it did look to more realistic minds then) that the crisis was embodied in Stalin, Mussolini, Hitler. And to explain *them* it is plainly necessary to adduce the particular circumstances of their environment

[3] W. Banning, b. 1888, "modernist" Reformed minister, Professor of Sociology in the University of Leyden 1946-1958; a leading figure among religious-minded Socialists.

[4] Albert Verwey, 1865-1937, poet and critic, leader of a group associated with his periodical *De Beweging*, 1905-19; Professor of Dutch Literature in the University of Leyden 1924-35.

and of their period. With not one word, however, does
Huizinga allude to these. Was he aware of what was in deadly
earnest being done and being prepared across the frontier?
One is almost inclined to doubt it when one sees how in his
letter to Benda of December 1933 he had noticed only the
folly of it all. Certainly, he realized the dangers of nationalism,
so he then wrote to the man who, in denouncing "*la trahison
des clercs*," had wanted to have all nations dissolved at one blow
into the universal state (where—significantly!—French was to
be used as the cultural language . . .). But, says Huizinga,
remember: "History, and the advantages of diversity!" I agree
whole-heartedly. However, he went on, he at other times so
inclined to take the gloomy view: "Have patience. The nationalism that you abhor is about to collapse in ridicule." And in
his conclusion once again: "The excesses of a demented
nationalism which the closing year has witnessed will conduct
it to absurdity and ridicule."

So he directs his indictment—as I already said—against our
own culture. It is from its decay that all our troubles result.
Culture, so he begins his argument, can exist only on condition
that there be a certain equilibrium between spiritual and
material values. This equilibrium is now disturbed. Culture
must be oriented ethically and metaphysically. "Thus, earlier
periods had as their generally accepted ideal: the honour of
God, however that might be interpreted, justice, virtue,
wisdom." For this has been substituted that which divides
rather than unites: "Well-being, power, safety . . . : all proceeding directly from the natural instinct, unrefined by the
spirit. The caveman already knew these ideals." The victories
of technique and of organization are celebrated. Huizinga is
ready to admit that there is something impressive in the
astonishing progress of the natural sciences, but the resulting
material progress can drag a civilization to its ruin. On the
basis of popular education, politics can by means of organization and propaganda work destruction. Is the effect of popular
education in itself so educative? does it not detract rather than
add to the people's wisdom? Popular thinking, so he believes,
is actually going through a crisis full of dangers of corruption.

Judgment has been weakened. The average member of the community has allowed the obtrusive culture apparatus and the cheap mass product to flatten and expropriate his notions, unfortified as they are by any more than superficial knowledge. The cinema Huizinga sees as playing a maleficent role in that process; and the radio no less. The critical turn of mind has declined. The cult of *life* has an anticultural tendency, for a culture of high quality must in a certain sense be oriented towards death. The state exacts adoration, to the detriment of all independence. Moral norms are consequently weakened, especially where actions by or on the authority of the state are involved. Where Nelson before Trafalgar appealed to "duty", men are now spurred to fanaticism with "heroism", and an ever more prevalent puerilism is put to use. The present-day theory of race proves, according to Huizinga, that men no longer listen to the veto of criticism. Cultural evidence of the decline is supplied by the loss of style and by the inroads of irrationalism.

"We witness the worst culmination of combined dangers that can threaten our culture. We have entered a state of affairs characterized by weakened resistance to infection and intoxication. The mind is being split. The means of exchange of thought, the word, is inevitably losing value as this development proceeds. It is distributed in ever more immoderate quantities ever more easily . . . Feelings of responsibility, seemingly strengthened by the slogan of heroism, have been torn from their base in the individual conscience and are being mobilized for the benefit of every collectivity that wishes to elevate its narrow view to be a canon of salvation and attempts to enforce its will . . ."

It is all very eloquent, and the admonitions deserve being taken to heart. But most of the charges put forward, and the worst of them, related in fact only to the countries where totalitarianism had triumphed. That cult of heroism, for example—Huizinga illustrates it with high-sounding placards he had seen in Italy. Did he expect that in Holland the N.S.B.[5] was going to win? When speaking of state absolutism and the

[5] N.S.B.: Nationaal-Socialistische Beweging (Movement) in Holland.

subjection of moral judgment to the interest of the state, he
quotes Carl Schmitt, one of the theoreticians of National-
Socialist public and international law, the inventor of the
friend-enemy formula. But he does not add the comment that
this was a concomitant of the infatuation then reigning in
Germany, and that not only he, Huizinga, but we, we Westerners, with the exception of some few unbalanced or
disgruntled individuals, still—heaven be praised—see things
in a different light. We heard him about the racial doctrine as
a proof of a decline of the critical faculty. Had *we* succumbed
to it? The moral sense in its entirety seems to him to have
been affected in the centre of its strength, and, after first
quoting some more German instances, he mentions as the
profoundest cause its relativation inherent in Marx's historical
materialism. Freud's influence he considers to be equally
pernicious. And as an illustration he then quotes from a
little textbook of morality with the aid of which the young
Soviet citizen is educated. The young Soviet citizen?! I am
not surprised, but did not Huizinga know that in our own
country the Socialist Party was just freeing itself from the
shackles of Marxism? Striking evidence, indeed, that our
society and culture still disposed of a good deal of resisting
power on their own account.

By lumping together the Western world, to which he himself
belonged with the whole of his being, and the countries that
had fallen under totalitarian regimes, Italy, Germany, Russia,
Huizinga committed a grave methodological error which
falsified his "diagnosis of the spiritual distemper of our time"
from the start.

The error was more than a fortuitous lapse. It was connected
with fundamental peculiarities of his attitude towards life and
the world. All through his *oeuvre* one can observe an unwillingness to bring into account, when dealing with the cultural
process, economic factors and also the purely political ones of
the state and of the struggle for power. Culture was to him
the service of what is nobler and more beautiful as it is carried
on by a small *élite*. In this way he saw the cultural process as
it were in isolation, obeying its own impulses, realizing its own

essence. I shall try to explain this attitude of mind later on. Here I observe only that it appears not only in his diagnosis but also in the treatment he recommended.[6]

For indeed—as I hinted before—he did point to a road of escape from the threat of ruin. He did so, one suspects, more from a sense of obligation not to give way to despair than from genuine conviction firmly rooted in his soul. It was a road, indeed, which to a sober eye like mine loses itself in metaphysical and illusionist mists. To him the only means of salvation was to reduce life to greater sobriety and simplicity, asceticism; men would of their free will have to renounce the superfluous and the meaningless with which life has come to be encumbered. For domestic relations within each separate country he sees a promise in the organic idea: a division springing naturally from pre-existing units. He dreams of a return (for that is what it would have to be) to "a noble relationship of service" so that the individual might, each "in his class", feel at home in the community and would there, "in his place", be happy in being "himself". In that way the foundations of culture would be stabilized. This is no more than dreaming, and also, the suggestion that Europe would come back to the Christian faith and at the same time learn to recognize the "rightness" of Islam and the "profundity" of the Orient (it is as if we were listening to Toynbee) does not impress one as more than a pious wish. But the high point of unrealism is reached in the solution he suggests for the international tensions which were soon to rend the world: "a far-reaching international benevolence." Indeed . . . "If only all men were wise"; if only the world were quite other than in fact it is . . .

[6] In his oration on the occasion of his transferring the rectorate of the University of Groningen, *In de laagvlakten der cultuur* (*In the Plains of Culture*), 1960, Professor P. J. Bouman, a sociologist, points to the exclusivist character of Huizinga's conception of culture in which only "the higher" is taken into account. Bouman then quotes some passages to show that Huizinga has occasionally "wavered as to whether he should not adopt a more comprehensive view", and adds: "Modern scholarly thinking is moving in the direction of a very wide, practically all-embracing, conception of culture."

But let us return for a moment to the diagnosis. In support of it, Huizinga constantly draws comparisons with the past. With an—one would almost say, wilfully—idealized past. Here his feeling out of tune with his own time led him to commit a second methodological error.

Or is it a fact that older periods present so luminous, for us so shaming, a contrast to the shortcomings of the present that we heard him enumerate? I could demonstrate, point by point, that while he paints the present in the darkest colours, where earlier times are concerned he contents himself with those convenient generalities under which imperfections, weaknesses, and abuses can remain withdrawn from our observation. When, for instance, he speaks of the honour of God, or of an orientation toward death, I feel driven to ask whether the average human being was ever touched so deeply by religion even when religion was far more indisputably powerful than it is now. We should in any case remember how little it was able to restrain the human vices of earlier generations. But Huizinga in his comparison never mentions this fact. When, to what according to him was so stabilizing and elevating a force in ancient times, a respect for "the honour of God," he adds the words *however that might be interpreted*, he glides indeed lightly over the religious differences which in the past used to give rise to ruinous divisions.

The evils happening around us today do not let themselves be relegated so unobtrusively to the background. Although—and I notice this in passing because it is so characteristic—Huizinga himself in "diagnosing the distemper of our times" does not devote one word to the evil of unemployment which had assumed such terrific proportions at that very moment.[7] His readers at any rate might easily allow themselves to be dazzled by the beautiful appearance of earlier stages of culture which he conjured up before them.

[7] Banning drew attention to this in the article in *Het Kouter* cited above.—It is true that Huizinga in his subtitle spoke of "the *spiritual* suffering" (suffering is a more literal translation than *distemper* used in the title of the book when it appeared in English in 1935), but did not unemployment have depressing and demoralizing effects in a spiritual sense?

Yet if he had searched the past for symptoms of folly and of spiritual or intellectual sloth as industriously as he did the present, how often should we have had reason to be surprised that Western civilization did not succumb long ago! For truly, there has never been a lack of iniquities and human deficiencies. History is largely made up of them. But—to use a word of Toynbee's for once—these shortcomings have always had the effect of challenges, and it is in struggling with them that the succeeding generations have confirmed our culture. Why should not the present generation do likewise? Verwey was right in pointing to Huizinga's lack of faith in the human mind as his fundamental error.

In the Shadows of Tomorrow was not Huizinga's last word on the subject. Again and again, in endless variations, he gave expression to the same ideas, with respect to both diagnosis and cure. Shortly before—I am confining myself for the moment to the thirties—he had already spoken in the same strain in a chapter "The Crisis of Culture" of his little book *Nederlands Geestesmerk (Characteristic of the Dutch Mind)*. Shortly after *The Shadows* he wrote a lecture *Der Mensch und die Kultur*, which was meant to be read at Vienna in 1938; in April 1940 he published, in the *Fortnightly Review*, an article "Conditions for the Recovery of Civilization." In between there had been a radio talk, "Neutrality and Freedom, Truth and Culture," broadcast in November 1939 (this was the only time that Huizinga let himself be heard through that pernicious instrument). In 1938 his great work *Homo Ludens* had been published, about which more in a moment. In 1941, that is to say during the occupation of Holland, he read a paper for the Academy at Amsterdam, entitled "On Change of Form in History." In it he contended that American history had become unpresentable to the imagination (incapable of being pictured) ever since the Civil War, because of, among other things, the dominance of the economic motive, and that the history of the rest of the world was moving in the same direction.[8] I

[8] The assertion is disproved—to mention one instance out of many—by the splendid work of A. M. Schlesinger Jr., *The Age of Roosevelt* (three volumes published 1957, '58, '60). The economic motive plays an

cannot see in these speculations anything but a crass manifestation of his aversion to the modern age. He compares this chaotic present, not with the equally chaotic reality of the past, but with the presentations of the latter as they have assumed form in the course of time and become current. Finally, he wrote during his exile in De Steeg, one more, fairly extensive, essay, *Geschonden wereld* (*Violated World*), which was not published until after his death and after the war.

It is worth noticing how he clung to his opinions even while events went on their ever more violent course. The paper *Der Mensch und die Kultur* could not be read in Vienna because unhappy Austria had fallen into the clutches of Hitler just before. Nevertheless, Huizinga would not hear of any "cultural schism", the term which seemed to many to sum up the situation, and he published his lecture unaltered, now that Austria had been enslaved, in Switzerland. "This pretended cultural schism is to a large extent no more than politically conditioned manufacture." *Politically conditioned?* That means apparently to him as much as to say: has nothing to do with culture. So here, too, he offers his specific: simplification of life, asceticism, and the rest. In the *Fortnightly* even, at a moment when his English readers were at war, he tells them imperturbably that "international good faith" is the solution and that it cannot exist without Christianity. (Because there had been no rivalries, no breaches of faith, and no wars in the Christian centuries? . . .) After the restoration of peace the world would be encumbered with generations spoilt by a lying propaganda. So, once more: sobriety, etcetera. In the radio talk of November 1939 he had indeed assured the Dutch listeners that neutrality was a beautiful thing. This was not for the first time: the same illusionist idealization of neutrality occurs in a newspaper article written in 1938 on the occasion of Queen Wilhelmina's celebrating the fortieth anniversity of her reign.

---

important role in this story, no doubt. But the author is constantly making us see the *men*, while the figure of F. D. Roosevelt dominates the scene. No question of "change of form".

I myself argued in December 1939, taking issue with the then Minister-President, De Geer, and the Leyden Professor of International Law, Telders, that our neutrality policy might be imposed upon us by circumstances, but that above all things we should not extol it as of positive moral value. "The great ideological contests in history," so I wrote, "have always realized themselves in wars as well. In this war, too, the ideological conflict does undeniably constitute the ultimate issue."

I quote this because it has to do directly with my subject. Huizinga was averse to this insistence that we should choose sides, or rather, that we had our appointed place on one side, even at that moment when there was no choice left for Europe than either to make an end of Hitler or to be ruled by Hitler. "Could one at this moment gauge the mood of the various peoples," so he ruminates in the radio talk of 19th November 1939, "the keynote would in every case be that of a profound sadness. Sadness at the downfall of so rich and beautiful a civilization as we have shared in." Huizinga did not usually admire contemporary civilization so whole-heartedly—we know it—but as regards that sadness: was it not rather that in Germany contempt for the noblest traditions of Western civilization was hammered into people's heads, while in England there reigned a determination to save them—for us too?

Meanwhile *Homo Ludens* had thrown a clear light on his mental attitude, although it is almost a *contradictio in terminis* to speak of a clear light in connection with the changing and gliding tints amid which he moved. A most remarkable book undoubtedly. A book such as can only spring from an unusual mind equipped with a tireless curiosity about the phenomena of life, with an immense erudition, with a vivid imagination. At first one lets oneself be carried along, thinking that the author is in his pricelessly entertaining fashion revealing a great truth, namely that culture, in the sense of giving shape to and ennobling community life, has in the early stages of human history owed a great deal to play, nay, that the coming into existence of culture cannot be imagined without play. In involuntary anticipation the reader expects—that is at least how I reacted—that he will be shown how, when culture gets more highly developed (Huizinga himself makes that distinction between primitive and highly developed states of civilization all the time), the element of play will come to fill a less essential role, and even that the growing predominance of seriousness is the sign *par excellence* of that higher development. Gradually, however, one becomes aware that this is not how Huizinga sees the problem. He is, on the contrary, out to efface the distinction between play and seriousness. It is as if he were being carried away by his subject and attached ever greater importance to the play element. Until, finally, towards the end of the book, one comes across what reads like a conclusion:

> We have by degrees come to the conviction that culture is rooted in noble play, and that in order to deploy her highest quality in style and dignity, she cannot do without that admixture of play.

Even the intercourse between nations and states should according to our philosopher of civilization be seen as a game. The entire argument seems to have served no other purpose— G. J. Renier made this remark in a review of the book—than to pronounce once more the verdict of guilty over present-day civilization, which has allowed play to deteriorate into puerilism. But has not the whole of the exposition been a play with an unreal and unworldly conception of culture?[9] A play outside what is earnest and crude in life, and intended by the author to screen himself off from these? Plato and Luther are called in to lend their authority to the representation of life itself as a game, a game of God. This does not do much to enlighten us mortals, who cannot unravel God's secret in history; but Huizinga seems to feel the more justified in eliminating from his consideration those unplayful political and economic factors.

[9] The book was dismissed as thoroughly unscientific, based on insufficient and sometimes erroneous definitions, by Prof. Buytendijk in *De Tijd*, 19 Dec. 1938.

Even in *Violated World*, written in 1943-4, we find him in
the same mood. Again we are treated to striking samples of
that comparison between *now* and *then* in which the shortcomings of the ancestors are concealed in order to bring out
our own more sharply.

Take for instance the degeneration of parliamentarism.
"Until some time after 1870," so he says, " the game of popular
representation, elections and parliamentary debate was in the
countries where it was practised played with a considerable
measure of seriousness, good manners, and dignity." (The
terminology *the game was played* is characteristic.) "Habits
like systematic obstruction, clapping desks, or throwing ink-
pots were not yet fashionable . . . The representatives of the
people belonged in large majority to a certain *élite*, whether
based on wealth, birth, or intellect. They brought good
manners along from their homes. They were wont to behave
decently and even formally. The press worked less quickly
than it does today and was less virulent . . . It is in a certain
sense the admixture of an element of aristocracy which makes
democracy possible, for without this it is always in danger of
being wrecked on the uncivilized behaviour of the masses."

If we were to detail the sins committed by the aristocracy,
for all its good manners, long before the period of parliamentarism, or if we displayed the worse than virulent pamphlets
of the seventeenth century, the *advocatus diaboli* would find
plenty of evidence that Western civilization has always been
in a bad way. For symptoms of decay he would not have to
wait until "the uncivilized masses" obtained their share of
power.

How exquisitely unfair can Huizinga be! For pages he
describes the "symptoms of degeneration, of decadence and
infatuation of political life" which manifested themselves
already in the last quarter of the nineteenth century. (This
dating of the phenomenon is in flagrant contradiction with
the utterance quoted above in which in November 1939 he
described the outbreak of war that had just occurred as
signifying "the downfall of that rich and beautiful civilization"
in which we had still had our share. But there is no end of the

contradictions in which he involves himself.) He goes on to point to the Dreyfus affair as an example. A miserable business indeed, but what has always struck me most in it was the courageous stand made by a small band of intellectuals, and I still regard their victory—in which no doubt less pleasant aspects obtruded themselves only too soon—as an encouraging sign of the vitality of our civilization.

But I have not yet mentioned the most astonishing—I ought to say really, the worst—token of Huizinga's blindness in *Violated World*. Writing in 1943-4 he does not show the slightest awareness of the powers of resistance manifested by Western civilization in the test of war. This racial doctrine, for instance, against which he had seemed to believe in 1935 the modern lack of critical capacity and the weakening of moral standards were making men defenceless—how splendid an answer had been given by the many (*many*, if it is remembered that human beings are apt, in any period of civilization, to shrink from danger), the many who had given shelter to persecuted Jews. Also, there were the working men of Amsterdam who in February 1941 went on strike in protest against the anti-Jewish campaign then just opening. This, one should think, ought to have shaken Huizinga in his view as if the working men, "less civilized" or "less educated," were no more than a deadweight on civilization, worse, a danger, now that they are trained by means of "organization" (that modern pest) to "soulless group egoism."

But in *Violated World* Huizinga is still of opinion that there will be a cultural emergency when the war is over; radio and advertising will have to be limited or abolished, and we shall have to give up much useless lumber, spiritual claptrap and material superfluities. Just as in 1935 (and we shall observe him in similar attitudes at much earlier dates) he rises for a moment in his conclusion—as it were in his own despite— "from the dark mood of seeing not much comfort in the near future of the desolate world that will lie before our eyes tomorrow." If only "the men of good will" scattered over the entire world can come into their own; and it will then be their task "to establish an international order of law among the

states" and realize, "on however modest a scale, a fair division
of goods and a social reconstruction of society." For a moment
then, with his last word, he suggests political and social reforms;
only, if one listens to him, they must come about all of a
sudden, without contest or fumbling, as a result of a change in
the mentality of mankind.

APPENDIX TO SECTION I

I have accounted it against Huizinga as a serious methodological error
that he is all the time trying to bring out the shortcomings of the present
by comparison with an idealized past. I have several times expressly
mentioned similar or worse shortcomings of the past, but I shall insert
here a number of further remarks or quotations to that effect—without,
of course, striving after completeness, and selected somewhat arbitrarily.
Yet they may serve to make the reader realize even more strongly how
false is that constantly indicated or suggested difference to the detriment
of our own age, and how easy it would be to draw up an "indictment"
against the past in the way Huizinga has drawn up his against the
present.

Huizinga seems to think that in the old days everyone was happy
within his class and the people wiser because there was no general
system of education so that the poor did not imagine they knew anything.
(Cf. above, p. 88) Hooft, the great seventeenth century historian of the
Revolt thought differently. We find him writing contemptuously about
wild rumours "which were eagerly received by the scum of the commonalty, who live from beggary or have it in prospect and are, like
the most part of the poor, of bad education, irregular habits and rude
and insolent speech; little notice is therefore taken of their babbling."

Huizinga asserts that earlier generations could realize a unity of
culture because they universally accepted as an ideal: "the honour of
God, . . . justice, virtue, wisdom", while in our time nothing is striven
after but "well-being, power, safety", which can only divide
(above, p. 191).

Was ambition for power a feeling unknown to William the Conqueror or to Louis XIV or to . . . but the names present themselves in
all periods. History is made up of wars, the slow building up of the
states that we know has never been able to dispense with war, and the
destructive as well as the constructive effect of these was largely determined, not by the mentality of men under the influence of a particular
"culture", but by the inadequacy or gradually increasing efficiency of
technique.

And must we regard the acquisitive instinct as an intrusion of recent
date? If we were to imagine it non-existent, what would remain of

history! It was an important factor in many of the wars. Let me only
recall the Anglo-Dutch wars of the seventeenth century and in the
eighteenth the Anglo-French contest in the colonial world (no more than
instances). Huizinga writes as if the acquisitive instinct were a specifically
democratic vice, which cannot go together with culture. I am rather
inclined to think that, with all its unpleasing possibilities, it has been an
indispensable factor in the development of civilization. It is at any rate
to be found present in the make-up of leading groups of former times
just as much as with the modern masses whose rise was watched by
Huizinga with so much uneasiness. I think—to take one instance out of
a thousand—of the novels of Jane Austen, who introduces us into a world
of perfect eighteenth-century *elegance* (her word), of refined and self-
assured culture. But how exactly was it known what dowry each girl
will command, and with how keen an attention was in the case of "a
good marriage" not only birth but fortune noted.

If one examines the relations between the propertied class and the
poor, the compelling force of the possessive instinct and of the privileged
position appears even more plainly. Marx's theories of the over-riding
importance of the class struggle, culture—including political opinions
and even religion—being no more than a superstructure of the social
establishment or even of the system of production, are presented in too
extreme and absolute a fashion. But they were not therefore mere
imaginings. The reader of Brugmans, *De arbeidende klasse in Nederland in
de 19th cenw* (1927). (*The Labouring Class in Nineteenth Century Holland*), or
of J. L. and Barbara Hammond, *The Skilled Labourer, The Village Labourer,
The Town Labourer*, (1917-20) will be struck not only by the horrible
conditions in which the proletariat then lived, but also by the indifference or complacency of the well-to-do and by the high-sounding
religious or philosophical or scientific-economic argumentations with
the aid of which they condoned that state of affairs or represented it as
justified by eternal laws. (See also Henri Guillemin, *Le coup du 2 décembre;*
1951.)

We can hardly picture to ourselves the misery and the coarse habits
of life prevailing outside the hermetically closed circle of the possessors
in the eighteenth and early nineteenth centuries. An English writer
wrote recently that the awful conditions are best symbolized by the large-
scale public executions and by the enslavement to gin. Indeed, Fielding,
who with his undaunted sense of reality understood where his age was
deficient in true humanity, said: "A number of cart loads of our fellow
creatures are carried to the gallows every six weeks." And as regards gin,
there was the notorious invitation chalked on the inn door: "Drunk for
a penny, dead drunk for twopence." In passing I mention the fourteen
or sixteen hours' working day of six-year-old children in badly ventilated
factories.

Matters like these ought also to be drawn into account when one
tries to estimate the value of a civilization. But Huizinga is mostly on the

look-out for the beauty of his élite's play. It is very rarely that he allows his attention to be withdrawn from that by phenomena of the kind I have alluded to. Nor does he seem to be aware of the material interests which determined that élite's attitude towards them.

But now what about the metaphysical orientation that he imagined governed life in earlier centuries? How is one to fit in the bestialized masses in that picture? In Holland the mob might attack Arminian gatherings and sack the houses of prominent Arminians, but this hardly proves them to have had any veritable conception of Calvinist doctrine. These men stood outside all higher culture, inclusive of religion in the true sense of the word. Nor should we nourish any illusions about the lower middle-class living above the level of that dehumanizing indigence. Indeed that the average individual in the past, two centuries, or five centuries, or ten centuries ago, lived for or by the faith, more than at present—I do not believe it. Where we get a glimpse of him—apart from the culture postulated or stylized by thinkers or poets or artists— he makes a very different impression.

I quote once more a passage by Fielding, who was, as we saw, far from being a cynic. In *Joseph Andrews*, of 1742, he shows us his truly good and truly believing parson Adams in conversation with an inn-keeper. Adams is startled to find that this man who, certainly, does not harbour evil intentions against his fellow creatures, is yet not too scrupulously truthful. He admonishes him to think of his immortal soul and that no momentary satisfaction counts beside what will be revealed hereafter. The host smiles, and says, lifting a glass to the hereafter: "He was for something present."—"Why", says Adams very gravely: "do not you believe in another world?"—To which the host answered: "Yes, he was no atheist."—"And you believe you have an immortal soul?" cries Adams.—He answered: "God forbid he should not."—"And heaven and hell?" says the parson.—The host bid him "not to profane; for these were things not to be mentioned or thought of but in church."—Adams asked him: "Why he went to church, if what he learned there had no influence on his conduct in life?"—"I go to church," said the host, "to say my prayers and behave godly."—"And doest not thou," cried Adams, "*believe* what thou hearest at church?"—"Most part of it, master," returned the host.—"And doest not thou then tremble," cries Adams, "at the thought of eternal punishment?"—"As for that, master," said he, "I never once thought about it; but what signifies talking about matters so far off? The mug is out; shall I draw another?"

Here you have the average man—I think of all centuries. Were Breero's peasants and millers different? Or the villagers and their priest in Reinaert?[10]

[10] G. A. Breero, early seventeenth century Dutch poet, famous especially on account of his comedies. *Van den Vos Reinaerde*, the thirteenth century epic, most famous work of Middle-Dutch literature, by a Flemish author.

I hinted in the text (see p. 195) that, while Huizinga wants us to see religion as guaranteeing in the old days unity of culture, on the contrary disagreements about doctrine created profound divisions. Let me illustrate this, too—although it seems hardly necessary—by just mentioning some concrete examples: the extermination of the Albigenses, the Inquisition, the suppression of Catholic worship in the Dutch Republic, the Synod of Dort and the expulsion of the Arminians from the Reformed Church and from political life, the expulsion of the Huguenots from France. Unity of culture?

I have no room even here to detail the sins of the aristocracy with their "good manners" vaunted by Huizinga (above, p. 200). A few remarks at random. Read, in La Bruyère's *Caractères*, the chapter "De la cour". It opens with the observation that "it is impossible to make a more honourable charge against a man than that he does not know the court: in that simple statement are comprised all virtues." And in confirmation read the letters of Mme de Sévigné, the *Mémoires* of Saint-Simon.

Huizinga regards aristocrats as indispensable in representative assemblies. In fact the observation of courteous forms of intercourse can hide a good deal of iniquity. Remember the corruption prevalent among English members of the House of Commons in the eighteenth century; the regents in the Dutch Republic had their own practices, which were not in fact more edifying. In public, too, good manners did not always prevail. Look up the sixth volume of Vaulabelle's *Histoire des deux restaurations* and enjoy his description of the way in which the priest Manuel, a member of the left, was prevented from speaking by ever fiercer interruptions from the right; how, amidst unceasing tumult, he was excluded by a majority vote and finally, while members shouted and reviled each other and almost came to blows, forcibly ejected by armed guards. This happened in 1823. Do not forget, moreover, Palmerston's famous speech on the Don Pacifico case in 1850. It is true that order was maintained in that debate, but Palmerston's triumph was none the less due to shameless jingo demagogy. The well-born gentlemen who at that time still filled the benches of the House of Commons displayed to the full that lack of rational powers of resistance which Huizinga would only expect from an assembly of uncivilized boors.

In his *Conditions for a Recovery of Civilization*, of April 1940, *Fortnightly Review*, Huizinga deplores "modern man's inaccessibility to persuasion." How is it possible to ascribe that peculiarity to modern man particularly! "Man is supposed to be a rational being", so he says: "If he really were, his mind when holding some opinion should yield to such arguments as proved its untenableness." Very true, and man does not too well conform to that condition. But did he in old times? Huizinga really believes so. He even adduces the period of the wars of religion as one in which the force of rational argument was demonstrated in individual conversions of Catholics to Protestantism and the other way round: which Fascist, which Communist, asks Huizinga, is amenable to conversion?! No doubt Fascism and Communism try systematically to cast out accessibility to persuasion—although, when one takes individual cases into account, apostasy is not unknown in their ranks. But are we moderns all of us either Fascists or Communists? And is not the leading fact about the wars of religion that men fought each other not with rational arguments but with arms?

One instance of a different order to remind ourselves that seventeenth-century man did not excel in accessibility to persuasion. A rational man was Balthazar Bekker, the Amsterdam minister of the Reformed Church, who contested the current belief in evil spirits or devils interfering in the lives of men. What was the reply of the South Holland Synod to his rational book of 1691-3, *De betoverde wereld* (The World Bewitched)?

"That all the classes (*meetings of a district's ministers*) and every member of the same detest the book unanimously and to the highest degree, as being full of offensive, pernicious and soul-destroying theses, going right against God's Holy Word and the formulas of unity signed by all ministers, brim-full of horrible mockeries and disgraceful distortions of the Holy Writ."

Bekker himself remarked, much to the point: "It is infinitely more easy to prohibit someone's books than to refute them."

Does it look as if the seventeenth century was so much more accessible to rational arguments than is the twentieth?

II

We have gradually seen taking shape—I have at any rate—the illusionist, unworldly attitude of mind that inspired Huizinga to his gloomy speculations. The two methodological errors that I pointed out: the overlooking of the fact that what governed the world crisis was the establishment, under very particular circumstances, of certain political regimes in certain countries; and the idealization of the past for the purpose of having an object of comparison against which the shortcomings of the present (largely imaginary ones) would come out as blackly as possible;—these two methodological errors do not so much explain that attitude as that they are produced by it. In order to make this clear we shall have to concern ourselves with Huizinga's earlier life and his earlier works. We shall have the help there of critiques levelled against him in his lifetime;

also of impressions published by friends after his death; and of some few studies devoted to him already. There is also his own autobiographical sketch written in the last year of his life: *Mijn weg tot de historie* (*My Road to History*).

In these retrospective reflections Huizinga mentions the first impressions that tempted him in the direction of history. They were evoked by a students' pageant in resplendent medieval costumes (he was still a child at the time) and by the collection of old coins he and his elder brother assembled. For a long time he felt no more than velleities. Toward the end of his university study, which was in the field of Dutch language and letters combined with history, he wanted to become a Sanskritist or expert in Indian religion. Gradually however, he felt his heart drawing him away from those distant and alien subjects back to the West, and particularly to the medieval West. The decisive moment—this, too, is characteristic—was his visit to an exhibition of old Netherlands art at Bruges in 1902. Life styled in art—that touched him in his inmost being. He approached history visually, with a hankering after beauty, beauty different from what his own time offered him.

In an article of 1954[11] J. Kamerbeek has strikingly expounded how the literary climate of his younger years had helped to shape Huizinga's mental outlook. *De Nieuwe Gids*, which at first had seemed to reveal to him life and the world, had almost immediately passed its zenith, but in Tak's *Kroniek*, which in the nineties had reacted against certain tendencies represented by the famous journal—against the unbridled individualism especially—, other of its tendencies were vivaciously continued. As a matter of fact Huizinga had begun by abandoning himself completely to the influence of Van Deyssel, the extreme exponent of the *Nieuwe Gids* spirit. That "boundless veneration of art and letters" that "high-literary cult of sentiment," that extolling of "the inner life" above

---

[11] "Huizinga en de beweging van Tachtig", that is to say, the literary movement of the 'eighties centring around *De Nieuwe Gids* (*The New Guide*), the monthly journal founded in 1885 by a group of talented young men in opposition to *De Gids*, by then grown staid and unadventurous. *Tijdschrift voor geschiedenis.*

everything, "above the sphere of study or profession,"—
later in 1942 (in his commemoration of his contemporary and
Utrecht colleague, G. W. Kernkamp) he might smile about it
as something "typically undergraduate," but it did fit in with
a trait of his being. And especially did he absorb the spirit of
opposition to the age, which moved the men of the 'nineties
as well as those of the 'eighties. This was in fact an international
phenomenon. Everywhere intellectuals, poets and artists
surrendered to feelings of estrangement from a society that
seemed practical and dull, governed by the machine, by the
arithmetic and the rationalism of science, by the bourgeois,
or by the masses. I mention Nietzsche. Kamerbeek quotes
Huysmans saying: "Depuis trois siècles le monde ne fait que
déchoir," and adds that the men of the nineties practically
adopted this view as the leading principle of their philosophy
of history. For while the immediate preceding revolutionary
period had been inimical to history, now, in the critical
examination of tradition, historical awareness woke up again.
I add: allied, in the case of some, and probably exactly those
with whom Huizinga felt akin, to a nostalgic mood, a neo-
romantic dreaming themselves away, into the Middle Ages,
or, as did Diepenbrock, the musician, into a past which he
saw surviving in the barbaric-hierarchic splendour of the
coronation festivities at Moscow in 1894.

In that same passage in the speech commemorating G. W.
Kernkamp, from which I quoted a moment ago, Huizinga
said, looking back, that this "extreme aesthetization of the
mind" emanating from *De Nieuwe Gids* "implied a certain
depreciation of scholarship" and that the intellectual life of
that young generation (to which he belonged himself) was,
"well considered, marked by a curious unsolved contradiction."
He adds that "this, nevertheless, did not in the least hinder an
intensive and personal devotion to study and scholarship." I
believe it. But it seems none the less certain that this
"aesthetization," this extolling of the inner life, to a large
extent determined the nature of what in his devoted labour
he sought for. Also, was it only his youth that was spent, as he
admits, in this "unsolved contradiction"? One of the principal

conclusions which my argument about his work will seek to establish is that the contradiction remained unsolved to the very end.

In his Groningen inaugural oration, in 1905, at the outset of his career as a historian, he speaks as if he had found the solution. *Het aesthetische bestanddeel in geschiedkundige voorstellingen* (*The Aesthetic Component in Historical Exposition*), that was the title. The aesthetic then, was no more than a component: examination and criticism, scholarly precision, are emphatically required: "the mining work of critical labour." But at the same time he draws a clear distinction, with grateful acknowledgment of Rickert and Windelband, between historical scholarship and natural science. A picture, an image, should be evoked, laws and generalizations are to be avoided, what matters is the particular; it is men, "who must not be reduced to a bundle of political or economic potentialities," but who are to be approached individually, with psychological imagination. We must remain aware "how vast and beautiful is the world around us."

Towards the end of his life the scales seem to have inclined even further toward the particular and the imagination. In his little autobiography, which was then written, he lays a more one-sided emphasis on the intuitive, I shall not say the *un-* or *anti-*, but the *extra-*scientific, character of his approach to history than he had done in 1905. The conception which was to dominate his most famous work, *Herfsttij der middeleeuwen* (*The Waning of the Middle Ages*, 1919), "not the announcement of what was to come, but the dying off of what had had its time," he now describes as having been a "sudden revelation," "a spark igniting the imagination." This sensitiveness to the fascination of decline in beauty was in itself part of the spiritual atmosphere in which breathed the *Nieuwe Gids*-men and their immediate successors. It is to be found with Kloos, it is to be found with Diepenbrock. In looking back, Huizinga says quite generally: history made an impact on his mind and soul "less as a solid, normal, scientific curiosity, than as an *hantise*, an obsession, a dream." His work never seemed to him to have "the character of a struggle"; the subjects "never faced him in the way of problems which he had to master."

There is no doubt that the sketch Huizinga here presents of his historical labours is heavily charged. The mental attitude that he professes is what distinguishes him most markedly among historians, but it did not govern him completely. He often acted in the other, in what he himself calls the "normal" way. *With* the intuition, *with* the seeking contact through the emotion roused by beauty, *with* the preference for objects of mood or quality not to be comprehended by reason, he did most certainly combine an organ not only for precision but for understanding in a sense different from what he had indicated in his Groningen oration. Years afterwards, in 1929, in a theoretical treatise "De taak der cultuurgeschiedenis" ("The Task of Cultural History") and in a brief essay "Een definitie der geschiedenis" ("A Definition of History"; I shall deal with both at greater length later on), he laid all emphasis, more than in 1905 and more especially than in 1943-4, on "accounting to oneself": a function in which reason must have the lead, and indeed an essential attribute of the scholarly cast of mind.

Much of Huizinga's best and most interesting work owes its existence to that desire for rational "accounting for". Yet it is often a little disturbing to notice that the two inclinations of the personality such as I have delineated them did not harmonize too well. Even when the rationalistic, the critical side, the side intrigued by the problem, takes charge, Huizinga remains, to use a phrase of Kamerbeek's "an irrationalist *mal repenti.*" In some of the writings, no doubt, the conversion appears to be complete and flawless. To mention one instance: in the masterly essay "Het probleem der Renaissance" of 1920.

Huizinga himself was of opinion, in the retrospective sketch of his life, that *The Waning of Middle Ages* was likely "always to be considered as the top of [his] production." And this is exactly the work in which this distinctive quality of the imagination commandingly and magically manifests itself. It appeared in 1919, but the conception, about which we heard him a moment ago, dated according to his recollection as far back as 1907. It thus became a vision deepened and enriched by many years of study during which he came to be on intimate terms with the phenomena that had fascinated him from the start through the subdued passion of his preference: the phenomena of the different ways of life of those generations, the phenomena of their psychology, of the unfamiliar forms in which these expressed themselves in the social as in the political sphere, all of it seen throughout in the tints of decline. But in this definition of what drew his interest, in which the social and the political factors never seem to have a significance of their own, at best serving as a framework, a limitation is indicated which struck his fellow historians at once.

It was particularly S. Muller Fzn who, with all admiration, gave voice to professional criticism. When at the end of his long article in *Onze Eeuw* (1920) he advised Huizinga to write a little "more simply", "as befits a calm historian", warning him "that literary laurels always have a suspicious colour for a writer of history," the philistinism is hard to bear. But the reservations he indicates from his historian's point of view are not therefore less wellfounded. He points to the uncertainty with which the author had treated the problem, mostly evading it in fact, of the relationship between the French-Burgundian culture of the court and the burgher civilization especially in the Dutch-speaking Netherlands. He criticizes the systematic neglect of economic and political factors. The violent party feuds of the *Hoeks* and *Kabeljauws*, by which especially the Northern Netherlands were torn in the fifteenth century, Huizinga tries to explain psychologically, as springing naturally from the quarrelsome temperament of that vehement medieval generation: he shrugs away the politico-economic conflict which was so obviously at the back of these troubles. He does not even seem to be interested in the great event of the establishment of the Burgundian state (or dynastic power), with the result that the Burgundian dukes, whom he pictures so vividly in their personal behaviour and peculiarities, do not in the end get their due.[12]

[12] Prof. Hugenholtz writes in his *Ridderkrijg en burgervrede*, 1959, that "modernity", "something new", was increasing in importance from the

How do we recognize here the Huizinga we saw emerge from his treatment of the crisis governing his own day in the 'thirties! The man who wanted us to look upon culture in isolation, as an exclusively spiritual process, flourishing or declining according to its own rhythm. The man who never faced the question as to which political and economic factors had raised National-Socialism to power, nor exactly where.

But in the same period of the long incubation of *The Waning of the Middle Ages* such profoundly differing work appeared over Huizinga's name as *Geschiedenis der Universiteit* (*History of the University of Groningen*, 1814-1914) in 1914, and *Mensch en Menigte in Amerika* (*Man and the Crowd in America*) in 1918. These publications afford indeed striking evidence of the variety of his powers as a writer of history and of the vastness of the field of his interest. The university history especially satisfied all that might be asked in the way of rational and scholarly method. And that subject, far from promising as it might seem at first sight, he managed to transform into a little masterpiece of cultural history. Simply by means of patient and loving attention, by means of a disinterested desire to understand these men—quite little men, often enough—within the framework of their time, that is in the wider framework of European intellectual life—and the author here gives evidence of unusual erudition—; but local circumstances too,

---

twelfth century on and was visible everywhere in the fifteenth. "Only, the group Huizinga had taken for his subject did not see it . . . What manifested itself as modernity was not to be found at the courts; the phenomena were in the first instance economic, bureaucratic, bourgeois. And since Huizinga did not deal with, and never meant to deal with, those aspects of life—and one cannot blame him for this, and those who did blame him were grievously wrong—, this modernity is hardly at all to be found in his book."

The way in which the problem is posed here does not quite satisfy me. One certainly cannot "blame" Huizinga for having wanted to deal with the court and knightly culture particularly. But that he neglected expressly to set out this limitation, that he did not draw the reader's attention to the contrast indicated by Hugenholtz (I am not suggesting that he should have given it elaborate treatment), does detract from the value as history of his magnificent book.

political and economic, are taken into account when necessary. The style, moreover, is as "simple" as Muller could wish, which does not prevent it from sparkling with life and wit.

But then *Man and the Crowd in America!* Side by side with the late Middle Ages in their romantic splendour and violent emotions, coloured by the sunset of a civilization that has come to seem to us so strange, and with the quiet, often somewhat provincial and self-satisfied sphere of academic Groningen during the last hundred years slowly changing over from eighteenth-century enlightenment to modern realism, he dared to cope with that youthful, seething society of America and its sharply differing forms and problems. What drove him to that study—and here the Huizinga of the 'thirties announces himself after all—was undoubtedly that he was already beginning to watch the development of Western civilization with misgivings, and in America he discerned some of its, to his thinking, most ominous tendencies in alarming force. The book has not for all that grown to be an indictment, as seventeen years later *In the Shadows of Tomorrow* was to be. It gives a richly varied picture, in which bright and hopeful phenomena have their place. Yet what will remain most vivid in the reader's mind is the spectre of "the mechanization of communal life" (so runs the title of one of the four chapters): man become the slave of the machine and of the organization. In one striking passage Huizinga admits that mechanization contains in itself a civilizing factor. Man must—"indispensable condition for becoming aware of his human value"—order the forces of society and of nature. But every improvement or refinement of the instrument "binds him anew to the blind power." And, one is inclined to ask, does the dialectical process then come to a stop? It seems clear at times that this is indeed what Huizinga means. "How," he says, "will the life of the spirit in this highly developed modern society escape the deterioration, the levelling and mechanizing, which are bound indissolubly to the commercializing of society?" As if the spirit did not dispose of independent power to react! As if culture did not, among other things, mean resistance against what threatens the spirit!

It should be remembered that Huizinga studied America at a somewhat unfortunate moment in the country's development[13]; and when a few years later he was able to see it with his own eyes, it was perhaps even worse off. In the notes he made of that experience, the despondent tone sounds more insistently. Since then, however, has not that reaction in which he found it so difficult to believe manifested itself overwhelmingly?

Meanwhile, *Man and the Crowd*, for all that the author's idiosyncrasy misdrew in it, is a wonderfully able achievement. The knowledge and the acumen, the subtlety of the observation and the bold vision with which connections are suggested between various aspects of American life cannot be observed without the most vivid admiration. But how puzzling seems that pessimism, coming from this despiser of the material, from this devoted servant of the spirit.

I said already that this pessimism had not only America for its object. Huizinga brought it with him from the contemplation of his own country, of his own Europe. "In the century in which we live," so he wrote, "mankind seems to become the helpless slave of its own perfect means of material and social technique." In the ensuing years his mood did not lighten. In 1921 Spengler's *Untergang des Abendlandes* made its appearance, and in the entire Western world, shocked by the first world war, disillusioned by Versailles, helplessly stumbling in economic distress, that book made an enormous impression. It did so on Huizinga. "Everyone who sees the mechanization of the life of the spirit and of the community as the phenomenon spelling ruin to our present world," so he wrote, "will find much to enlighten him." But he also finds much in it to revolt him. *The system*, upon which as upon the bed of Procrustes Spengler fits his historical presentations, was unacceptable to the historian in Huizinga. "Whoever still feels the need to know about the things of the past what we can truly know of them, whoever loved things in their own

[13] It should also be noted that the historians Turner and Beard, to whom Huizinga liked to listen, at that time could still pass for authoritative. Their views have since been seriously devalued.

singularity even when it is inexplicable and irreducible, will not surrender to the magician." Moreover Huizinga's humanity was repelled by Spengler, by the man's philosophy of power, by his Germanic racialism. And so he concludes his article by stating that "Spengler's book has in a homoeopathical way had a curative effect on me, freeing me in some little measure from my own dark despair about the future of our civilization: his hopeless certainty made me feel that I still had hope and did not *know.*"

It still sounds passably dejected. And his near-despair made him turn to and cling to, most unexpectedly, the comfort that Wells's *Outline of History* might furnish. He reviewed that book in the same article, "Twee worstelaars met de Engel" ("Two Strugglers with the Angel"). He could not but find Wells's *system* as unacceptable as Spengler's. Wells, the illusionistic humanist and rationalist, had but "small sense" of "art, cult, and rite" and so belonged to a species of men for which Huizinga really had little use. But after all the criticism to which he subjected the book, Wells charmed him by "his great mildness, his boundless confidence, his firm hope." To me the long passage which he quotes in support, Wells's fervent announcement of a new world after the deplorable failure of the old, sounds equally unhistorical with the rest. But in fact the whole of that famous piece of Huizinga's—and indeed it is written with irresistible fervour and vividness—proves only that he found himself in a labile state of mind.

We see him seek a way out of "despair." For one moment, in that same year, he imagines he has found a guide in Seillière, the French philosopher. Seillière looked for the cause of the malady of culture in the undue strain put upon two of the three life forces that he distinguished and for which he had his own names: *imperialism,* the desire of each human being and of each group for self-realization; *mysticism,* the sense of living and working by the grace of a higher, a supra-rational, supra-human principle. The third force, which ought to keep the others in control, is *reason,* a term which Seillière does not interpret rationalistically, but by which he means the capacity of observing limitations with the aid of the experience and wisdom of our ancestors. The weakening of the last-named force, and the over-straining of the first two, coming to light in the forms of nationalism, socialism, and aestheticism, all have, according to Seillière, their origin in romanticism.

He gave expression to a wide-spread mood: it is well to recall the fact, because it helps to place Huizinga. In France there was not only Maurras, the preacher of what he himself called "classicism," although in his hands it degenerated into a nationalism that could not be more "over-strained." But there was also his disciple, who soon parted ways with him, Pierre Lasserre, whose *Le romantisme français* (1907) for all its exaggerations amounts to an impressive indictment. In America there appeared in 1919 Irving Babbitt's *Rousseau and Romanticism*, animated by a closely related spirit. For Seillière also, Rousseau was the fatal figure *par excellence.* He opposes to the fashionable aberration an attitude of stoicism and preaches self-control on the basis of a rational traditionalism. He closes on a note of pragmatic optimism—indispensable if one is to persist in striving after improvement.

Huizinga, in the article he devoted to him, follows his exposition on the whole with agreement; he even sees in the philosopher's emergence a proof that the role of the French people as guide and pioneer is not yet played out. But the conclusion leaves him doubtful.

"May we hope it? Is not man's thinking power too badly paralyzed under the double influence of the supremacy of sentiment on one side and of the mechanization of culture on the other? . . . Society overwhelms us with impressions, cheap and mass-produced. The influence of strong and pure minds has lost in effectiveness because blind and mechanical organizations feed the masses gratis with surrogates and poison. The spirit has been plebeianized and our poor brain can no longer cope with the world." (I remark in passing that he would not, *could* not, surpass this in the 'thirties; the word *gratis* is revealing!) "The only way out seems to be through a strong resorption of culture: limitation, simplification, our entire world of notions more severely shaped. Has Western humanity sufficient control over its mind to see to, in the way

Seillière proposes, the purification of its civilization itself?
Or will it have to be done by a succession of catastrophes?
. . .

It is the programme of 1935 *in optima forma*. But Huizinga
still has something to add: "At all events, let us strive. This is
the lesson taught us by Seillière's earnest works." However,
how does one strive for the realization of so completely unreal
a programme? One can go on uttering laments and admonitions, but if one takes one's stand on these negative principles,
so detached from the time, it is impossible to interfere to any
purpose in developments.

Huizinga did not, during the remainder of his life, mention
Seillière more than once or twice in passing. Yet I believe that
the Frenchman had made a permanent impression on his
thinking. More sharply than before he seems from now on
aware of the dangers of romanticism. With respect to nationalism and socialism he was sufficiently on his guard already,
but in overstrained aestheticism too he now saw an enemy.
Applying to history the powers of reason, with aristocratic
and stoic restraint, that, he feels, is the way for him to *strive*
and combat the diseases of culture.

III

These were the ideas he elaborated in some treatises on the
theory of history collected in a volume under the title of
*Cultuurhistorische verkenningen (Explorations in Cultural
History)* in 1929. These essays are not among his best work,
for all the subtle and arresting remarks one comes across in
them. But in connection with my subject they are of importance
—also on account of the sharp attacks they elicited from three
younger men.

Huizinga begins by defining the history of civilization as an
attempt to distinguish forms of life which take shape under the
hands of researchers and thinkers. The concept of *development*,
borrowed from biology, he rejects. Elsewhere, but not unconnected with this, he ranges anthropomorphism, the staging of
historical abstractions under the guise of human beings, among

the greatest dangers that threaten true historical understanding.

Meanwhile he has entered upon a long digression about another danger, namely that "history for a larger public might fall into the hands of an aestheticism-cum-sentimentalism proceeding from literary aspirations, working with literary methods and directed toward literary effects." This is the introduction to an—I should almost say, tempestuous—outburst against the genre of the *vie romancée*, which had then suddenly come into fashion. A concession, so he thinks, to the feeble romanticism of our levelled-down society, to the plebeian love for sentimentality and "passionism," to the diminished capacity for concentration of the reader, enslaved to time-wasting diversions—a disloyal competition with the professional historians.

At the same time he recognizes as an element, and "a very important one," of the process of "becoming aware historically" the emotion, related to art or religion, which he dubs "the sensation"—a term which Van Deyssel had introduced for his own purposes and which it is indeed curious to see cropping up here; the more so since the argument as a whole means a definite break with Van Deyssel's influence. For, note well: "The form in which modern civilization can know the past is that of critical scholarship." True history must be stoic, must not indulge in pity with all the world's sorrows, must observe a certain sceptical reserve.

When Huizinga next comes to giving practical advice, there are also some points that arrest our attention: "For the time being the history of civilization finds enough to do in determining the particular forms of historic life. Her task it is to draw up a special morphology before she should venture upon the general." For periodization she had better use a colourless, merely chronological terminology, instead of, for instance, the Renaissance, the period of the Baroque, and the like. "There is plenty of time before we should come to describe entire civilizations round one central notion. Let us for the time being be above all pluralistic."

In another treatise, a paper read before the Amsterdam Academy in this same year 1929 Huizinga tried to define the conception of history. Every civilization, so he said, produces its own form of history and must do so. It is work demanding "inexorable seriousness," for, as he had already asserted in the other piece, the element of play, so prominent in literature, is lacking *in toto* in history-writing. A statement that surprises coming from the future author of *Homo Ludens*. And this is how he formulated his "concise definition":

"History is the spiritual form in which a civilization accounts for her past." One advantage of this definition that he stresses is: "It provides a way out of the dilemma of either the more intellectual or the more visual character of our historical knowledge."

It is the dilemma that I observed already never ceased worrying Huizinga, and while he asserts that he here leaves it intact, I feel rather that with the term "accounting to oneself," and indeed with the distribution of his accents in the whole of the preceding argumentation, he comes down unmistakably on the side of the "intellectual". The factor of "the sensation", which as we saw he did not pass by in silence, to which on the contrary he still seemed to attach great importance, does not find a place in his definition. He now speaks of "a way out". I should not want him to have made a *choice*, but a *connection* was indeed required. Evidently he had not yet *solved* the problem, as can indeed be seen throughout.

Now this was the central point against which the three to whom I alluded already directed their criticism, Ter Braak, Van Eyck, Romein—no contemptible adversaries.[14]

[14] Menno ter Braak, 1902-1940 (committed suicide on the day of the capitulation), critic, took a leading part in the definitive reaction against *Nieuwe Gids* æstheticism. (*Verzameld Werk* published after the war.) His friend and ally Du Perron, 1899-1940, an even more impetuous fighter than he, and author of at least one outstanding novel, died of a heart attack on the same tragic day. My essay on the two, mentioned below, is reprinted in my volume *Reacties* (1952).—P. N. van Eyck, 1887-1954, poet and critic, succeeded Verwey as Leyden Professor of Dutch Literature in 1935.—Jan Romein, 1893-1962, Professor of History at the University of Amsterdam 1939-62. About him see the little essay below, pp. 241-248.

Ter Braak, to take him first, in an essay "Huizinga vóór de afgrond" ("H. before the Abyss"), mocks at the older man's caution, his desire to ensure his safety. This "pluralism" for instance, and then "for the time being": for the time being no philosophy of life! He discerns in his exposition a return to the old, the antiquated, objectivist historiography against which the despised literary genre, the *vie romancée*, meant a welcome reaction.

I am still of the opinion which I expressed in an essay devoted to Ter Braak and Du Perron in 1951, not only that Ter Braak valued the significance of that genre too positively, but that he followed all too easy a line in arguing as if, now that we are agreed on recognizing a subjective element in all history-writing, the brakes may be loosened altogether and we can be subjective to our heart's content: all that we can provide is after all no more than myths . . . Dangerous, too, is that state of mind, to be explained, partly at least, as proceeding from the resentful exaggeration of a man who had himself resigned from Clio's service. Not without some amusement I notice now that at one moment he interrupts his somewhat frivolous philosophizing to assure us "that the historian bears a responsibility toward his facts," thus making a concession of the kind he takes in such bad part from Huizinga, when he sees him forever retreating from definite positions just taken up.

That Huizinga does not choose between the two principles, Ter Braak regards as a shortcoming. I have already said that I differ here and I agree with Huizinga even when, in his (belated and on the whole not very strong) answer to the three (for all three make the same point here), he says that "the entire thinking process of the historian takes its course through a series of antinomies," and among these that of "the subjective and the objective."

And yet I am struck now to observe how often Ter Braak hits the mark in indicating Huizinga's hesitations, evasions, contradictions. Even before I re-read his essay, I had come to be more keenly aware of these than I was when writing in 1951. Huizinga's angry rejection of the "disloyal competition" of literary history-writing seems to me now to be undeniably lacking in measure. Indeed, here too I am driven to suggest the explanation "resentful"; it is the anger of the man who shrinks from his own inclination in that direction and who moreover too often lost his balance under the influence of the fear and hostility with which he regarded his age.

If Ter Braak did not go beyond making light-hearted play (so at least it seemed on the surface) with Huizinga's confusions and uncertainties, Van Eyck went all out for him in grim earnest and with murderous sarcasm. His article makes heavy reading (as is usual with him), but if one manages to work through the awkward constructions and the long sentences, it turns out to be an important contribution.

Naturally, for him too the first butt is the assigning of a lower place to the imagination and the extolling of critical scholarship, though better than Ter Braak he makes it clear that he does not want to deny the latter its due. We saw that Huizinga in the 1929 volume represents history as free from all element of play, while literature is permeated with it. But much worse was an utterance in another essay, which Van Eyck quotes: "A literature must never take herself wholly seriously. For when she imagines herself to be mounting the heights of supreme Wisdom and leaves the bounds of the playground, she will forsake her glory." Bitter was the indignation of the serious-minded poet. The sallies against the *vies romancées* he could (unlike Ter Braak) dismiss with a shrug: what is at issue here is mostly "bad history and bad literature." But Huizinga had asserted that even "literature in general" is inclined today to magnify the element of passion and that the critics will not on any account have the standards of morality praised. And now Van Eyck retorts, briefly and cuttingly: "The judgment of a layman, even where the *Nieuwe Gids* period is concerned." And on the passage quoted first: "He forgets the royal works of the creative spirit"—a pronouncement with which he also meant to efface the sharp line of cleavage drawn by Huizinga between literature and historiography.

In his reply to the three critics—not until 1935—Huizinga admits that Van Eyck had "drawn his attention to a *lapsus memoriae*." When he, Huizinga, in distinguishing between history and literature, had asserted that the first-named "is entirely lacking in the element of play [he] was for a moment forgetting [his] own view, expressed since," and so he now corrects: "is *almost* entirely lacking in." *Expressed since* refers to his rectoral oration of 1933, which was a kind of rehearsal, in brief, of the ideas to be published in maturer form in *Homo Ludens* a few years later. The problem at issue here is only adumbrated in that oration and what strikes me most in it is the account, towards the end, of a conversation with a colleague on the scientific side. When this man said: "I believe that for you even science and scholarship are a noble game," "I was startled," confesses Huizinga, "I answered with a half-hearted *yes*, but within me I heard the cry of *no!*" On second thoughts, in the oration, he saves himself from his embarrassment by quoting that word of Luther's, of which I observed before that it does not really make us any wiser. *His own view*, he said to Van Eyck. Did he have anything so positive? He rather seems to be groping round in uncertainty.

Another point is that of anthropomorphism. We know how decisively Huizinga rejected that device. But, observes Van Eyck, in the very definition he submitted to the Academy he sins against his own precept. Does he not describe history as "a spiritual form in which *a culture* accounts to itself for its past"? Does he not add: "We cannot abandon the demand of scholarship without forsaking *the conscience of our culture*." Whereupon Van Eyck: "One can only forsake one's own conscience. Not our culture, but our historians have a conscience that can be forsaken." And he argues that in Huizinga's phrasing there is implied the demand that the modern historian should subordinate his labours to his conception of modern culture. And he adds: "The fact is that Huizinga assumes the existence of *one* contemporary culture and not only considers it possible to know and define the nature of that culture, but is positively convinced that he has discovered that definition, so that he can summon all present-day cultural phenomena before his, or our civilization's, judgment seat."

A question of fundamental importance arises here, and I shall now on my own account expressly pose it.

Huizinga is inclined—even though he speaks quite differently on many occasions—to present contemporary culture or the culture of an earlier age as a unit by itself, an inclination of which the anthropomorphic way of expression is unconscious evidence. Listen to the following. Huizinga regards the sham history which is so successful nowadays as a danger, because historical science must not be borne by a band of esoteric scholars alone: "It must rest on the foundation of a historic culture, which is the property of all civilized men." My first query here would be: "Only of all *civilized* men?" Van Eyck asks (and this too is an obvious query): "Of *all* civilized men? Can there not be two varieties of culture simultaneously?" It is true that Huizinga himself in another passage accepts the possibility of differentiation: "according to different nations," and within each of those again "according to groups, classes, parties"; whereupon, so he thinks, "there follows automatically the corresponding differentiation in the form of history-writing." But in this way the concept of culture assumes an even more tyrannical character. The unending variety, the contest between numerous views, of which our culture is the resultant shaped in our comprehension—Van Eyck's mentioning "two varieties" is far from doing justice to reality as I see it—, are obscured and the historian's personal liberty of judgment gets impeded.

But into what a confusion does Huizinga land himself—Van Eyck points it out mercilessly—when he attempts to determine the task of historical scholarship within contemporary civilization! First he lays it down that historical scholarship shall be stoic. Then, that our civilization, of which he also had said that it tolerates no other form of knowledge with respect to the past than that of critical scholarship, "shall be democratic, or it shall not be." Next, that "the people is always anti-stoic." Finally, "history may become democratic, it must remain stoic." And he adds: "It is questionable whether the construction of present-day cultural life leaves any room for a historical science which as donor of culture will dominate over the literary apperception of the past."

Indeed, there remains little else than such a dejected and doubting conclusion once one has got stuck in such incompatible convictions so positively expressed. Huizinga, it is true, says bravely that "historical science must venture to enter into competition with all that talent, fashion, and intellectual sloth throw into the scale of literature." Van Eyck is not impressed. He characterizes Huizinga's attitude with the word passivity. And how *could* Huizinga "venture" when he has weakened his position by mistaking a possible ally— true literature—as an enemy! "Impotent dreaming, which will not turn the tide, that is all he does, instead of co-operating, with clear perception, in throwing up a dyke." Thus Van Eyck.

Romein wrote after Ter Braak and Van Eyck. He also speaks of confusions and contradictions, of rashness and retreat, a retreat "into a *clair-obscur,* leaving behind all sharp-lined, exact opinions." Romein employs for a large part the same arguments as the two other critics had done, sometimes strengthening them; but at the same time he introduces a new point of view.

It is, naturally, the point of view of historical materialism. Bartstra, in an article of 1938, reviewed more especially the relations between Huizinga and Romein. He contrasts very tellingly: the indeterminism of the one, aiming at nothing but the enrichment-through-observation of the history-writer's personality, conquering the eternal uncertainty and the doubts accompanying his contact with the past through ethical speculations, which remind Bartstra of nothing so much as of the well-meaning sermons of modernist Protestant preachers; and the determinism of the other, who possesses a perfect certainty and sees in history the means for serving the realization of the final purpose known to him; "dangerous onesidedness," as Bartstra puts it, who remarks also that this attitude of mind little fitted Romein for approaching Huizinga's characteristic qualities with patience and comprehension.[15]

My attitude toward the Romein-Huizinga "dispute" is not fundamentally different from Bartstra's, but, since I am now dealing especially with Huizinga and his indictment of his age, I shall confine myself largely to what I have found to be illuminating in Romein's criticism. Not that I shall not repeatedly have to make reservations on particular points.

When for instance Romein misses in Huizinga's definition of history the relevance to the present which is indispensable for all history-writing (he naturally quotes Croce in this connection), then, although I am far from underestimating the significance of history for our own life, I cannot help querying the word *all*. When he is pleased with Huizinga's recognition of the inevitability of subjectivity and especially with his connecting particular subjectivities with groups (sectional cultures), I on the contrary, as I explained above, not only feel that Huizinga's argument in this passage involves questionable consequences, but must especially shake my head, or smile, when Romein among those group-subjectivities awards a decided preference to the socialist, "or more exactly,

---

[15] "Indeterminism" undoubtedly fits in with the whole of Huizinga's vision upon history. Nevertheless, in 1924, in an address to American students at Leyden, discussing one of my earliest expositions of the view that the sixteenth-century split of the Netherlands had been caused, not by innate differences between the populations, but by the fortuitous events of foreign intervention and military operations, he had spoken as follows: "I for myself am inclined to side with those who regard historical development with the eyes of determinism, rather searching the past to find why things have come about as they did than to prove— what theoretically always can be proved—that they might have fallen out otherwise too."

I took position at once against this statement of principle in an article in *De Gids*, 1926; reprinted 1930, 1946, 1960. In 1938, in a review of his *Science of History*, I recalled his statement and placed over against it what he wrote now: "The historian must stick to an indeterministic point of view with regard to his subject . . . Only by retaining an open mind for the boundlessness of possibilities can he do justice to the fulness of life." Personally, of course, I found, and find, the latter statement wholly satisfying.

E.H.   H

Marxist," brand; indeed, he goes further and asserts that the inevitable subjectivity can best be overcome, even though always only partially, with the aid of the historical-materialist method, which directs the attention especially on "the zones where determination applies." When Romein, continuing, describes Huizinga's opting for "colourless names for periods" as "a mere smoke-screen" to hide the colourlessness of his own theoretical position, I can no more willingly follow him. No doubt the description of an *Idealtypus* of culture (Max Weber's term, with which Romein here operates) can yield splendid results: we need remember only Burckhardt's *Kultur der Renaissance in Italien* and Huizinga's own *Waning of the Middle Ages*. But to lament "the pulverization of the image," as Romein was to do some ten years later in his inaugural oration, has always seemed to me senseless. Romein reproaches Huizinga for having in his article (of 1920) "The Problem of the Renaissance" merely demolished Burckhardt's vision without, not even later, erecting an image of his own devising in its place. "The counterpart of *The Autumn of the Middle Ages* [this is the literal translation of the title known in English as *The Waning of the Middle Ages*], *The Spring of the Modern Age*, has remained stuck in *The Problem*." Let me say only that in my opinion that article "The Problem of the Renaissance" is a splendid piece of work, which gives profound intellectual satisfaction, "the liberating word" as Enno van Gelder has said of it, a triumph of critical scholarship. It shows with what mastery Huizinga, if he was so minded, could practise the craft, which, truly, we must not forsake, neither for the literary or Nietzschean certainty of Ter Braak nor for the historical-materialist certainty of Romein.[16]

[16] H. Schulte Nordholt in his doctoral thesis (*promotor* Prof. Romein) *Het beeld der Renaissance* (1948) devotes a note of over three pages to Huizinga's article. He deplores the "pulverization" (Romein's term), but the weakness of his position comes out when he writes: "If a writer does not believe in the possibility of a rebirth, that is to say, of a change involving the complex in its totality, happening *per saltum* and being *final*, then he will see every image falling to pieces in his wavering hands. And he will not only fail to see God's Kingdom, but not a

But I can go along with Romein in the criticism he levels at Huizinga's precept to confine the task of cultural history to "specific morphology"—"for the time being" at that, an additional clause with which (to make in passing a remark of my own) he seems to be adducing that ostensibly humble pretext of *Vorarbeit*, which in an earlier paragraph he had denounced. He now suggests a number of subjects: the Garden, the Road, the Market and the Inn; the Horse, the Hound and the Falcon; the Hat and the Book—all these in their cultural functions. There is here plainly something of that abdication which Ter Braak and Van Eyck too had noticed.

When, however, Romein attempts to explain this passage by Huizinga's mental attitude, we notice an accent differing from that laid by the two literary men. By proposing these "harmless subjects," he says, Huizinga degrades history to the level of a game—he who had just declared so proudly that it, in contradistinction to literature, is lacking in the element of play, that it must be "inexorably serious". A game? Instead of a struggle. For, says Romein, "great historiography is a fighting weapon; or at least a fighting testimony." Huizinga "has succumbed to his Erasmian need of a safe neutrality." His subjects are "deliberately turned away from the aspirations of our time and confined to the quiet of his study, where the plebeian tumult of the street does not penetrate, and the antistoic struggle for a crust of bread is not perceived." And Romein quotes Huizinga's dictum "that history must not indulge in pity for all the world's sorrows." Pity? asks Romein; apparently it does not occur to Huizinga that history might engage in a struggle.

Let me here insert the remark that, while fully admitting the justification of the factor of struggle in history-writing, I

---

single kingdom will he see, not that of the Renaissance either. Iridescent fragments, glittering splinters, that is all that will remain." The "image" of the Renaissance is here postulated by a faith. Huizinga's criticism levelled against it *must* be rejected, because otherwise that faith—the faith in sudden and final turns in history—might be affected. But why should we allow that faith to be forced upon us?

should not, as Romein does, make it a condition of great history. His introduction into the debate of the social motive, however, I think is completely warranted. I only wonder whether it is sufficient to speak of Huizinga's "need of a safe neutrality." We heard him call upon the historian, in 1905, to remain aware "how vast and beautiful is the world around us." A few years after *Explorations in Cultural History* he wrote, in his *Wetenschap der geschiedenis* (*Science of History*, 1934-5), that "to let oneself be engrossed in history is a form of enjoyment of the world"; he wants to "lose himself in the contemplation" of the past. Even though, deeply shocked by the spectacle offered by "the world around" him, he had as early as 1921 abjured aestheticism; even though, calling in the aid of all forces of rational control, *stoicism* had since become his favourite word; in his heart he still wanted that history should reveal to him, *truth* no doubt, but also *beauty*. His reactions were those of the disappointed aesthete.

True, it seems undeniable that the aesthetic satisfaction, and no less the aesthetic repulsion, were largely socially determined. Even in order to explain the confusions in Huizinga's philippic against the aestheticizing sentimentalism of a certain kind of literary historiography, Romein emphasizes the social aspect. According to him Huizinga came to find himself in the wrong camp "out of dread of democracy". Huizinga could not recognize in "the people" any potency for culture; he quotes the conclusion of Rostovtzeff's *Social and Economic History of the Roman Empire*: "Is it possible to extend a higher civilization to the lower classes without debasing its standard and diluting its quality to the vanishing point? Is not every civilization bound to decay as soon as it begins to penetrate the masses?"[17] A question that may well oppress us, according to Huizinga, and indeed it reverberated gloomily within him. "Our culture," says Romein, "about which

[17] Romein reproaches Huizinga for having ignored another statement made by Rostovtzeff immediately before: "Our civilization will not last unless it be a civilization, not of one class, but of the masses." This does indeed throw a different light on the passage quoted by Huizinga, who did not, however, take up this point in his reply of 1935.

Huizinga is talking all the time, *naturally* is in course of disappearing, but the thought can oppress only a man who does not or does not want to perceive the new culture behind it (which is the old one at the same time)."

Again I can go in the direction here pointed by Romein, although I do not like this terminology of "the old" and "the new" culture: I find too much in it of Huizinga's own, so to speak, absolutizing conception of culture, even though Romein by that somewhat confusing clause about it being "the old one at the same time" tries to meet the objection. I should rather say that the composite of forces and tendencies which in our observation or our conception or our imagination appears as an entity that we call culture, is from its very nature subject to constant alteration. The component factors change places in their mutual relationship, each grows either stronger or weaker, or varies its direction. We need not for that reason doubt the continuity of the process, and the awareness of this which history can teach us is in itself a quality of culture and an invigorating one. But Huizinga felt oppressed by the changes he noticed, part of a natural development though they were. His heart was wedded to a state of affairs which he, wrongly, identified with "our" culture; a state of affairs that he wanted to see stablilized, but that was in fact "in process of disappearing"—which did not at all mean that culture was disappearing. Above all he detested the larger share taken by the masses and all the phenomena inevitably accompanying that development.

Here then we have, in my opinion as well as in Romein's, a decisive point for the explanation of Huizinga's mentality. This interpretation is confirmed by numerous utterances, not in the later writings only, which I have already quoted. Ter Braak and Van Eyck certainly gave evidence, in their reactions to *Explorations in Cultural History*, of having noticed this factor, but they laid the emphasis elsewhere nevertheless.

They saw the celebrated author of *The Waning of the Middle Ages* shrink back from his own success. It was the men of letters who had applauded him, the professional historians had maintained reserve. With them now, with critics of the kind of S. Muller Fzn, he wanted to rehabilitate himself. In his reply of a few years later, in which he passed by many of the objections advanced, Huizinga scouted this interpretation decisively. "I have never bothered about suspicions of unscholarliness. I work and write as it is given me." This is a protestation in which I believe unconditionally. His work, his convictions, his outlook upon life, were too closely tied up with his deepest nature for him to have wanted to adapt them to the pleasure of his critics, or of his professional colleagues however highly esteemed. The unmistakable change, and the contradictions, must have welled up from a much deeper source.

The stoical and rational, anti-romantic doctrine of Seillière, whence he sought support from 1921 on, agreed with part of Huizinga's being, but there were, and there remained, other needs urging his soul.

Romein, as we saw, in speaking of Huizinga's need for safety, slipped in the qualification "Erasmian." I see another problem here. Not long after Huizinga's death, in 1946, Romein wrote that in his book on Erasmus (1934), Huizinga had in fact painted himself: "wavering between the opposing sides, the non-fighter."[18] But with how little sympathy did Huizinga approach Erasmus, and on this very ground! He actually reproaches him, as did Dürer, for not having chosen for Luther. It is not because wavering between the parties or keeping apart from the struggle appeal to me that I have never found this particular book of Huizinga's satisfactory. I see Erasmus in quite a different light, and he seems to me to have been misjudged by both Huizinga and Romein. Erasmus's true greatness lies, not in that he wavered, but in that he consistently refused to take sides with either of the two absolutisms which were then threatening Western civilization. But Luther's absolutism, Luther's, who in Erasmus saw Reason incarnated and on that score hated him so passionately,[19] was able to charm Huizinga. Luther, as he says in another connection,

---

[18] "Huizinga als historicus" (1946), in *Tussen Vrees en Vrijheid*, 1950.
[19] Lucien Febvre, *Un destin; Martin Luther* (1927), p. 257-8.

"whose word has at times the sound of eternity."[20] Erasmus, on the other hand, left him cool. Between reason and mysticism, too, there was in Huizinga's make-up an unsolved conflict.

I myself wrote in 1946 that in his personality and mind we seem to discern "a floating, a conscious weighing and probing of subtle distinctions, a trying to make extremes go together, which did occasionally rouse his critics to impatience. Understandable—although what we have here before us is Huizinga's deepest being, which constitutes his irreplaceable value."

Yes, this judgment I can maintain. That "conducting a conversation with himself" (as I put it in the same article), that unending, unsolved struggle with himself, those inclinations in incompatible directions, make him interesting. "Subtle versatility rather than closed systematism"—to quote once more my own words of sixteen years ago—"the advantage is unmistakable. In fact it placed him in an attitude towards life and towards history which can surprise ever anew. One may differ, one may observe that he differed from himself. But one feels all the time in contact with a human being, with a mind, and one feels enriched even in opposition."

All this I can still say with conviction, and yet, after my renewed and more thorough study of the work, I feel that the contradictions of the state of mind may suggest less extenuating terms. In *Explorations in Cultural History* we see not without concern the signs of an irresolution, an inner confusion, which betray a profound dichotomy. The connection of this with the systematic hostility toward the development he saw the world going through is evident. By giving such prominence in his analysis to the social motive, Romein has undoubtedly made a contribution. It is there that I too find the decisive factor: in the irritation, in the uneasiness bordering on panic, with which he observed the progressive democratization or, as he put it, plebeianization, of society. It was this feeling that threw him out of his balance in his intellectual

[20] Towards the close of his rectoral oration, 1935.

life as well, so that he was apt to warp relations and to mistake proportions.[21]

IV

"True historical interest presupposes a certain detachment from the present." So Huizinga wrote in 1926, in the preface to his volume *Ten Studies*. It is a debatable thesis. But the curious thing is that Huizinga did not at all conform to his own precept.

I have shown all through that he was on the contrary closely tied to his present—through opposition, through disapproval, through constantly saying "no," through near-despair (the word he used as early as 1921). He added to the statement quoted above that the historian "must possess a certain lightness and coolness of mind." This cannot be applied to all great historians. And what about Huizinga himself? Yes, in much of his work one will find that quality, and it can strengthen both the charm and the persuasive power. But his profound alarm about the present could at other times crush or scorch that lightness and that coolness.

I said a moment ago that it could make him lose sight of the proportions. How obvious is this in the hot-tempered attacks on literary history-writing. But when one looks through the four or five thousand pages of the *Collected Works*, without skipping the smaller pieces, the indignation about the use of *doctorandus* as title, about simplified spelling, about the multiplication of universities and technical high schools, about the Dutch flag, which one can see in so many different colour combinations and which some fail to take down at sunset— all that seems at times just a little comic. The interest was intense, but it covered a limited area. In the impassioned effusions of the 'thirties about the decline of our civilization

---

[21] Anyone who has read T. S. Eliot's *Notes towards the Definition of Culture* (1948;1962) will be struck by the similarity between his basic views and Huizinga's. In the presentation there are no doubt considerable differences, not all due to Mr. Eliot's anxiety to make concessions and to avoid giving offence to modern democratic feeling.

we have seen how large a part of life remained outside it and how as a result the picture was distorted.

But it deserves noting that Huizinga's tie with the present should not be described in negative terms only. His irritations and his glooms were the counterpart of positive and fervent feelings of attachment, always, of course, towards the social order or forms and institutions fitting in with his conception of culture, or which he saw as requisite for it, to the exclusion— this too we have seen—of much that had at least as valid a claim to recognition. I mean the forces of dynamism and of change, in which he would see nothing but destruction.

Huizinga's ideal of culture was that of an *élite*. This *élite* had not only its intellectual outlook, it had its social structure. As a member of that community he felt "being himself within his class," he appreciated that "noble relationship of service," words which I quoted above. To observe the habits of that group, to conform to its conventions, that he did with convic- tion and gracefully. The articles or addresses of homage or commemoration such as he wrote or delivered on numerous occasions are always idealized, free from even the lightest reservation or criticism. The "inexorable seriousness" of the historian of which we heard him speak is sometimes wanting in these pieces. It was to him a game. When Ter Braak and Van Eyck explained his shrinking back from *The Waning of the Middle Ages* and from imagination generally by a desire to be accepted by his Leyden circle as a normal university scholar, they misjudged him (as I said above); but this unmistakable social trait in his way of living must have led them into their error. Ter Braak, mocking at his longing for safety, pictures him at a Faculty meeting, at the editorial board of *De Gids*, with pinnacles in the shape of honorary "promotions", not forgetting the one by which Princess Juliana received a doctor's degree.

I did not know much about that particular "promotion." The speech delivered by Huizinga on that occasion has not been included in his *Collected Works*. I had to look it up in the Yearbook of Leyden University. I confess that it startled me a little, and I can enter into the feelings of the Utrecht

Professor of Ancient History, Bolkestein, who in the *Socialist-ische Gids* of 1930 protested against it as an offence against "the respect due to scholarship." Huizinga's newspaper article of 1938, on the occasion of the forty years' jubilee of the reign of Queen Wilhelmina—I mentioned it above as representing Dutch neutrality at that critical juncture in so illusionist a light—was also couched in that somewhat high-flown style. We have, so he assures us, passed the years of the war (of the first war) safely and honourably, "under the firm hand of Her who bore the highest responsibility for all the difficult decisions." Here speaks neither the historian nor the expert in public law, here speaks the panegyrist.

Discussing, in his *Homo Ludens*, the Baroque, with its "desire to exaggerate," "to be understood as proceeding from a strong playful element in the creative urge," Huizinga cites as an example Grotius' dedication of *De iure belli ac pacis* to Louis XIII of France, who is there in the most extravagant fashion lauded to the skies for his widely famed sense of justice. And he speculates: "Did Grotius mean all this?—Was he, then, lying?—He played, with the others, on the instrument of the style of his age."

Can this be said of Huizinga himself as well? Yes, provided it be added: the style of the age as he understood it, but which had in fact got hopelessly out of date, as is proved by Bolke-stein's protest.

"A safe history" in order to make sure of "a safe life." Thus Ter Braak rails at the end of his article. It is putting it unkindly. The choice that he demands Huizinga shall make, could not be a choice for Huizinga. Ter Braak argued all too one-sidedly from his own point of view. Combining the two tendencies caused tensions for Huizinga, but if he constantly operated with cautious reservations (*cautious*, a word that infuriated Ter Braak), it was certainly not so much in order to secure safety for his life as not to detract from critical truth.

"Huizinga is no fighter," said Romein, who later on added: "Huizinga was no thinker." A thinker in the sense of a man whose thinking opens up new fields, and who manages to build up his finds into a well-composed whole—no, this

Huizinga was not. *The Science of History*, of which one thinks for a moment, is after all not sufficiently original. *Homo Ludens* rather impresses one as a brilliant but wrong-headed improvization. Huizinga was no thinker, but he was a *remueur d'idées*. It is a joy—I often am truly impressed—to see him moving in the world of ideas, making subtle distinctions, striking comments, unexpected applications. The spectacle is the more attractive for being so unusual among us Dutch historians. But we have observed how, from year to year and sometimes in one and the same argument, he could tie himself up in contradictions.

As regards: "he is no fighter"—I should think that in the last decade of his life (after Romein had uttered that verdict) he did reveal himself in that capacity in a surprising way. He fought, it is true, for something that was not worth the effort: for the conservation of that "rich and beautiful culture" from before 1914 (you will remember the phrase), without taking notice of the oppressive and soul-destroying conditions out of which the masses were only just beginning to struggle upwards. But he fought also against the National-Socialist madness, for the spiritual values which had become consolidated in the imperfect society of earlier generations, and in that fight I can still gratefully honour him. He did not, in my opinion, fight with the most effective weapons. His mixing up the phenomena in Germany and in Russia with what filled him with concern in his own world was an error, and a bad one. But he fought.

His error was connected with his blindness for certain realities of life, for politics, for economics, for social evils. I have tried to demonstrate that blindness with the help of his writings, but after his death his friend Heering testified to it expressly in a little book, *Huizinga's religieuze gedachten:* "a deficiency of social feeling," this, he says, was one of Huizinga's limitations. He could not work up any interest, so he himself admitted to Heering on one occasion, "for social or political plans of reform." He turned away from the whole of that sphere of care and struggle; and culture, as he understood it, stood apart from it. *Homo Ludens*, with that excessive and questionable elevation of play, was inspired by that aversion. Only in noble play did Huizinga feel at home. There he could realize his dream of a world in which the struggle would shed its rudeness and be transformed into a rule-governed tournament with which material interest, gain, improvement of living conditions, would have nothing to do. Of a safe world as Ter Braak and Romein put it—I seem to be coming quite close to them after all.

I have discussed Huizinga primarily as accuser of his age, and in that capacity I have not been able to say much in his praise. My attitude toward *Shadows of Tomorrow, Violated World*, and the numerous smaller essays of the disturbed 'thirties and early 'forties when he appeared in that role more particularly, has been largely negative. The state of mind, the direction of his interest and of his indifference, which led him to his errors there, make themselves felt in the historian's work also. Less perhaps than in any other branch of study can a separation between the man and the scholar be made in historiography. So some of the more strictly historical works, too, I am inclined to put aside as errors: for instance *Homo Ludens* and *Change of Form in History*, both dating from that last period when the obsession with decline and ruin and the rancour against his own time had taken complete control over his mind. In other of his publications I observed weaknesses which stem directly from the mental attitude I have sketched. There is *The Waning of the Middle Ages*, which for all that remains a masterpiece; *Erasmus*, which retains great beauties; the works on theory of history, like *Science of History*, which I have always enjoyed and which despite its shortcomings is full of wise and perceptive remarks. But besides there is much that will always be admired without these reservations: I mentioned the *History of Groningen University*, 1814-1914, and "The Problem of the Renaissance"; I add now *Holland's Civilization in the Seventeenth Century*; but the list is far from being exhausted with these titles.

With all this work he remains an imposing figure in our Dutch historiography, and especially, he remains, not on account of that historically flawless work alone, but with contradictions, prejudices and all, an *uncommon* figure. Those eight volumes of the *Collected Works* sparkle with life. I have not scrupled to speak my mind about him and the defects of historical vision. In doing so, I have in a way rendered him my homage. He does not leave me indifferent. I remain convinced of what I wrote in 1938 in a review of his *Science of History:* "We have but one Huizinga."

III

ON SOME CONTEMPORARY
HISTORIANS (MAINLY CRITICAL)

1. Jan Romein, or Bowing to the Spirit of the Age

There is something both uncommon and attractive about the personality of Jan Romein (born 1894; Professor of History at the University of Amsterdam from 1939) as it is revealed to us in his latest volume of essays, *Commissioned by the Age*[1]. He moves by preference among great problems, and his intellectual intercourse—as a reader, I mean—is by preference with great minds. This cannot be said of all historians, and indeed a historian does not need that particular quality to make an outstanding contribution to the historical discussion. But Romein here obviously obeys a deeply felt want, and it is enough to give him something distinctive. What makes him attractive—and this, too, sets him apart from the every day type of our profession—is the intensity of his struggles with those great ideas and the sincerity with which he reports on them. For that is characteristic of his work. He does not build a proud and imposing system in accordance with a project preconceived in the cold transparency of an intellectual universe. He is a seeker. His heart impels him as much as does his mind. His examination of history, his conception of what it can give and of how it may best be approached, his discoveries and his doubts—it all means something to him in his life, and in his essays there transpires something now of his hope, then of his disappointment or of his uneasiness. They have something to tell us on a different plane from that of mere curiosity about the past.

A seeker—after steady truth. In fact, he imagines that the remedy against his tormenting vision of dizzying chaos is to be found in Marx. He often testifies to this belief, but he

[1] *In opdracht van de tÿd.* On Romein cf. footnote on p. 219.

belongs to those whom the revelation of truth does not once
and for always satisfy; he must labour to experience it every
day, he must put it to the test. And this is what he does in these
essays, in a charming fashion, confidential, disarmingly frank,
obviously yearning after what is noble and good. He does it
in a thoroughly human style, at times sensitive in a way
bordering on the coquettish, but also shot through with
flashes of humour.

This testing of a truth postulated by the heart makes a
spectacle both fascinating and instructive. Convincing, however, if that is to mean that the result will every time seem to
the reader as conclusive as it does to the author—convincing
it can be only to those to whom the same revelation has already
been vouchsafed, to his companions in the faith. Terms as
here used flow automatically from the pen when this work is
discussed. By its nature it is related to writings giving an
account of the experiences of religion.

The first essay is from this point of view the most important.
In it the central problem of "certainty and uncertainty in the
science of history" is treated. One can readily go along with
the author as long as he describes the uncertainty that is so
obviously inherent in history and the inadequacy of the various
methods with which it has been thought this could be overcome. "We cannot, however, forever linger at the inn called
Zero and must proceed. How?" A statement, and a question.
But should we not, with respect to what is denied and
affirmed so unhesitatingly, first of all like to know *Why?* and
Why not? Why can we not stay on in uncertainty? and who
has told Romein that we must—or can—proceed? The
answer, in fact, is not far to seek: because Romein finds
uncertainty unbearable, and because he hears his soul cry out
that the certainty without which it feels itself lost *must* exist.
So he goes out to seek, and (as indeed it is written) he finds.

And what is the certainty he offers us as the result of his
reflections? He begins with a twofold assumption which he
does not attempt to prove. The past has an objective reality,
which, moreover, has sense; which sense we can get to know
through and by way of our mind. Especially the last point,

which he seems practically to take for granted, would seem to stand in need of some serious argumentation. *Can* we know this sense? know it in a way that amounts to certainty? For Romein apparently it is enough that he wants to, that he must; therefore he can.

But how?—Here Croce's dictum points the way for him: "All true history is history of the present." This is how Romein himself formulates it: "Objective is, and certainty gives, *that* history-writing which is in agreement with the spirit of the age." (Let there be no mistake—he means: with the historian's age.)

Romein admits that he does not write down those words without "some trembling," and he expects "a cry of protest." I must say that, for my part, it is especially the way in which he overcomes that trembling and tries to silence that protest which makes me stare.

Romein knows, and he says, that the present spirit of the age will be succeeded by a different spirit of the age, and that the devotee's certainty will thereby be superseded. Does he then acknowledge the relativity of his certainty (of "the certainty as I understand it")? His entire argument is intended to turn that relativity into an absolute.

For that purpose the conception of "the spirit of the age" must be simplified and fixed. For Romein there is at every time but one spirit of the age—or rather, there are two, the true one and the false. Only *he*, at any rate, can claim objectivity or certainty who, as our author puts it, "has made the right choice." But how is one to know that one is not in error? At first sight it might be thought—thus Romein lets us share in his cogitations—that only the future will decide this point.

I cannot see on what grounds we should have to let the future judge on true or false. Moreover, the future? The future is a most variable entity. Romein here clearly gets himself involved in difficulties. To which future, how far distant, must we defer the judgment? He adduces the striking instance of the German historians who saw the past in the terms of Bismarck's "Little-German" solution of the unity problem, and in their lifetime this did indeed command the future. Must we therefore call them objective? By Romein's own standard we know better now. The ever-continuing shifts in the development of the ever-moving times have indeed opened our eyes to a thing or two. And has the development come to a stop even now? Besides, the historians who read the past by the light of a policy that was indeed to triumph did not have the field of history all to themselves. Must we conclude that the true spirit of that age was after all represented by their critics because a more distant future seems to be putting them in the right, or at least, showing the fallacies in the outlook of the others? and must we therefore accept these critics as the better, or even greater, historians? Klein-Hattingen greater or more famous than Treitschke? For fame with posterity, too, supplies Romein with a criterion by which to judge the historian's true significance in his own time. He may be right in thinking that the historian becomes "truly famous" only after his death and that only then can his greatness appear. But neither his fame nor his true greatness is determined, and no more is the view we take of his objectivity or of any time-bound certainty that he may offer, by his being representative of the true spirit of his age. Many other factors, differing among themselves, will count in the final reckoning.

But indeed, the comfort that the future may give is not enough for Romein. He wants to know *now* that he is on the right track.

> After the choice between the true and the false spirit of the age has been made, it appears possible to check it in another way than with the help of the future alone. The choice can be checked by the *inner* certainty of the historian who made it, on condition, however, that the choice was the right one. For—and this is most noteworthy—this inner certainty, this, so to speak, higher peace of mind of the historian who made the right choice creates (and *because* he made it) the psychological condition that will help him when writing history to overcome his other, personal and group, subjectivity. . . . [And a little later he avows:]

As for me, I have made that choice. I see the true spirit of our own age in the emancipation struggle waged by labourers and peasants, and as long as it lasts the critical method of knowledge that goes with it is the dialectical-materialist. It is that method, therefore, that in my opinion guarantees, for us, the largest possible measure of knowledge about the past.

Romein, in other words, not only has the conviction of his social-political conceptions, but he knows that, taking his stand upon them, he possesses the only true view of history that our time affords. He is certain. Certain with an inner certainty that can never be the part of other-minded men. So while *he* can overcome personal or group subjectivity, those others, who—perhaps against their better judgment, against their better nature—follow the false spirit of the age, live in a constant unrest caused by self-reproach; and blinded by egoism or hatred, doomed to indulge their passions of partiality, they will never find that radiant inner certainty.

It is worth noting that Romein appeals to Groen van Prinsterer, the mid-nineteenth-century Calvinist and anti-liberal, who wrote: "It may sound paradoxical, but it is true: only he who chooses a side can be impartial." And indeed, Groen too was a man possessed of an inner certainty that the truth concerning his own time and concerning the past had been revealed to him. Whether it was the truth that was to be confirmed by the future I leave to Romein to judge; the question must worry him more than it does me; I suggest to him that he reread *Unbelief and Revolution*.[2] In any case, Groen was a famous, and if not a great, an important historian. But not a historian, really, who impresses us as having been remarkably objective. He began by representing the Prince of Orange as a hero of the faith, then he revised that interpretation, without being able essentially to alter it, under the

[2] *Ongeloof en Revolutie* was based on lectures given in 1845 and 1846. In it the author derived the Revolution, which he saw still continuing its nefarious work, from the rejection of Christianity springing from the philosophy of the Enlightenment.

influence of the criticism advanced by writers who, if *he* had
a monopoly of the true spirit of the age, must have been sadly
devoid of it. To how untenable a picture of the Earl of
Leicester his partiality made him cling down to the end of his
life, can be seen in *Maurice et Barnevelt*.[3]

"The certainty *as I understand it*," so Romein wrote—and
we can now see how badly needed was the qualification
—"does not exclude, but on the contrary includes, doubt.
This is in accordance with the experience of psychology
telling us that the strongest believers are the strongest doubt-
ers."

There is no trace of this inclination to doubt in Romein's
title, in which the writer gives us to understand that the age
commissioned him to compose his book. But what strikes me
above all in the passage just quoted is the comparison, which
is in effect an identification. Romein's conception of history
is a faith. His conviction that he has the true view of the past,
and others, dominated by the false spirit of the age, the false
view, is not a thesis that can be proved, it is not even liable to
discussion: it is a faith.

Finding this faith formulated as we saw it done by him—
averring that the true spirit of the present age consists in the
emancipation struggle of labourers and peasants—one is
inclined to add that it is a hopelessly short-range faith. I am
quite ready to agree that this emancipation struggle is a
phenomenon characteristic of our age; I trust that it will prove
fruitful. But the abundance of life does not let itself be
imprisoned in so narrow a definition. There are contrasts of

---

[3] This book of Groen's old age—it appeared in 1875—attacked the
interpretation of the church and state crisis of 1617 to 1619 given by
Motley in his *Life and Death of John of Barneveld*. To Groen, Maurice was
the hero who had preserved the life principle of the Dutch Republic,
orthodox Calvinism, which the old "advocate," Oldenbarnevelt, had
jeopardized by the protection meted out to Arminianism. Moreover, he
traced the issue, which to him was at all times the one of essential
importance, throughout the history of the Republic and recalled the
polemics in which he himself had been engaged in his lifetime to vin-
dicate its true significance. See in my *Reacties* (1952), the essay "Groen
contra Motley."

endless variety on all sides—exceeding or crossing this only aspect that Romein is willing to observe.

We are confronted here, and not for the first time, with a peculiarity of the author that is connected with his deepest being. In another essay in this same volume he quotes a "thesis" appended to his doctoral dissertation (of 1924): "The science of history must accept history-writing as its final aim, and history-writing must concentrate on the historical account, or story."

Striking words indeed, and Romein says he still agrees with them. But why, then, do we now receive from him so little "historical account, or story"? Why has he given his heart to what he calls "theoretical history"? I regret this, for although a historical account impelled by so emotional, and at the same time, so narrow a faith would not be likely to excel in objectivity and could hardly embody more than a fragment of the spirit of our own age, its inspiration might lend it pace and fire, and even those otherminded men whom Romein abandons to the contempt of posterity might be grateful for the light thrown, if only on an aspect of, the truth about the past. But no, Romein the historian seems to be succumbing to the danger of allowing his mind to be so engrossed by general conceptions that the historical sense for the concrete, for the particular, for the multiform and the refractory to system, is escaping him.

"The conception of the spirit of the age is so vague." This, so he says, is the objection that will be raised against the considerations he propounds. He continues:

To this I must reply that the historian always works with vague notions. Race, people, nation, state. Nobility, bourgeoisie, small middle-class, proletariat. Republic, monarchy, dictatorship, democracy. Feudalism, capitalism, socialism, fascism. Renaissance, baroque, romanticism, liberalism. Where is the historian whose hand will not hesitate when venturing to define any of these conceptions? But where, also, is the historian who will refrain from using them as being too vague? The historian must work with vague notions because his object does not admit of exact ones.

The problem, however, presents itself in a totally different fashion from that suggested by Romein. The historian does not work with notions or conceptions primarily, but with representations, or delineations. What vagueness there is in conceptions must become exact in his concretization. The notion *monarchy* is vague. But in a history of Louis XIV we must get a clear picture of what monarchy was under him. The true historian will feel some diffidence in the, indeed unavoidable, employment of vague generalizations. He will at once be ready with questions, with criticism; he will desire greater precision and do what he can to supply it.

And so I conclude that the reckless employment of the term *the spirit of the age*, the simplistic distinction made between *the true* and *the false spirit of the age*, the presumption of measuring every writer of history by his being an adept of either the one or the other—I conclude that all this making play with a conception of indeed so vague an import must be called thoroughly unhistorical. If Romein did not content himself with a general presentment of his idea, but tried to apply it in particular cases, the results would probably provide an ironic comment on his all-saving theory of certainty. The rightness of a historical representation, and the greatness of a historian, depend on many factors, among which are prominent those of personal qualities and personal ways of thinking not simply to be derived from the historian's intellectual position with regard to his own age.

How dangerous is this doctrine according to which objectivity is not a capacity to be acquired, or approached, by dint of labour and discipline, but a state of grace obtained once and for all by adhering to the doctrine itself! How must it, and in what treacherous ways, strengthen the temptation, to which we are all of us exposed, to let our cherished fancies and our constructions have the better of the facts!

(1947)

2. *Othmar F. Anderle, or Unreason as a Doctrine*

I will frankly confess that I read reviews of my books with a good deal of interest. In the course of a lengthening life, in which hardly a year has passed without some publication or other, I have had innumerable reviews in half a dozen countries. There were some that annoyed and some that infuriated me; others pleased or even delighted me; a good many, laudatory as they might be, moved me to no more than a shrug.

But I have seldom experienced the mixed feelings of astonishment and indignation giving way to sheer amusement that were roused in me on reading a review of my *Debates with Historians* in the solemn pages of the leading historical journal of Germany, the *Historische Zeitschrift*.

The writer, Othmar F. Anderle, is a fervent admirer of Toynbee, and his article is concerned mostly with those essays in my volume in which *A Study of History* is criticized. But indeed so full of Toynbee is the writer's mind that even when I write about Ranke, Macaulay, Carlyle, and Michelet, about the American Civil War and Talleyrand, he imagines that I am indirectly tilting at the prophet.

Now, none of this very greatly disturbed me, but what I thought extraordinary is that Toynbee's apologist should admit the correctness of practically the whole of my criticism. When I point out the errors in the factual foundations of Toynbee's superstructure of theory and generalization, he thinks I am in the right. Even when I assert that the whole method is faulty and that Toynbee's repeated insistence on proceeding empirically and arriving at conclusions by a concatenation of proved facts is no more than makebelieve, he agrees. In fact, he considers my opposition to be the most careful and wellfounded statement of the many that international scholarship has made against Toynbee.

But now Herr Anderle brushes aside all the defects in the great work as irrelevant, and because I seem to consider them important and indeed conclusive, rates me down for an antiquated representative of out-of-date "classical" scholarship. I reveal myself as being a mere stickler for the correct statement of facts, a despiser of theory and generalization, a man blind to the greatness of this startling new panoramic vision. Toynbee, according to Anderle, is helping to bring about a revolution in historical scholarship, and only if we will do homage to the principle, *Credo quia ineptum, quia absurdum*—I believe because it is preposterous, because it is absurd—shall we be allowed to enter the brave new world this revolution is opening up for the elect.

The argument reveals a state of mind with which it is impossible to argue. Was I right in saying that the ultimate feeling the article aroused in me was one of sheer amusement? At any rate, when the next issue of the *Historische Zeitschrift* brought an article in which Herr Anderle gave his views on Toynbee's work at greater length, and when the issue after that presented us with a third article, in which he set forth his own theory of history (in both I came in for renewed denunciation), I began to think, not only that the joke was growing rather wearisome, but that, after all, the matter should perhaps be taken seriously.

My protracted dispute with Toynbee has from the first exceeded the limits of strict historical scholarship. I have championed against him not only, as Anderle will have it, the canons of the profession but—that, at least, is how I have felt about it myself—the vital traditions of Western civilization.

Nothing is more absurd than to suggest that I, or historians in general, believe in nothing but facts, that we despise theories of generalizations as such. History must reveal to us a meaning in life, or we are not worth our salt. History, as I have expressed it on another occasion, is a key to life, as is art or literature.[1] But history has its own methods and obligations, and although

[1] See below, in "Looking Back," p. 401.

it will not get far without imagination or intuition, it must always accept the control of reason.

There is in the whole of the Western world, as there has been before, a movement of revolt against the claims of reason. Toynbee's great work, and the popular acclaim that greeted it, were signs of this, and I have done what I could to point out that behind the pretence of scientific empiricism there was the reality of emotional and defeatist fantasy. I was not, truth to tell, alarmed overmuch, because I believe that our civilization, which has no more distinctive feature than its rationality, disposes of abundant powers of resistance to master (again, as it has done before) these stirrings of impatience and petulance within its own fold. But Herr Anderle goes one better than Toynbee. He dispenses with the pretence and boldly invokes the principle of Tertullian, which has undeniable greatness in its own sphere, but which, when applied to history, cuts at the foundations of scholarship and clear thinking.

When a great European historical review, not once but three times running, allows this doctrine of unreason to be proclaimed in its pages, one has an uneasy feeling that among the custodians of our heritage some are not fully aware of the dangers that beset us. The powers of resistance of our civilization are, I said, abundant. The rational approach is among its most effective weapons of defence. We must be careful of it.

(1958)

3. Herbert Butterfield, or Thinking at Two Levels

The leading idea of Herbert Butterfield's *Man on his Past* (1955) is that of the importance of the history of historiography. Four lectures included in it were delivered under the auspices of the new Wiles Trust at the University of Belfast. In these we are first shown the history of historiography in historical perspective. The origin of the notion in a more significant form than that of a mere listing of books and authors is traced back to the Göttingen School of History in the decades before and after 1800. Quotations from Gatterer (1760), Schlözer (1785 and later), and Rühs (1811), bear out the conclusion that these men were the spiritual forebears of Ranke and Acton.

The importance of Germany's contribution to the emergence of the view of history that we have come to consider as characteristic of modern civilization is beyond dispute; the recognition that historiography is itself governed by the process of development is a natural concomitant of that view. So it is not surprising that the second essay deals with "The Rise of the German Historical School." The third, on "Lord Acton and the Nineteenth-Century Historical Movement," is again largely concerned with German ideas, which it was Acton's ambition to introduce into England, although at the same time he set his face against the consequences of relativism and acquiescence to which "historicism" so easily led, and insisted on the need for upholding the independent and unchangeable standards of morality.

The fourth lecture, "Ranke and the Conception of 'General History,' " deals with general history as much as with Ranke. We are given disquisitions of the author's own on the problem of the importance of foreign policy, the idea of Providence, the Renaissance, and the division into periods.

Finally there are two essays, published earlier, one on "Lord Acton and the Massacre of St. Bartholomew" and the other on "The Reconstruction of an Historical Episode: The History of the Enquiry into the Origins of the Seven Years' War." In these the author gives samples of his own of the history of historiography in connection with concrete questions.

The first thing that must be said of this work is that it is the product of profound and meticulous research and testifies to a remarkable erudition. The accounts of the origins of the notion of a history of historiography and of the rise of the German historical school are particularly useful since they show—once again—that what one is accustomed to look upon as a revolution and to associate with a few great names, had in fact been long prepared, and prepared by "little men," or men, at least, whose names have been forgotten.

One aspect of the general history of historiography which has Professor Butterfield's special interest is the treatment of individual historians. "Since the Second World War," he writes, "three men in particular have been repeatedly examined, both in Europe and in America," Ranke, Burckhardt, and Acton.

Personally I believe that the attention lavished upon Acton in England sometimes surprises Continental historians. That extraordinary devourer of books and scribbler of notes, whose *magnum opus* never got written, produced only essays in a style that has been described as "crabbed, tortuous, contorted, elliptic and allusive."[1] In his voluminous private notes, no doubt, he often found for his unceasing and profound reflections phrases of an unforgettable quality, and Professor Butterfield deserves our thanks for having culled so many more from those mysterious black boxes in the Cambridge University Library. How could the idea inspiring the history of historiography be stated more pregnantly and more simply than when he says: "To teach to look behind historians, especially famous historians." And how can the opposition

[1] Lionel Kochan, *Acton on History* (1954), p. 36.

to historicism, which he welcomed with such fervour, be better expressed than in a note unearthed by another recent student of his work: "Resist your time—take a foothold outside it."[2]

The treatment of Ranke is admirable. To approach him from the angle of "general history" proves really fruitful, and in a few pages not only the special qualities of the great historian, but the various aspects of the concept "general history" (European and world history, western European history, the relations between political and cultural history, nationality, power and the moral factor) are illumined.

On one point I think Professor Butterfield goes too far along with Ranke. He confesses to having felt shocked at first when he found Ranke arguing that " in spite of Goethe, German culture and German cultural influence gained their great momentum with the rise of German power and confidence in the nineteenth century," and then: "Yet when I reflect on the cultural leadership which the United States and Russia have come to enjoy since the Second World War . . . I am staggered to see how such matters are affected by a mere redistribution of power." I am not at all sure that it is right to speak of "cultural leadership" of the U.S., however highly I esteem the American contribution to our common Western civilization. But I am quite sure that it is wrong to speak of a "cultural leadership" of Russia. I write under the fresh impression of the wilfully one-sided and propagandist Russian contributions to the proceedings of the International Congress of History recently held in Rome.

But perhaps the author will brush this evidence aside as irrelevant, for he, who devotes so much attention to Ranke and Acton, does not seem to rate history very high as a cultural force. In trying to establish the usefulness of the history of historiography he takes a somewhat narrow ground. He speaks as the teacher of history, he considers the equipment of the research student, he hopes for the unravelling of the bewildering entanglement of researches in certain fields. For the two practical examples of his own application of the method, too,

[2] Op. cit., p. 97.

he has (in the two essays alluded to above, the fifth and sixth in his book) chosen problems of a concrete and factual nature.

Stress might have been laid on matters of wider significance. As for instance that, every personal view of a historical episode or figure being to a certain extent one-sided or biased, more of the fundamental truth may be revealed when we watch the everchanging interpretations offered by successive generations of historians,—no mere kaleidoscopic sequence, but one in which every next picture will be seen to have incorporated elements of the preceding ones, a gradual conquest of reality over myth. Also, how much do historians unconsciously reveal of the spirit of their own times! The ideal history of historiography would be a contribution to the intellectual, social, and political history of the times in which the works were written. Moreover, the historian as the exponent of contemporary tendencies has often exercised a direct influence on the development of ideas, conditions, and events.

This, of course, Professor Butterfield knows as well as anybody, but he regards this influence with suspicion. He dwells on the case of the post-Rankean school in Germany which, as he puts it, misled the German people. And he concludes that particular story with a reflection of even wider import: "It would seem that the decline of religion gives undue power to history in the shaping of men's minds—undue power to historical over-simplifications, and multitudes of young students have even come to the study of technical history in the expectation that it would help them to shape their fundamental views about life. It is an expectation that is often disappointed." (Curiously enough, according to Acton, as recorded by Professor Butterfield himself: "history lay at the basis of European religion," and if what Professor Butterfield means is not really "history" but "historical over-simplifications," the question might well be asked whether many of these were not inspired by religion.)

"Technical history"—what our author means by this becomes clearer in another passage. "Technical history," the kind of history that we can teach and that, when we write it, will pass the tests of scholarship, "is a limited and mundane realm of description and explanation, in which local and concrete things are achieved by a disciplined use of tangible evidence." Professor Butterfield is here concerned to place the concept of Providence beyond the reach of the "technical historian." "Thinking at different levels" is what he advises.[3]

In his *Christianity and History*, when apparently he was thinking at the other level, he explained the defeat and destruction of Germany in the second world war as the divine punishment for the sins of the German people. The explanation required the concept of "vicarious punishment," for is it not obvious that many Germans were not guilty? The fact that other countries, I mention only the Baltic countries, which had not sinned (insofar as sinlessness is humanly possible), had to suffer as grievously and are still suffering, remained without explanation.

At any rate the technical historian, according to *Man on His Past*, "is arguing in a circle if he thinks that his researches have in fact eliminated from life the things which for technical reasons he had eliminated in advance from his consideration." But do historians have to eliminate things in advance? Professor Butterfield now even switches over from religion to literature and maintains that "the poet, the prophet, the novelist and the playwright command sublimer realms than those of technical history because they reconstitute life in its wholeness. The history of historiography may help us to keep the technical historian in his place."

This is a view of history which I for one can never accept. History must claim the whole of life for its province. It is hampered by a deficiency of data, admitted; the human mind is incapable of embracing even those which it can gather and of bringing them into a stable equilibrium, of that too I am fully aware. I do not claim that history will solve the riddle of our existence. But the true historian, whose mind has been touched by the great revolution in historic thinking which Professor Butterfield so well describes, does not come to his material as a technician, or not *only* as a technician, but as a human being. He will eliminate nothing in advance. He will

[3] Compare the remarks made by De Marans, quoted above, p. 181.

never expect to reach the absolute, but he will strive, despite his handicaps, with all his soul and mind, like the poet. He will in his way be a servant of truth, like the preacher or the prophet. He will not mind being put in his place, but he will not belittle history, nor will he be discouraged.

I know that this is just stating view against view. I am, however, grateful to Professor Butterfield, not only for his excellent specimens of technical history, but also for the shock he has made me experience by his philosophy, a shock which is to me confirmation of my own belief that history cuts down to the deepest issues of life.

(1956)

4. Geoffrey Barraclough, or the Scrapping of History

It so happened that I read Barraclough's *History in a Changing World* immediately after another volume of essays, *Six Historians*, by Ferdinand Schevill, which was published posthumously. I shall write here only of the first-named work, but it is impossible not to remark upon the contrast presented by the two.

Professor Barraclough, who for a number of years occupied the chair of Medieval History at the University of Liverpool, recently succeeded Arnold Toynbee as Research Professor of International History at the University of London. His essays, fifteen of them, for the most part quite short, give evidence, no less than do those of Schevill, of a vast range of learning. But instead of a firm rooting in the Western cultural tradition, and the balance and mellow understanding characteristic of the older man, we find here a restless dissatisfaction with the old ways of historical scholarship, carping—wildly, as it seems to me—at prejudice, convention, antiquated methods, and calling on us to cast all our textbooks on to the dustheap and learn the world's history anew.

For Barraclough, "historicism," is the enemy. Historicism, which sees history as a process of continuity, to which one period is as important as another, by which everything is judged according to time, place, context, and environment, etc.; I abridge the eloquent passage.

No doubt such tendencies have at times been promoted by historicism, but it seems to me absurd to write as though they constituted the prevailing attitude among historians of the last generation. Historicism is not for me a term of reproach, for I regard these demoralizing and deadening kinds of relativism as excrescences. I find its true significance in the fact that it enables us to feel ourselves, not enslaved by the past, but in touch with it—a touch that is invigorating as well as restraining.

But here comes Professor Barraclough to bid us study the periods of crisis, of change and revolution, for continuity is a delusion and we are ourselves in just such a period of crisis, which makes all our inherited notions of the past "irrelevant." What exactly does the new prophet mean? In his introduction he lays much stress on the immorality of historicism, but his own philosophy, as he develops it in a variety of contexts, is not preoccupied with morality or the free choice of the individual, but with power.

Western Europe has lost its dominant position: America, Russia, Asia, now make world history. Let us not shrink from the conclusion, then, that we have been wrong all along in picturing to ourselves a world history centring on Europe. So runs Barraclough's argument.

The loss of the dominant position is indisputable, though to suggest that "in the late twentieth or in the twenty-first century Europe is destined to enjoy (if that is the right word) something not unlike the colonial status which in the eighteenth and nineteenth centuries it imposed on Africa, much of Asia and the New World," seems to me just shock tactics unworthy of a serious historical argument. But admitting that the dominant position is gone and irretrievable, does it follow that in our view of the past, when the dominant position was undeniable, Europe must no longer be seen as the central force in world affairs?

To me it seems obvious that the peoples of America, Asia, and Africa, all of whom have been deeply and permanently affected by the enterprises and traditions of western Europe, will for a long time need to study the history of that region in its period of greatness if they want to understand themselves. But it does not seem obvious to Barraclough:

The traditional Europe—the Europe of our history books, the Europe of Louis XIV and Napoleon and Bismarck—is dead and beyond resurrection, and we may disabuse our minds of the illusion that there is any special relevance, from the point of view of contemporary affairs, in studying these neolithic figures.

It was in 1943, when Stalingrad was relieved by the Russians, that Professor Barraclough suddenly awoke to the fact that he had misspent his life. Why, he asked himself, had he and all Westerners been so blind to the actual distribution of power? It was because he, who knew a great deal about the machinery of the papal chancellery in the thirteenth and fourteenth centuries, knew nothing of the Piasts, the Przemyslids and the Ruriks; because, in short, he knew nothing of eastern European history. This strikes me as an extraordinarily naïve remark. In the first place, why wait until 1943? And although the victory at Stalingrad may have been an unanswerable power pronouncement, was it the natural culmination of a process beginning with the Przemyslids and the Ruriks? One has only to read the story of the 1941 campaign to realize how uncertain were the chances of war and how near Stalin came to ruin. Would we then have had to accept Germany as the true centre of world history and rewrite everything accordingly?

It is not only the decline of western Europe's world position, it is the rise of Russia and of Communism which often makes our "universalists" give way to what I regard as a detestable defeatism with respect to the vitality and prospects of Western society. They are so obsessed with the idea of change that they no longer care to preserve our heritage. Their outlook is akin to that truly revolutionary mentality that Croce, twenty-five years ago, described under the name of "anti-historicism":

> That feeling that true history is only about to begin, and that we are at last escaping from the bonds of false history and struggling into freedom and space.

I used the term "our heritage." *The European Inheritance* is the title of a three-volume collective work that appeared in England two or three years ago. Barraclough devotes a largely sarcastic article to it, the title especially moving him to scorn. Though some of his remarks are to the point, his bias appears in the use he makes of Geoffrey Bruun's gloomy description of the state of affairs, especially in France, after the miscarriage of the Revolution of 1848 and of the 1871 Commune: "A runaway technology; the implicit contradiction at the heart of liberal philosophy: the unresolved contradiction between political equality in theory and economic inequality in fact; the confident premises were no more." All this is quoted from Bruun, Barraclough seeming to forget that it is related to one particular period. Indeed the final sentence of his paragraph, "When the end came, old Europe's last breath was a sigh of relief, as it concluded the unequal struggle, cast aside its burden, and gave up the ghost," is *not* based on Bruun, though the reader must think so.

Has old Europe indeed given up the ghost? One might maintain with greater justice that the twentieth century, which has seen the ruin of Europe's power, has also seen a new proof of the vitality and resourcefulness of its society and civilization —seen it in the welfare state, which has largely resolved the distressing contrasts of the preceding century. But the welfare state comes in for nothing but sneers from Barraclough:

> In Russian eyes today [he said in a lecture] Western society is a weary, decadent society, the relict of a dying bourgeoisie, which has lost faith in itself and is incapable of renewal from within. To you, luxuriating in the manifold delights of the "welfare state," this may seem a curious and perverse judgment.

He does not actually say that he considers the judgment sound, but this is the impression one gathers from his many pronouncements. And indeed he tells us in so many words that our civilization has nothing to look forward to but gradually being superseded by "the coming civilization," of which he can already see "the dim shape." Elsewhere he bids us take comfort from the thought that "European values, though they may be modified and re-assessed, will not perish, because they are embedded in both American and Russian civilization."

Yet he warns us not to think of America as an integral part of western European civilization. He is at pains, on the contrary, to argue that Russia is more truly of Europe than most of us are inclined to believe. He does not, in fact, seem to find much to choose between America and Russia:

> Already the Soviet Union and the United States have their European satellites; already eastern Europe can only defend itself with Russian help against American domination [!], and western Europe can only defend itself with American aid against Russia.

Power, I said, is the dominant factor in Barraclough's view of the world. Nowhere in his book is there a clear indication of the true nature of the Soviet system in which we are to be glad that "our Western values" are being "embedded." The tendency of this latest prophecy of a historian (in a book, let me add, abounding in acute and stimulating remarks) seems to me pernicious.

(1957)

5. *Soviet Historians Make their Bow*

For a full week in September 1955 the Tenth International Congress of History was assembled in Rome. Two thousand historians of all nationalities discussed, in I don't know how many sections, innumerable subjects. Before leaving home they had received six heavy volumes containing elaborate reports, and at Rome there waited for them a seventh, with brief summaries of the communications to be delivered orally. It would be an impossible task to survey the activities of the Congress as a whole. But one fact was of so unusual, and at the same time, of so arresting a nature that it still dominates my memory of that crowded week: there were Russians there, flanked by Poles, Hungarians, Czechs, Rumanians, and they were anxious to give an account of themselves.

Into the babel of voices they certainly introduced one that was distinctively different. Unfortunately, it is impossible to affirm that they added to the possibilities of a real exchange of thought. On the contrary, the most remarkable feature of their contribution was that the Russians did not really take part, and obviously were unable to take part, in that argument without end which is to us of the West the study of history. No doubt this is what one would have expected, but to have one's untested expectation so abundantly confirmed is a significant experience. They had come just to *tell* us—for they were certain that they had a monopoly of true historical method and true historical insight, revealed for all time by Marx and Engels. They were unshakably certain that the materialistic conception of history is the indispensable condition for history being raised to the status of a *Science*; with the aid of it alone can work be produced that will be both *progressive* and *objective*. These latter terms, which at first sight do not seem to go together too well, they would reel off confidently in one breath—for it is part of their doctrine, not only that history is governed by the development of the means of production and is essentially the history of the class war, but also that its direction is *determined* toward a future of pure democracy, of a classless society.

When I speak of *them* in the aggregate, I only echo their constantly referring to *us*: "We Soviet historians"; "the school of historical materialism to which I belong"; and so on. In the West, however, all of these axioms are still problems: one historian may accept more of them; another, less; a third will reject them altogether. Most of us will count spiritual or instinctive factors in history in addition to purely materialistic ones. There will be fairly general agreement that these various categories are somehow interdependent, but there is nothing like a *communis opinio* as to the order in which the connection makes itself felt. The different factors will be differently apportioned. As regards the course of history, Western historians may hope or fear, accept or doubt; few will affirm that they *know*. They are far, then, from constituting a unanimous chorus, and here we have the first and principal characteristic of the performance and the testimony of the Russians at Rome.

Or rather—a unanimous chorus?

A close phalanx is what they appeared to be. Their leader was A. L. Sidorov. His contribution to the activities of the Congress was a survey of Soviet Russian historical problematics and achievements.

"Soviet Russian historiography," so he tells us without mincing matters, "continues the materialistic tradition, which has found its most consistent and fullest expression in Marxism." Led by it, Lenin in his writings "has explained in a new way all major events of Russian and modern world history." Nothing less. Also: "It may be said with certainty that the materialistic conception of history has completely triumphed in our country and is universally recognized by historians of both the younger and older generations."[1] As for this last positive assurance, I do not for a moment doubt it. But it does not seem to strike the Russians that what we are confronted with here is an extraordinary phenomenon, which cries out for historical explanation.

Truth to tell, their own recipe for historical explanation is easily applied, and one guesses that for them Sidorov's first sentence says everything: "Soviet historiography came into existence, after the great revolution of October 1917, in the conditions of the new socialist society." But *is* there no more to be said? The spectacle of this intellectual discipline, of this well-drilled array of historians all trotting obediently through the same curious processes of thought, all pretending to master the refractory material of mankind's historical vicissitudes by the same formulas—it not only rouses the disgust of anyone who has not had his thinking moulded by Soviet dictatorship, it makes the outsider ask questions to which no satisfactory answers will ever be forthcoming from those well-schooled adepts of historical materialism and its special kind of dialectics.

How much compulsion has been needed to achieve this state of affairs? Is there any Soviet historian left who, in the privacy of his study (if he has any), thinks differently? Are there any younger men trying to widen their outlook by surreptitiously scanning the writings of unorthodox ("reactionary," "bourgeois") Western historians? Do not doubts stir in the brain of one or another of these speakers who, after having arrived in Rome with passport and all in order, is now proclaiming with brazen forehead the Marxian truths, doubts that perhaps he hardly dares to admit to himself?

And as regards the future, of which these lights of Soviet historical scholarship dispose so masterfully—does it really belong to them? Is their "history" really destined to become *History*? Have they discovered the means by which to shackle once and for all the human mind, which, as Burckhardt said

[1] I follow the English translation of the pamphlet distributed at the Congress. The version in Volume VI of the official Congress publications is in German.

(a reactionary bourgeois if you like, but somewhat more besides!), is "a worrier" (*ein Wühler*)? I cannot believe it, and what strengthens my disbelief is that very disgust with which the achievements they so confidently offered us have filled me.

I have heard them. But I have, more especially, read them. In Volume VII of the Congress publications there is to be found, for instance, another brief theoretical treatise, by Madame Pankratova, agreeing completely in both thought and terminology with Sidorov's survey. "We start from a materialistic view of history [so she tells us] in which history is conceived as an objective process, at the base of which lies the development of the means of production of material goods." Proceeding in that way one will learn "rightly to understand the laws of history and how these are to be applied in order to solve the problem of the present." Western historians get lost on unscientific paths, as did Spengler, who drew a gloomy picture of the past, and Croce, Beard, Collingwood—all submerged into subjectivism or pessimism. And what can be worse than the opinion, suggested in the American *Report on Theory and Practice in Historical Study* of 1946, that history is unknowable!

A worse case of mixing up representative and unrepresentative names (Spengler!) and of neglecting shades and subtleties of opinion, it would be difficult to imagine!

Sidorov has an explanation of this reluctance of Western historians to deduce laws from their observation of history and to speak dogmatically about the true meaning of history: it is because they are afraid of the future; it is their way of trying to halt history in its march and to delay social progress. Indeed, according to Madame Pankratova, "the study of history shows that socialism is the normal result of the entire preceding development of society, the result of the struggle of the mass of workers for their liberation." If, by looking at realities and refusing to shut up one's mind in the schematic, one realizes what is meant here by "socialism" and the "liberation" of the workers (another author will give me occasion to come back to this point), there is indeed plenty of reason to be afraid. Fortunately, the equation of Soviet society with the future requires a violent mental somersault, which there is no need for us to imitate.

But what about the practical achievement, the works of history *in concreto*? Sidorov follows up his theoretical introduction with an enumeration of what is being done in Russia in the field of historical study. Judged by the numbers of research workers and the variety of their subjects, an impressive show of arms. The proclaiming of generalities is not all; historical sources are being ransacked, and no doubt much of that technical work will be useful. Nevertheless it does remain subordinated to the preoccupations, to the *idées fixes*, of the system—that this is so, Sidorov affirms with pride at every turn. But, as a matter of fact, we were put in a position to form our own judgment at leisure. One morning it was announced that in Room Thirteen Soviet Russian historical literature was obtainable, and I managed to get hold of some eight booklets, in Russian, with translations into one of the Western languages (Sidorov's paper was among the lot, with translations into all three). Of the rest I only mention Khvostov on the Franco-Russian alliance of 1891, Nikonov on the origins of the second world war, Stepanowa and Lewiowa on the struggle for a united Germany in 1848 and 1849, Volgin on humanism and socialism.

Here, then, Soviet historiography shows the West what it can do, and it is a pitiable exhibition. How frightful is the superficiality, and at times, downright falsification resulting from that dogmatism, that wilful one-sidedness, that parrot-like repetition of the same formulas all over again!

Take for example Nikonov. He begins (as they all do) with a grandiloquent proclamation of theory. The origins of wars can only be ascertained correctly and scientifically (how fond they all are of the word "scientific"!) by a veracious analysis of concrete historical facts. Fine! Who would not applaud so virtuous a statement! But wait a moment. The field on which "science" is to operate is at once drastically restricted. To begin with, the attempt to explain wars by man's biological or psychological make-up is not allowed to pass for "scientific." It amounts to "calumniating mankind." To represent kings or rulers as responsible for the outbreak of wars, too, is to indulge in a fable from the unscientific phase of historiography. Chance is ruled out: to admit it into the picture would amount to rejecting history as a science. In order to be scientific one has to believe in the goodness of human nature, in mass movements as the true motive forces of history, in the obedience of those movements and consequently of history to laws, and in a few more axioms. Accept them, and you will *know*. In a tone of triumph Nikonov assures us:

> Modern historiography investigates all historical phenomena, wars included, in their organic connection with the concrete socio-economic conditions of the development of society, [and thus] determines and discloses the objective laws of the historical process. History has become a systematized science. . . . Modern progressive historical science, and Soviet historiography particularly, proceeds from the fact that every war is the result of preceding economic and political development, the result of the home and foreign policy of the respective classes and states.[2]

And he goes on once more to reject specifically every explanation based on fortuitous circumstances of a phenomenon so patently "law-governed" as war.

In the whole of this passage one detects a polemical undertone against Western historians, not mentioned by name, but in the aggregate untouched by grace and unenlightened. The implied criticisms are, to begin with, unfair. There are few of us who will try to explain everything by man's corrupted nature, or by the ambition and lust for conquest of rulers, or by chance; there are few also who will not include in their argument "the concrete socio-economic conditions of the development of society." The only thing is that Western historians—or had not I better say "good historians"?—will not take the all-too-easy way of confining their attention to one order of factors. They will as a rule offer pluricausal explanations. Factors of a spiritual nature will not be left out of account, and although ideas at times seem to us to be a

[2] I quote from the official English version.

reflection of social or economic conditions, we shall recognize in them a vital principle of their own, one capable of overcoming such conditions. To strike a balance between factors belonging to different orders is indeed our insuperable difficulty. And so, we are often led, not, as Pankratova blames the writers of the American report of 1946 for being led, to the verdict that history is *unknowable*, but indeed to the admission that in the final, all-embracing judgment there will necessarily remain a quantum of arbitrariness. This modesty might more justly be called scientific, while Nikonov's crude one-sidedness and his boast that he and his party have mastered the laws of that immense happening of mankind's life on earth strike me as in the deepest sense unscientific and unhistoric.

But indeed, Nikonov's essay, following upon his pompous introduction, has no other purpose than to lay the responsibility for the second world war on the shoulders of "the reactionary politicians" of the West. Everybody knows—and disagreeable truths of this description can be safely uttered on this side of the Iron Curtain—that Neville Chamberlain, supported by considerable conservative groups in England and France, carried on a very questionable policy, at the back of which fear and distrust of Soviet Russia were undeniably present. To suggest that the ruling circles in England, France, and the United States, driven by their capitalistic interests, "were unwilling to halt the impending world war" is nonetheless a monstrous distortion of what actually happened. How recklessly Nikonov can let his preconceived notions prevail over "concrete facts" appears when he writes that the Munich agreement was greeted with indignation "in the democratic circles of the various countries." Take England. Who was more indignant than Winston Churchill, Leo Amery, Duff Cooper?—to each of whom, in Nikonov's terminology, the description "reactionary politician" would apply. "The peoples," so he goes on, undaunted, "realized that the deal with the aggressors at the expense of Czechoslovakia was fraught with the gravest consequences to peace." "The peoples" indeed! the masses, that deified figure in the theory of Communism (*only* in its theory, however)—what was more striking in those tragic days of 1938 than the naïve enthusiasm with which the peoples everywhere acclaimed Chamberlain as the saviour of peace!

But the reactionaries, the capitalists, *must* be the guilty ones, and to the exclusion of the rest. Granted that fear and distrust of Russia had an unfortunate effect in the critical days of the summer of 1939. But in every "scientific," or more simply, honest discussion of the crisis the fact will have to be recalled that there were only-too-real grounds for that fear and that distrust. Those feelings were alive particularly in Russia's unhappy neighbouring countries, which have since been conquered and assimilated; and this constituted for the leaders of the West an objective obstacle (apart from personal sentiments or prejudices) to a consistent and straight-lined course of policy.

But to admit this extenuating circumstance on behalf of the West would amount to allotting to Russia at least a share in the responsibility. Now this can never be allowed. Over against the guilty West, Russia must appear in pure nobility. The Nazi-Soviet non-aggression pact of August 1939 is therefore represented as an act of self-defence which was forced upon Russia. In order to stifle all objections to that interpretation (which is at best a half-truth), Nikonov has been careful to avoid all recognition of the altogether exceptional, the lawless and inhuman, character of the Hitler regime. To him it is merely a variant of the capitalist system. He never notices the essential difference between National Socialism and the political and social conditions prevailing in west European countries.

Only a man caught in a system that turns a blind eye on the pluriform reality of peoples and of individuals can write like this. But there is more. This system compels its adherents to defend through thick and thin the rulers who profess it, or make use of it. "Science" has nothing to do with this. What goes to shape the picture is really not even the system; it is, clothed in Marxist formulas, an intention that is purely tactical. It is the determination always to appear to be, and always to have been, right; and to supply to the Kremlin—

whether smiling or frowning—what it needs in its struggle
with the West.

The tactical intention is transparent, and it becomes even
more so when in another one of these Soviet historical booklets
we find the Franco-Russian alliance of 1891 discussed in a
surprisingly different tone. Czarism and the French Republic
of those days were of course capitalistic powers of the deepest
dye. In spite of this, Khvostov sees in their alliance the illustration of a constant historic truth, namely, that "the peoples"
of France and of Russia need each other against the menace of
German militarism; both are aware of this, and each cherishes
for the other "ineffaceable sentiments of sympathy."

It is no accident that the language into which Khvostov's
essay was translated is French. The author conceived it with
an eye to the anti-German feelings and the fears still present
in French opinion, feelings and fears to which, when it suits
them, the French Communists also appeal. A Marxist confession of faith is not lacking—practically all these writers on
special topics feel bound to begin with one. "The school of
historians to which I belong," says Khvostov, "the Marxist,
takes for a starting point the fact that in the transition from the
nineteenth to the twentieth century, capitalism was entering
upon its last stage, that of imperialism." And again: "The
Marxist historian starts from the fact that under capitalism the
various countries go through unequal stages of development."
This latter thesis, which is taken straight from Marx (as is the
earlier one), has to do service in the whole of this literature to
smooth out such obstacles as the system may encounter. But
in Khvostov's argument the categories of Marxism—the
production process as the determinant of events, the class
struggle, the inevitable selfdestruction of the capitalist system
—seem to have receded to the background altogether. The
essay is a piece of national propaganda and nothing else.

These tactical manoeuvres[3] are facilitated by the confusion
of thought which Marxist determinism has engendered in

[3] Signalized by Dr. R. van 't Reve in his little book *Sovjet-Annexatie
der klassieken*. His observation of these manoeuvres in the field of literary
criticism is a help towards understanding what goes on in historiography.

Russian heads. Determinism will not work in human relationships,[4] and so its adherents are forced to use subterfuges in
order to maintain it in theory while evading it in practice.

When, for instance, the ladies Stepanowa and Lewiowa deal
with the German revolution of 1848, they indulge in vehement
exclamations against "the treason" of the liberal middle-class
and against "the cowardice and indecision" of the lower-
middle-class democrats, who refused to be dragged along by
the socialist revolutionaries. It is very questionable, so it seems
to me, whether at that juncture the social revolution ever stood
a chance against the conservative forces entrenched in the old
dynastic states. I am quite ready to admit that the dissensions
breaking out between the three oppositional groups hastened
its failure. But do not the Marxists themselves hold that these
dissensions were determined? Why then these words heavily
laden with moral reproach? It is not even necessary to think
in the strict terms of materialistic determination to realize that
the liberal middle-class and the smaller bourgeoisie acted in
accordance with class convictions. If the story of 1848 and
1849 is told so as to make it appear that "the people," in the
Marxist sense, would have been able to dominate the German
revolution and that on the other groups rested the moral
obligation to admit this and to follow in the people's track,
clearly something from the historian's own philosophy is
forcibly imposed upon a period to which it is in fact alien. This
is a completely unhistorical way of proceeding—always to
approach the past with that one query and to overlook the
problems as they presented themselves to the contemporary
generation in their own rich setting of ideas and strivings.

But the Soviet historians are on the watch all the time—they
say so themselves every now and again, and several of these
publications deal with nothing else—for popular movements,
popular revolts, revolutions: these in their eyes constitute the
real, the beneficent motive power in history. Every expression
of doubt as to the people's capacity to govern is to the Soviet
historians an attack on what they consider to be an eternal
truth. Sidorov says this in so many words when Mignet writes

[4] As Isaiah Berlin remarks in his little book *Historical Inevitability.*

in this way about the years of the French Revolution. Similarly, according to Stepanowa and Lewiowa, in 1848, only Marx and Engels saw matters in their true light—and this not only for the future, but for the actual historical moment itself. How much more natural, however, is the traditional view that, given the entire course of events, these two men badly misjudged the situation and that, moreover, if 1848 made anything clear, it was the prematureness of an attempt to let "the people" govern.

But even as regards the future! We heard Madame Pankratova exult in the liberation of the masses. Volgin quotes, with a reverence hardly less than would be due to Lenin, a dictum of that other great doctor, Stalin: "What is the essential feature and the effect of the fundamental economic law of socialism? It is to assure the maximum satisfaction of the ever-growing material needs of society, by continually increasing and perfecting socialistic production on the basis of a superior technique." And Volgin adds, proudly, that in this formula no mere utopian society is sketched any longer. "The realization of the elevated humanitarian aims posed by it is assured by the fundamental principles of the Constitution of an actually existing socialist state, the U.S.S.R."[5]

What beautiful reading is made by the passages that Volgin goes on to quote—and what a gap between them and the reality of life as lived by Soviet man! In no case does the gap yawn more widely than where clause 123 seems to suggest that it is "the people" that governs. Regarded "objectively" and "scientifically," developments in Russia since 1917 would

[5] This is according to precept. To utter doubt with respect to the actual existence of the socialist society would be an unforgivable heresy. On October 9, 1955, after this article had been written, I read in the newspapers that Molotov had made a bad *faux pas* by stating in a speech that "in the Soviet Union the *foundations* of a socialist society are already in existence." In a letter to the periodical *The Communist* Molotov has since confessed to having committed "a theoretical error": the nineteenth Party Congress had found that the party had already succeeded in building up a socialist society; that all that remained to be done was "to build up a communist society by way of a gradual transition from socialism to communism."

almost seem to confirm the opinion of that "backward," if not "reactionary," Mignet, who wrote over a century ago that "the people" is not capable of governing. For is it not the fact that the masses in Russia *are* governed, and with a heavy hand, by a group, or a clique, asserting that they are called to carry out what will redound to the masses' well-being and what they *ought to* want—what indeed has been hammered into their heads as their salvation and their dearest wish for so long now that perhaps they hardly know any better?

And are Soviet cultural needs really being satisfied? One shudders when one reads Sidorov triumphantly citing the printings of historical textbooks. There are those that run to 15,500,000, to 18,600,000, copies. All, we may assume, composed on patterns designed by these masters. Brainwashing on a gigantic scale! One can hardly expect the masses to be able to resist so well organized a "satisfaction of their cultural needs." But may we not hope that among Russian intellectuals, the intellectuals of a nation that not longer than a few generations ago produced so rich a literature, so humane, so open to all problems—that among them doubts will occasionally stir? One really does not need to have been schooled in historical method to be struck by the crooked logic, the contradictions, and the dull, lifeless colouring, the poor quality, of this kind of history writing.

A few opinionated intellectuals will not bring about a revolution, I know. But I believe that they can keep a spark aglow, from which, under a favouring constellation, and after a development the "laws" of which I shall not presume to guess at—let alone to lay down—a beneficent fire might be kindled.

I believe it. Indeed, I, too, have a faith. Not a faith in Marx or any other prophet; not a faith, either, in historic materialism or any other system. But a faith in life, a faith in the human spirit.

(1955)

POSTSCRIPT

At the Twentieth Party Congress, held in Moscow in March 1956, Mr. Khrushchev delivered his famous speech revealing the tyrannical character of Stalin and his regime. One would expect that this must have given Soviet historians furiously to think. Had they not been taught to regard Stalin as a doctrinal guide no less authoritative and reliable than Lenin? But indeed, at the same Congress, Mr. Mikoyan said in so many words that the history of the October Revolution and of the Communist party had been misrepresented, not by "reactionary," "bourgeois" historians of the West, but, under the influence of Stalin, by Soviet historians themselves.

These same men whom I had heard lecturing us on our "unscientific" methods, and telling us with inimitable self-assurance how we should go about things, were thus, on coming home, reproved by a politician who may not be a historian but whose authority to decide what is orthodox and what heretical history they will not for a moment dare to dispute. They were reproved, and at the same time instructed to present the party and the government with more acceptable history. One can imagine them writing away laboriously in a feverish attempt to obey orders.

A very unsettling experience, one would think, and it must have added to the trials of these unfortunate men that the mood of the Kremlin has kept going through dizzying changes since. Is it possible that they remain unshaken in the belief that Communism knows the answers to all the riddles of history? I am afraid that they will go on docilely convincing themselves that every new version is, no less than was the previous one, in strict conformity with the precepts of historic materialism, that is, of *Science*.

(1959)

6. Toynbee's Answer

Arnold Toynbee has surprised us all by laying yet another big book before us, in which, presenting it as the twelfth volume of his *Study of History*, he sets out to meet the criticisms levelled at that great work. In a footnote to his Introduction he refers to a passage in my review of his volumes VII to X, in which I observe that he never answers and is not likely now ever to answer.[1] He is no historian, I said, but a prophet, and prophets do not answer. "I take this argument of Geyl's to hold good in reverse," so Toynbee now remarks. "In this volume I *have* replied to my critics; therefore I cannot be a prophet after all."

Let us see.

No doubt the book is another impressive achievement. 674 pages. Some 170 critics are listed and observations made by every one of them quoted and discussed in the text or in footnotes. All this in the course of arguments which often sweep far beyond them and which, after all that was already to be found in vols. IX and X, again build up an explanatory comment on the work as a whole, on its method and on its tendency. Explanatory, and naturally enough most of the time apologetic—although the fact that the four volumes of 1954 were conceived in a spirit differing essentially from the pre-war six leaves the author unworried.

Indeed, Toynbee was quite frank about that at the time. In the years between vol. VI and vol. VII he had been converted to a new religious conviction with which went a new vision. He now says that in the system of civilizations such as he had

---

[1] *Debates with Historians* pp. 207-8. (I quote from the Fontana Library edition, London, 1962.)

established it in the six volumes he must acknowledge his then sceptical attitude towards religion as one of the determining factors. I must admit that I had not noticed any scepticism in those early volumes, and although Toynbee quotes one or two critics who had pointed it out even before the appearance of the sequel, I am still puzzled by his assertion. Not that I was not struck as every reader of vols. VII to X must have been by the shift of mental attitude and consequently of interpretation that had taken place between 1939 and 1954. The crucial problem was how to understand the relationship between religion and civilization and only in the later part of the work was the first place indisputably assigned to religion—nor was it the Christian religion any longer.

A momentous change of front undeniably. To me it even seemed as if the whole of that empirical investigation, in which in the pre-war volumes it was claimed that the laws governing the historic life of mankind had been revealed was now unceremoniously pushed on one side by the author himself. He, however, did not draw that conclusion; and now again, with all the adaptations, in spite even of explicit admissions of having been wrong and concessions to criticisms on specific points, the rest of his theses and his method are in the main and in all essentials maintained.

It is the same Toynbee who is here holding forth. The capacity for labour and the mental energy, the learning also, rouse the familiar feelings of awe. The amplitude of the manner asks for powers of endurance as before. One stands amazed at the variety of facts and arguments that he drags in. Again one hesitates between impatience and admiration. Admiration, yes—for the insatiable zest, for instance, with which he connects his expositions with problems in the spheres of sociology, philosophy, theory of history. The tone is mild. Those poor, short-sighted Western historians, imprisoned in their technique, who were executed so unmercifully in vol. IX, are now, even when they have not spared him the severest strictures, dealt with quite charitably; although, naturally, their shortcomings are still remembered. And even Western civilization itself, the butt of so much animosity some years ago, receives from time to time a few kind words, in between the depreciations—for in fact, here too, there is no essential change.

But another question has to be faced. Has the criticism been, I shall not say, refuted, but has it been answered? I feel, on the whole—no.

I cannot dream of dealing exhaustively with this full, rich book, humming with problems. I must make a selection, and it is obvious that I should ask, first of all: how have *I* been answered? If it needs an excuse that I should allow myself to be guided mainly by this personal curiosity, I can observe that the points against which my earlier criticisms were directed are indeed points of fundamental importance. Many others have in fact occupied themselves with them, and their arguments, as I now find them quoted by Toynbee, have often not only confirmed my own views, but have sometimes deepened my understanding of them through lucid expression or in other ways.

I

First of all then—I have always placed this in the forefront—this empiricism, which has always seemed to me a mere disguise of his apriorism. In all stages of the life of civilizations, in their origin, their growth, their break-down and after that their generations-long disintegration ending in their dissolution, he discerns forms appearing regularly in accordance with what he sometimes proclaims to be laws. Those phrases of his, as challenge and response, withdrawal and return, the nemesis of creativity, do at times correspond with realities of historic life; they do make an appeal, they can stimulate the imagination. It is especially the attempt to systematize them and to subject to them the whole process of civilization which invites criticism. The examples he adduces, taken from all countries and from all centuries, would not, in the face of the immense multiplicity of mankind's unruly history, prove much if they were stated correctly. Of several I have somewhat elaborately demonstrated that they are fallacious, that violence has been done to the realities of history in order to make them confirm the imaginative formula or law.

It was these passages to which I drew Toynbee's attention when in '55 I challenged him to *reply*, instead of, as he had done in his vol. IX, to decry Western historians wholesale as industrious delvers in their little professional plots. Let him prove that, for instance, his reading of nineteenth-century Italian history, which according to my demonstration[2] did not warrant the conclusions he built upon it—in connection with the nemesis of creativity—was right after all; or to do the same for his reading of North American history, which I argued was hopelessly wrong[3], so that his laws and large theories—in connection with challenge and return—fall to the ground. But, so I went on: Prophets won't take the trouble to show that their critics are wrong.

And indeed, with regard to his fantastic Italian and North-American history Toynbee preserves silence, even now. I had also criticized,[4] with valid arguments, his exposition of the rise of Holland—this, too, in connection with challenge and response—and his excursion about English history,[5] according to which England has spent the period of 1558 to 1914 in "withdrawal", only to "return" the more forcibly.

On this last point alone do I get a reaction.

"Geyl's criticisms of my account of English history are telling, besides being witty. They prove me wrong on a number of incidental points, but, as far as I can see, they leave my thesis still standing. With Geyl's aid to help me steer clear of some pitfalls into which I have stumbled at my first attempt, I believe I could produce a revised version of my thesis that would be acceptable to Geyl himself."

How charming! One feels a little reluctant to have to state that one is not yet satisfied. But really, the points were more than "incidental" and the entire thesis rests on nothing. The answer, in other words, is no answer.

On specific objections, then, even when he mentions them, Toynbee remains in default. But he fills pages[6] with quotations

---

[2] *Op. Cit.*, 137-40. [3] *Op. Cit.*, 177-82. [4] *Op. Cit.*, 121-2. [5] *Op. Cit.*, 131-2.
[6] Vol. XII, 41-7.

from a variety of authors, which, looked at a little closely, are not always relevant, in order to confirm the usefulness of theories which can be confronted with the facts only afterwards. But who will doubt this? Toynbee often represents his adversaries as being more naïve than they really are; after which he can deal with them the more easily.

Several critics have taken him to task for taking episodes out of their context, with the result that their significance is distorted. Thereupon he sets up an argument to the effect that this consequence of distortion is less likely to happen in his case than in that of many other present-day historians. For is not he trying to view Reality as a whole?—well knowing, alas, that "it is a grievous limitation and a radical defect of the human intellect that it is incapable of apprehending Reality as a whole". . . . In any case, "the charge of denaturing Reality by taking episodes out of their context" must, "I should have thought, hit with considerably greater force the school of specialists which is the predominant school among present-day Western historians."[7] He only betrays here his habit of overlooking the reality of smaller contexts—not only national, but local, limited in time, episodic.

Similarly, "the charge that my citation of examples is selective has to be dropped, because it applies, not just to me, but to everyone who tries to test a theory." This is again evading the real problem, which is one of observing a measure, of keeping a balance. The actual charge is that Toynbee passes by all too light-heartedly the multitude of phenomena of a different tendency which will not fit into his system. This was the trend of all my four expositions mentioned above, which surely might have been rebutted before we are invited to drop the charge.

Toynbee denies in so many words that he can be described as "schema-bound". He declares himself to be "ready at any time to modify or abandon any of my hypotheses if I am given convincing reasons." As a matter of fact he does so a number of times in the course of his survey, mostly in connection with the origins of later configurations of the Asiatic civilizations.

[7] Vol. xii, 248.

There he is apt to go into typically professional or technical considerations. Generally only smaller aspects of his great system are here involved and the main lines remain untouched. In one chapter, nevertheless, the debate goes a little deeper. Toynbee there deals with the criticism of the English geographer Spate, at present professor at the National University at Canberra. Even though he considers it unfounded in one particular, it has, so he declares, set him thinking and he admits:

> that, when we are reasoning in terms, not of abstractions, but of phenomena, we are never in a position to guarantee that we have succeeded in insulating the relevant points, all of these, and nothing but these, and are consequently never in a position to guarantee that the entities which we are bringing into comparison are properly comparable for the purpose of our investigation . . . However far we may succeed in going in our search for sets of identical examples on either side, we shall never be able to prove that there is not some non-identical factor that we have overlooked, and that this non-identical factor is not the decisive factor that accounts for the different outcomes in different cases of what has looked to us like an identical situation but may not have been this in truth. [8]

He then quotes from a letter Gilbert Murray wrote to him thirty years ago after reading his first volume in typescript a passage of similar tendency and admits that he might at that time have given it more attention. He would not then "have offered so vulnerable a target for Spate's shot-gun."

Does he realize that in these admissions the condemnation of his great work is implied? Does he renounce it—as indeed he implicitly renounced the first six volumes with the change of front revealed in the next four? Not really. In the conclusion of this same chapter he comforts himself with the reflection that in human affairs mathematical certainty is after all not attainable.

[8] Vol. XII, 325-6.

"Our understanding of what lies behind and beyond the phenomena may however be valuably increased by conclusions that get no farther than being probable, or even than being no more than possible, approximations to the truth."

To me, who have described history as "an argument without end," [9] this sounds acceptable enough, and indeed among those who practise the sciences of man it is a fairly commonly held opinion. Only—when one recalls to one's mind the positive tone of the great work; the triumphant conclusions following upon historical expositions so frequently incomplete, tendentious, untenable; the self-assured boasting about "our now well-tried empirical method"; those extraordinary tables also, which caused me and other critics to exclaim: one feels that in this way that approach to truth, that argument, is not very effectively served, or even, is not served. And indeed, it was not the boldness of the imagination, of the theorising, of the comparisons, of the suggested lines of human development, that aroused criticism; it was the weakness of the factual foundation, the frivolity of the conclusions; coupled as it all was with the pretence of a strictly logical proceeding from proof to proof resting on observation.

When I say "pretence", I do not, of course, mean that I imagine Toynbee is purposely deceiving his readers. He himself indignantly rejects the suspicion as if he had ever consciously made selections to suit his purpose, and, he adds, "I doubt whether any other scholar ever has either." I agree. Even the most passionately partial historian, wildly misrepresenting the facts, will rarely, if ever, be consciously deceiving his readers. All he will do, and nothing is more human, is to let his mind be controlled by his constructive imagination, by his zeal for a great or for a new idea. The phenomenon, no doubt, common as it may be, is remarkable in the case of Toynbee, because he disposes at the same time of so subtle a critical capacity. But when one sees how it can be silenced by his creative urge, the explanation of bad faith would testify to a sad deficiency of psychological insight.

[9] *Napoleon For and Against* (English translation 1949), p., 16.

All these virtuous declarations, too, which one meets so frequently in the new book and with which his critics can so cordially agree, Toynbee means them sincerely, I have no doubt. Their very frequency is to me an indication that the—indeed severe—criticisms of the professional historians have not left him unshocked. Yet when in a paragraph especially devoted to the conception of "facts" in history he has to deal with observations made by Ernest Barker and myself, the reflections into which he wanders off are less "virtuous"; he now seems to be out, rather, to rule out of court as narrow minds, imprisoned in the immediately observable, those who want to correct him on facts. (This character of the professional historian was known to us already from his somewhat irritable polemics with the *genus* in vol. IX.)

From one of my articles he quotes: "The facts are there to be used"; then: Toynbee's facts "are not facts, they are subjective presentations of facts." From which he goes on to deduce that in my view "the authentic historian is a collector. He is like a man scrambling up a torrent bed picking up, on his way, the boulders that he finds deposited there."[10] No, Toynbee continues: "Facts are not really like boulders that have been detached and shaped and deposited exclusively by the play of the forces of non-human nature." After which he quotes against me, for instance, from the 1954 *Report* of the Social Science Research Council's Committee on Historiography (N.Y.) the following: "Facts do not speak for themselves";—"The criterion of selection is not inherent in the data; it is applied by the historian." Sentiments with which I wholeheartedly agree and which I have voiced myself in similar statements on more than one occasion. Indeed, when I said "The facts are there to be used," I meant exactly this, and in case the sentence by itself does not make this clear, let me here insert the passage from which Toynbee took it:

> I don't mean that the historian should (as he is sometimes advised) stick to the facts. The facts are there to be used. Combinations, presentations, theories, are indispensable

[10] Vol. XII, 229.

if we want to understand. But the historian should proceed
cautiously in using the facts for these purposes . . . he should
remain conscious . . . of the element of arbitrariness, of
subjectivity, that necessarily enters into all combinations
of facts, if only because one has to begin by selecting them;
while next, one has to order them according to an idea
which must, in part at least, be conceived in one's own
mind."[11]

Indeed I am far from being the collector of facts, assembling
them haphazardly and passively accepting them, such as
Toynbee pictures me. That is not to say that I can go along
with him when, continuing his argument, he makes facts
dependent on the hypothesis which has "engendered" them.
A statement, this, which makes a far from "virtuous" impression. It would seem very difficult to square with the following
observation made by Bagby:

We shall only be able to judge our scheme when we have
applied it to the actual facts of history.[12]

Yet Toynbee expresses his complete agreement with Bagby's
view, so that now, for a change, he accepts the independent
existence of these "actual facts".

The contradictions into which he allows his defensive
position to force him would have a dizzying effect if one did
not get used to them. He devotes an entire chapter (13 pages)
to "The Issue between Trans-Rationalists and Rationalists."
If one remembers the bitterness with which in his earlier
volumes he pictured the "neo-paganists" as the underminers
of our civilization, one is surprised to see him now exerting
himself to advocate a truce, or a compromise, between those
two groups. He uses clear language, nevertheless, when he
says: "I am now more alive than I once was to the limitations
of the human reasoning powers."[13] The definition of rationalism which he gives in a later section is: "a belief in the

[11] *Debates with Historians*, 166-7.   [12] Vol. xii, 166, footnote 1.
[13] *Op. Cit.*, 75.

human intellect's capacity to apprehend Reality."[14] Here,[15] curiously enough, he had, in a footnote, given that same definition, but with the additional words: "to some extent"; which really makes an enormous difference. In the radio debate I had with him in January 1948, and this is even more curious, Toynbee had ranged himself against me with those extreme rationalists of his second definition in the present volume. He reproached me with having too little confidence in the human mind because I had argued that it was incapable of embracing the multiplicity of historic phenomena with sufficient certainty to order them in so ambitious a system as his own.

Is history really too hard a nut for science to crack? When the human intellect has wrested her secret from physical nature, are we going to sit down under an *ex cathedra* dictum that the ambition to discover the secret of human history will always be bound to end in disappointment?"[16]

This sounds rather differently from what we hear from him now. Must we conclude that this turning away from rationalism took place only after January 1948? But even more extraordinary is it to find him expressing agreement with a statement of Dawson's, according to whom human history "is impatient of the neat system of laws and causal sequences for which the rationalist is always looking, and that the mysterious and unpredictable aspect of history is a genuine and immovable stumbling-block for him." For the rationalist! System-building now is, apparently, a rationalistic vice. Or rather, it is a vice to which rationalists are given. Where, then, does Arnold Toynbee stand?

The pattern of his own mental attitude is not, when one hears these various statements, becoming any more systematic. In so far, however, has he I think remained true to himself that, differing in this from many rationalists (if this word must do service), he cannot humbly be content with uncertainty. Here is the origin of his patent confusion. His heart drives

[14] *Op. Cit.*, 313   [15] *Op. Cit.*, 72, footnote 3.
[16] *The Pattern of the Past* (Boston, 1959), 80.

him to triumph, no matter how, over our incompetence and over the facts. Our incompetence which irks him so much: we heard him lament our "grievous limitations" in this respect[17]. He is unable to accept our humanity such as we are born to it.

II

Stuart Hughes is, I think, justified in counting Toynbee among "the new Spenglerians".[18] But however strongly he may have been influenced by the German prophet of doom, not only does Toynbee speak from a profoundly differing philosophy of life (averse to violence as against adoring violence), he has, deliberately and strongly, reacted against the method. Of this his attempt to work not by intuition only but empirically was the first consequence, and he appeals frequently to this characteristic of his investigation in order to mark the distinction between Spengler and himself. I stick to my opinion that his empiricism is largely outward appearance. Another point on which he repeatedly expresses dissent from Spengler is that of the latter's identification of civilizations with organisms, of which the individual human beings are but parts. In his third volume already, for instance, he opposes to Spengler's view his own ("the empiricist's"), according to which "a civilization is . . . a dynamic process or movement or *élan*."[19] The rejection of Spengler's determinism, of his *saeva necessitas* of dissolution, follows as a matter of course, and indeed Toynbee does express his disagreement from this philosophy at length and emphatically.

But does not the entire system as he unfolds it in *A Study of History* conflict with these assertions of principle? Those laws by which according to him the development of civilizations is governed, that fixed order of stages through which they all have to go (albeit each in a tempo of its own)—can these conceptions be applied to anything but to Spengler's organisms? And as regards the *saeva necessitas*, it is true that Toynbee

[17] Cf. Above, p. 8.   [18] *Oswald Spengler* (1952), 137.
[19] Vol. III, 383.

does not pronounce an unconditional sentence of death on our Western civilization, the only one of his twenty or thirty which is still showing signs of life. But in his schema he had observed as following upon a "breakdown" that long-drawn-out period of "disintegration" (which I confess that, after all his expositions presented with breathless conviction and staggering erudition, I cannot discern as anything so distinct or so regular); and during all those many years "the leaders of the stricken civilization are unable to meet challenges successfully: they can at best obtain a respite, but after every crisis the situation re-emerges, worse than it was before, and in the end the dissolution of the broken-down civilization cannot be averted."[20]—"Now I submit"—so I wrote ten years ago already[21]—"that it is small use telling us you are a believer in man's free will and particularly in the freedom of human beings composing a civilization to respond to challenges when in fact you make an exception for this protracted period of disintegration."

And indeed, in the conclusion of his sixth volume Toynbee had written that the "element of uniformity in the rhythm of the disintegration process", as shown by an investigation of the history of civilizations, was "apparently so definite and so constant" that "we have almost ventured to cast the horoscope of one civilization that is still alive and on the move."— He means ours. The forecast to which he alludes could not have been anything but dissolution. He had suggested all along that Western civilization had suffered its breakdown as early as the sixteenth century, since which time we find ourselves in the disintegration stage, and of this his system knows but that single, tragic ending. However, he had only *suggested;* also, he had *almost* ventured. This latter term of caution means no more—he says so explicitly enough—than that only one chance remains to us, that of the miracle of a return to the faith we have so disastrously abandoned. I reminded him of all this in our radio debate in January 1948.

[20] This is my own summary of Toynbee's system: *Debates with Historians*, p. 157-8.
[21] Immediately after the fore-going "summary".

In his reply Toynbee reproved me for mistaking for gloom his courage to acknowledge our danger and for seeking shelter in an illusionist optimism while shutting my ears to the call for action.[22] To which I, in my turn:

"Have I been saying that we are not in danger? And that no action is required? What I have said is that Toynbee's system induces the wrong kind of gloom because it makes action seem useless." Had he not spoken slightingly of "our hotly canvassed and loudly advertised political and economic maladies"? To the loss of religion alone our precarious position was due, and so there was one way towards salvation left: "allowing ourselves to be reconverted to the faith of our fathers." And here Toynbee exclaims: 'You see, I'm not so gloomy after all.' Perhaps not. But if one happens to hold a different opinion both of the efficacy and of the likelihood of application of his particular remedy, one cannot help thinking that he is but offering us cold comfort . . . To most of us this is indeed condemning all our efforts to futility."

On this occasion Toynbee said only, but this quite positively: "I don't believe history can be used for telling the world's fortune." The awful warning of Spengler's dogmatic determinism had made him, so he said, extra cautious. When I thereupon recalled again the tendency of his system, giving expression to my relief that he was not yet sentencing us to death, he said, a little shortly:

"No, I think we simply don't know, I suppose I must be the last judge of what my own beliefs are."

Need I explain that this reply did not set my mind at rest? I was left with the unsolved contradiction between those repeated asseverations and the none the less clear implications of what he had written. And now his new big volume does not carry me any further.

He now invites me to quote the passage where he speaks of his investigations as undertaken in order to forecast our future. I recalled a moment ago his *almost* drawing the horoscope.[23]

---

[22] *The Pattern of the Past*, 83.

[23] Prof. H. Kraemer drew my attention to *Civilization on Trial*, 1948, on what the world will be in 2047, 3047, 4047.

I add, from that same conclusion of his analysis of the disintegration process, the very last paragraph, where he leaves no doubt as to his being practically certain that we find ourselves in that stage. Even so, "we cannot say for certain that our doom is at hand, and yet we have no warrant that it is not; for that would be to assume that we are not as other men are." (So certain is he of the validity of the comparison he has drawn up with other civilizations overtaken by disaster as the conclusion of their disintegration.) "But there still is the divine mercy. We may and must pray that a reprieve which God has granted to our society once will not be refused if we ask for it again in a contrite spirit and with a broken heart."

Is he leaving our will free in this passage? He leaves us free to be converted, but for nothing else.

I am reminded of what Isaiah Berlin wrote, in 1954, in his little book on *Historical Inevitability*. He there surveys the numerous opinions, widely differing among themselves, but alike in holding that human behaviour is governed "by factors largely beyond the control of individuals," as for instance "by the 'natural' growth of some larger unit—a race, a nation, a class; or by some entity conceived in even less empirical terms: a 'spiritual organism', a religion, a civilization, a Hegelian (or Buddhist) World Spirit; entities whose career or manifestations on earth are the object either of empirical or of metaphysical inquiries—depending on the cosmological outlook of particular thinkers . . . It is true," Berlin adds, "that the more cautious and clear-headed among such theorists try to meet the objections of empirically minded critics by adding in a footnote, or as an afterthought, that, whatever their terminology, they are on no account to be taken to believe that there literally exist such creatures as civilizations or races or spirits of nations living side by side with the individuals who compose them; that they fully realize that all institutions 'in the last analysis' consist of individual men and women and are not themselves personalities, but only convenient devices—idealised models, or labels, or metaphors . . . Nevertheless these protestations too often turn out to be mere lip-service to principles which

E.H.   K those who profess them do not really believe." And among the writers of this category he also mentions—"somewhat hesitantly"—Toynbee. I can understand that hesitation in the light of these deprecating assurances repeated by Toynbee so frequently and so earnestly that one cannot help being impressed for a moment.

In his new volume he is even more lavish of assurances of this description. He quotes Bagby, for instance, a man of a totally different mental structure from his own and who is among his most outspoken critics, but for whom he testifies respect; he quotes from him the following: "Cultures do not do anything. Only people do things."[24]

And with this Toynbee now professes himself to be in agreement,—after ten volumes in which human beings are all the time depicted, reacting to challenges, no doubt, but nevertheless obediently moving in accordance with the general pattern of the history of civilizations from tabulated stage to stage, and during disintegration powerless, generation after generation, to find the right answer.

It is the practice, after all, that counts, and no wonder that the "virtuous" protestations have not restrained many writers from uttering criticism analogous to mine. Marrou, for instance:

"The twenty-one 'objects' of which his theory seeks to give an account are nothing but abstractions treated as realities (*réifiées*); this powerful effort embraces nothing but phantoms."[25]

Others have pointed out passages where civilizations are actually staged in the guise of human beings. Toynbee now advances an excuse for the anthropomorphic terminology he admits he has occasionally employed:

"With the vocabulary at our disposal, this is sometimes almost impossible to avoid." Is it indeed so harmless? I quote a passage from vol. I.[26] When explaining his projected study of "civilizations" he argues that the chapters in the history of one and the same society (i.e. civilization) resemble the succes-

[24] Vol. XII, 115.   [25] *Quoted, Op. Cit.*, 232.   [26] Vol. I, 44.

sive experiences of a single person; the "affiliations" and "apparentations" between one society and another resemble the relations between parent and child." He notes *a resemblance*; he does not *identify*. But one must also note that it cannot have been the limitations of our vocabulary that brought him to make that most dangerous comparison, which he goes on to elaborate.

Let me also recall a passage which I quoted in an earlier article of mine[27] and in which he, dealing with the territorial development of North America in the seventeenth and eighteenth centuries, shows the course of events being controlled by one of those entities which elicited the mockery of Isaiah Berlin: History (with a capital), or Clio. History "permits," History "re-asserts her ascendancy," History "keeps a watchful eye" or "indulges in a caprice," History "led the people of the U.S. to lose a desire."—"History, in short," so I remarked in my essay devoted to vols. VII-X, "exempts the historian from the trouble of looking for rational or factual explanations. It is obvious that rational or factual criticism can have no meaning for a man privileged to share the confidence of this selfwilled Muse and that no discussion with him is possible."

Toynbee has dozens of references to one or another of my critical reviews of his work, but of this passage he has taken no notice.

We saw that Western civilization, if we are to believe Toynbee, is in a bad way. I have more than once subjected this attitude of his to criticism—and I have found myself in good company.

I have observed, first of all, and described it as one of the most unmethodical features of his method, that he does not do justice to its composite character, in fact hardly, or never, discusses the problems involved. All through his work he adduces, in dealing with Western civilization, examples from the particular histories of the Western peoples as if Western civilization as a whole were thereby characterized. In that

---

[27] *Debates with Historians*, 207, footnote 23. The passage referred to occurs in vol. IX, 297-8.

way, so I said,[28] one can prove anything: some national variety will always present you with something, somewhere, that lends itself to support whichever argument you are conducting. In referring to my criticisms on this point, Toynbee passes by this last remark. But our sharpest conflict in this connection occurs when he rejects my contention that National Socialism cannot be regarded as a normal product of Western civilization.[29]

Fundamentally, this dispute is still connected with the difference of opinion about what a civilization—or what Western civilization—really is. Toynbee believes himself entitled to reproach me (and Hans Kohn, who had made similar comments) with lacking the courage to face painful but undeniable facts.[30] Our liberalism (Kohn's, Geyl's and his) is a product of Western civilization, but must not the same be said of those ideologies that are so abhorrent to us? Was not Hitler an Austrian—he says, surprisingly, "a Sudetenlander"—, Mussolini a Romagnol, Marx and Engels Rhinelanders, settled for a long time in England? Did not the Russians and Chinese get their Communism from the West?

In other words, all that is thought or done by Westerners, is characteristic of Western civilization; I should almost say that in Toynbee's historic imagination—in spite of his approval for Bagby's dictum—it is Western civilization that thinks it or does it. But if one really believes (this too we have heard him say) that Western civilization is no more than "a dynamic process, a movement, a striving"—I once put it: a struggle—, then one will not blindly stick this label on to everything. One will reflect, firstly, that the Communism of Marx and

---

[28] *Op. Cit.*, 153.

[29] I mention in passing that I blamed in particular "the demagogic manner" in which Toynbee in his Vol. VII, p. 305, writes as if the humane spirit of Frazer, as evidenced in the first decade of this century, had since been driven out by the racialist, demonic, violent spirit of Rosenberg. Is the spirit of Rosenberg now in the ascendant in the West? The suggestion is absurd. (*Debates with Historians*, 199.) This specific, and to my mind incontrovertible, point is not taken up by Toynbee.

[30] Vol. XII, 532.

Engels (whom in fact it shocks me in my historical sense to
see lumped together with Hitler and Mussolini)[31]—that it was
exactly in Russia and in China that their Communism
developed these barbarous tendencies. Secondly, that Mussolini in Italy and Hitler in Germany could come into power
only with the aid of exceptional political and economic circumstances which confused the masses and threw them off their
balance, and that their regimes were overthrown without
leaving any lasting impact on the cultural and political
mentality of their countries. They were barbarians, in revolt
against the best traditions of our part of the world. It is
undeniable that they made a shameless use of noble ideas
belonging to our heritage or falsified them for their purpose.
In the life of the spirit the greatest and most constructive
systems of thought bear within them the possibility of
perversion.

But how is it possible to overlook that the resistance—in
Toynbee's own England, in a country like Holland, overrun
and reduced to impotence—appealed to the true traditions of
Western civilization which the totalitarians despised and
rejected, and that it found them a source of moral strength?

In another passage, aimed at me particularly, Toynbee
asserts that the Nazi movement was a modern Western
phenomenon "that should have pricked the bubble of modern
Western complacency."[32] Again he indulges here in that not
very profitable debating style in which one starts with misrepresenting the adversary's position. "Self-complacency"?
At the moment a grim clinging to the conviction that we were
making a stand for the noblest part of our heritage; afterwards
a joyful realization of the fact that the storm had been overcome, even in the country where it had started. This is something very different from self-complacency and it is a good
deal better than the irresponsible statement that Toynbee

[31] In Somervell's abridged edition of the first six volumes there is an
even wilder jumble of the most heterogeneous names, put together for
an equally demagogic effect: "When Descartes and Voltaire and Marx
and Machiavelli and Hobbes and Hitler and Mussolini have done their
best to dechristianize our Western life . . ."; p. 401.

[32] Vol. xii, 628.

permitted himself in his vol. IX:[33] that Hitler had been right in thinking that "the World was ripe for conquest" and that we were saved only by "an accidental combination of incidental errors in the measures;" more, that, seeing "Mankind's patently increasing defeatism and submissiveness," "any future would-be world-conqueror" is not likely to be "so clumsy as to let the same easy prey escape for a second time."

In any case I know full well, as do all who live sincerely by our tradition, that the ideal of Western civilization we try to serve has not made angels of us. It is an aspiration, hallowed by the labours of many generations, even though they, too, have frequently gone off the track. It is an aspiration which has always been and is still exposed to reactions from inside. If these at times seem menacing, this must only incite us to be prepared and to persevere. At the time of the national-socialist aberration there were too many in my own country as well—I mention only Huizinga[34]—who treated us to gloomy admonitions as if the evil was in fact the culmination of a process of decay of which they imagined to detect the symptoms all around them. Toynbee now admits, in one of those apologetic concessions which drop from his pen so frequently in his new volume, that since he cried alarm (not against Hitler, but against ourselves), the menace has been warded off, and yet even now it suits him to dub "the cold-bloodedness and highpowered organisation" of the totalitarian movements "typically modern-Western."

III

Speaking about his method as I was still doing in the last paragraph, I had insensibly come to consider the spirit animating his work, his system, and his expectations of the future. And indeed, that spirit is largely responsible for the unhistorical features of his method.

Toynbee quotes my characterization of this spirit, written

[33] *Op. Cit.*, IX, 502. Cf. *Debates with Historians*, 190.

[34] See especially his *Shadows of Tomorrow*, 1935, about which see the essay "Huizinga as Accuser of his Age" on p. 188 of this volume.

in 1955: "His dream is the unity of mankind in the love of God. Or rather, his dream is to participate in that loving vision and see its approach and realization." Here is his comment: "I am grateful to Geyl for the insight with which he has perceived what I feel, and for the sympathy with which he has described it." I feel again some embarrassment in the face of so amiable an acknowledgment. Must I question the word *sympathy*? No, it is true that the grandeur of that vision and the sincerity of that surrender have to me a disarming quality. But only for a moment, and only for the man, for that most remarkable specimen of (to speak in his style) *Homo Occidentalis*. In the historian's activity this mentality expresses itself in consequences which I as a member not only of the profession of historians but of the community at large, of Dutchmen, of Westerners, of world citizens, consider to be pernicious.

At a conference in America, not long ago, I was confronted with the thesis that in the sciences of man *the true* and *the pseudo* cannot be distinguished, as they can be in the sciences of nature. I would not accept that.

Of course I do not dispute, so I said more or less, that history does not yield absolute truths not subject to doubt. There are, and there will always be, contending schools of which one would not be justified in saying that one represents history to the exclusion of the others. But they can all feel united in respect for the true method. With that true method I mean (to quote Professor Werkmeister) "the scholarly punctiliousness in dealing with facts, the desire to provide rational explanations on sound, logical, or, simply, honest argumentation."—"In contradiction to this," so I continued, "history, that is, a view or an interpretation of the past, can be so dominated by fanaticism, by an emotion, by the craving for a system, by the desire to make it a preface to the future, or rather to the picture of the future of which the historian's mind is full, by detestation, also, of the existing world and of the direction in which it seems to be moving—that all these safeguards of the true method are thrown to the winds."[35]

[35] *Scientism and Values*, edited by Helmuth Schoeck and James W. Wiggins; D. Van Nostrand Co., 1960; p. 156.

I must have thought of Toynbee when I spoke like this. I had, in fact, said something similar in my last criticism of his work.

When a man comes to the past with a compelling vision, a principle, a dogma, of such magnitude and emotional potence as Toynbee's unity in the love of God, with a system which causes him to reduce the multitudinous movement of history to one single, divinely inspired current and to judge civilizations and generations by one single criterion, rejecting most of them, and incidentally his own, as unimportant—that man can write a work full of colour and striking theories, glowing with conviction and eloquence, but no history.[36]

So completely is Toynbee taken up in his dream that he measures the whole of history by it. Occasionally he gives utterance to very virtuous principles, in this connection too. So after another analysis of his own spiritual development (he had already taken us into his confidence in the earlier volumes; for all his fondness of self-analysis, however, it seems to me doubtful that he knows himself so well as he imagines), he reflects that one's own standards and outlook are very largely the product of one's heredity and one's environment and concludes that "this recognition of the relativity of any set of human standards and values . . . should make one more charitable and open-minded towards the set that we find in other people. . . . Open-mindedness, charity and sympathy are . . . priceless virtues."—"It is true that we cannot study our fellow human beings' standards intelligently unless we realize that these have a value of their own, which we should be misrepresenting if we insisted on interpreting it in terms of ours."[37]

This is the current doctrine of modern historians, who do not, thereby, surrender the right, or repudiate the duty, finally to form a judgment of their own, a judgment which will however still contain the element due to the historical approach. But now see, by the side of this theory, Toynbee's

[36] *Debates with Historians*, 201.   [37] Vol. xii, 62, 64, 65.

practice. His theory will then take on the appearance of a mere *captatio benevolentiae.*

I said Toynbee measures everything in history by his dream. That is to say, unity; and love; in the last instance, religion.

The first victim he sacrifices to unity is the national factor. And to love: force. If he said no more than that the division of Europe into sovereign power states has led to catastrophes and that it is high time for us to reflect and to learn limiting or restraining the excesses of the modern idea of national sovereignty as well as the ever more destructive use of the instruments of war, I should, with the large majority of thinking men, agree with him. But he rejects both nationality and force from the beginning, they are to him manifestations of original sin. "Matter and force, two ugly and potent factors."[38] That they are potent, more than he was ready to believe while writing his earlier volumes, he now admits, even though he still thinks that spirit and love are superior in strength—a proposition that seems acceptable when one concentrates one's attention on the development of civilization. But how revealing it is that to him *matter* and *force* remain just *ugly*.

Every separate organization in the course of the ages, first the Greek city state, next federations, finally the great powers of modern times, are to him infringements upon his ideal of unity. The idolization devoted to these "ephemeral institutions" by the participants is by him visited all along with the bitterest disapproval—although they could hardly be expected to be cognisant of his ideal. Even when, for instance, a federation might seem to mean a step forward out of the preceding fractionized chaos, he is of opinion that only later developments will prove whether the men of that distant past deserve our praise or rather our blame because in fact they were building up, albeit on broader foundations, a new particularism which would imprison succeeding generations. Herodotus quotes Solon to the effect that for a valid estimation of any phenomenon the attention must be directed to the circumstances in which it finds its end. So before praising the Netherlands experiment of the Union of Utrecht (which he takes as

[38] Vol. xii, 616.

an example) we must be sure that we, we in our time, or our descendants, will win through to the happy finish of world unity.[39]

Let me add in passing that his treatment of the particular case of Utrecht is typical for his habit of expecting to find valid arguments in his impressions gathered from the mere surface of past events and all the time looking down on "the specialists." Those Netherlanders of 1579 become in his account quietly deliberating political thinkers, whose decisions we are entitled to call either wise or short-sighted. While in fact they were men severely pressed by menacing circumstances, which moreover affected some in a different way from others, men doing what was possible or could not be helped doing at that moment.

But speaking more generally, is not this treatment of history in flat contradiction with what we heard him recommend a moment ago?—that we must recognize something of value in the standards of earlier generations and should be misrepresenting them if we insisted on interpreting them in terms of our own time! Toynbee sketches Gibbon as a historian. [40] A genius, but who took his own standard of rationalism to judge men and their actions by it so exclusively that he could see in believers nothing but either knaves or fools. "The relativity of Gibbon's outlook interposed a psychological barrier between the historian and the great majority of the figures passing across his stage." One might describe Toynbee as a Gibbon in reverse. [41]

When he argues that modern nationalism was apt to go

[39] Vol. IV, 251, 316.

[40] Vol. XII, 80.

[41] In 1955 I remarked that in Toynbee's work "every civilisation is judged by a standard foreign to it." "But this," so Toynbee rejoins, "is true of all historians, including Geyl himself." (Vol. XII, 68, footnote). This may in an absolute sense be arguable, but it is again a question of measure. On the preceding page, Toynbee had written that "we must try to maintain all the time a difficult balance between two attitudes, both . . . indispensable . . . , though they may be mutually exclusive in logic." Exactly, and my objection to Toynbee's treatment of history is that (as we have seen on a sufficient number of occasions) this balance gets lost.

off into dangerous one-sidedness and extreme ambitions; that the power states such as they had been generally built up, reckoning with no interests but their own, led in our time to consequences catastrophic for the state of our Western community; and that, therefore, this tendency must be restrained; I agree whole-heartedly. When he remarks in passing that now at last "mankind is beginning to grow together into a single family," I can't help saying: dreamer! But he even believes that with that consummation the moment will come when mankind will arrive at a unanimous judgment on the various civilizations, then dissolved in the universal state, and whose conflicting moral standards can then be tested by that unanimity. Was I wrong when in an earlier article[42] I spoke of "the idol Unity, which is, Moloch-like, to devour national traditions"? I am relieved to think that this horrifying universality is no more than a phantasm, or a nightmare. But in the meantime Toynbee is already judging the past in the name of that Moloch.

In what I said about the Union of Utrecht I indicated already how badly the realities of the history of our poor human kind as it actually goes can in that way be realized. Instead of either wisdom or deliberate malice the past offers most of the time the spectacle of a wearisome struggle of conflicting interests or with blindly resisting circumstances; of a giving way or a coming to terms, which we had better not too easily look down upon from the height of a doctrine thought out in the safe seclusion of our study.

Unity, however, is not Toynbee's only criterion. There is also *love*. "I hate war," he says.[43] Who doesn't? But he, moreover, regards war as a senseless business and wants to see history governed by spiritual forces alone. All force, as I said before, he detests. In his six volumes he denied expressly that force had ever exercised any decisive effect. He even resorted to the most specious argumentation (I showed it[44]) in order to exclude the factor of force from the process of the dissolu-

---

[42] *Debates with Historians*, 209.   [43] Vol. XII, 610.

[44] In connection with the ancient American civilizations. See *Debates with Historians*, 133-4.

tion of civilizations. On this point he now makes a concession.
But even now he will not admit that force can have anything
but a destructive effect.

"I do hate war." "It is an unhappy but undeniable truth
that, during these last 5000 years, mankind has spent on war
by far the greatest part of the hitherto meagre surplus . . . that
we have succeeded in wresting from non-human nature."
That may be true, but what can we do but accept the past as
it was enacted? But Toynbee *deplores* the coming into existence
of the great power states into which Europe is divided. We
heard him already *deplore* that the human intellect is so
defective. Is it not as if he would like to re-create creation?
A creation without *matter*, without *force*, with men (if they
still might be called that) capable of apprehending spiritual
Reality—that is the sort of creation he is yearning for.

The true historian, but also the true statesman, and even the
true reformer, begins by taking the world and mankind such
as they are. Only within certain limits of daily reality, shaped
as it is in part by historical tradition, can we understand and
can we work effectively.

Now on these points of national variety and of force or
power we must surely begin by accepting that nature and
human disposition pose certain inevitabilities. In the excesses
to which these are apt to lead we need not acquiesce—on the
contrary, civilization springs from the resistance with which
we meet them—, but we must not therefore overlook the constructive, the socially and culturally positive possibilities inherent in the inevitabilities themselves. National communities
evidently—let us be prepared to accept this from the centuries-
long experience of mankind—belonged to a stage which
historical development could not avoid. And if these formations
entailed a great deal of suffering, how can it be denied that the
smaller groupings were at the same time beneficent and that,
generally speaking, variety has been a blessing? So much of
culture is connected with this that it must be called reckless
not to try, in the transition to wider associations (and *a
fortiori* to universality), to preserve these riches stocked in
history.

Toynbee himself now says somewhere that he can feel for an equipoise between the national and the international. But as so often, this is but an ineffective remark. In fact he still sees in the national no more than the parochial, the illusion of being worth more than the others or of being alone in the world. Here again he polemicizes all the time with extreme positions which reasonable defenders of the national conception reject as decisively as he does himself. And the same is true for the problem of force. The admission which his critics have now wrung from him, that force has sometimes destructively interfered with the course of a civilization, is not enough. It does not even count for much, for the denial here bordered on absurdity. The indispensability and the positive significance of force must also be admitted. I recall Pascal's great saying:

La justice sans la force est impuissante; la force sans la justice est tyrannique . . . Il faut donc mettre ensemble la justice et la force.

I venture myself to pose a syllogism:

Without a minimum of social order civilization cannot come into existence or flourish.

No social order is thinkable without its being able to appeal to authority, in the last instance to force.

Civilization cannot come into existence or flourish without the aid of force in the background.

Historiography, including the historiography of civilization, which excludes on principle the factors of nationality and of force; which proceeds, not from the realities of the past, but from a dream of future universality, must fail.

But Toynbee glories in his freeing himself from all that he esteems to be doomed traditions, but for which he can only substitute his dream. This is what he calls his "intellectual independence." One is amazed at the self-deception which allows him to preach to us—in his estimation supercilious and self-satisfied Westerners, or nationalists incapable of looking outside their "parish"—the wisdom of "a minimum measure of detachment from the toils of relativity." His own detachment does indeed exceed the minimum. Or rather, it takes on the shape of a systmatic ignoring, or rather detraction of all that he feels would divert him from the universal and from religion.

Religion now is the highest, indeed *the*, subject of history, and the civilizations are subordinate to it—that is the great change that was suddenly revealed by volumes VII-X. Bagby's view that Christianity had evolved along with Western civiliza-tion is one that consequently he emphatically rejects.[45] He sets religion apart from all inferior reality, from all "social or cultural shackles". This means that the historian in him is left indifferent by social or economic factors; although one can't help thinking that this attitude does not wholly spring from religious sentiment, probably not even primarily. From the West, too, he has detached his religion. Christianity could not but make in his eyes too parochial an appearance. So he has sacrificed it to his universalism, and while he still feelingly honours Christ, he immediately places Buddha by his side. A harmony of the four higher religions, that is where the world's salvation has to come from.

Western civilization itself—for all that he assures me that he is not lacking in appreciation for it[46]—he is in fact still only too ready to belittle and he pursues it with bitter reproaches (we have seen some of it, far from all). Exclusivism, feelings of superiority—this is what occupies the central place in his indictment. As regards the smaller, national, groups, they are according to him governed by this same mentality, which in their parochial setting makes an even more offensive and a foolish impression. All these "claims to uniqueness" in which his Englishmen indulge meet with spirited rejection on his part. One can only applaud. Only, how he exaggerates! He draws the entire picture out of proportion by writing as if this were about all that national distinctness has to offer. Of the particular and irreplaceable of English cultural traditions, or for that matter of French, German, Italian, Netherlandish, he has not a word to say. "I do not know English history and do not love it," he says.[47] And he continues as if it contained nothing but that

[45] Vol. XII, 92. [46] *Op. Cit.*, 628. [47] *Op. Cit.*, 630.

false claim to uniqueness. One looks in vain for names like those of Elizabeth or Shakespeare, of William III or Locke, Pitt or Burke, Gladstone or John Stuart Mill—names indeed which occur but rarely in the entire ten volumes. Here English history seems to culminate in the riots at Notting Hill, which "were in the news at the moment when I was writing these words,"[48] coinciding with the wretched incidents of Little Rock and South African "apartheid." And so Arnold Toynbee does not love English history. He has detached himself from it. He has risen above it. He soars in the vacant heights of this dream of unity in the love of God and from there looks down upon us all.

I mentioned that he desires from us "a minimum measure of detachment from the toils of relativity," meaning that we should not take the national as an absolute.[49] He adds a footnote which I cannot admire. "This conviction of mine, too, is controversial. Geyl, for instance . . ." In this way he creates the impression that to me the national is the standard for all things, that (as I put it a moment ago) I do not wish to look across those narrow limits. He goes on to quote me in the following manner: "Geyl, for instance, feels that Toynbee's 'ostentation of detachment from his own heritage' is 'prideful,' 'sinful,' and 'ridiculous'." Obviously these remarks of mine never meant that I do not regard some "detachment" from one's own heritage as needed for a sound study of the history of mankind. My statement was a retort intended to turn against himself the charges he is accustomed to level against us, short-sighted and self-opinionated Westerners. Hence these words loaded so heavily with moral reproof and which as a rule come more readily from him than from myself. And finally, I had not written; "ridiculous," but "at times slightly ridiculous."[50]

And in the end, I must maintain that passage without qualification. "Prideful," yes. The thought that one can divest oneself from all one's earthly limitations, that one has attained to an "intellectual independence" which can do without any ties with natural group connections or tradition, that one knows better than all preceding generations—this is a prideful thought

[48] *Op.Cit.*, 632.　　[49] Vol. xii, 584.　　[50] *Debates with Historians*, 197.

and at times one can't help feeling just a little ridiculous. When I said earlier that Toynbee, for all his explorations in his own spiritual development and for all his analyses of the influences to which he has been exposed, yet falls short at times in self-knowledge, I was thinking of his being so obviously unaware of this peculiarity, which he would according to his own code consider a serious defect. I do not overlook the delight in biting sarcasm that guided Trevor-Roper's pen in writing his brilliant article in *Encounter*. But this is where he was in touch with reality, and Toynbee's comment: "no comment", is not enough.

IV

When in his last section, entitled "Ad Hominem" he deals especially (for over a hundred pages) with the personal factor such as it appears in his critics' strictures, Toynbee does me the honour to take me "for the spokesman of the jury" when calling on him "almost plaintively" to reply.[51] I just remark in passing that "plaintively" is not the right word; irritably, or impatiently, would be more like it, accompanied by an acquiescent shrug in the knowledge that prophets don't answer.—Am I now satisfied?

From what I have written it has become clear—indeed I hinted as much at the start—that there are many points on which I cannot feel that I have been answered. Sometimes my closely argued objections have simply been passed by; or also, the answers were not really answers: too superficial, addressed to what I had not said, evasive. The critical observations of other scholars have often been treated in similar ways. And yet, when I try to summarize my impressions of the big volume as a whole, I must say that Toynbee appears to be more "amenable to reason" than I had expected. He admits repeatedly having been struck by solid arguments, certain parts of his system he even abandons or at least adapts. On the whole he is visibly doing his best, and there is something attractive in the mildness with which he bears himself under the pelting he receives from so many sides.

[51] Vol. xii, 575.

He is doing his best to take part in the discussion he has set going, to take part not only by means of oracular pronouncements from the height of his "independent" point of view, but on a footing of equality, as a searcher after truth as we are all of us. He is doing his best—I do indeed believe that he has seriously striven—, and yet his performance is but little effective. For all his concessions he is still just as much caught in his dream, and the obsession of his mind prevents him from perceiving how truly shattering much of the criticism he receives has been.

He has not really answered most of it. He is doing his best to be a historian, but first and foremost he still is a prophet.

IV

REFLECTIONS OF A EUROPEAN

1. The Idea of Liberty in History

The idea of liberty can assume widely different forms as it is applied to different domains of life. I shall confine myself to the domain of history, that is, of the aspirations, the fates, the struggles, of men living in community.

Just by way of contrast, not in order to embark upon theology, I begin by noting what liberty meant in the Bible, especially in the New Testament. Evangelists and apostles all use the word in the same sense. "The truth shall make you free" (John 8:32). "The Son shall make you free" (John 8:36). To be free means: "Free from the law of sin and death" (Rom. 8:2). "Where the Spirit of the Lord is, there is liberty" (II Cor. 3:17). "As free, and not using your liberty as a cloak for maliciousness, but as the servants of God" (I Pet. 2:16).

The liberty that is here meant is a moral, a spiritual conception; it is a psychic state. In history, on the other hand, the idea of liberty refers primarily to man's relations with other human beings or to the community; it is a political conception.

The first Christians indeed honoured authority and the State, but they did so as outsiders: political intentions did not enter their heads. Later, when the State became theirs, and, later still, when Christian states took shape, this mentality could not remain dominant. Yet it continued to exist, and, fundamentally unpolitical as it was, politics were sometimes measured by it, with unfortunate or paradoxical consequences.

I am thinking of St. Augustine and his doctrine of the *civitates*, one of the faithful, the other of those who live after the flesh. This latter he seems to identify with the State, whose rulers, proud and divided by quarrels, strive after greater power by conquest, using God at best as a device to enjoy the

309

world; while the faithful live in love and use the world to enjoy God. The *civitas terrena* will perish; the *civitas caelestis* will inherit eternity. Augustine's vision, marked as it may be with spiritual conceit, has grandeur. And as regards the political consequences to which I alluded, inherent in this doctrine is the danger that it will divert its followers' attention from politics, that they will look down upon earthly turmoil with self-satisfied contempt.

This consequence may be found unmistakably in Luther. More than a thousand years later, his *Liberty of a Christian Man*, that famous treatise of 1520, a powerful testimony of faith, seeks freedom in surrender to Christ and nowhere else. The Christian does not need the State. The State, on its part, must not meddle with men's souls. Apart from that, its power is unlimited; and again, apart from one reservation, the Christian, too, must submit to authority. The rulers are God's jailers and executioners. "God is a great lord, that is why he must have such noble, highborn, and wealthy executioners and executioners' servants, and it is his gracious pleasure that we shall call them gracious lords, throw ourselves at their feet, and be submissive to them in all humility."

The Christian's withdrawal into his spiritual life, quietly leaving the authorities to their task, which consists of nothing but the disciplining and chastisement of the wicked, represents an attitude of mind by which Lutheranism has certainly inhibited, not promoted, the cause of secular, or political, liberty.

But the European world took its traditions not only from the Bible, and Christianity itself could not stay within the narrow confines of this conception of the State. Side by side with the line that I have indicated, there is one that has its origin in the pre-Christian civilization of Greece, one, moreover, to which the Church had adapted its theory of the State long before Luther's time. I am not thinking of Plato, whose system, it is true, centred on an idealized state on earth, conceived, however, in no less arrogantly absolutist a sense than was Augustine's kingdom of the elect, and claiming liberty as its own monopolist prerogative. I am thinking of Aristotle's

Politics, in which he proceeds from the simple observation that man is a social being. This view was adopted by Thomas Aquinas, the great thirteenth-century philosopher of the Roman Catholic Church. And it was enough to prevent the self-righteous isolation of the faithful and their indifference towards the State from becoming a current proposition in general Christian ethics.

The implications were of immeasurable importance. As soon as the State was accepted as an institution naturally appertaining to man, interest in its organization was bound to be aroused. Thomas follows Aristotle also where the ancient philosopher distinguishes three forms of political constitution: monarchy, aristocracy, and democracy. Discussing the merits of each, he concludes in favour of monarchy. Monarchy become despotism is, he admits, the worst polity imaginable; but the advantage of one-man rule, if the king sincerely tries to promote the common weal, is that it engenders harmony and through harmony that order, or quiet, which is the State's highest aim. A much more positive definition, this, than was Luther's chastisement of the wicked!

The word "liberty" is not used with any emphasis by Thomas. It *was* by Aristotle. Liberty, so he wrote, appears to flourish particularly in democracies. Too often, however, it is the liberty to act as you please. And it is an error to think that to live in accordance with one of the other possible constitutions is to be considered slavery. Order, whatever the polity, means the security of the individual.

A contrast is making its appearance: liberty, order. Indeed, much controversy had raged about this contrast in ancient history, and in the later Middle Ages, too, it dominated the political struggles of the Western world. Thomas, so much is plain, has chosen order. The same can be said of Erasmus, in whom I see the line of Aristotle and Thomas continued. There is no trace in Erasmus of that Augustinian contempt for the world and its potentates. Far from indulging in the cynicism of Luther, who in his personal assurance of grace took pleasure in seeing rulers play the executioners to the wicked and honoured them for it as the performers of God's awful judgment, Erasmus lovingly sketches the portrait of the Christian ruler. He must be like a benevolent father; he must not only punish, but admonish and teach. He must not act arbitrarily, but be the embodiment of the law. More, Erasmus would like to see monarchy softened with a certain admixture of aristocracy and of democracy; *sic volo sic jubeo* he abhors.

The word "liberty" does not occupy a central place with Erasmus either. He was a monarchy man, as indeed were, then and for generations to come, most intellectuals. They distrusted the unreasoning multitude and feared that popular liberty would interfere with theirs. But a liberty of a different kind than that of pure democracy had been inherited from the political arrangements of the Middle Ages, and by and large it was this that the monarchy in its striving after expansion of power found in its path—I mean the liberty of privilege, the particular liberty, the liberties (for here one should really use the plural) of groups, of corporations, of towns and provinces. When from the theories expounded by Luther and Erasmus, mutually so widely differing, one comes to the reality of their day, it must be noted that it was *this* conception of liberty that was the issue of much contest. Traces of it are indeed to be found in Erasmus's treatise, where we saw him attempt to make the monarchy come to terms with it. The combination, or mingling, of the two which he recommended still actually existed, although not always leading to harmony.

In the centuries after the great migrations, serfdom had formed the sharpest contrast to personal freedom in the areas of Germanic settlement. The serfs had for the most part won their freedom, but the free had forfeited a good deal of their liberty. The feudal system as it came to cover the entire empire over which Charlemagne had reigned may be likened to a pyramid of subordinations. Personal loyalty in exchange for protection was its leading principle. But it did not for long retain the simplicity suggested by my parallel. Great ones made themselves practically independent. Other relations of dependence crossed the original ones. And gradually, exceptions, or exemptions, were conceded. The towns, the monasteries, broke loose from feudal cohesion and obtained their own charters, their privileges, their "liberties"; privileges became the prized possessions of many groups.

To these exceptional positions, to these particular distinctions, the conception of liberty became almost exclusively attached. For the state, or states, that had originally continued the tradition of the Roman Empire this process of feudalization, subsequently complicated by the privileges, meant little less than dissolution. But in the late Middle Ages a movement in the opposite direction set in. Rulers, influential over wide areas, like France, or over parts of a wide area, like the German Empire, were trying to restore princely power and began building up the centralized and bureaucratic states from which the modern states were to spring. And this led to that struggle between liberty and order which I mentioned before.

The liberty of privileged groups, corporations, or districts, should not be disposed of as mere egoism, disorder, a caricature of liberty. It meant something real. A striking token of this is the vigorous life springing up under these auspices in the towns. Yet the falling apart into separate areas, and within these areas, into more or less independent parts, the inequality of groups, each with its particular status and rights, constituted a hindrance for the development of Western society. In the struggle between liberty, as represented by feudalism or privilege, and order, as represented by the rulers, a struggle that was carried on for many generations and with varying success in the whole of western Europe, the modern observer will not find our conception of liberty a ready criterion by which to determine his preference. Each side made its contribution to the future as we know it.

Take Netherlands history. The Act of Abjuration, by which in 1581 Philip II was deposed as sovereign of the Netherlands provinces, is still so largely ruled by the idea of the privileges that it appeals less immediately to us than does the American Declaration of Independence two centuries later, in which liberty is proclaimed in more general terms. Yet in the older document, too, the love of liberty in general speaks with unmistakable accents. This document has its honorable place in the European history of liberty.

The subjects [so it was said in the famous preamble] were not created by God for the sake of the Prince, to be subject to him in all that he may ordain, whether it be godly or ungodly, right or wrong, and to serve him like slaves; but the Prince [was created] for the subjects' sake, to rule over them after right and reason and to protect them, like a father does his children and a shepherd his sheep.

And if he does not do so, but instead of protecting his subjects tries to oppress and overcharge them, to rob them of their old liberty [mark the singular], privileges, and inherited customs, and to treat them like slaves, in that case he must be considered, not as a Prince but as a tyrant and may, particularly by the country's States assembly, be deposed and replaced by another.

Their "old liberty"—but immediately after that—their "privileges, and inherited customs." The Netherlands revolution of the sixteenth century was not, indeed, one inspired by a general or abstract ideal (I leave aside the religious motive, which in the early stage of the crisis was of secondary importance); it was not intended to found a State in which liberty was to be carried through to its logical conclusion. It was intended to safeguard what was prized as an old possession.

The Act of Abjuration has been explained as proceeding from Calvin's constitutional doctrine set forth in his *Institutes*. And indeed, although expressly rejecting a change on the ground of theoretical preference or purely rational argument, Calvin approves of resistance under the conduct of inferior historic magistrates when existing rights are being violated. But the drafters of the Act were not so Calvinistic. I should rather say that both they and he proceeded from the same medieval tradition of liberty, one that was firmly rooted in the Netherlands, both North and South. It was even the fourteenth-century Charter of Brabant, the Joyous Entry, that supplied a particular inspiration for the Act of Abjuration (both Flanders and Brabant were still represented in the States-General that passed the impressive decree).

At the same time it is worth noting that Calvin, in marked contrast to Luther, did accept the State as a domain belonging to God's positive order and in which the Christian therefore had a task to fulfil. This alone is enough to explain how the Calvinists, so much more than the Lutherans, have been able at times to do something for the cause of liberty.

The Netherlands revolt, at any rate, was not one that in principle aimed at a renovation; it was a defensive revolution. Consequently, the Republic to which it gave birth north of the rivers can, considered purely in its constitutional appearance, be called a medieval survival. Provinces and towns, each equipped with its particular liberty; the rights of the citizens guaranteed by old privileges and supposed to be protected by authorities themselves deriving their power from old privileges and in whose election the townsfolk had no say: our conception of liberty is not satisfied by this oligarchic constitution of the old Republic. And yet it must not be overlooked that in the struggle against Philip II's despotism the general idea of liberty had obtained a strong sway over Netherlands political thought.

But whose liberty? Liberty to do what? These are the questions that must always be asked, and the replies could not always be edifying. The cynical but sharp-witted mid-seventeenth-century chronicler Aitzema taunted the Frisians, whose province was always backward in contributing to federal expenditure, with their habit not only of exclaiming indignantly at every attempt to make them pay more, but of accompanying their resistance with grandiloquent boasts of their famed liberty: "Libertas, et speciosa nomina," he comments (Liberty, and more such specious terms).

In France Louis XIV gave expression to similar sentiments with regard to the current conception of liberty. In his *Mémoires*, written for the benefit of the Dauphin, he explained that to promote the well-being of the people at large, to protect the little man's interests against the nobility or the urban magistrates and their egoistic use of privileges, one single authority is needed, raised above all and shared with no one, inviolable; only thus can the absolute king carry out his noble task. Many intellectuals were inclined to agree, some on the same high idealistic grounds, the majority, however, rather because they feared a democratic liberty that seemed to them tantamount to the worst possible tyranny.

We are now in the presence of a widespread state of mind. I hinted at this when discussing Erasmus. Shakespeare thought likewise. Even an early seventeenth-century Dutch patrician like Pieter Corneliszoon Hooft, the great poet and historian, looked with some regret upon the beneficent monarchy in France. And much later still, Voltaire expected everything from that monarchy, on condition, of course, that it would be "enlightened," and he kept hoping against hope that it would prove so. Those to whom culture was the highest good expected the absolute monarch to protect them against the mob, the populace, which might break loose and destroy everything. It was in particular the susceptibility of the masses to religious fanaticism which roused the intellectuals' feelings of contempt as well as of fear.

The classical example is the English philosopher Hobbes, who, shocked by the spectacle of the civil war in the 1640's, developed a theory of the state which was to exercise an immense influence.

What was the object, Hobbes asks himself, for which men in the condition of nature concluded the State contract? (For he makes use, like most of the seventeenth- and eighteenth-century theoreticians, of the fiction that the State was created by a deliberate agreement.) What was their object? To escape into security from the misery of "the war of all against all" (the condition of nature was, according to him, nothing better). Given man's unruly nature, power is required for that purpose, and in order to be effective that power must be unassailable, raised above all discussion. By that (imaginary) treaty, therefore, men completely and irrevocably transmitted their rights to the State. To the State they have since owed their security, their life, their society, their civilization, their law. Good and evil, unknown in the condition of nature, exist only thanks to the State. The State decides what is good and what is evil, what true and what untrue Errors containing the germs of

revolt must be suppressed; the State will see to it that the
universities teach only the true doctrine.

Even for this horrifying system Hobbes enlists the help of
the patient word, "liberty." It is a mistake, he says, to think
that liberty should consist of lawlessness or should require
that authority be unable to issue laws out of the fullness of its
power. And in any case: "The measure of liberty must be
calculated after the well-being of the citizens and of the State."
A good deal of harmless liberty, harmless to the State, will, so
he reflects, remain, and he does not grudge the citizens that
boon. It will even flourish the better when, thanks to the State's
all-powerful character, penalties have been fixed for good and
all, and arbitrary measures have become unnecessary.

But is not it likely that this all-powerful State should consider, occasionally, or even frequently, an arbitrary measure to
be good? In that case, nothing would be left to the citizens,
and to Hobbes himself, according to his theory, but to
acquiesce, or rather, to agree. *Leviathan* is the title he gave to
his book. The State that swallows all, indeed. Totalitarianism,
the denial of liberty.

I spoke of the immense influence exercised by Hobbes's
theory. One sees the traces of it even in a country where the
tradition of the liberty of liberties was strongly embedded, as
it was in the Dutch Republic. Take Spinoza.

Spinoza's philosophical conception of liberty could not but
make his mind susceptible to the attraction of Hobbes, although
at the same time it caused him to preserve a certain independence. "Free is, not he who acts upon his individual pleasure
but he who can wholeheartedly live in accordance with the
precepts of reason." If Spinoza regarded the all-powerful
State as indispensable for liberty, he therefore at the same time
postulated that it should behave rationally. But to say that he
postulated this is saying too much: he *hoped* for it. And when
he, who was personally not only rational but humane, attempts
to smooth out the rough edges of Hobbes' system, his treatise
takes on the nature of a plea rather than a doctrinal exposition.
He describes all dictation on matters of inner conviction as
"violence"; he judges a government to act unjustly towards

its subjects if it lays down what should be accepted as truth or be rejected as untruth. That the government is entitled to do this, however, he does not question. "We are not now speaking of its right, but of the wisdom of its actions." He seeks comfort in the thought that no government is likely to be rash enough to offend its subjects, knowing, as it must, that its right only lasts as long as does its power (this, too, is pure Hobbesian theory). And Spinoza is happy in being able to point to the example of tolerance given by the wise rulers of Amsterdam.

He did not, like Hooft, indulge in an aberration into monarchism. He reposed confidence in the actual rulers under whom he lived, the patricians (the "regents"). To them he applied this high theory of the absolute nature of authority. Nor was he the only one to do so. Even more rigidly absolute was the sovereignty claimed for the States of Holland by the lawyer Graswinckel. The brothers Jan and Pieter de la Court, in their remarkable pamphlets, went no less far, although they permitted themselves inconsistencies, casting glances in the direction of democracy, using the *word*, at least.

It is a striking fact that all these men were faithful followers of De Witt, and that the great Grand-Pensionary and his friends in these same years called their regime the regime of "True Liberty." This elicited a good many sarcasms at the time, and also from later historians. The phrase does indeed appear paradoxical when it is remembered that among the citizens there was widespread displeasure at their complete exclusion from all political control. This "True Liberty" was the liberty of the new sovereign, the States assembly. "Their Noble Great Mightinesses" wanted to be free from the supervision of a stadholder, which might easily have become princely absolutism; free, also, from the interference of the commonalty, of the stupid, shortsighted masses, which allowed themselves to be incited by the ministers of the Reformed Church.

Now, every time the people raised their own democratic demands against this oligarchic liberty—and the history of the Dutch Republic is thickly sown with disturbances of that very tendency—they recalled the theory of the Act of Abjuration. The prince for the people's sake, not the people for the prince's sake, was its great tenet, and this was now directed against the new oligarchic sovereignty claim. The patricians were reminded that they wielded power for the people, not for their own interests. And for this course, too, liberty was invoked.

All through the two centuries of the Republic, "liberty" remained a great word. It was a word to which the Dutchman liked to lay claim for himself and for his nation, and it made him look down with a feeling of superiority on the slavery of the French, the Germans, the Italians, of all peoples living under despotism. In spite of the theories put forward at the time of De Witt, people and patricians were generally one in this. The Hobbesian doctrine had no more than a passing influence. The patricians might often be presumptuous, but they did not generally forget that their rule bore a representative character. This had in fact been expressly stated, in the early phase of independence, by the States of Holland in its famous Deduction of 1587. Representative, although not elected: to us this may seem surprising, but in the Middle Ages, and in the early modern period, "representative" and "elected" were not felt to be necessarily connected.

Until at last, late in the eighteenth century, the tradition of the Act of Abjuration and the Deduction was merged, quite naturally, with the new formulas of the people being free only if it is consulted or elects its rulers to carry out its wishes. In the American Declaration of Independence these new ideas, of course, occupy a central place; but yet, even it can be read as a late-eighteenth-century version of the Act of Abjuration, a modern confirmation of the old tradition of liberty originally wedded to privilege and to history.

The influence of Hobbes, however, was not wiped out by this development. It even appears most strikingly in Rousseau's *Contrat social*, of 1762. But before I come to that, I shall consider in its wider European aspects the counter-current that I have just been noting in the Dutch Republic.

Two great names present themselves: Locke and Montesquieu.

Locke wrote in order to justify the Glorious Revolution of 1688. A king dethroned because he was violating the constitution. According to Locke, and this is the essential point, the subjects on entering upon the State contract had *not* transmitted all their rights. Men had had rights in the condition of nature already, and it was to safeguard these so much the better that they had formed a State equipped with no more power than was needed for that purpose. Life, liberties, and property, these were what mattered, and if the government laid hands on these, it laid hands on the State contract to which it owed its existence and no longer *was* a government. Resistance consequently became lawful.

Observe that this is precisely the argument on which the Netherlands Act of Abjuration was based. Locke stands indeed squarely in the tradition of medieval liberty, but by virtue of his generalizing way of thinking and arguing, and no less because the transaction of 1688 gave rise to the durable English constitutional monarchy, he also points into the future. The modern term "liberalism" can be applied to him without seeming overly anachronistic.

This is even more true for Montesquieu. Montesquieu wrote under the impression of the derailment of absolute monarchy as he had witnessed it in Louis XIV's last years. Those fine-sounding phrases in the young King's *Mémoires* about a task for the benefit of the people, how little did the practice of the reign agree with them! Power policy had become all, and endless wars had exhausted the country and hindered all useful reforms. Versailles, where the court was established in 1682, had isolated the monarchy from the nation. In the view of independent-minded Frenchmen, it no longer was the ordering, and when necessary, reforming, power—although Voltaire, for one, in spite of all disappointments, clung to this view almost to the last. It had become a despotism, enamoured with its own greatness, stifling all independence, growing more and more arbitrary.

The theory of the State, then, as Montesquieu developed it, was inspired by the wish to safeguard the nation from this despotism. Putting it positively, what he wanted was liberty,

liberty for the individual—actually, he was primarily thinking of the well-to-do bourgeoisie—liberty resting on a feeling of security. The laws, and the State, should keep their hands off certain fundamental rights, freedom of thinking and speaking, freedom to do everything that is not harmful to fellow citizens or to the community. But how to obtain that the State should stay within those limits? By dividing authority and at the same time strengthening organs that might resist it.

Not for Montesquieu, then, the one, indivisible, absolute authority advocated by Hobbes and so many others. On the contrary, Montesquieu wanted to have the executive, legislative, and judicial functions established as three separate, mutually independent parts of government; the *trias politica*. The exaltation of sovereignty, in which rulers and writers were on all sides indulging, was an abomination to him. Authority was not to be simply derived from the pretended right of sovereignty. It could not will after its pleasure. The highest resort to him was reason, crystallized in law.

But moreover there were the historic bodies of inferior rank, to which he assigned in the life of the nation and of the State a role of essential importance. First of all the *parlements*, the courts of justice, manned by the *noblesse de robe*, to which Montesquieu himself belonged. He even went so far as to defend the vicious system under which the councillors' seats were purchased or inherited, because this engendered in the *parlements* an independent *esprit de corps*. Besides, there were the provincial States assemblies, urban magistratures, guilds, clergy—all these *corps intermédiaires* (to use Montesquieu's own expression) were useful in that they might resist all-too-importunate intrusions of central authority.

It was a broadly devised system. Reason, as we saw, is the ultimate, the decisive criterion, but to Montesquieu reason is not necessarily opposed to history. On the contrary, he likes to call history to its support. Consequently his system is, like Locke's, related in spirit to the Netherlands Act of Abjuration. But, again like Locke, Montesquieu nevertheless spoke for the future. His theories for the moment lent support to his class, the members of the *parlements*, in its opposition to the arbitrary actions of the monarchy under Louis XV, an opposition that a generation later was to create the situation from which the great Revolution sprang; but when I affirmed Montesquieu's significance for the future, it was not of this that I was thinking. Rather does his advocacy of the *parlements* reveal a reactionary trait in his thought. The *parlements*, which did so much to create the revolutionary situation, never for one moment dominated the Revolution, which was immediately directed against the privileged, that is to say, against *them*, at least as much as against the monarchy; and in fact all of those *corps intermédiaires*, to which Montesquieu attached such importance, were brushed aside by the Revolution.

In the American Revolution, Montesquieu's influence made itself more directly felt or rather, in its sequel, the fashioning of a constitution to take the place of the Articles of Confederation. The separation of the powers, which actually came to be a feature of that constitution, was advocated by Madison with arguments borrowed from "the celebrated Montesquieu."

But the French Revolution very soon turned away from Montesquieu and let itself be inspired by the unhistorical, absolutist spirit of Rousseau. Montesquieu's time, however, was to come when the Bourbon restoration seemed to have written off the radical interpretation of the Revolution as a failure. It was partly to Montesquieu that nineteenth-century liberalism owed the strength of a certain tendency characteristic of it, a tendency that had been presented with great force by Burke, in his famous *Reflections* (1790) when the Revolution had only just begun. Liberty? Yes, but liberty as an inheritance from our ancestors, liberty in historic forms; no nicely thought-out system, no abstract (or as Burke himself put it, metaphysical) argumentation taking no account of fact or circumstances. Because of his passionate detestation of the Revolution, all this has a strongly conservative bias, as presented by Burke. That he is, nevertheless, fundamentally a liberal, becomes clear at once when one places him beside a counter-revolutionary thinker like Joseph de Maistre, who, writing in the early years of the Restoration, openly mocks at

liberty; or like the great Dutch eccentric Bilderdijk, who wrote,
as early as 1793:

> The cheering subjects of a king,
> That is where liberty flourishes.

Montesquieu and Burke stand at the beginning of a line that
was to be continued by Mme de Staël, Tocqueville, John
Stuart Mill, Lord Acton. Of a liberalism, in other words, that
was concerned about the danger threatening liberty and
civilization from the levelling effect of a new despotism, that
of the masses. Not that they, as in *their* time Erasmus or
Voltaire, looked for protection to an enlightened monarchy,
but they attempted to impregnate democracy, which they
accepted, with respect for law and reasonable moderation.

But not Rousseau had been the greatest preacher of liberty of
them all? With what vehemence, in the very opening para-
graphs of his *Contrat social*, does he take Grotius and Hobbes
to task for having assumed men capable, by the founding
contract of their State, of transmitting their liberty to a
monarch or to a small number of rulers! No! exclaims
Rousseau—for even in this succinct, almost pedantically
positive, little book the new personal and emotional tone with
which in his earlier works he had made so deep an impression
breaks through every now and again—no! "To renounce one's
liberty means to renounce one's quality as a human being, the
rights of humanity, one's duty itself."

What could be more promising! But note that Rousseau goes
on cold-bloodedly to assert that only one social contract is in
agreement with nature, namely the contract by which each
and every partner surrenders himself totally, with all his
rights, to the community. From that moment on, this community is the sovereign. Upon the sovereign no fundamental
law can be imposed. Nor is this necessary, for since *this*
sovereign is composed of all the individuals having made the
contract, it has not, and cannot have, any interest opposed to
theirs. The General Will (*la volonté générale*), by which the
State under this contract is governed, is always right and pure.
"Whoever refuses to obey the General Will, shall be compelled

to do so by the whole body; and this means only that he will be *compelled to be free.*"

This, then, is the liberty that Rousseau at the outset so strikingly proclaimed to be the distinguishing mark of human dignity! He is back with Hobbes, of whose influence he, while denouncing him, carries the indelible imprint. The General Will in the place of the monarch, but equally absolute!

And now let us try to understand what Rousseau means by this General Will. It is not necessarily the will of the majority. The majority can have been misled. Separate groupings, parties, churches, those *corps intermédiaires* that in Montesquieu's eye rendered such useful services in helping to protect liberty—according to Rousseau all they can do is divide and confuse the community. The General Will, however, is the will towards the general weal; this will, Rousseau assures us, is present in all men whether they know it or not, and it can therefore be safely assumed never to err. It remains in all circumstances the sovereign expression of the community's true will; it *is* the community's true will.

This, too, points into the future. Towards the immediate future of the Revolution at its most violent, when Robespierre, with his small group of Jacobins, was unshakably convinced that he was the embodiment of the General Will ("inaltérable et pure") and that he was by it entrusted with the task of exterminating all who seemed to endanger the realization of the ideal State. But it also points into a much later future: towards all the minority dictatorships that we have seen, and are still seeing, in action.

Not long ago a French Socialist had a conversation with a member of the Central Committee at Moscow. "You tell me," so the Russian countered his arguments, "that only where the individual has a right to give utterance to opinions opposed to those of the government can liberty be said to reign. This may hold good for a middle-class state, where people and government are contesting forces. But how is it possible with us for an individual to hold opinions different from those of the government? All that we have is at the disposal of everybody. We are the government of the people; we *are* the people."

This is completely in agreement with Rousseau's doctrine. The State is a community into which the individuals have been completely merged. That State can never wish for anything that would go against the interests of its members. It represents the General Will, and the General Will is always right. If an individual wills differently, he must, for the sake of his liberty, be coerced.

It seems a far cry from Rousseau to the Soviets. I am not suggesting that this Moscow Committee member had read the *Contrat social*. But Rousseau's spirit, Rousseau's *trick*, this horrifying adulteration of the word "liberty," this argument leading to the conclusion that the citizen must find his liberty in the submission of his will to the State—to the democratic State, it is true, the State founded by the surrender of each to all—this Rousseauan doctrine has become the property of quite a school of thought, and it has come to the Russians via intermediaries. I am thinking in the first place of Hegel.

Hegel, too, saw the individual merged in the community, in the State, able to realize himself only through the State, and only thus finding his liberty. In his imposing system history is a development of the Absolute, thinking itself towards liberty—the ultimate goal. The way this happens is through a struggle of States, now this one then that being the elect of the Absolute and bearer of the Idea of History. Germany, Prussia, had been designated by the Reformation to attain the goal, as it was understood in his, Hegel's, mind.

The vision of St. Augustine's work, I said above, was one of grandeur. How are we reminded of Augustine here! Hegel's *Absolute* is Augustine's *God*, and the predestined goal of liberty towards which Hegel's Absolute is thinking itself is St. Augustine's predestined Day of Judgment, when he and the like-minded faithful will inherit the Kingdom of Heaven.

Hegel's "liberty" is, like that of Rousseau, a mere philosophical, or rather, romantic liberty; a liberty in the prophet's imagination. In reality the term is made to palliate a veritable enslavement to the State; and in Hegel's case, to war. For to him it is war that necessarily marks the stages of development.

Many men have since operated with this "liberty" paradox,

and to suit very different purposes! There was Treitschke, who saw the triumph of liberty in Germany's victory over France in 1870, a victory willed by history. And there was Marx, who announced that triumph for the day when the proletariat should have wrung supremacy from the bourgeoisie and have founded the classless society.

"A community," so we read in the Communist Manifesto of 1848, "on which the free development of every individual will be a condition for the free development of all." The whole of previous history had been, in Marx's view, a struggle, not, as for Hegel, between peoples or States, but between classes. The bourgeois rule, under which men were still living at that moment, was in all ways objectionable and rotten, it must and it would be forcibly overthrown, to make room for the pre-destined final state of affairs.

The belief in one solution, the only and final one, to be forced through irresistibly, be it by Providence, by Reason, or by History, after which there will be no more strife and prac-tically no more history: this absolutist trait all these ways of thinking (St. Augustine's, Rousseau's, Hegel's, Marx's, and that of the Moscow Committee man) have in common. And it is this very characteristic—absolutistic, simplistic, fatalistic, and, I add, unhistorical, however much its presentation is accompanied by rummaging in the storage rooms of the past—it is this that lends these systems their power to impose and to fanaticize, and at the same time, charges them with deadly danger to liberty.

"There are two schools of democratic thinking," Professor Talmon of Jerusalem wrote not long ago, and he distinguishes them as the Liberal and the Totalitarian. One regards politics as a matter of trial and error and leaves a large domain of life outside its sphere; the other assumes a sole and exclusive truth in politics, and its messianism pretends to embrace the whole of life. "Both schools affirm the supreme value of liberty. But while one finds the essence of liberty in spontaneity and the absence of coercion, the other believes it to be realized only in the pursuit and attainment of an absolute, collective purpose."

I need hardly say that I belong to the Liberal school—liberal of course not in any party sense. Not only does the other attitude seem illusionary to me, but I see in it the negation of liberty. And yet I must add that by this other road, too—at the cost of heavy shocks and of a deplorable waste of energy, no doubt—mankind has sometimes made headway. Moreover, whenever it took this dangerous turning (for that at the very least it must be called), it was practically always the blind obstinacy of conservatives, or perhaps the shortcomings or hesitations of fellow democrats of the other school, that had tempted it to do so.

The liberty of the privileged under the *ancien régime*, and later on, that of the propertied bourgeois class continuing their tradition, was before everything *their* liberty. Nineteenth-century liberals too often shut their eyes to the fact that the propertyless masses, left to the free working of economic laws, were bound to be anything but free. These are undeniable truths. And this implies that Marx's criticism was up to a point justified and had its relative usefulness. The social struggles of the nineteenth century have made a contribution of irreplaceable significance to liberty. But that the cause of liberty would be lost without resistance by counterforces grounded in civilization and history—I for one am firmly convinced of it. Tocqueville's conservatism is at times somewhat obtrusive; in Mill's thought the neglect of the State and community factor constitutes a weakness; yet the emphasizing of the value of an *élite* by the one, and the other's insistence on the need for individual diversity and for totally unfettered discussion, count in the history of liberty.

I shall not dream of attempting to draw up, by way of conclusion, a definition of my own of the idea of liberty, or of "True Liberty." There have been too many such attempts already. Of the results some appear to me to be no more than impudent sophisms. Others do strike a chord. But to sum up in a formula the conception of its numerous aspects and implications—personal liberty and liberty in relation to the community, political liberty and liberty in social and economic terms—one formula, one definition, one recipe? I feel unequal to the task, and what is more, I believe that it is impossible.

Liberty in the full sense of the word cannot, in the imperfect society in which we imperfect beings live, exist. All that we can do is to strive after conditions in which as much liberty as is practicable will be attained. To strive—not by abolishing history and making an entirely new start. "Liberty": this word, full of wisdom, was spoken by Lord Acton, the Englishman who devoted a long life to collecting materials for a *History of Liberty*—which he never wrote: "Liberty is the delicate fruit of a ripe civilization." To strive, in the path opened for us by preceding generations, making use of their achievements, learning by their mistakes. To strive, and if need be, to fight. For unless they had the courage to stand up for it, liberty has never remained the lot of men; and that to fight, or to be prepared to fight, may still prove the only way to retain of it as much as we have, the years in which we live have made abundantly plain.

(1956)

2. *"Hitler's Europe"*

The first volume of *Hitler's Europe* (edited by Arnold and Veronica M. Toynbee; issued under the auspices of the Royal Institute of International Affairs, London, 1954) is a co-operative work of seven hundred large and closely printed pages; I count nine contributors, apart from the two editors, of whom Professor Toynbee opens the volume with ten pages of introduction. In six parts we get accounts of the fateful six or seven years—in Germany, politically and economically, in Italy, in France, in the smaller countries of western, and in those of eastern Europe. An additional volume, of over three hundred pages, contains documents.

I cannot, of course, dream of trying to criticize in detail each of those parts and their several chapters. There are aspects with which I am insufficiently familiar, but besides, I am sure that you would soon get bored if I attempted to deal with the book in that fashion.

Speaking quite generally, I have found most of the chapters both informative and absorbingly interesting, and the book as a whole stimulates a number of reflections. But before I can try to lay some of these before you, I feel I must relieve my mind about the chapters on Holland and Belgium. I confess to being astonished that the Royal Institute of International Affairs should have entrusted these chapters to a writer who does not appear to know the language of Holland, which is also the language of the majority of the Belgian people. It is to this deficiency that I put down the errors and general super-ficialness of Viscount Chilston's account of what the Hitlerian occupation amounted to in those two countries.

A very great deal of serious, scholarly work is being done in

Holland on the history of the occupation. The State Institute for War Documentation, in Amsterdam, which exists solely for this purpose, has brought together an immense collection of documents pertinent to the subject of the occupation; monographs have been published, and are still being prepared, under the Institute's auspices. How is it possible that Chatham House has not consulted the able experts in charge of that great work?

Confining himself to German sources and the few Dutch sources available in German or English, the author has been unable to establish any real contact with the problems. All that he has to say on the evolution of public opinion under the occupation, on the part played by the Queen while in exile in England, on the resistance movement, gives but a blurred, and at times, seriously distorted, picture.

As regards Belgium, because a large portion of the national sources is in French, he has been able to give a more consistent and more penetrating account. Only, his inability to take any notice of what has been written by the Flemings has resulted in a deplorable one-sidedness. What, for instance, is one to think of the following statement?

> In view of the undeniably closer kinship of the Flemings with the Germans in the matter of race and language it was not unnatural that the Nazi movement should have deeper roots in Flanders than in Wallonia.

If "kinship . . . in the matter of race and language" really was the decisive factor, how does Lord Chilston explain that the *Dutch* National Socialists remained so completely out of touch with the realities of Dutch national life? The fact is, of course, that among the Flemings there had for a long time existed a sense of grievance with respect to the Belgian state, French-administered, and favouring French as it did, a sense of grievance that could be worked upon in a moment of crisis. It is true that the most glaring injustices had been remedied, but nationalist resentment often survives its immediate cause (need I remind you of South Africa and of Ireland?), and in any case it leads quite easily to dabbling with National Socialist theories and to adventures in association with the self-styled avengers of the wrongs inflicted by the alleged imperialist nations. This side of the story is not even mentioned by Lord Chilston. Nor does he state with sufficient emphasis that, even so, the large majority of the Flemish people proved obstinately refractory to National Socialist teaching, and while he gives the names of a few French-written Belgian underground papers, he does not mention a single Flemish one. Let me assure him and his leaders that the Flemings did have an underground press of their own.

But I must come to the more general reflections to which the work as a whole gives rise.

What *was* Hitler's Europe? It was in fact no more than a part of Europe conquered and held in a stifling grip while the conqueror went on fighting for more, and finally for bare life. There was much talk in the early stages, of a New Order that victorious National Socialist Germany was going to found, a United Europe, united not only for Germany's but for its own good. Mr. Clifton Child brings out very clearly—it is one of the interesting points of his excellent chapters on Germany —that Hitler himself never believed in this fine talk. What he was after was the expansion of German power and the establishment of German supremacy over as many subject peoples as he could manage. For international consumption he could at times speak the high-flown language of the New Order as well as anybody, but in the circle of his intimates he once said in a burst of confidence: "Why proclaim German aims to the world? As far as our might extends we can do what we like; and what lies beyond our power we cannot do in any case."

We have here perhaps the fundamental reason why the Germans could not during the four or five years of their supremacy make any lasting impression upon the occupied countries of Europe. Suppose that they had taken seriously the conception of a European unity which the propagandists loved to proclaim. One can imagine that on those lines something might have been wrought with which, for better or for worse, the liberators and the liberated of 1944 and 1945 would have had to reckon. As it was, no planning, no large-scale political or social reconstruction was possible, nothing that might be termed a *policy* for the occupied territories. Nothing but subjugation, oppression, exploitation. And as soon as the occupied nations gave signs of having discovered that the occupation meant indeed no more than the advancement of the interests of the occupying power, all they got was worse subjugation, worse oppression, and worse exploitation.

The parallel with Napoleon's conquests readily presents itself, and Professor Toynbee, whose mind runs so naturally on parallels, does, in his introduction, mention it. He is, in my opinion, inclined to take Napoleon's European unity too much at its surface valuation. I am not forgetting that the Napoleonic occupation did have a policy, and that it did leave lasting results behind. But that Napoleon was in many ways Hitler's prototype becomes, I should think, clear when one remembers that he, too, might be described as the conqueror for conquest's sake, the conqueror who would not state his aims because he never knew if he could not go beyond them, the despiser of ideology too, ever ready to use phrases that might result in procuring him useful dupes—such as the unfortunate Poles.

But where Toynbee seems to me to go more definitely wrong is when he identifies the purely personal policy of the disastrous maniac Hitler with the Prussian tradition. To talk of "a Prussian tradition of finding no pleasure in the acquisition of power without savouring this by tasting blood," or of "Hitler indulging in the Prussian pleasure of offensively asserting his domination over satellite states and conquered peoples," is mere rhetoric, replete with prejudice. I have no call to defend the Prussian tradition wholesale, but I cannot help remembering how Prussia, when she acquired, at the peace of Vienna, the western German territories of the Rhineland and Westphalia, managed to weld these into her system; and the same happened after 1866. Mere denunciation of Prussia, in view of such facts, appears woefully inadequate. Indeed, Professor Toynbee here seems to depart from the argument of his own contributor, for Mr. Child insists, as I hinted before, on the purely personal nature of Hitler's naked power policy. Far from representing it as the resultant of a deeply rooted historical tradition, he opposes to it "the proposals for the re-organization of the European continent along the more liberal lines occasionally suggested by the German publicists."

It is at all events one of the central problems of Hitler's Europe, this conflict between the attraction exercised by certain tendencies of the New Order and the growing disillusionment attendant upon the practice of the conquest. There had been, in the late thirties, in most countries a weariness of the weaknesses of democracy and of the confusions and calamities resulting from the political and economic anarchy in which Europe seemed so hopelessly stuck.

That the opportunities offered by this state of mind of the victims were missed, is not to be explained by Hitler's individual opinions or peculiarities alone. His was not the only influence accounting for the completely amoral, immoderate, destructive tendencies of the National Socialist movement, for its *nihilism*, to use Rauschning's description of it. There were many, in all the conquered countries, who never for one moment were under any misapprehension as to the evil nature of the New Order suddenly imposed upon them by brute force and making ready to shape their lives. Yet in the first weeks, or months, of complete discomfiture due to resounding, and as it then seemed irretrievable, defeat, people experienced a kind of relief to find themselves still alive and the German soldiers not the fiends they had seemed while the battle was raging; the public at large was to a certain extent malleable, the New Order did in some ways appeal to it. It took the peoples, in all the occupied countries, some time to wake up to the hard truth that there was no possibility of compromise with the conquerors or with their system.

It would be interesting to draw a comparison between developments in the various countries. In a book in which these are treated separately by various authors one cannot expect this comparison to be fully worked out. But in reading the chapters of *Hitler's Europe* I was struck by similarities and differences; every now and again I felt myself faced by the problem: Why was it that things took this turn here? Why did they assume so different a shape there?

I indicated one particular factor that made itself felt in Belgium: the peculiar position of the Flemings and their feelings, or the feelings of a radical group among them, with regard to the Belgian state. There was another factor there: the most unusual position of the King, who personally acted as commander in chief. When he thought the hour had come for a capitulation, he elected to stay with his army and rather than retiring to England and heading a refugee government there, as at that moment the Queen of Holland was already doing, he became a prisoner of war. There is no doubt that King Leopold's unfortunate decision was immensely popular, just as there is no doubt that the flight of Queen Wilhelmina and her government had been viewed by most Dutchmen with feelings of dismay and indignation.

I can well remember how men who had always professed (and professed in all sincerity) love and reverence for the House of Orange talked bitterly of desertion and betrayal. It was left to a minority to reason with them—to men who had not, perhaps, been very zealous royalists, but who had studied the international situation and cherished no illusions about Hitler and his crew. We had to explain what after a while became so obvious that it needed no explanation any more: that the Queen and the government would have been powerless, under the occupation, to prevent anything; that the Germans would have tried to use them as tools; that it was only in England, last remaining free spot in Europe, that they could preserve the continuity of Dutch sovereignty and prepare for a better future.

Yet it was not, as Lord Chilston thinks, the example set by the Queen which revived the feelings of self-reliance and of fortitude among the people of Holland. There was a hard core in the traditions of Dutch society and of Dutch civilization which needed no outside incitement. It was nevertheless a great and inestimable service that the Queen and the government rendered the nation by their going away and by their determination to stay away until Holland had been freed. And here the Queen played her personal part—I can think of no better word than: manfully.

One automatic effect of there still being a Dutch government was that it prevented the setting up in the country of a lawful government under German supervision, round which all the forces of defeatism, of compromise and collaboration, might otherwise have gathered.

As happened in France. The story of Vichy, as told by Professor Cobban, is an instructive, although a depressing one. The old Marshal, enjoying his triumph in the midst of defeat, partly through vanity, partly out of an honest but stupid hatred of democracy, presents a far from pretty spectacle. Yet that of the intriguers by whom he was surrounded is worse. Then there were the colonial governors sheltering behind legality and taking pride in carrying out the orders that were the price Vichy had to pay the Germans for its semblance of independence. But what makes it all so particularly humiliating an episode is the fervour with which the majority of Frenchmen indulged in a veritable cult of Pétain as the saviour of their country, because in the turmoil raging all around them he seemed to be securing them the comfort of peace.

The Dutchman cannot help congratulating himself that the history of those years in his country did not present the exact match of all this. But he should not therefore imagine himself to be immune from the weaknesses shown so glaringly in France. We were saved from the most insidious temptations thanks to the timely departure of the Queen and her government. And even so, the problem of collaboration remained, and people's attitudes towards it were often enough similar to those that can be observed in France. Indeed, everywhere, the reactions of the public will be found to have been similar; it was the different circumstances—different in France from what they were in Holland, different again in Belgium or in Denmark—that turned them into different channels.

But everywhere, there was this fundamental fact: people in responsible positions could not altogether refrain from co-operation with the invader. Their individual desires to withhold from him all services that could even remotely be construed as assisting him in his nefarious practices had sometimes to give way to considerations of the immediate welfare of the population. Exactly at what point co-operation became collaboration was a question that could not be answered offhand. It was apt to involve serious-minded and patriotic men in the most painful conflicts of conscience.

Resistance and nothing but resistance, resistance caring nought for all these nice distinctions and considerations, was a great moral asset. In France, too, it helped to save the soul of the nation. But it must always and everywhere be the affair of a minority.

I have broached a question here which can still arouse the passions of people in all the occupied countries. It is a great question, a question touching deep-seated chords of feeling. I can say no more about it now, but I am sure that later historians, too, will consider it to be one of the most fascinating as well as most trying problems of Hitler's Europe.

(1954)

3. *Opening Lecture (October 1, 1945)*

When, on October 1, 1945, I lectured to my students for the first time since my transportation to Germany as a hostage five years earlier, I felt that the occasion required some introductory remarks of a general nature. I had no thought then of publishing the little piece I prepared, and I had even completely forgotten it when I happened to come across it some eight years later. I then included it in a volume of essays published in 1954 under the title *Historicus in de Tijd*.

If I have now thought it worth translating, it is not because I believe it will add much that is new to the views on history which I have already expressed on several occasions. But the circumstances in which it is set and to which it is a response do perhaps impart to this confession of faith a peculiar quality of immediacy.

(1960)

It is five years ago since I last lectured in this building. On October 7, 1940, I was arrested by the Sicherheitspolizei, and when I was released, on February 14, 1944—nearly three and a half years later—I had in the meantime been dismissed from my chair by the Reichskommissar.

So it is like a new beginning for me to be able to address you once more.

I have asked myself whether, under the impression of what we have been through, I shall speak to you differently from how I used to, whether the spirit of my teaching, of the information and the guidance I shall try to impart to you, will prove to have undergone a change. I believe not. Oh, certainly, events have not passed by without leaving their imprint upon me. You will occasionally, in what I shall from now on have to tell you, hear the echoes of the fight that we have all of us fought. But a different attitude towards life, a different attitude towards history, that is not what you must expect from me. The air resounds with admonitions: everything must now be changed, so we are told from many sides; the older generation and its wisdom have had their day. It is at moments as if people regard the catastrophies by which we have been struck as the doing, not of Hitler and his armies, but of our own short-comings; as if civilization and society in this country before May 1940 were rotten through and through; as if salvation can come only through a new generation prepared to try new ways.

Now this is of course no more than hollow talk, and I haven't the slightest fear that you, as you are seated here before me, representatives of a young generation, are looking at me sus-piciously or arrogantly, thinking in your own minds: Now what can this old fogy still have to tell us? Let me at any rate give you plain notice that what I can give you is the same I tried to give before the war. I have not been renewed or made over, I am still what I was—at least I hope so. I am not ashamed of my past; I am not appearing before you in a pen-itential mood. The best service I believe I can do you, and I hope with all my heart that I may to some extent achieve it, is, through my teaching, to put you in touch with the old civiliza-tion that the fury of National Socialism assailed and threatened, but God be thanked, did not extinguish. Through my approach to historical problems, through the whole of my mental attitude towards history, I hope to do my bit towards restoring and reviving old cultural possessions that in five years of oppression have shown their soundness and resilience.

Perhaps you attended, a week ago, in the Aula, the meeting called to found the "Civitas Academica," and very likely you supported the declaration of principle to the effect that the University must not stand apart from public life, that scholar-ship and science have a social task to perform. I am myself cordially of that opinion, but really I did not discover it only in the course of the last five years. The study of history in particular has in my eyes always had a social, a national, function. I have always been profoundly conscious of this, and I believe that before the war my teaching was already animated by that thought.

But let us take care. The community, the nation, have claims upon us; but we cannot give to the community and the nation the best that is in us if we don't cultivate our individuality. Science, and also the study of history, has a social, a national, function, granted; but it can only fulfil it if it scrupulously maintains its independence and proceeds undeviatingly in accordance with its own laws. Those precious acquisitions of our civilization which I said a moment ago I hoped to help you in restoring to their previous freshness from the ignominy and the neglect of the years behind us, are precisely those laws and the respect for them; it is the true historic spirit as it has been evolved in generations of European civilization. I have no doubt but that we, you and I, not in the least troubled by our belonging to different generations, shall be able to find each other in that service and shall be able to co-operate in concord toward the mental recovery that is needed after the malicious attempts at confusion and subversion that we have experienced.

I don't want to confine myself to generalities. What do I mean by the laws of the study of history, by those invaluable cultural possessions in the guard of our profession, which during the occupation were exposed to disregard and to distortion and to which we must be true if we want to be good Dutchmen and good west-Europeans?

I mean the sense of criticism, the courage to apply criticism, the fearless use of our rational capacity, daring to go where it leads us, even though in effect this may at times seem to put a distance between us and those verities that we can every day hear being proclaimed as eminently and obligatorily Dutch, or it may be, west-European. You know how National Socialism tried to enslave scholarship, and particularly history, to its pet ideas, to its myth. National Socialism had nothing but scorn for the independence of scholarship. History had to prove the cohesion and the worth of the People, the greatness and the power of the *Reich*, or of the Germanic Race—or rather, those great truths were to be taken as starting points, they were sacred, not to be tampered with, but to be glorified. The historian bold enough to criticize was denounced as a heartless individualist, a traitor to his nation. We take our stand against National Socialism, we prove our faith to our national traditions of culture, when we dare to think for ourselves, when we apply criticism, when we serve scholarship in accordance with its own laws, regardless of persons, regardless of people or nation. That is the first duty of historical scholarship, criticism, again criticism, and criticism once more. A hard duty at times, for it may bring us into seeming collision with other duties and loyalties. But in reality by being true in this respect, we are true to the highest values of our civilization, that is to say, to our noblest traditions, to what we owe before everything to our own people and our nationality.

Without allowing ourselves to be misled by current views we should search fearlessly for the reality behind conventional terms, behind nationalistic or party phrases. "L'histoire est une fable convenue"—there you have a cynic's statement, but insofar as it contains truth we must not acquiesce in it, we must attempt to dig more deeply, and our first task in doing so will be to apply criticism, to look at the facts dispassionately and unafraid, to use common sense. To train us in this exercise is one of the great gains that the study of history holds out for us, and I do not mean for the individual historian only, but for the community to which he belongs. It is salutary that there should be a group of men schooled in that discipline by which the dangerous clouds of fine-sounding words and of thoughtless repetition, of romanticism and of mental laziness, can be dispelled. This is one of the great social functions of—in a sense of all study, but I believe that the study of history is particularly important from this point of view.

I lay so much stress on this aspect because some of the effects of the deceitful and crafty propaganda carried on by National Socialism against the true scholarly spirit, against criticism, against the intellect, are still with us. *Intellectuals* is a word that still has to many ears a somewhat suspicious sound. *Rationalism* evokes the idea of *cold; criticism*, of *destructive*. But let us try to look at what has happened to the world collectively, as if from a distance, and we shall see that the most cold-blooded despotism and terrorism that have ever reigned, and the most terrible danger of destruction that has ever threatened European civilization, were made possible by a systematic extolling of instinct and passion above reason, by detestation and contempt of criticism. Reason and criticism are among the bulwarks of Western civilization.

But this is not all. A sense for criticism is necessary. But no less needful is a sense for tradition, love for what has grown, love for what is distinctively ours, or to put it more briefly, love and respect. Is there an insoluble contradiction between the first requisite and the second? Certainly not, although undoubtedly there is a tension. In any case, as it seems to me, this sense for continuity, the capacity for discerning it and the zest for bringing it out, constitutes an equally indispensable feature of the historic attitude. And it, too, is a precious feature of the civilization that has helped to shape us, to which we belong, and which after the brutal outrages of revolution and fanaticism we must patiently try to nurse and to develop.

Reason and criticism are factors we cannot do without, but they are not enough. Even he who stands up for the rights of reason and criticism, and, more, maintains that they belong to our most valuable cultural possessions, will know nowadays, that the great creative forces of life, of society and civilization, lie elsewhere. Rationalists such as flourished in the eighteenth and nineteenth centuries are an extinct species. Nobody will nowadays regard the world as a mechanism driven by reason alone and to be controlled by reason. How shall we name those great creative forces? How shall we approach them? I am not lecturing on philosophy, and this is a question I don't feel called upon to deal with. Ask various individuals or groups of our national community, and the solution will assume sharply differing shapes. Here come into play deep springs of personal conviction. Our Dutch civilization, the whole of west-

European civilization, is long past the phase of one interpretation of life common to all.

But this I think I may say, that the study of history can strengthen in men of divergent religious or philosophic sentiments a feeling of—how shall I put it? I have already used the words *love* and *respect*, and indeed I think that they render better than any the historian's attitude of mind. Without indulging in romanticism or mysticism, unbefogged, after having given to criticism its full due, we can by the spectacle of history feel fortified in our love for life, in our respect for life. The true historian may detest deception and violence with all his might, yet, placed before the great currents and upheavals of history, he will not scoff, he will not rage, he will feel awed; before everything, he will attempt to understand. In the manifestations of communal life, in that ceaseless alternation of the noblest intentions and the direst lapses, he will see more than did the eighteenth-century English thinker who described history as "the dreary record of the crimes, the follies, and the miseries of mankind." It is not as if I should want the historian to see everything in a rosy hue, to lay aside his intellectual or moral standards when contemplating the men of an earlier age; far from it. But the historian will learn to see those men in their human surroundings, and he will understand that the imperfections of both are the concomitants of that human imperfection of which he and his time still have their share.

History does not only fashion that understanding and participating attitude of mind in the most general way with respect to life and humanity; it calls forth feelings of kinship with the group to which the spectator belongs, it strengthens the sense of community. With understanding grows love for what one is part of, and a more profound and firmer love as it is free from illusions. A feeling of kinship, moreover, that can do without the incentive of hatred. Hatred for another people is not a historic state of mind. Hatred for oppression and cruelty, certainly; hatred for crime and deception. But the historian who seeks the support of reason and of criticism knows how to make distinctions, and the rejection of an entire people, or of that people's civilization, which is in so many ways intertwined with European civilization as a whole, cannot pass muster with a true historic appreciation.

In resuming my lectures after the liberation, I had to unburden myself of these general reflections. We stand at the opening of a new era in the history of our country, in the history of Europe and the world. If that is taken to mean that *tabula rasa* has been made and that we are starting afresh, history would be a subject that could have little contact with reality and with our actual problems. But that is a view I resolutely reject. In this new era the past will be seen to be continuing. Every revolution has imagined that history, so to speak, began with it, but when the dust clouds of upheaval and destruction settled, the uncommitted spectator was able to observe how many of the old trends were going on under the new surface, how much of the old framework of society and of civilization had resisted the impetuous passion for renovation. So it will be now, and more so even than was the case, for instance, after the French Revolution, because, although the material shocks have this time been more violent, Europe was not, as was the case in the eighteenth century, enamoured of the new ideas even before the crisis, and when Hitler triumphed, these ideas, instead of being sucked in and assimilated by the conquered people, were on the contrary resisted and rejected.

History, then, will carry us to the sources of what still is our civilization, the civilization of our time. And it is a work of restoration, it is a work of reconstruction, to devote attention to our past, to study history. It is not an escape from the present, it is strengthening ourselves for the struggle that is calling us.

I tell you so, and I hope that you will feel it yourselves, or will learn to feel it. But this does not mean that I want to impress upon you that in your study you should be continually animated by present-day preoccupations. Not a bit of it. On the contrary. Plunge into the subject, work hard, stick to the laws and the rules of the subject, exercise your powers of criticism and of discrimination, treat the problems as technical problems. The other thing will come, if it can come, of its own accord.

Bringing the University closer to life—about which we heard so much at the meeting of the Civitas Academica—does not mean that we, in studying history, must all the time be on the lookout for the actual, the practical, the national, or whatever it may be in the sphere of interest of the community. If you have followed my argument that the historic attitude itself— the critical faculty, the sense for discrimination as well as for connection and continuity—that this true historic state of mind is in itself a precious asset for the national as well as for the wider European community, you will understand that I can urge you to give yourselves to the subject, to the study, simply, without distracting commitments, with wholehearted devotion. That, once more, will be reconstruction; that will be making your contribution to the restoration of our civilization.

4. *The Vitality of Western Civilization*

The great problem of our day is that of the salvation of Western civilization.

Let me tell you at once that you will not hear me speak in an alarmist fashion. Prophecies of downfall, laments about the decline of Western civilization—these are moves in the under-mining tactics of its assailants. My theme will be, on the contrary: the vitality of Western civilization. But we must not hide from ourselves the fact that our life and our work lie under the shadow of a total menace, a menace from the outside, from Russia and her Communist or semi-Communist accomplices in our midst.

It is our duty, in the face of this menace, to maintain our position. A task that is perhaps all the harder because we must not expect the sudden and rousing challenge of a war: the atom bomb is the paradoxical safeguard of world peace. What is needed is an alert spirit of resistance to the insidious en-croachments of a system that, in spite of all we now know of its practical effects, still casts a spell over backward or badly apportioned groups, over absolutistically inclined minds, and that turns to its advantage all our weaknesses, economic and social, but more especially, intellectual and psychologi-cal.

That is why it is worthwhile to examine a little more closely the campaign of pessimism and self-criticism which has the effect, whether intended or not, of weakening our morale. A variety of tricks are employed in that campaign. Pessimism even at times takes on the appearance of optimism and adopts a tone of cheerfulness and hope. Not that this is required on

all occasions. There is in human nature a trend that responds
to visions of ruin and decay. Against them the divine promise
of eternal bliss can shine with greater radiance. Take Augustine, take Bilderdijk, the great early nineteenth-century Dutch
counter-revolutionary poet. But even Spengler's unadulterated
pessimism found a receptive public.

The course of the world's affairs has not so far followed the
prophecies of doom. The generation that accepted Spengler
as a prophet did, it is true, live through a severe trial of the
West, but instead of this trial leading to dissolution, Western
civilization came through it triumphantly. One has only to
cast one's mind back to those anxious years before the war
when the outlook seemed so gloomy: that powerful Germany,
led by a lunatic—its ambitions aimed at the very pride and
value of our life. The most oppressive phenomenon in those
days was the fumbling, the disunity, the wilful blindness,
among the peoples of the West. The economic depression,
which had done so much to bring Hitler into power, the
paralyzing unemployment—there were moments when all
this seemed irremediable.

But see: the war roused the spirit of resistance. Our civilization turned out to be possessed of profound reserves of
strength. England's example proved fruitful because in the
rest of western Europe too, the traditions of freedom and of
human dignity were still alive. And the greatest miracle of all,
the most hopeful happening, was when, after the collapse, the
German people too came to their senses. After the destruction
of their cities and the exhausting and upsetting experience of
an inhuman regime and its savagery, German society was
seen to have preserved the life germs of its better past. The
German people were able, after that evil dream, again to
unite with the West. History triumphed over the nihilistic
revolution.

Yet our problem had not been solved. The Soviet Union
had moved into central Europe, and it seemed to be western
Europe's turn next. In fact, history hardly knows solutions.
As a Dutch poet puts it:

Drama without a dénouement; every decision
glides over into a resumption of the plot.[1]

In any case, the plot of National Socialism had had an
ending that we may count as a striking proof of the West's
powers of resistance and of recovery. And this especially
because there was more than a mere having survived a threat,
more also than the reviving of the historic German people.
I mentioned the economic distress and unemployment in the
'thirties. Today the Western peoples have succeeded, in spite
of that destructive war, in raising the general well-being of
their masses and at the same time in guaranteeing to the
common man a security such as he has never known before.
The welfare state is not, of course, a sudden postwar product.
It had been prepared in a long period of social strife. It is now,
at any rate, a striking testimony to the inventiveness, the
creative power, and the humanity of our civilization. In the
new contest that we face, the economic base of our civilization
constitutes, moreover, a considerable element of strength.

Generally speaking, I think it is a fact that prophecies of
doom supply no objective indications about the vitality of the
periods in which they are pronounced. They must be explained by the subjective state of mind of their authors, or by the
reaction of those authors to social phenomena that signified
less than they imagined.

One might well ask whether the phrase "decline of a civilization" has any sense. A civilization is an extraordinarily
composite phenomenon. Moreover, it is subject to incessant
shifts and changes. Here old branches will wither away; there,
at the same time, new foliage will be sprouting. We cannot
expect contemporaries, not even the most learned sociologists,
to be able to comprehend the whole in a balanced view and to
speak of *flourishing* or *decaying* stages in a way that has
absolute and universal validity. To pronounce the prognosis
"hopeless" will always be a risk, and even with a "hopeless

[1] The Dutch poet quoted is myself. The lines are taken from one of the
sonnets I wrote during my internment, see below, "Looking Back," pp.
400/1.

unless" (*unless* whatever the observer happens to have thought of as a remedy) one is presuming upon the sovereignty of the inexhaustibly inventive future.

Why then, these recurring fits of discouragement or dissatisfaction? Our civilization draws on the resources of a rich past, but it keeps on changing. Without change no life, and this is a sign of health. Nevertheless every change, however salutary for the community, or however salutary in the long run, will disturb individuals or groups and will indeed actually cause them hurt or damage. Here is a plentiful source of those complaints against the age which were indeed heard in previous ages just as they are in our own.

In the middle of the nineteenth century an optimistic belief in progress was prevalent. The triumphs of human reason were celebrated; science, technology, opened glorious prospects. Yet even then one can perceive a constant voice taking the counterpart and uttering the most dismal warnings. This very belief in man's independent power to determine his fate was regarded by some as proof of impending disaster. I might quote De Maistre or Carlyle or the Dutch Calvinist thinker Groen van Prinsterer. But instead I shall let you hear that voice as it is raised today.

The religious-minded man today is shocked by the ever-advancing de-Christianization. Over against this, the triumphs of science, and the multiplication of material goods, count for nothing in his estimation. Sometimes he even regards them as a snare and discerns tragic evidence of man's sinfulness in allowing himself to be deluded by the semblance of power over "all the realms of the world and their delight." I quote a contemporary Dutch Catholic writer: "Wealth has spread over a large part of the earth." When he adds "the wealth against which the Gospel warns us," he explains that the *attachment to wealth* is meant, the *striving after wealth*. "This desire, which has mastered mankind more than ever before, constitutes the veritable desert of God's Absence."

Now has desire for material well-being really mastered mankind more than before, and is it causing us to neglect the spiritual? If every prophet of doom, denouncing his age from whichever system of thought it may be, is inclined to invoke the comparison with the past, it is because the past lets itself be fashioned or simplified in the way that suits him. Past reality may get lost in the process, but the contrast needed for the effect will be obtained. The *historian* knows—or should know —that in the ages of the supremacy of the Church, or of the churches, man was at least equally tied to the material; that his childlike or dogmatic faith did not guard him against passion or avarice; that the social arrangements with respect to property, public authority, and the dispensation of justice were accompanied by an oppression and a cruelty from which one might at least as readily conclude God's Absence. It would be an unwarranted, in the deepest sense unhistorical, conclusion. But this is true also for the present. Forms have become different. Dogma and organization have lost much of their power over the spiritual. But that is not the whole story. The service of knowledge and of social justice and its rationalization can satisfy the need for the spiritual in a way that I imagine is in harmony with God's plan no less than was, in the ages of faith, the Council of Trent or the Synod of Dort.

But another motif governs the protests against the spirit of the age. Progressive optimism in the previous century dominated especially the minds of those who believed in and continued the rationalistic and humanistic tendencies of Western civilization. Among those very men a reaction manifested itself from before the middle of the century on. Tocqueville and J. S. Mill were concerned. Burckhardt, Renan, Flaubert, Taine, expressed bitter aversion to the development they witnessed. The year 1848 gave the first rude shock to bourgeois liberals. The Paris Commune of 1871, coming on the heels of the crushing defeat administered to France by Germany, made an even more profound impression, and not on the French only. While Nietzsche launched his imprecations, Jakob Burckhardt withdrew in stoical resignation. Fruin, too, the great nineteenth-century Dutch historian, who at first was all satisfaction and confidence, in the later decades of the century gave way to gloomy forebodings.

Numerous are those who nowadays would be inclined to think that these fears have come true. A friend wrote to me, not long ago: "Our century is a calamitous century." I replied: "Certainly, the twentieth century cannot exactly be called an idyll. But that is a description which, when you look at the history of mankind, no century has ever deserved. And true calamitousness does not reside in the measure of human sorrow, in the numbers killed in battle or murdered. It should appear in the irremediable dissolution of human society. Well, as far as I am concerned, I am struck rather by the astonishing power of resistance and resiliency that has been displayed—in the West; but is not that our world?"

In fact, there is more than power of resistance. The social reforms alone show undiminished creativity. But these very reforms explain the disgruntlement of so many intellectuals, then and now. The nineteenth-century men I mentioned were frightened and embittered by the rise of the masses. They feared the consequences it might have for international relations, but more especially for conditions at home.

Civilization seemed to them to be safe only with a social *élite*. It seemed to them the property of the aristocratic or well-to-do bourgeois group to which they themselves belonged, and they could not help thinking that its fate was bound up indissolubly with their own. And as for *their* position, it was indeed menaced. Swiss democracy did not win so quickly as Burckhardt, as early as 1846, was afraid it would. The Commune, which threw Renan, Flaubert, Taine, into paroxysms of fright and fury, never came anywhere near success. Yet in the whole of the succeeding period, and until today, the well-to-do bourgeoisie felt uncomfortably threatened in their pre-eminent position in society.

Now the same fact can be stated in the reverse: we can observe that the masses were being gradually raised out of the pitiable and dehumanizing conditions in which, during the heyday of aristocratic and bourgeois civilization, they found themselves. And did civilization suffer a corresponding loss? Were humanism and education ruined, as prophesied by Treitschke and Renan? Did our society become a *waste land*,

and we ourselves *stuffed men* or *hollow men*? to use the words of
T. S. Eliot—in whose case one can wonder whether it is his
Christian faith or rather his aristocratic feeling of life which
makes him seek comfort in such wholesale condemnation.
Ought the present state of our civilization to be characterized
as *quantitative* in contradistinction to the *qualitative* civilization of the past?

It seems to me that there was something lacking in this
nineteenth-century civilization that overlooked so light-
heartedly, or condoned with such fervour, the misery around
it. The utterances of aversion to the people, the arguments
that civilization needs a substructure of poor and docile wage-
earners, which were heard on all sides, were really sadly
devoid of that humanism these prosperous bourgeois imagined
was their monopoly. Their qualitative civilization was without
at least one quality, a quality by which, at least by the potentiality of which, Western civilization has always been distinguished. I mean a sense of responsibility for the whole of
the community. Here is an organ of our civilization which a
development, accelerated in our reputedly calamitous century,
has strengthened, resulting in a heightened sensitivity and a
finer perceptivity.

Of course I know the usual complaints. Technology exposing
mankind to self-destruction; the progress of science leading
to narrow specialism; films and television estranging the
rising generation from serious reading; art broken away from
tradition, desiring nothing but immediate reflexes. There
even are plenty of talented young men who take delight in
systematically extolling anxiety and absurdity as the hallmarks
of true artistic feeling. This mentality truly denies some of the
most precious tendencies of our civilization. But let ever so
many critics be eager to praise that wild talk as the purest
profundity, I see in it no more than the ephemeral after-effects
of the shocks of war and revolution, and I am quite sure that
it will not affect the main current of development.

Perhaps every one of those complaints contains a grain of
truth. I am not singing a song of praise of our times the
burden of which would be "All is as it should be, sleep well."

I want, on the contrary, to rouse and to warn. I mention weaknesses, and no doubt there are more. But I know no greater weakness than when the constant changes to which our thinking and our ways of life have to adapt themselves, or which they have to overcome, are met only with a sigh of fatigue or a revulsion of fear. True, every change is apt to disturb us in our customary train of life and to confront us with problems. But we should not expect civilization to be served up to us like the sweet fruit to the inhabitants of the Land of Cockaigne. Civilization means struggle. And struggle we do.

To me the present spectacle of that struggle seems downright impressive. In the command of matter, in the knowledge of human life, social as well as individual, Western man is making progress as never before, and every discovery, every new theory, every shift in conditions causes tensions that necessitate provision. I say, "Western man," for it is he who continues to lead in these respects, and if Russia at times seems to be in front in the technological sphere, the regime of compulsion which prevails there calls into being tensions that are concealed rather than solved. The contrast between the semblance of unity there and the continual controversy here does not denote strength as against weakness. Our liberty, with all its drawbacks, is sure proof that Western civilization is very much alive.

But no doubt the process of democratization and removal of inequalities, which is far from having come to an end, will continue to offend groups that are still in a better position than many to make themselves heard. Here we still have, together with the uneasiness of organized believers, a source of alarmist opinions about the voyage on which History is taking us and of fears that Western civilization will not come through unharmed.

But now I come to a third factor, which serves more than anything else to create, in some, feelings of frustration, of lost greatness. I mean the demolition of the overseas position of the western European countries, the rise of Asia and Africa, and coupled with this, the weakening of Europe's power in world politics. The time when world history seemed to revolve around Europe is gone. Beside the United States and against Russia the voice of western Europe does not count for much any more in the neutral world of countries recently come to independence. This is a development that is being used by people of radically different outlooks for radically different arguments, all tending to prove that Europe has no future.

There are, first of all, the convinced colonialists, who keep on declaiming about the halfheartedness and feebleness with which in the critical years from 1945 to 1949 our democratic regime abandoned the bastion, and about the betrayal of the West committed by the United States. Suez was to these men a new proof of the degeneration of the West, while France's obstinate fight in North Africa seems to them a last chance, in which, however, they can hardly believe any more. In short, a "calamitous century."

I cannot, of course, go into any detail about these questions. It seems to me, leaving on one side the blindness displayed by American political leadership and all possibilities of compromise or gradualness that may thereby have been neglected, that we were faced here by an ineluctable development. The colonial peoples had been shaken out of the immobility of their social conditions by their Western rulers: intellectually, too, they had been touched, set in motion by ideas and slogans with which we ourselves made them acquainted. Add the suicidal wars in which the European countries involved themselves, and the position of mastery, even of leadership, became untenable.

But does this course of events, and does this issue, imply a death sentence on Western civilization?

This civilization may have been stimulated by its colonial expansion and its position of world power; it has thereby been led into errors and illusions as well, and at any rate, it never owed its essential values to that development. And similarly, even our economic prosperity—the miraculous revival after 1945, or rather, after 1948—has taught us that we can do without that artificial support. Looking at the Netherlands alone:

E.H.   M

the rebuilding of the devastated cities, the bold Delta scheme for mastering the estuaries and securing the low-lying land, the almost revolutionary industrialization, the search for new markets; and no less, the control of the social and cultural consequences of those material changes—it all gives plenty of scope to our energies. We can resign ourselves to putting the colonial episode behind us.

And as regards world power—we Dutchmen lost our modest share of that some centuries ago. It is helpful to observe that our national civilization was not thereby doomed. Shall we not conclude from that experience that Europe, too, can lose her world supremacy without necessarily losing the vitality of her civilization?

Provided, once more, that the Atlantic peoples—we western Europeans and Americans—remain conscious of having in common the task of self-preservation against the system entrenched so powerfully in the Soviet Union and which would prove inconsistent with the fundamental principles of our civilization. For democracies, co-operation is always difficult, and there is only too much disagreement in the Western world.

This is partly due, no doubt, to the gloomy speculations I am tracing and which have unsettled too many minds.

Take, for instance, Professor Barraclough, a year or two ago appointed to Toynbee's London professorship of international history, previously known as a sound medievalist. In his book *History in a Changing World*, of 1954, Barraclough warns us that the history we have learned and practised has lost all sense. He himself was converted to the realization of having wasted his life, as suddenly as was Saint Paul on the road to Damascus, by the spectacle, in 1943, of the Germans being compelled to raise the siege of Stalingrad. Russia was thereby revealed to him as the great power of the future. He regretted the time he had spent in studying the papal chancellery or the emperors in the thirteenth and fourteenth centuries: owing to that, he now knew nothing of the Piasts, the Przemyslids, the Ruriks, or of Casimir the Great of Poland. "Farewell to Europe," is the title of one of his lectures, and he contemptuously dismisses Louis XIV, Napoleon, and Bismarck as "neolithic figures," completely irrelevant for any purpose today. *The European Inheritance*, the title of a collective work recently published in England, is to him a senseless phrase: "The old Europe has given up the ghost."

Now this kind of writing simply revolts me. As a historian I protest against the denial of a truth to which history owes its irreplaceable value: the indissoluble concatenation of the ages. As a European I detest the defeatism. And then the implied proclamation of success as the supreme standard of values! Must we see the whole of history culminate in the Kremlin because the Russians won at Stalingrad? It was a near thing if Hitler did not bring off his *coup*, and in that case I suppose Barraclough would have told us our first duty was to search the past for the signs of the Third Reich.

I do not close my eyes to the change we see materializing. It amounts to a revolution. I know, too, that contemporary events of this magnitude do not leave our view of the past unaffected. We now see in Louis XIV, Napoleon, and Bismarck, in addition to all that they were besides, the unconscious contrivers of the present-day collapse of European power. But one thing I hold firmly: that we are still Europeans and that our past, including those great national power fanatics, contributes towards shaping our present; that in us there lives the tradition of a great civilization, great and beneficent in spite of all the shortcomings and errors which are inseparable from human nature; and that it is our task to go on working towards the prospects and within the confines set to us by that tradition.

All this is nowadays obscured in theorizings propounded from many parts. *Eurocentric history writing* has become a term of reproach. We are told to practise *universalism*. But because Europe does not now hold the central place in world events, must we therefore forget that for a long time it did? And does not that period still in many ways affect the present? But indeed, as a basis of history writing, universalism seems to me impracticable. The stage is too wide, the action on it too confusingly varied. If one wants to depict it all in an intelligible connection, one will have to survey it from a point of view, and how can anyone in doing so detach himself from his country and civilization?

That would be a superhuman effort, and what is more, one that would go against human nature. I am quite ready to admit the right of Indians or Chinese to write the world history that suits them; but equally firmly I stick to the conviction that we Europeans are entitled to, and need, the world history that will help us to discern more clearly our place in the well-nigh incomprehensible whole. This does not in the least mean that everything must be seen in subordination to the European interest, or that admiration must be reserved for what was done by Europeans. Nor does it mean that European or Western civilization should, or can, be interpreted as a rounded-off entity on which no outside influences have made, or are making, themselves felt. But how can a human being—and the historian must not, above all, try to pass himself off as anything but a human being—allow his mind, shaped in his own cultural environment and by its centuries of sustained action, to be dissolved in an unorganic and anarchic *world* without losing hold of his most fertile life-principle? We must approach world history through the smaller formations in which we grow up. To each of us his national history, to all of us the history of our Western cultural community, must provide a point of departure and always a point of orientation.

But now read a man like Professor Locher of Leyden University, who does his best, unmistakably, to remain critical and matter-of-fact. Even he proposes that we should prescribe extra-European history as a subsidiary subject to (mark well!) our best students; and he wants time to be found in the secondary schools—at the expense, inevitably, of the study of the Greek and Roman world out of which our own civilization has partly sprung (and let me remind you that Greek and Latin still are compulsory subjects in the secondary classical schools in Holland)—to familiarize our next generation of intellectuals with . . . with what? with China? with India? with the Arab countries? with Russia? That there are specialists studying those civilizations does not satisfy him. I remark in passing that I regard such studies as an enrichment of the intellectual life of our community, and no civilization has, and has had for a long time, so wide a curiosity as ours. But to extend this to the school programmes, as Locher imagines should be done, could, I fear, lead only to a disintegration of that intellectual life and to hotchpotch in the pupils' heads.

However, this is nothing compared to the naïve illusionism to which the true universalists abandon themselves. They form a numerous host, and their influence is felt in an even wider circle. I shall have to say something about Toynbee and the Amsterdam professor Romein—a Marxist, and at the same time, curiously enough, a fervent admirer of Toynbee. But first of all a few words about the Moral Rearmament enthusiasts. The caricature presented by them in such deadly earnest will sharpen our eyes for the unhistorical features in the views of those historians.

I suppose that many of you will have seen those delightful periodicals. We got one in Dutch as well recently. How charming are those pictures! The happy, beaming faces of all those Filipinos, Negroes, Chinese, Burmese—they call up before our inner eye a better world than the one we know. And indeed, I read: "Will Asia lead the way?" Nothing is expected any longer from poor Europe. Nothing but *repentance* for former *pride* and *self-sufficiency;* and now *humility.* "We have plunged mankind into two world wars. We have exported materialism. . . . Humbly we ask you, Asia and Africa, to forgive us."

I grant that pride and self-sufficiency, and also the wars, are evidence of the wickedness of human nature which even Western civilization has never been able, and never will be able, completely to check. But that human nature in Asia and Africa contains nothing but this irresistible kindliness so ably pictured by Mr. Buchman's photographers—I can't believe it. I shall not enumerate the sanguinary despotisms in the Oriental world of former days; nor the murderous outbursts of religious fanaticism or the terrible social abuses still to be noticed today. If I recall them, it is not in order to argue that these peoples are incapable of anything better. But those better potentialities will not be realized at one stroke by congresses where world citizens in picturesque attire utter, and cheer, amiable platitudes. Only by strenuous labour, by generation after generation struggling with stubborn traditions and prejudices, will progress be made—as has been the case with us.

This fundamental error, this lighthearted overlooking of history and decreeing that everything will be different from now on, I also find in Toynbee and in Romein, his Marxist admirer in Holland. And these two men similarly belittle the part that western Europe can still play. The present commotion in the until recently colonial world proceeds—both Toynbee and Romein admit it—from the impact of Western civilization on the forms of social life prevalent there. But what did we bring them? What have we still to offer? According to Toynbee only the Russians have a faith to import, that is their advantage over us: a faith derived, however much distorted, from Western civilization. All that *we* have is technology: "a stone instead of bread." It is exactly what we heard the Moral Rearmament man say: "Nothing but materialism."

Isn't it astonishing that Toynbee keeps silent about the sense for social justice which has led to those profound reforms in the West during the last few generations and which did undeniably inspire the civil servants of England, of France, and of Holland in the East to attempts at alleviating the oppressive feudal arrangements there? But even more astonishing is it that in another passage, concerning Turkey, Toynbee himself observes that what the revolution in that country has borrowed from the West is "the sense of fair play and moderation in politics which, we Westerners believe, is one of the good gifts that the West is able to give to the world." Astonishing, because he forgets this later when he speaks so bitterly of "a stone instead of bread."

What is the key to this contradiction? It is that Toynbee in his heart nourishes an urge to ostentatious depreciation of his own side, an urge to disparage and impeach. Worse, on one occasion he went so far as to write that we must not expect another escape as was the last war; mankind's patently increasing submissiveness makes it certain that a future would-be world conqueror will find us an easy prey. A heart taking pleasure in a pernicious defeatism. And with Toynbee this heart scores off the mind every time.

The same can be said of Romein. He has in the last seven or eight years given much of his attention to the relationship between Europe and Asia. In his case, too, the resulting picture testifies to an unresolved conflict between his knowing and his wishing. His wish is to make us believe that we, that the whole of our aggressive Western society, have misbehaved towards the gentle East, which has never committed aggression against Europe; and that for us it is now time to come to resipiscence. It would be enough, in his view, if we remained neutral between an America playing with thoughts of war and a peace-loving Russia. That is what history demands of us, but he is afraid that we shall not have the strength even for that modest role. Need I point out that western European neutrality would indeed be *enough* . . . for Russia and Communism to triumph?

But the astonishing thing, in Romein's case, too, is that elsewhere he does give a realistic sketch of the monstrous feudal conditions in Asia at the time the Europeans came to know it, and that he even admits that the invaders contributed something to their improvement. But yet again, when speaking for an audience at Gadjah Mada University, at Jokjakarta in Java, he lets himself be carried away to exclaim: "Asia has in its history known higher triumphs than can be bestowed by martial glory, triumphs in the works of peace!" Europe, apparently, has not . . .

And yet the cultural influence exercised by the West upon the East is a leading theme of Romein's argument. He has summarized his vision of world history in one of those attractively brief formulas with which he loves to operate—and he is particularly proud of this one—formulas that may seem, at first sight, striking, but to which the rich variety of historic life will always refuse to adapt itself. He starts from the assumption that the communal life of all peoples in its early stages bore the same features everywhere. This is the Common Human Pattern. From it *the European peoples* gradually deviated. So here we have the fundamental secret of Western civilization, that it is a Deviation from the Common Human Pattern (I hope you hear the capitals). Now, however, the Awakening of Asia, brought about unintentionally by those aggressive and interfering Deviators, has set in motion a process of assimilation. The world is being Westernized, soon the Deviation will be a deviation no longer. In principle, and lately more particularly under the influence of Soviet Russia and of the United States, it has already been accepted by the whole world. In principle the world is one already.[2]

In 1955 I heard, in London, Toynbee deliver the speech on "World Unity and World History" which soon afterwards he repeated at The Hague with Romein acting as chairman. I said to Toynbee when he had concluded. "You spoke of mankind being one large family. It doesn't look much like it." To which he retorted like a flash: "No, it looks more like a slaughter-house." He meant, of course: We must. It is our only alternative to annihilation. And this is also the idea of Romein. To me it seems a depressing idea: our only alternative—a phantasm!

For this Westernizing of the world, this removal of that extraordinary Deviation—can it take place so readily? Civilization is no currency, which will retain its value when passed on to somebody else. It is a commodity shaped in the course of centuries and tied indissolubly to its possessor, to his history, to the qualities and capacities that are proper to him and that also owe their existence to his experiences and those of his forefathers, to their exertions and tribulations. The civilization of a people is but the aggregate of those qualities and capacities, of those memories. It is a product of history and powerless without living contact with history.

How lightheartedly did the Americans believe, after the war—and numbers of Europeans likewise—that colonialism only needed to be demolished and the West might count on the Asian and African peoples as sympathizers and allies. Actual developments brought a good deal of painful disappointment.

[2] An essay by Romein on the Common Human Pattern (in English) was published in the issue of *Delta* that followed that in which the present lecture was first published.

A passionate nationalism, quick to take offence, was among the first fruits of Westernization—a strange introduction to the one-world paradise that in the imaginations of Toynbee and Romein seems as good as realized.

But now the explanation has been thought of that the cause of the trouble is in the poverty and "underdevelopment" of the ex-colonial world. Let us remedy that, and everything will be all right. I have all sympathy with the policy of assisting the underdeveloped countries, but it is already beginning to dawn on the supporters that even here, in that apparently technical and material sphere, matters are not so simple. The assistance does not yield much result if the technical abilities of a population fall short (and in most cases they do, inevitably) and if, moreover, the class contrasts within the underdeveloped area (and most of them suffer from that evil) direct the assistance into wrong channels. (This was pointed out in the inaugural oration recently given by the new professor of non-Western economics at Leyden University, Dr. Brand, who speaks from the experience of his work with the United Nations Department of Social Affairs. A book on the subject from his hand is soon to appear in English.)[3]

Here again history will not be ignored. Impatient idealism is doomed to sterility. Hollow optimism is as dangerous as is the most destructive pessimism.

The optimistic and the pessimistic speculations I have discussed agree in this: all of them tend to disparage the vitality of Western civilization. A state of mind is encouraged in which whenever a cultural phenomenon is discussed without reference to Asia or Africa, the word *hubris* is thrown at the speaker; and the more bitterly so, of course, when he has dared to mention the backwardnesses or imperfections of Oriental societies. And one who professes love for the grandiose tradition of Western thought, or of Western poetry, will be called a *Western chauvinist*.

[3] This book has since appeared, under the title *The Struggle for a Higher Standard of Living: The Problem of the Underdeveloped Countries* (The Hague: Van Hoeve; Glencoe, Illinois: Free Press, 1958).

There is something thoroughly unhealthy in that habit of depreciating our own spiritual heritage. The West has no faith any more, it is asserted, and the accusers vie in offering, one this, the other that, which might serve. As if an ideology could be plucked from the air! No faith? Well, I believe in ourselves, in our own tradition, which with its tireless experimenting and trying out changes, gives evidence that it still has something to offer to the world.

But in any case, even if, either because overpowered by an alien force or owing to our own shortcomings, it might have to pass through another time of trial, to us it will still remain an indispensable source of strength. All those other faiths are no more than wishful thinking, and they divert attention from the devoted labour and the incessant struggle which are needed.

Strife is the law of life. I am far from suggesting that we should underestimate the deadly character of a third world war. We must avert that catastrophe with all our capacity. But by breaking faith with Europe and her past, by cringing before Russia, by hollow confessions of guilt with respect to the peoples of Asia, we shall not show that capacity or avert threatening misfortunes.

A calamitous century? It is a century that makes demands on us. And in spite of the lamenters and the dreamers, I see around me heartening signs of the will to respond.

(*Valedictory oration pronounced by the author in the Aula of the University of Utrecht on the occasion of his retirement from the chair of Modern History, May* 31, 1958.)

5. The Historical Background of the Idea of European Unity

European unity. We hear the cry on all sides. Everyone agrees that the times demand its realization and implementation. This can be argued on political or political-strategic, as well as on economic grounds. The organization that is being planned, and is already partially effectuated, is related to those orders of ideas and in the practical discussion of its realization considerations derived therefrom prevail. Yet at the base of it all there lies the fact of a spiritual affinity which, across distinctness and discordance, reaches far into history.

With this cultural cohesion there were in former days connected certain political, or ecclesiastical-political, institutions, which although seemingly imposing, were actually decaying and increasingly impotent. And although there was no lack of attempts to renovate them or to found others in their stead, the history of attempts at European unity can never give much encouragement to the strivings of the present day. It presents a series of failures, and one will even detect in it a tendency of "going from bad to worse." But we must not turn to history for encouragement only. It is equally salutary to allow history to show us the limits set to our ambitions. Not that we need be satisfied with an admonition to be cautious. The demonstration of "from bad to worse" may make us conclude that "if we don't show sense, the worst will be upon us." Therefore: "We must." I don't believe for a moment that the future will simply bow down to our imperative, but that does not mean that we should abdicate. This mood of "it never came off, but this time we shall see that it does come off" may inspire fresh attempts that will perhaps help to fashion the future. There will be less chance of disappointment to the extent that we have a clearer perception of the limits of our capacity.

It has sense, then, for the present in which we live, for the problems with which we struggle from year to year, to consult history—primarily in order to refresh and strengthen our awareness of that cultural cohesion on which in the last resort we must rely. History is a vital need of culture.

Let me begin by stating that our European civilization springs from two historic roots: the Graeco-Roman tradition and Christianity. There is nothing novel about this statement. One hears it repeated to satiety. But that does not make it less true or less important. Yet, when one tries to elaborate it in detail, one has to work one's way through a maze of complications and contradictions, by a twilight very often in which the outlines seem to be blurred. This observation will not cast doubt upon the simple thesis that I stated, but the centuries-long process through which the synthesis of the Graeco-Roman and the Christian came into being is far from characterized by simplicity. Every account of it will differ from every other and be marked by the particular preferences and opinions of the observer. And when developments unfold the diversity by which the cultural cohesion is manifested in cultural forms of its own (I am of course thinking of national forms), when the all-embracing Christian unity is torn asunder and faith itself weakened in consequence, the multiplicity of possible presentations and interpretations is certainly not diminished.

I shall first of all indicate—very briefly, and with an almost shameless neglect of shadings and distinctions—what was the heritage of Greek culture.

In the Homeric world already one is struck by the appearance of clearly marked personalities and by the keen attention given to the individual. The Greeks themselves were conscious —in a somewhat later stage at least—of the contrast they presented in that respect with the Asiatic Orient, the world of power states, of despotisms, of arbitrariness and subjection. What they defended against the Persians was, in their own estimation, liberty. The victories of Thermopylae and of Salamis created a respite of some generations, during which the Greek spirit could work on. Its most distinguishing quality—the Oriental civilizations had a brilliance of their own and often displayed a striking technical inventiveness, but in this they were lacking—was the mathematical exactitude of its thinking, its aptitude to appreciate the fact and to subject it to criticism. Plato and Aeschylus still make a glorious appearance, but the modern mind feels a more direct affinity with Thucydides and Aristotle.

In the Roman Empire, in which the independence of the Greek cities and small states was dissolved, the Greek mind— to quote the well-known phrase—conquered its conqueror. The riches of Greek civilization were given shelter in the Empire, and its influence could then spread over a much wider sphere than previously. The Romans, too, had in their republican period valued political liberty, but it was an aristocratic liberty, and by the time of the emperors, little more than its memory was left. Yet the Roman Empire had its contribution to make. Even when it had fallen apart, the organization of power itself, the administration, still proved in its after-effects a fertilizing influence. Especially significant for the future was Roman law, and indeed it was closely bound up with the other factor. After the interruption of the Dark Ages it was dug up and put to practical use, and its firm theoretical foundations and clear definitions, its formulas and modes of argument, formed ties between the Western peoples almost as firm as those of their common Christianity.

Now as regards Christianity. This, too, was able at first to spread within the confines of the Roman Empire. It might be thought that with its renunciation of the world, and directed as it was towards eternity and the hereafter, it offered the sharpest contrast imaginable with the mundane and human traits that seem to be so characteristic of both Greek and Roman civilization. Not, in fact, the sharpest imaginable. The Christian religion has been described as the most Western of the many Oriental religions or mystery cults that in the latter days of the Roman Empire wooed for the soul of a population menaced by decline and ruin. If it took hold, it was because of the unique importance it assigned to the human personality, while the equality of all before God which it preached was to prove a positive and dynamic strengthening of tendencies already present in the Greek city and in the frigid, matter-of-fact law of Rome. It was, in any case, one of the great facts in the development of Western civilization that in the later Middle Ages not only was Roman law "received", but that also the Church, in a way, "received" ancient thinking.

"After a long contest and in a process taking some generations"—I quote from the Dutch Cardinal De Jong's *Manual of Ecclesiastical History*—"and which was completed by Thomas of Aquino, the Aristotelian philosophy, purged from errors, was placed in the service of theology." All this was a truly European achievement. The language used by the theologians, the lawyers, and generally speaking, the scholars, continued to be Latin. This facilitated exchange from country to country. And who does not know that it was the monks who, industriously copying old Latin texts of all kinds, contributed to the salvation of the treasures of ancient culture until succeeding generations reached the stage where they could put them to advantage—there were indeed several stages, the great Renaissance of the fifteenth century being long preceded by similar movements.

I have boldly traced a line from Homer to the fifteenth century. Taking into account all the shocks and revolutions, and moreover all the new departures and goings astray, one can observe continuity. Not until the last phase did this civilization assume forms that we immediately recognize as being our own, but we may say that it is the early history of our European culture that I have been talking about.

Let me point out, however, one aspect that from this point of view constitutes at first sight a difficulty. The geographical delimitation of the process of development I have sketched has been subject to very considerable shifts. (I apologize for the word "sketched", which has to my own ears far too pretentious a sound. I shall indeed, after dealing with these geographical changes, have to say a little more about the political and ecclesiastical history of that early period. But first the shifts in the geographical compass.)

The world of the Greeks had exceeded Greece, but remained bound to the Mediterranean. The Roman Empire, in which Greek civilization found a refuge and in which it so profoundly affected the original human element, still had the Mediterranean for its axis. Asia Minor in the East, and on the other side of the water, North Africa, belonged to it. To the north it stretched towards the Alps and the Rhine, even towards the Danube and the lands of the Black Sea. This, then, was the territory where Christianity was to strike roots, soon recognized, even fostered, by the emperors' authority. But the imperial power falls into dissolution. From their still "barbaric" central European home, the Germanic peoples, crossing the rivers, invade the Empire. The invaders are assimilated, but political unity is broken up. Only in the East, with Byzantium as its centre, does the Empire maintain itself.

In the West, in Gaul, the kingdom of the Franks has been formed; Rome is now only the see of a bishop, who, however, manages to become acknowledged as the head of Western Christendom. The split is confirmed when Charlemagne, in 800, has himself crowned emperor. It is a split, but at the same time an attempt to continue the tradition of unity. And in so far Charlemagne is indeed the true representative of the civilization built up in the Roman Empire, that in expanding his reign across the Rhine he also expands Christianity to these Germanic regions, which had never known imperial sway. After his death, when his ostensibly old, but in fact new, empire is divided, it is even there that the imperial dignity, with its claim to representing unity, is transplanted. A hollow claim at least in terms of politics. And as political unity kept decaying, the cohesiveness of the European world was more and more embodied in the Church and its supreme pastor in Rome. I say "of the European world," for it was to Europe, west and central, that the civilization whose vicissitudes I am trying to trace was now practically confined.

Russia, which was Christianized from Byzantium—let us say in the tenth century and mention the dukedom of Kiev in order to give our thoughts a momentary hold—went through an entirely different political and social development from that of Latin-Christian Europe (to which belonged, let me remind you, Poland and Bohemia, that is, Czechoslovakia). Yet Russia cannot on that account be considered Asiatic and excluded from Europe. Christianity made its influence felt there in different forms—it showed for one thing much less resistance to state despotism—but it did make its influence felt; and ancient civilization penetrated as well, although less profoundly no doubt, through the medium of Byzantium. Let us say then that Russia was a variant of general European civilization, which—to cast a glance into the future—was able in the eighteenth and nineteenth centuries to approach the West, only to take up in our time an attitude of bitter and dogmatic aloofness.

North Africa and Asia Minor, on the contrary, were completely alienated. From the seventh century on, the dynamic Mohammedan movement managed to detach those regions from Western civilization and Christianity. Europe herself was menaced and directly attacked. The rise of an aggressive power on Europe's southeastern border heightened the feeling of solidarity between what had already become independent European powers. The Crusades were a striking sign of this.

The Church, in the early Middle Ages the strongest factor for unity in all spheres of life, could play a particularly active part in this development. It not only dominated thought, without, as I pointed out, barring pre-Christian forms, but it disposed of the only effective organization on the European scene. The Pope exercised his spiritual authority over all rulers; and in spite of the bitter contest over competence between the papacy and the imperial power (which was now in fact confined to central Europe), this had real significance. The Holy See had not yet become so exclusively an Italian institution as it was to be later on. And in any case there were the monastic orders, whose unifying influence made itself felt perhaps even more directly.

The oft-quoted phrase *respublica christiana* must not, however, be taken in too literal a sense. It denoted a vague, and mainly spiritual, conception. Politically it served at most an aspiration which was never realized. There was never anything like a regular, permanent organization embodying the European feeling of kinship. The period resounded with endless quarrels and fights between Christians, on a local scale mostly, because effective action in a larger context was beyond the capacity of the loosely constructed communities. The later Middle Ages indeed, saw the rise, very gradually, of somewhat more strongly organized separate states.

This was a development that spelled danger to European unity, but it is idle to complain. It was an indispensable stage. The medieval world lacked the resources needed for the establishment of an authority over the whole of Europe. For the time being nothing more could be expected than the formation of states of some size, within whose domain local particularism or chaos could be superseded and order guaranteed. No doubt new tensions were thus created, which were to prove increasingly violent and destructive, down to the times in which we live. Disputes and wars between these ambitious new formations were inevitable, and from them the unity of Europe was to suffer worse shocks than from the small-scale scuffles of the preceding period. Yet even now the awareness of a common bond between otherwise hostile nations was not extinguished.

And this although simultaneously the influence of the all-embracing Church was growing weaker. The Renaissance was not anti-Christian. Yet within the Church wholehearted dedication was sapped by abuses, while in the world outside, thinking was not ruled by its initiatives as exclusively as before. Thought was to some extent secularized, although it is worth noticing that in those terms, too, the idea of European cohesion and homogeneity was expressed. Machiavelli, for instance, in *The Prince*, contrasts Europe and Asia. In ancient times already, he saw Asia personified in Darius, the despot, all the rest being no more than slaves; while in Europe *many* shared the work of government. In Machiavelli's own day he personified the same contrast in the Great Turk, the unreservedly despotic Sultan, and in the King of France, who could not rule without the aid of his barons. Machiavelli no longer mentions the *respublica christiana*, nor does he seem to hanker after unity: the numerous states in Europe, each with many men sharing responsibility, create a courage and talents such as are not to be found in Asia. To all appearances, he does not consider their fratricidal warfare too high a price for that advantage.

But the Renaissance was not to be all. Soon the Reformation burst over Europe, and the Church, of old the guardian, even the creator, of unity, was torn asunder.

Thomas More, who refused to take an oath to Henry VIII's supremacy over the English Church and who was therefore brought to the block, was a martyr not only to the cause of papal supremacy, but also to England's historic partnership in a Christian Europe. (This is how an English historian, not himself a Catholic, puts it.)

The Reformation did indeed stimulate and intensify the process, which had long been gathering strength, of the formation of absolute and sovereign states. The religious wars of the late sixteenth and early seventeenth centuries contributed to this development and moreover created other than purely religious ambitions and contrasts. Their violence and destructive effect was such that even Machiavelli, had he lived to see them, could hardly have taken them so lightly. Even before those wars, Erasmus had sounded a very different note: Peace, peace! had been his deep-felt wish. Grotius's *De jure belli et pacis* was inspired by the same sentiment. Erasmus, however, had not gone beyond philanthropic, pacifist preaching. Grotius, basing himself (curiously enough) on the work of Spanish Jesuits particularly, constructed a complete system of international law which was to be valid for princes and republics alike and which was to make it possible to identify the unjust war and to brand it as a crime. The questions of *who* was to do this, and *who* was to intervene —to prevent or to punish—he left unanswered; indeed he hardly posed them. The author's ideal aim, the establishment of an international community ruled by law, was not brought any nearer to practical realization by his famous book. Yet the mere thought of a generally acknowledged international law, which was its message, served to strengthen the common bond.

The division of Europe into Protestant and Catholic did not apparently make an absolute separation any longer: that is what we may conclude from Grotius's building upon foundations laid by Spanish Jesuits, and indeed from the respectful attention given to his book all over Europe. There are many signs of the European idea still living in men's minds. Towards the close of 1646 Charles I, in his turn head of Henry VIII's national church, was a prisoner of his own people. And now he addressed himself to the other Christian rulers, who were at that moment negotiating peace at the Münster Congress, reminding them that his cause was theirs also and exhorting them to come to his aid when peace had been restored. It was indeed an appeal to a shadowy solidarity, and it found no response.

Nor can it be denied that after, no less than before, the peace of Münster, in the actuality of international politics, the cause of unity fared worse and worse. In the cultural sphere, too, there was more than only the schism in the Church, which had, when it was the one and only Church, tended to impart a single general direction to the underlying variety. The dominance of Latin had long been weakened, and the prestige of literature in the popular languages was increasing all the time. This was only one aspect of a development that sprang, as it were, automatically from the operation of states embracing much larger entities and affecting people's lives much more profoundly, a development of national consciousness within each particular state. In the episode of Joan of Arc one sees an early sign of this. How strongly and articulately does it speak in Shakespeare! And in Holland, a generation later, in Vondel!

But it is in the *politics* of the seventeenth century that the movement away from universality can be observed most strikingly. It was the century of Richelieu, and in its second half, of Louis XIV: the sovereign state that was a law unto itself, that strived systematically after more power, more prestige, more territory—the great minister, and after him, the

Sun King, "le grand roi," as his admiring subjects called him, were its most conspicuous personifications, and they regarded the glory and the advantage of the wearer of the crown as the glory and the advantage of the entire nation. *National* glory and *national* advantage were the stakes for which the century's indefatigable power-policy, and its wars, were carried on. And no room was left for any thought of the interest of Europe. Europe was no more than the field of contest where every contestant was intent upon nothing but his *own* preservation, his *own* gain. At most, Europe could figure as a unity in the overstrained ambition to shine with a lustre superior to all other rulers, to establish a *universal monarchy*. This was the mood that was also prevalent at the Emperor's court, and one can observe it, if not, naturally, with the same wide-straying tendency, in princes like the dukes of Savoy, the electors of Brandenburg, and many others.

France furnishes the most striking example because it was the most powerful among the states that had emerged from the medieval confusion, and because in the course of time the others began to feel menaced by Louis XIV's insatiable land hunger. And so the very excesses of that unbridled ambition, that policy inspired by the most exclusive national and dynastic interests, tirelessly intriguing, thinking out combinations, and interfering, if not directly resorting to arms, did in the end evoke a manifestation of European solidarity.

I am thinking of the coalitions that William III spent his life in trying to build up in order to restrain France. That generation was still inclined to see the real danger arising from the Catholic versus Protestant contrast. To the Dutch, Louis was the persecutor of the Huguenots; what mattered now was to defend the Protestant religion, at home and in the whole of Europe, against his aggression. In 1688 William III set out for England as the champion of that country's *liberty and its Protestant religion*. The Catholic Hapsburg ruler at Vienna, however, was the great rival of Louis, and the coalitions were mixed Protestant and Catholic. When Protestant-Catholic co-operation was aimed at, the fear that statesmen could openly advance was only that Louis was out for *universal monarchy*. In 1707 the English Parliament declared—and nothing could be more in harmony with William III's way of thinking—that it meant to stand up to Louis for the sake of *the liberties of Europe*. The European solidarity to which the English Parliament thus appealed was, after the Glorious Revolution and after Locke, of a different conception from that which had occurred to the mind of Charles I in his hour of need. This word *liberties*, however, was far from denoting a universally admitted principle. The principles of dynastic prerogative and of popular co-responsibility would still have to wage a bitter contest, in which indeed the latter principle was to gain the upper hand. However, now, at any rate, solidarity could consist in nothing but resistance to the one most powerful, in the instinct of self-preservation of the numerous independent weaker ones. Peace and security were sought in a balance-of-power system.

It was exhausting work to have to lead those coalitions. Was I justified in describing them as a manifestation of European solidarity? William III at one moment grumbled about his Englishmen, who cared so little about what happened on the Continent and seemed to imagine that they were alone in the world; then again about his Dutchmen, who preferred to make themselves small in their little corner, hoping that the storm would spare them; and all the time he was plagued with the particular demands of the Emperor and of the petty German and Italian princes on the anti-French side and with their mutual rivalries. These coalitions themselves bring out the weakness of the sentiment of European community of interest in the existing disruption into sovereign states.

The danger of French domination was averted—for the time being. But the eighteenth century still had no better system for the organization of Europe than one of combinations keeping each other more or less in check. What did the balance of power mean? In the instruction of a French ambassador the answer was given as it were with a shrug: "C'est une chose de pure opinion" (all interpret it in accordance with their own views or interests). And the great French historian Albert Sorel (late nineteenth century) concludes: "There was no

Europe, there were but nations and states." And to be sure, one war succeeded another. Prussia now is the most dynamic player in that game, but the situation was not a little complicated by the conflict between the colonial ambitions of England and France in Asia and America. Principles of law were much invoked in international relations, and theoreticians, following the example of Grotius, filled many books on the subject. But the moral norm that Grotius had placed in the centre was lost sight of, and Vattel raised state sovereignty into an absolute. The Polish partitions, for which Prussia, Austria, and Russia conspired in time of peace, were an insolent negation of that order of law which was still given the homage of words and in which the small states sought their security. The first partition, in 1772, created considerable alarm among them.

As a matter of fact, there were thoughtful men everywhere who understood that something was wrong. It was a time when there was a good deal of thinking done, critical thinking. The Enlightenment undertook to apply the standard of reason to all phenomena, national and international. If the spectacle of practical politics must make one sigh "There was no Europe," an examination of intellectual life will on the contrary evoke a clear picture of true European homogeneousness.

This new spirit is seen at work everywhere—in fact it was in many respects no more than the acceleration or intensification of older tendencies. Society had long been undergoing shifts and changes as a result of which inherited institutions and customs were often felt to irk. Everywhere an ambitious middle-class had grown up. With veritable passion the existing state of affairs was criticized and the desire for reforms rationalized. From the late Middle Ages on, the rulers, with the wholehearted co-operation of their lawyers and ministers, had already dared, within certain limits, to lay hands on traditions and to carry through reforms. The period was now marked by the Enlightened Despots, who carried on this work with a new zeal and in spheres hitherto left alone. Even Russia, where that broad middle-class was lacking, had been by Peter the Great, and was now by Catherine, opened up for this Western influence. Everywhere the Enlightened Despots were applauded by the philosophers (as the leaders of the Enlightenment were called in France).

Intellectually, or propagandistically, France played a leading role from the middle of the eighteenth century on. This was partly due to the position the French language had acquired among the aristocrats and the intellectuals of all countries, so much so that it had almost become a European *lingua franca*, a substitute for Latin, which was more and more losing that position. The conceptions and the methods, however, were no specifically French possession. They resulted from the centuries-long process to which all peoples had made a contribution of their own—of late, and very particularly, the English. The Germans, the Italians, the Dutchmen, who proved receptive to that great movement and went enthusiastically along with it, cannot be dispatched as mere disciples of either the English or the French. Among them, too, this spirit worked from the inside. There was a concordance of views and aspirations arising naturally from each nation's particular as well as from the universal-European development.

The intellectuals of the period were aware of this. Each might feel warmly for his own country and at moments of international tension side with it unhesitatingly, yet each knew that Europe constituted a cultural unity. Burke, who, of course, cannot without qualification be called a spokesman of the Enlightenment, said that in manners and education, in the modes of intercourse and in the entire conduct of life, there was from country to country so much similarity that no citizen of Europe could be wholly an exile in any part of it. Montesquieu went even a little too far when he described Europe as one state composed of several provinces. Another remark of his is, on the contrary, very true: "What all countries of Europe have in common is a spirit of liberty, which has always made it difficult to subject them to an alien power." And Voltaire says it most strikingly of all: "Europe is a kind of large commonwealth, divided into several states, all of which support the same principles of public law and politics, unknown in the rest of the world."

In France the spirit of the Enlightenment developed in a

more vehement sense and acquired more radical tendencies than elsewhere; soon the Revolution set to work to carry through reforms more thoroughgoing and less respectful of old traditions than those of the Enlightened Despots in Prussia, in Austria, in Belgium, in Russia. Why precisely in France? No single answer will fit that question, but let me concentrate on one of the many factors that any full explanation will have to consider: in France the monarchy was not enlightened and had allowed the reforming task that it, too, had somewhat fitfully attempted, to get completely stuck. In fact, the Enlightened Despots elsewhere had not been so enterprising or so consistent but that in their countries, too, the French example was bound to make an impression. The French Revolution, moreover, presented the dramatic aspect of a struggle for the ideal of liberty, a struggle against despotism as such. This could not but evoke a response among the peoples that were governed despotically, in however enlightened a sense.

What I want to bring out is that in the period opening in 1789 the unity of Europe, its unity in the sphere of civilization and society, was strikingly demonstrated; more, was strengthened and deepened. Especially if it is realized that the period was not exclusively dominated by the Revolution. The Revolution has largely shaped the future, but the resistance, too, has left profound traces. And this resistance was equally firmly rooted in European traditions. It is the contest between rationalistic reforming zeal, whipping itself up to excesses, and traditionalist conservatism, tainted with class interest and selfishness no doubt, but nevertheless representing an indispensable form of life—it is this contest, to which the Restoration did not put an end, in which divided Europe once again attested its essential unity. Action and reaction were both European, and both fruitful. If one tries to think that thought through, one is presented with the conclusion that Europe realized herself even in the wars to which the Revolution gave rise. Paradoxical as it may sound, I can accept that conclusion.

II

I shall now look a little more closely at the significance of the French Revolution for our problem—the problem of European unity. Before everything, I want to underline the fact that the Revolution in its first phase presented itself in the conceptions and the terminology of the Enlightenment, the thinking of which was so markedly universalist. Reason, common to all men, undertook to lay down what was good for all men. The preamble to the famous "Declaration of the Rights of Man and of the Citizen" of August 1789 spoke, not for the French citizen, but for mankind. It meant indeed to brush aside what had grown up historically in favour of what, from before the formation of states and governments, before their abuses and misdeeds, had always been, and would always remain, the rights of man. Not long before, England's rebellious North American colonies had introduced in similar terms the declaration by which they announced their independence to the world. There has been a good deal of dispute as to how far the French was an imitation of the American declaration. I believe that we must explain the similarity by the fact that all peoples of Western culture (and the Americans who were in revolt against England can safely be regarded as Englishmen) shared the cult of reason and natural rights typical of the Enlightenment. This makes it at the same time understandable that both these declarations, and particularly, of course, the French one, made so profound an impression upon the European peoples.

I said a moment ago *universalist*, and I have now switched over to *European*. The Enlightenment may have progressively become more anti-religious; it built on the foundations inherited from Christianity. In its absolutist attitude of mind this becomes manifest. It demanded the entire person and the entire world. Thus it was that the French in their initial ecstasy did not reckon with frontiers, and thought, not beyond France only, but beyond Europe. *Mankind*, that is how the enthusiasts felt it, was reborn in 1789. In practice, however—and is it not natural? for in practice history does not allow itself to be disposed of so easily (we experience this truth today at every turn, as our predecessors have experienced it in their time!)—in practice the influence of the enthusiasts remained limited—for the time being, if you like, but certainly for a long, long period—to the countries where men's minds were prepared for it, where they had already been touched by the Enlightenment, that is to say, it was limited to Europe. Anacharsis Cloots, *l'orateur du genre humain*, remains a figure of fun.

But as far as Europe is concerned, then, did the spirit of 1789 lead to a strengthening of the sentiment of unity? For that is where my argument seems to tend. Everybody knows that the contrary is often maintained, namely, it is maintained that it was the French Revolution that created nationalism—nationalism that was to prove the greatest threat to European unity. Well, I admit an element of truth in that thesis too—although I do not agree that the Revolution *created* nationalism; let us say, stimulated, stirred to a particular virulence. We are faced, then, with two opposing tendencies both of which can be attributed to the Revolution.

It is a fascinating spectacle to see how in the thinking and the acting of the men of the French Revolution the two tendencies appear in close conjunction: how nationalism was fed by universalism, until the latter ideology, sucked empty, was thrown away. What facilitated the transition from universalism to nationalism was messianism. In their early enthusiasm the French wanted the entire world to share their happiness, but they could not think otherwise than that *they* should bring that boon to the others. They were carried away by an exalted feeling of having a mission to fulfil. They promised support to all peoples seeking liberty—but it must be *their* kind of liberty. When it comes to war—war with the monarchs as it was termed—the old and all-too-human ambitions of the French monarchical policy spring to life in the hearts of the revolutionaries: the cry of *the natural frontiers* drowns out that of humanity. The passion of the Revolution allies itself automatically with the passions that always accompany war, and the struggle with hostile Europe, a Europe, blind, backward, slavishly attached to its evil traditions and its princes (that is how French enthusiasm sees it), becomes a popular cause such as wars under the old regime had seldom been. Some of the conquered peoples—the Belgians, for instance—would not understand what blessings the conquerors showered on them. It is small wonder that the horrors staged during the Terror turned the original sympathy for the self-styled liberators into feelings of suspicion and aversion. But such peoples were with a heavy hand "forced to be free"—to use a horrifying phrase of Rousseau's.

When Napoleon enters the stage of history and curbs the Revolution, nothing is left of liberty at all. But did he not attempt to unite Europe? Purely and simply as a conqueror. Even so, there were those in Europe who were ready to accept him and his enforced and despotic unity. In Holland, for instance, the orthodox Protestant Bilderdijk, in the days of the Republic a fervent supporter of the House of Orange, prophesied in 1806, in his *Ode to Napoleon*, that the upshot of all the suffering would be salutary. Dirk van Hogendorp, too, the brother of G. K. van Hogendorp, who was to play so courageous and statesmanlike a part in the insurrection of 1813 and the restoration of Dutch independence, in 1808 applauded Napoleon as the hero who would give the world peace. Germans and Italians joined in that chorus.

The large majority of the French themselves for a long time venerated Napoleon as the man who not only had established order in their country and won it glory, but who spread the beneficial principles of the Revolution over Europe. Pitt, who at the Lord Mayor's banquet of November 1803 spoke those famous words, "England has saved herself by her exertions and will, as I trust, save Europe by her example," was in *their* view the leader of the English aristocracy and of the powers of darkness everywhere. English liberty in those days was certainly far from perfect, yet the consciousness of fighting for liberty was by no means alive among the aristocracy only.

In the end, Napoleon's coercive rule proved unable to found a firm system of European unity. It goaded the peoples, the Germans, the Spaniards, in 1812 even the Russians, into

open resistance, or at least, it fostered feelings of resentment
and aversion; it made the peoples aware of their own particular
natures, interests, aspirations; in short, against French
nationalism it called into being multiple nationalisms.

The first thought of the victors at the Congress of Vienna
was, naturally enough, to organize Europe in order to prevent
a new period of war. But after the downfall of Napoleon
Europe was the prey of an indescribable confusion and fermen-
tation of minds. The nationalist movements had been directed
against a France that still pretended to be the bearer of the
principles of the Revolution, and they had thus sought strength
in historical, religious, legitimist, conceptions. But Napoleon
had at the same time been the military despot, and so the
revolutionary ideology had done service together with or
against the other. How easily it could now be mobilized against
rulers who bluntly interpreted the Restoration as meaning a
return to the untenable conditions of the past, against rulers
who, as in the Hapsburg monarchy and in Italy, were alien to
the populations!

The Holy Alliance, concluded, at the initiative of Czar
Alexander, between himself, the Austrian Emperor, and the
King of Prussia, was intended to be the nucleus of the desired
organization of Europe. Quoting Holy Writ, the partners
testified to the most complete community of interests, in which
their peoples were to share: they were to form *one Christian
nation*. The true aim was, however, to restrain whatever might
still stir of the diabolical tendencies of the Revolution. In spite
of all the fine phrases, Metternich turned the Alliance into an
instrument of espionage and suppression, using it in the
provinces of the Hapsburg monarchy, and outside it, in the
German Confederation and in Italy, against all democratic
or nationalist movements. England, little more liberal under
Castlereagh, acceded by a separate treaty. As early as 1818
France, now under Bourbon rule, was admitted as a fifth
partner. Congresses were held regularly to maintain strict
supervision over the affairs of all countries, to prevent, in
other words, the Revolution from raising its head anywhere.

It was, as it were, a last attempt on the part of that dynastic

Europe to which Charles I in 1646 had made his vain appeal. At that time it had hardly had shape, and now that it did constitute itself it proved unable to master the spirit of the time. After Castlereagh's death, England, under Canning, freed itself from Castlereagh's reactionary tendencies. The English government openly disapproved of the expedition undertaken by France—where reaction still had the better of revolutionary stirrings—at the instigation of "Europe", to suppress a rising against the King of Spain. With regard to the revolt in Greece and to the collapse of Spanish rule in South America, too, Canning followed a line of his own. The solidarity of the great powers had thus fallen apart even before, in 1830, the Bourbons were chased from France. The reign of Louis Philippe, the Citizen King, did not in the long run satisfy the radical elements, and in the forties a powerful revival of revolutionary sentiment manifested itself, and raised echoes all over Europe.

A moment ago I spoke of "the spirit of the time." But I must not be understood to mean that there was no ideological counter-current. I recall Ranke, to whom the states—not the peoples—were "ideas of God"; in the state alone the individual can realize himself, even without any democratic share in the responsibility; power is the primary quality of the state. Yet from our point of view there was a positive element in the mind of the historian whose work was to do so much to shape political thinking: he believed in Europe. He saw the power game of the great European states controlled by an eternal equipoise and European civilization benefiting from their variety and their struggles. An optimism that was to be sadly put to shame by what later generations had to suffer.

As a matter of fact, this kind of European idealism stood outside what was coming to be the reality: the development of popular nationalisms. The existing state formations in Central Europe—in Italy, in Austria and Hungary, in Ranke's own Germany—became the butt of the aspirations once stirred up by Napoleon: the clamour now was for a state based on each particular nationality, covering the whole of a linguistic area. *The people* and *a share in the government*, those were the slogans. Everywhere, national movements allied themselves with liberal or radical sentiment, sentiment tracing its origin to the Revolution. And here, too, the universalist thinking of the Enlightenment and of the Revolution was in evidence, although practically speaking, once more, *universalist* meant *European*. The synthesis of nationalism and Europeanism was embodied in Mazzini. The passionate Italian nationalist and republican looked beyond Italy. He maintained close contacts—mostly in common exile—with the radicals of other oppressed and dissatisfied nations, and with them he dreamed of: away with kings; Europe a federation of free republics!

The Communist Manifesto of 1847—"Proletarians of all countries, unite!"—belongs organically to the same state of mind. To Marx, however, nationality was but a category of capitalism and fated to be superseded with it. In his view it was only the fight against the bourgeoisie that counted.

In February 1848 revolution broke out in Paris. The memories of 1789 and 1792, revived in the preceding years in a flood of historical writings, by Buchez, by Lamartine, by Louis Blanc, by Michelet, now demonstrated their dynamic power in actual fact. Messianism was always an important factor; in practice it meant: French conceit; French chauvinism. "When Providence desires an idea to inflame the world, it kindles it in the soul of a Frenchman." So says Lamartine. And Michelet: "France believes that she cannot render a greater service to the world than by presenting it with her ideas, her ways of living, her fashions." And it should not be thought that he disapproves or writes ironically. He *glories* in this "assimilation des intelligences," this "conquête des volontés"; according to him this is something quite different from the mere egoism of Rome's, or England's, imperialism.

We see again how Europeanism might slip over into a dangerous kind of nationalism. Meanwhile, in Poland, in Italy, in the German Confederation, the cry of national liberty, national unity, rises to a higher pitch: the growths of history are to be drastically corrected. And the French revolutionaries acclaim what they consider to be the effect of their example. All European nations will be liberated, all united in fraternity.

Failure was followed by disillusionment. The middle class,

which had after all the tempestuous courses of the Revolution of 1789 in the end pocketed the gains, maintained itself now too and presented a bold front to the future. But when we think of European unity, the striking fact is that the historic power consolidated in the states so dear to Ranke's heart did indeed hold the field. It is true that in Italy and in Germany the movements for national unity bided their time and were in the end to prove irresistible. But here, too, the lead was no longer with the idealists, deriving their thought from the Revolution and striving after a synthesis with Europe. It had fallen to men devoted to that same historic power, men who only *used* nationalist enthusiasm and who did not regard Europe with any feelings or aspirations of fraternity, men to whom Europe was (as it had been to Richelieu and Louis XIV) a field of contest, where combinations could be devised to create constellations enabling them to bring off their *coups*.

What was at hand was the time of Cavour, and above all, of course, of Bismarck.

Bismarck had in 1848 resolutely opposed all those revolutionary doings of the German nationalists who had wanted to dissolve Prussia into a liberalized, or even radicalized, Germany. All he wanted was to serve the state and the King of Prussia. He was as little satisfied with the German Confederation as were the enthusiasts for German unity, for in it Prussia played second fiddle to Austria. In any case, he never believed that solutions could be obtained as a result of popular excitement and eloquence: "blood and iron" was the only way. The power policy he had carried out in the sixties, as the King of Prussia's minister, he continued after 1870 for the Emperor he had helped to make. First its aim had been conquest, now it was consolidation, but as regards the fundamental principle—that his royal, now imperial, master's interest must come before all other considerations—there was no change. The sensational successes of his policy, even before 1870, dazzled the German liberals and made them forget *their* principles. The historians moved away from Ranke's European view and began to take the interest of Prussia, as the predestined creator of German unity, for the standard by which to judge all things. Treitschke, who had started as a liberal, later proclaimed the tenet: "To cultivate its power is the state's highest moral duty." Unconditional submission to the purpose of power, this now came to be an article of faith in Germany, and one result was—especially after Bismarck's gigantic personality had gone—that the army, or the officer's caste, acquired a dominant position in the direction of the state.

For the European idea this development meant a regression. And at the same time, in France the loss of Alsace-Lorraine left an unappeasable sense of grievance. The feud between the two leading powers of the Continent poisoned the entire European atmosphere. In France, too, there grew up a nationalism of a much more virulent kind than Louis XIV's primarily dynastic policy or than the nationalism of the Revolution which, chauvinistic as it became, still retained an element of idealism. This new nationalism indeed set itself squarely against the ideology of the Revolution. The messianism of those heroic years, so it was now argued, had contributed towards bringing about France's weakness. It was time to stop this madly generous, this ruinous, devotion to the salvation of *the world;* France must think of herself.

In Charles Maurras's *Action française* this new attitude found its most uncompromising expression. "La France seule" was one of his slogans, and it could not be put more briefly and more pointedly. In the Dreyfus affair Maurras had considered the question of guilty or not guilty of less importance than the safety of France, which was guaranteed only by the army: no doubt must be cast on the honour of the devoted officers' corps for the sake of a Jewish intruder. The *Action française* glorified *le grand siècle* of Louis XIV as a source of inspiration for the present; the movement advocated a return to the Monarchy: the Republic, according to its teaching, was a revolutionary and impotent abortion. This, while the Republic was preening itself on having concluded an alliance with Czarist Russia, which exposed Germany to the danger of a war on two fronts.

The *Action française* never succeeded in cutting a figure in practical politics. It exercised, nevertheless, a powerful influence over the public mind. Intellectual circles took Maurras very seriously indeed. The sham logic he presented with bitter passion somehow touched deep springs of the French soul.

The French-German feud was at the basis of the intolerable tension prevailing in Europe, but there were several hearths of unrest, especially in the southern-Slav world, where rising national sentiment began to clash with existing arrangements. Austria-Hungary felt itself menaced and looked upon Russia as a possible enemy. The great powers were allied in two groups, and although peace was for a long time preserved, a mad armament-competition kept nerves on edge. In 1899 a peace conference assembled in The Hague. The initiative had been taken by the young Czar Nicholas II, and what he had had in mind originally was to bring about a coming together of all the states that were willing to make world peace secure. "Stupid blunder of a young dreamer," was Kaiser Wilhelm's private comment; "grist on the mills of socialists and antimilitarists." But for decency's sake the conference could not be declined. It became a hollow show. The German representative declared, bluntly, but at least frankly, that his country did not feel oppressed by the cost of armament and that the German people discharged their military service with feelings of pride and satisfaction. The conference was to have met again, but the Boer War, which broke out in that same year, 1899, caused the plan to be shelved.

The acutely nationalistic mood was not confined to Germany and France, not to the Continent. In England men like Gladstone and Cobden, much as they differed in mental structure, had had this in common: the conception of Europe meant something to them. With Joseph Chamberlain, nationalist conceit and self-righteousness came to prevail in a particularly offensive manner. It is true that a revival of the liberal outlook soon followed, and in France, too, attempts were made to temper the international contrasts. But the catastrophe, prepared by a generation of power politics and nationalist narrowness could no longer be averted.

E.H.   N

The war of 1914 to 1918, with its mass armies deadlocked in the murderous trenches, with Russia thrown into revolution and Austria-Hungary in dissolution, shook Europe more violently than even the Napoleonic wars had done. At the Congress of Versailles, as at Vienna a century before, the victors felt that an attempt must be made to prevent a repetition. The League of Nations, planned by the peace treaty, was in a way a counterpart of the Holy Alliance. If the Holy Alliance had failed, it was largely because it was so blunt a negation of the principles of the Revolution, which, related as they were to some of the oldest and most distinctive features of European civilization, had proved too powerful for a merely conservative "restoration." Now the war had been waged by the western European powers under the slogan of protection of democracy against autocracy and militarism, even before the idea found its prophet in the president of the great extra-European power that came in the last stage to intervene in European affairs, for the first time—and decisively.

Wilson came to Versailles with definite conceptions about the principles that ought to govern the drafting of the peace treaty; he had formulated them in advance in the Fourteen Points. He also had a project for the League of Nations ready: it was in his idea to clinch the arrangements to be laid down by the peace treaty and to insure permanency. The exhausted European victors could not but listen with due respect to the man who seemed to command the unimpaired strength and wealth of America. Why did it all once more end in disappointment?

The Fourteen Points had been dictated by a well-meaning care for the interests of a peaceful world community. But it proved not so easy to translate them into practice. Historic insight was too completely lacking in Wilson's mentality for him to foresee that old prejudices and blind sentiments would put up strenuous resistance and that the truths he preached would be interpreted variously in various countries. The Italians and the southern Slavs, for instance, each claimed that the right of self-determination supported their cause. The French and the English could not at once get the better of the hatred and suspicion of the Germans into which they had worked themselves up during the war years. The French were inclined to look for their security, as of old, in a weakening of the redoubtable neighbour country even though it might now disguise itself as a republic. They wanted the Rhineland, at least the Saar district. The English public joined in the chorus claiming crushing war-indemnities. Wilson, with his generalizing and moralistic preoccupations, was helpless in the face of such unregenerate manifestations.

He spoke of "American principles" that he advocated. According to him they were "the principles of mankind" and they *must* prevail. The tone of messianism is unmistakable. It was not the French, this time, who knew, but the Americans, and so they were *called*. But the sequel shows once again how easily this spirit can turn into the most selfish nationalism.

Coming home with the result of the Congress, in which little was left of the Fourteen Points, and with the League of Nations project, which must still put everything right, the President was abandoned by his own people. The mood of the American public was no less self-righteous than was his own, but its conclusion was to wash its hands of this incorrigible Europe, quarrelsome and divided by nationalisms. The Senate voted down the League of Nations, and the United States withdrew for many years into a sterile isolationism.

Not only the United States, Russia too stood aside. For a long time the Western powers regarded the Russian Revolution as an irregularity that was bound to be straightened out sooner or later. On its part, the authoritarian minority rule that had become established in that country interpreted the slogan "Proletarians of all countries, unite!" in so dogmatically one-sided a manner that an absolute separation from the rest of Europe came about.

By themselves the western European powers were unable to make a success of the League of Nations. Such paper arrangements cannot in one blow change the course of history. Zealous Europeans said at the time—and they still say—that the League of Nations could not do it because it had not been fitted out with supranational authority. But that nostrum won't cure everything either. The forces that make history come from the bottom, and in Europe they were indissolubly tied (and still are, of course) to the nations and states that, with their several interests and traditions, composed the European community. In order to understand the failure of the League of Nations the observation of its organizational weaknesses will not help much: the political conditions and feelings actually prevailing in Europe will have to be examined. It will then be noticed that, certainly, the cultural cohesion maintained itself, also that many in all countries realized the danger threatening all of us and urged the necessity of international co-operation, but that nevertheless there was still, as a legacy from the preceding period, in each country a large public opinion passionately cheering on its government's unrestrained selfishness.

The most pernicious phenomenon was the ever-rankling Franco-German feud. Instead of giving a fair chance to the German Republic (of Weimar), seriously trying as it was to master the evil tendencies of the Wilhelminian period, the French kept making things difficult for it; especially the French, but the English, too, often behaved unwisely in this respect. Practically, western policy encouraged the German nationalists of various descriptions in their reckless opposition to what they denounced as the weaknesses of their own German government. This German opposition inveighed against the humiliations that the treaty of Versailles was still inflicting upon Germany; the economic crisis by which the country was being overwhelmed, too, they explained as an effect of the treaty. An impassioned nationalism burst forth.

We now see the fateful figure of Hitler rising up. I pay a tribute in passing to Stresemann and Briand, who still did what they could to avert the disaster; I mention Locarno. But National Socialism did come into power. And glorifying race as it did, clamouring for a strong state that, inexorably one, was to make the German will prevail at whatever cost, it was the denial of all European order, of Europe itself.

I quoted Maurras's saying, "la France seule." In 1932,

shortly before the *Machtübernahme*, I attended a students' congress in Germany and got acquainted at first hand with the National Socialist madness. Among my most vivid memories is the abhorrence with which I heard Count Reventlow's contumelious rejection of the entire conception of Europe. There was no sense in it, there was no such thing, there was only Germany: Europe was a phantasm invented to paralyze the courage and the energy of a great nation.

Well, we have seen to what all this led the Germans and the world. Europe was renounced not only politically, but culturally and morally. Triumphant National Socialism amounted to a veritable revolt against Western civilization, to its negation.

In the end, however, Europe did have a place in the National Socialist imagination and in the National Socialist propaganda, but only as an object of conquest and of domination. And it is to be noted that many people outside Germany hoped—you will remember my pointing to the corresponding phenomenon in the days of Napoleon—that the longed-for unity of Europe might in this fashion be realized. So spoke our Dutch N.S.B.-ers (members of the Dutch "National Socialist" movement), and there are a few left who still do. But there were men of an entirely different outlook who were impressed by this slogan of European unity. They deluded themselves into believing that the excesses did not belong organically to National Socialism: they would not last. No doubt, authoritarianism was the very essence of the German dynamism that seemed to be changing the world. But they were prepared to sacrifice democratic liberty to this idolized unity. A strong impetus was given to this way of thinking in 1941, when Hitler made war on Russia. "Europe united against Bolshevism," was the cry then raised. In that enchanting vision the national particularisms of Europe could appear insignificant. England? Did England *belong* to Europe? Had not England at all times been the enemy of European unity? Had not England thwarted the great work time and again—as it was trying to do now?

Actually England was then making a stand, as it had done against Louis XIV and Napoleon, for the salvation of

European liberty. William III, Pitt, Churchill—they form a sequence. And what is Europe without liberty? I have stressed how from the beginning liberty has been the guarantee and the hallmark of Western civilization. One of the most fertile forms in which the resulting diversity appears, is the national. No unity can be allowed to stifle or to blur it—or disturbing reactions will result. Diversity, that is how the great Swiss historical thinker Burckhardt put it in 1869 (without expressly mentioning the national, but it is implied in the passage): diversity, the struggle between individual forces, and the harmony arising out of those various sounds of tendencies, groups, and individuals, this is the essence of European civilization.

> It is menaced by only one danger that might prove fatal: that of an oppressive mechanical power, whether on the part of a conquering barbaric people or of the aggregate means of power within its own confines mobilized in the service of one tendency.

This is how the large majority of the Dutch people felt it under the occupation, and more intensely as the visitation lasted longer. In France, which went through an unprecedented moral collapse and where Pétain had concluded his unholy pact with the victor, men's minds were divided much more profoundly. There, moreover, a factor rooted in history was at work: the old distrust of England, mixed with envy. To range Churchill in one sequence with William III and Pitt would probably be regarded by a Frenchman with very different feelings than I meant to evoke.

Nevertheless, in the last instance the mood was determined everywhere by the aversion and hatred the occupying power roused against itself with its increasingly brutal methods. In the end we owed our liberation to the stubborn perseverance of the English people and the overwhelming power of the United States.

But what about the problem of European unity after the downfall of Hitler and his system? Was the story of the years after 1918 to be repeated and the German people, while trying amid the ruins to recover its senses, to be confused and goaded into fresh outbreaks of fury by the nationalist ambitions of the others? Even in Holland there was wild talk of annexations at the expense of Germany. For a few years France persisted in its eastward expansionist ambitions—I am thinking of the Saar region. But the acute menace presented by Stalinist Russia, whose power now stretched westward down to and across the river Elbe, made the aid of what remained of Germany indispensable. The antagonism between Russia and the West (that is to say, Europe, insofar as it was still free, and the United States) soon paralyzed the organization of the United Nations, which had been meant to be an amended League of Nations. From the point of view of my theme the United Nations hardly comes into sight. The League of Nations, too, had been projected for a world organization, but the European powers and their mutual relations had held the stage at Geneva. In the United Nations, Europe was submerged in the mass of extra-European countries animated by a new consciousness of their importance. But in fact the Russian vetoes undermined the effectiveness of that grandiose enterprise. At any rate, it could not play a part in the organization of Europe. Only America made its influence powerfully felt once more.

In these circumstances a deliberate endeavour to reintegrate Germany into the West soon won through, and it is one of the most auspicious phenomena of recent years that this process has followed so smooth a course. The most beneficial aspect has been the settlement of the Franco-German feud that had for generations dominated the European scene. An atmosphere has been created in which it is possible once more to work with some hope for the unity of Europe (of a Europe, it is true, suffering from an amputation on its eastern side).

After all periods of war this idea emerges: after 1815, after 1918. The lesson has been more severe this time; the ardour is more intense; the chances are more favourable. The fact that there is, compared with earlier periods, a larger measure of consensus on democracy—due to the experience with National Socialism as well as to the new menace of Communism—is, in particular, an inestimable gain. Something has been achieved already. I am thinking of the Council of Europe and the European Parliament at Strasbourg; of the Organization for European Economic Co-operation; of the North Atlantic Treaty Organization, too, even though the leading part in it is played by the United States. It is more, and it seems more solid, than anything that was built up on earlier occasions.

And the Europe of "the Six"?

I have repeatedly given expression to my doubts about the wisdom as well as the practicability of that undertaking. I think that for the smaller partners (the Benelux countries) it contains downright dangerous possibilities. This does not belong to my subject. But I want to indicate very briefly how my view of the history of Europe, as I have unfolded it very sketchily here, leads me to these doubts.

The first thing that fills me with astonishment is that the creators of the association of "the Six" have presumed to claim for it the name "Europe," and that the Europe enthusiasts exultingly applaud an arrangement that may well turn out to have prepared a cleavage in Europe. This small Continental Europe has never been on the order of the day in history except under circumstances unacceptable for the true European. If we seek the unity of Europe in liberty, it is absurd to leave England outside, England, which has on three occasions stood in the breach for the liberty of Europe—and the last time the most glorious.

Speaking generally, throughout the unceasing changes to which conditions and ways of thinking are subject in the course of the centuries—and our generation has lived through some dizzying changes—I am struck by the persistence, the stubborn durability, of fundamental characteristics. The belief of the idealistic or revolutionary mentality that we can at a given moment begin, so to speak, on a clean slate, is a dangerous illusion. Such, for instance, is the idea that the French and the Germans are from now on nothing but Europeans. They are still, respectively, Frenchmen and Germans, and so are we Dutch still Dutchmen, and it is right that we should, and we must, be. But can we make our influence felt with regard to the powerful nations to which we have tied ourselves by the treaty of Rome? Does not our enthusiasm for the idea of supranationalism impede us in our freedom to watch over our interests?—more than it does them? Do the articles of the treaty leave us room, for instance, to promote the extension of the association that our government assures us it desires, but that seems to hitch every time on the unwillingness especially of the French? I shall no more than mention the directly elected parliament that is in course of preparation and that to me seems to be a most questionable experiment. Not only because it is likely to prove an unsurpassable obstacle to the English, but in itself: how is it possible to expect reliable guidance from so heterogeneous a body, one whose members will be drawn largely from nations that have not made a conspicuous success of parliamentary government at home?

Enough of questions. The historian is no prophet. The future is to him an impenetrable mystery as it is to all of us mortals. But for all that, history sharpens the eye for possibilities and impossibilities, and I shall be satisfied if I have made you feel for a moment that the past—*not*, holds us enslaved—thank heaven, no!—*but*, that it participates.

(1959)

POSTSCRIPT

From 1953 on I had watched with misgivings the establishment of a closer relationship between "the Six." Not because I am opposed to European federation, but because a partial federation from which England and the Scandinavian countries (to mention only those) are excluded seems to me not to advance that ideal, but on the contrary, to place a very serious obstacle in its way.

I know as well as anybody that England bears a large share of the blame for the development that we are now witnessing. But I have felt all along that our statesmen, for their part, were shutting their eyes to the dangers of the course in which they engaged; and the enthusiasm for the treaty signed in Rome displayed by the fervent supporters of the European idea in our midst seemed to me incomprehensible. To listen to them, indeed, the association of "the Six" was only a beginning, made necessary by England's hanging back, and in the end it would be seen to have promoted a more truly European solution.

These explanations and excuses could never convince me. I was, and still am, afraid that, on the contrary, the block that has been formed will evolve a particularist sentiment, supported by vested interests growing stronger with every year that passes. I am afraid that, under cover of a devout use of the name "Europe," a dangerous division of Europe is being prepared.

This is not what the Dutch statesmen wanted, or want. But in this association with states of so much greater strength, their wishes can already be seen to count for little.

I have repeatedly expressed my "unorthodox" views on this matter.[1] In 1959 I devoted the address I was invited to give at Harvard on Commencement Day to the subject.[2] For years mine was a somewhat lonely voice in my own country, and if many of my compatriots now seem to be waking up to the unfortunate consequences of the Common Market, it is becoming increasingly clear that there is now very little we can do to avert them.

One can still hope that England will realize that the Continental block her policy of abstention has allowed to be constituted may in the long run weaken her own position, not only economically, but (and I am inclined to think, especially) politically. There are at this moment signs of a change in English public opinion. Have those who used to say that the association of "the Six" would act as an incentive and would

[1] "Onorthodoxe bedenkingen over Klein-Europa" was the title of an article I published in *Het Parool* in January 1954, when E.D.C. was on the tapis. I had it included in *Studies en Strijdschriften* (1958).

[2] See the *Harvard Alumni Bulletin*, July 4, 1959, and *The New Leader*, August 31, 1959.

prove to have been only "a beginning" been in the right after all? If England does join, I shall be only too happy to apologize to them. But I am still afraid that this will not happen unless "the Six" will adopt a somewhat more forthcoming attitude, and I am also afraid that not all the partners will be as ready for concessions as will be Holland.

(1960)

SECOND POSTSCRIPT

Over two years have elapsed since I wrote the above Postscript for the American edition. A new situation has been created, or rather, the true meaning of the situation in which we find ourselves as a consequence of the treaty of Rome has been dramatically revealed by President de Gaulle's slamming the door against England at his press conference of January 14. It is no exaggeration to say that consternation and indignation were universal in Holland. And the worst part of it is that nobody has a clear answer to the question which now insistently poses itself: What can we *do*?

(1963)

V

LOOKING BACK

Looking Back

When I was asked to talk to you tonight I said that if the committee would not object, I meant to talk about myself. A man who has just completed his seventieth year may be allowed this luxury. I am in a reminiscent mood. And I have a good many memories to draw upon.

If I may say so by way of introduction, I have a feeling that my life has been a happy one, in spite of all the sorrowful moments and all the difficult circumstances that I have known; and much of my happiness I have found in what I always used to describe as "my own work," as distinct from the functions more directly attached to my professorship, which has indeed also given me a good deal of satisfaction. But "my own work," my writing, my creative work—that is where I shall inevitably place the emphasis when I survey my life. And my creative work shall always be indissolubly connected with the part I have, from time to time, taken in politics, in the exchange of thought or the controversy about great questions in the public life of my own day.

I was aware of a desire to express myself at a very early age. The same observation has been frequently given a different twist—sometimes in a friendly manner, sometimes with caustic undertones—by suggesting that I have from boyhood on been animated by burning ambition. But are the two motives mutually exclusive? I think not, and however critically I look at myself I cannot doubt that in my case the first one was perfectly genuine.

It was not history to which I immediately turned as my natural form of expression. At first I wished to be a poet—in

my *gymnasium* years at The Hague. Next, a novelist—in my
first years at Leyden. I had chosen "Dutch language and
literature" as my main subject, and while history was not in
those days admitted in that capacity, it was an obligatory
subsidiary to "Dutch." How little I knew of history—although
I had been really interested, at the *gymnasium*, by Van Aalst's
history lessons—appears from an incident that has stuck in
my memory. It happened in my first year at Leyden. An older
student showed me his books. One he took from the shelf:
there, he said, lay his true interest. It was Fruin's *Tien jaren*,[1]
and the name, not only of the book, but of Fruin, was completely new to me.

History soon gripped me. Yet I continued for a few years to
ride two horses at once, and it was not until Verwey[2] to whom
I had sent the manuscript, dismissed a novel of mine with a
shrug that I decided: I must choose. Afterward the thought
would rise occasionally: Verwey! But was he the man to judge
a novel?

Nevertheless history had won. Writing poetry—it had been
sonnets, mostly—I had given up long ago; my faith in that
work had gradually withered away. History, then, as a second
—or third!—best? Failed as a poet and as a novelist, and now
a historian for want of something better? No—here too, I am
inclined to reject the all-too-simple contrast; and this much is
certain, I never rued the choice, and, then and all through my
life, I had a strong feeling of having found my calling.

Not that early aspirations were therefore completely stifled.
The contrary became clear during my internment at Buchen-
wald.[3] Suddenly interrupted in my habitual work and torn
from my routine, there sprang from me, to my own surprise
and delight, a series of sonnets, and also a novel. You may smile
when I mention those sonnets. I belong to a different genera-

---

[1] *Ten Years of the Eighty Years' War* (1588-98). This book, which
appeared in 1857, when Fruin was thirty-four years old, is still regarded
as a classic.

[2] Albert Verwey, 1864-1937, a leading poet and critic.

[3] October 7, 1940 to November 1941, when the group of hostages to
which I belonged was transferred to Holland; I was released from
internment only on February 12, 1944.

tion from the men who now dominate the scene of poetry and of poetic criticism, and since my poems are strictly and regularly constructed and have a clear and sometimes incisive meaning, these younger men are inclined to regard them as not really poetry. I can only say that I take my sonnets very seriously myself and that I reject the new fashion in poetry as wholeheartedly as they do a tradition that I am sure it is not in their power to kill, however successful they may be in confusing the minds of their docile readers.

But you will *certainly* smile at my mentioning my detective novel. I remember very well how, when I came home from my internment early in 1944, and the rumour of that peculiar indiscretion was spread about, more than one colleague asked me, with concern even more than with astonishment: "Are you going to publish this under your own name?" Yes, indeed I did, and I am still glad to have, with my historical work, a volume of sonnets and that "lighthearted" tale laid in the river country that I love, standing to my name.

History, nevertheless, became and has remained the ruling interest of my life. History such as I have always understood it: not an inventory of dead people and dead things, but a key to life—as literature, too, is a key to life. Not long ago I found in a review of one of my latest publications a passage quoted from the preface to my first, that is, to my doctoral thesis of 1913. I was much struck—for I had completely forgotten the passage—to find this idea already forcefully stated then. It has continued to inspire me.

Life in its fullness, life in all its shadings and aspects. This is one reason why I have never shrunk from contact with politics, why, on the contrary, I believe that history can benefit thereby. Not that history should *serve* politics. The position of bondage is not for her. History has her own laws, and only by remaining true to those can she match herself with life. *Distance* is her contribution to life, but without *contact* it can never be a contribution of much value.

Fate smiled on me when I was appointed, in 1913, correspondent of the *Nieuwe Rotterdamsche Courant* in London. I had not disliked schoolmastering, at the small *gymnasium* of

Schiedam (summer 1912 to December 1913), but what wider prospects did this correspondentship open up for me! The work first of all. I owe a great deal to this journalistic episode for my formation. The introduction to men and to conditions in another country—and a great country—the need to write quickly and intelligibly, was a basic training. Especially so in those blessed times when a foreign correspondent—at least at the *N.R.C.*—had latitude both as to space and as to expression of opinion. I could let myself go, I could write as much as I pleased and on anything that struck my fancy. Politics was, of course, an obligatory topic, but then, politics interested me very particularly.

And also, entrance into the Anglo-Saxon world was in itself an event in my life. I had not dreamed of this a year or two before, when I had been granted a travelling scholarship and had spent six or seven months in Italy, in Venice more especially (first half of 1912), where in the Frari archives I had collected the material for my thesis. I had had visions then of a future devoted to Italian history, literature, art. But now I was drawn westward.

I was to spend twenty-two years of my life in London. After the 1914 war, which I "did" for my paper (what an experience!), I became the first incumbent of the newly founded chair of Dutch Studies at the University of London. History could now come into its own. Not that the first years were not very difficult. A young and untried man, with an out-of-the-way subject, having to find his way in that enormous, self-sufficient, and indifferent organization! But after a while the position began to give me very real satisfaction. I came to feel at home in the English academic world; I made friends there; every year a few students placed themselves under my particular guidance. Yet how intensely, as the years went by, did I begin to hanker after a return home.

I taught Netherlands history; I wrote Netherlands history; and just about the time of my entering upon that first professorship I began to follow, with passionate interest, the development of affairs in Flanders and of the relationship between Holland and Flanders. I had grown fond of London; I was happy in my position and circle there; but my heart was across the water.

My first contact with the Flemish problem dated, in fact, from 1911, my last year at Leyden, when I had attended a Flemish students' congress at Ghent. The profound impression the experience made on me[4] is evident in a long essay I got accepted by the serious-minded, conservative, professorial monthly *Onze Eeuw*. That impression was never effaced; yet my residence in England, and then, especially, the war, had for a while cut me off from what went on in Flanders. But now I got immersed in the counsels of the newborn Flemish Nationalist movement as intimately as if I had been a Fleming.

This too—but the reflection I am going to make came to me only after the event, for at the time I took it all with too whole-hearted a devotion—was training for a historian. "The captain of the Hampshire grenadiers," says Gibbon in his auto-biography, after having described his activities in that capacity, "has not been useless to the historian of the Roman Empire." So from my association with a nationalist movement, from the internal quarrels and intrigues, from the enthusiasm that was liable to deteriorate into fanaticism, from the moderation that might become flabbiness, from the derailments and dis-appointments, and from the permanent achievements, I learned a good deal that has somehow helped to fashion my writing about the past.

It has for many years dominated my life, this Flemish question. From London I crossed over to Holland several times a year. I could manage to do this because the Batavier Line had, as its contribution to the Dutch chair, granted a permanent free pass to the professor. In Holland the Great-Netherlands Students' Union,[5] a small but active group

[4] Compare what is said on this point in *Debates with Historians*, pp. 228.

[5] The organization was called Dietse Studenten Bond. The word *Diets*, an archaic word for Netherlandish, was revived in those years by the adherents of the Great-Netherlands idea. It has since fallen into dis-repute owing to its similarity to *Duits*, that is, *German*, a similarity that seemed ominous when later on a number of "Dietsers" gravitated towards

promoting closer relations with Flanders, provided me with a platform. And no less frequently I lectured to Flemish students or academic and other organizations in Flanders. My relations were with the Flemish Nationalists, the radical wing of Flemish movement, the group of my generation.[6] At first my closest connection was with Dr. Antoon Jacob, whose acquaintance I had made at the students' congress in 1911. I now visited him several times in the prison at Antwerp where he was kept from 1919 to 1924 for his "activist" misdeeds during the war. I still possess a large batch of his prison letters. An impressive personality! He was my junior by a year or two, but from the cell he acted as my teacher of Flemish Nationalism. Even before he was set free, however, I began to detect in his mind a rectilinear quality that roused me to opposition. Soon Herman Vos became my most intimate ally. Next to him Rik Borginon. These two were successively to lead the Flemish Nationalist "fraction" in the Belgian Chamber. Both were intellectuals of a high calibre; both were, like Jacob, of my age or a little younger.

In the 'twenties and 'thirties Flemish Nationalists were somewhat undesirable connections in the eyes of the Belgian authorities, and also of Dutch public opinion at large, as well as of the academic and the official world. In Holland all Flemish Nationalists and Great-Netherlanders were lumped

---

National Socialism and in the end collaborated with the Germans. It is hardly necessary to say that no such proclivities were intended or even thought of, by the original "Dietse Studenten" in the 'twenties.

[6] Flemish Nationalism had come into action during World War I in two distinct forms. One was the "activism" of those Flamingants who used the presence of a complaisant German occupying authority to carry through reforms that were indeed long overdue. Secondly there was the clandestine, but at one time powerful, organization of Flemish soldiers at the front who resented being commanded by officers ignorant of their language. After 1918 the Activists were prosecuted; many fled the country, settling in Holland (some in Germany). In the practice of Belgian politics there soon took place a merging of the forces of Activism and of Frontism. The common appellation now became Flemish Nationalism. See A. Willemsen, *Het Vlaams Nationalisme, 1914-40* (Utrecht, 1958).

together in the same reproval: revolutionary elements, a
threat to the very existence of the Belgian state. That my
closest associates were not extremists was not noticed, nor that
I myself was throughout those years carrying on a fight on two
fronts. On the one hand I found ranged against me the
indifference and the misapprehensions governing the minds of
my fellow Dutchmen, and on the other hand the recklessness
of the extremist groups among the Flemish Nationalists and
of the hotheads in the North who took their cue from them. I
used to remind audiences of the Great-Netherlands Students'
movement of the "European order," and I warned them against
indulging in irredentism. And all the while I polemicized
indefatigably against the preachers of total unadulterated
nationalism, against the weekly paper *Vlaanderen*, the organ of
the group gathered around that typical scholar-fanatic De
Decker, a Flemish exile (now teaching Latin at an Amsterdam
gymnasium).

In *Vlaanderen* De Decker and his associates tried with bitter
persistence to make the movement as a whole toe the line of
their "integral" Great-Netherlands programme. "Death to
Belgium! A Great-Netherlands state!" [7] As I saw it, the activities
of these men hampered or paralyzed the attempts of the
Flemish Nationalists in the Belgian parliament, who of
necessity worked within the reality of Belgium, and who were
indeed achieving something there, if only—and to me it
seemed much—by putting "Belgicist" Flamingants, like Van
Cauwelaert the Catholic and Huysmans the Socialist, on their
mettle. It has indeed been the most tangible result of the
Nationalist clamour for a federal system that it helped the
"Belgicist" Flamingants to obtain from the Chamber, about
1930, a number of "language laws." Divisions within the
ranks of the Nationalists, so it seemed to me, must slacken
the pace of actual reform, and I was more intent on attacking
these doctrinaire troublemakers of the *Vlaanderen* weekly and
their partisans in Flanders than were the parliamentary
Nationalists themselves, than was Vos particularly, who was
inclined to laugh at these adversaries and shrug off their

[7] This is what was meant by the cry "Politiek Groot-Nederland!"

"nonsense." His feeling of superiority and his contempt were intellectually understandable enough. But politically his attitude had fatal consequences, for those men did undeniably undermine his prestige with the rank and file in the country, with the young men particularly. His disdainful silence was apt to be interpreted as embarrassment or weakness.

But however strongly I opposed the false logical consistency of the doctrinaires, neither in Brussels nor in The Hague was there much inclination to draw a distinction between moderate and radical in the Great-Netherlands movement. In 1929 I was made to feel it as far as Brussels was concerned.

I had been invited to give a lecture in three Flemish towns. I had received warnings from more than one side (there had even been statements to that effect in Belgian newspapers) that the Belgian government had decided that I should not be allowed to speak. In London, at the Belgian exhibition of ancient painting, I had happened to meet Vermeylen, the well-known writer, at that time a Socialist Senator, and he told me that the warning was meant. I gave him to understand that he ought not to acquiesce in such a thing, and he did do his best in Brussels, but (as he wrote to me) without result. I went all the same. In Antwerp and in Ghent I was not interfered with. But when I came to Louvain, with the same speech, of my usual historical kind—and it had not, on the two earlier occasions, caused the Belgian state to shake on its foundations—here, in the hall of the hotel where I was to have dinner with my friends before the meeting, a little old gentleman came up to me. "Have I the honour," so he began, in Dutch, "to address Professor Geyl from London?"

The question flashed through my mind: Is this an admirer, or is it the police? It was the police. Orders from Brussels: he showed me the paper. "In French," I said: "Against the law." But of course that did not alter the situation. I was allowed to dine with my friends and was then, with unfailing politeness throughout, conducted to the train out of Belgium to Holland. (A few years later I met with a similar contretemps. On that occasion I was expelled together with a member of the Dutch

Chamber, Moller, and the well-known novelist Antoon Coolen. That excellent Coolen, a child in politics, simply could not understand what was happening to him!)

But in Holland, too, the distinction between moderate and radical was not generally made, although I must say that I had no reason to complain of the press reactions to my expulsion in 1929.

This could not leave me indifferent. The affair might have had very unpleasant consequences for me. In London I combined with my professorship the position of an unofficial press-attaché. There would be a great deal to tell about my experiences in that function too: how I wrote articles, for instance, to explain the Dutch case in the long-drawn-out Scheldt dispute with Belgium in the decade following the war, articles under my name, under a pseudonym, at times under somebody else's name; how I tried to influence editors. I received for that work a salary from the Dutch Foreign Office —and I needed that supplement to my somewhat scanty professorial stipend. Our Foreign Office—if I may say so— really valued my work in England, but my activities in Flanders were always regarded with suspicion. The Plein [8] was always completely lacking in understanding of the value to our own country of the potentiality for Dutch civilization in Flanders. When the question of my lectures in Belgium cropped up in 1929, the Foreign Office had explicitly warned me not to give occasion for an incident. And now I had risked it, and the fat was in the fire.

The train that was to take me from Louvain to Holland stopped in Antwerp, and there I got out to devise with Vos the way in which we were to give publicity to the affair. When I arrived in The Hague, the Dutch press was in possession of a leading article written by him in his paper *De Schelde*, in which the offensive, incomprehensible action of the Belgian authorities was denounced in his most dignified and tactful manner. I myself made straight for the Plein. Attack is the best way of defence. I had a talk with my friend Van Kleffens,

[8] The square in The Hague on which the Ministry of Foreign Affairs is situated.

who was at that time chief of the Political Section, and I demanded that an explanation should be exacted for the ignominious treatment meted out to a reputable Dutch citizen and scholar. Van Kleffens explained that this would hardly be possible since the Dutch government itself set too much store by its right to expel undesirable aliens without stating grounds. But the conversation took place in an atmosphere of good humour.

In my own mind I made the observation that apparently, without having in the least departed from the line that I felt was dictated to me by principle, I enjoyed a reputation for moderation. A little to my surprise. Not that I want to decline that praise—if praise it is, and on the whole I think so—but in certain circles I knew I was regarded as a difficult customer, too readily spoiling for a fight. In certain circles, and especially among my fellow historians.

A few years afterward, when political conditions had already profoundly altered, the old confusion of thought concerning my association with the Flemish Nationalist and Great-Netherlands movement still appeared to prevail—in the University of Utrecht, in the Faculty of Letters.[9] Here a vacancy was created by the retirement of G. W. Kernkamp, Professor of Modern History. A vacancy on which I had had my eye for years. Here was my chance!

The Faculty has to make the first recommendation. In this company, consisting at that time of not quite twenty men, several, for no other reason than that I was associated with a nationalist movement, regarded me as little better than a National-Socialist. In consequence of my long residence abroad, they hardly knew me personally. They judged by a reputation that had very little to do with reality. My historical work? Hardly any attention was given to what I had written on other subjects, but my polemical essays directed against the

[9] Dutch universities embrace seven or eight "faculties," each faculty being concerned with a particular field of study: theology, science, law, medicine, etc. The faculty of letters is perhaps the most heterogeneous one of all, embracing not only languages and literatures, Dutch and foreign, ancient and modern, Oriental and Western, but history, geography, psychology, philosophy.

Little-Netherlands interpretation of our history and against the complementary Belgicist interpretation—and also my *History of the Netherlands People*,[10] of which by then two volumes had appeared (1930, 1934), covering the period down to 1688—had given me in the profession, not of course without exceptions (and they were notable exceptions), the reputation of a man abusing history for political purposes. A disturbing element.

In the early 'twenties I had already questioned the authority of Fruin, next that of the leading men among the living, of the generation that was now in control, that preceding my own: my masters Blok and Kalff; then Colenbrander, Japikse, Huizinga, Brugmans; and in Belgium the great Pirenne. Pirenne was admired quite uncritically in Holland, and I never gave more offence than I did in 1927 by my review—I must admit cutting, but in substance incontrovertible—of the sixth volume of his *Histoire de Belgique*, dealing with the late decades of the eighteenth and the early decades of the nineteenth century. Then, in 1933, there had occurred the sensational affair of the plagiarism committed by a well-known professor of history,[11] an affair about which I shall say no

---

[10] *Geschiedenis va de Nederlandse Stam* (Vol. I, 1930; Vol. II, 1934; Vol. III, 1937), reprinted in two large volumes (1947-8); a new volume dealing with the period appeared in 1959. The portion on 1555 to 1609 appeared in English under the title *The Revolt of the Netherlands* (1932; third impression 1958); 1609 to 1648 under the title *The Netherlands Divided* (1936); a new edition of this latter work and a further instalment covering the period from 1648 to 1702 are in preparation (the title to be: *The Netherlands in the Seventeenth Century*, I and II).

[11] In January 1933 the leading monthly *De Gids* came out with a long article in commemoration of the fourth centenary of the birth of William the Silent. It was written by the Managing Editor, Professor of National History at the University of Leyden. In a letter published in the press, signed jointly by my friend Van Eyck (my successor as London correspondent of the *N.R.C.*, a well-known poet and critic, in 1935 appointed Professor of the History of Dutch Literature at Leyden) and myself, it was pointed out that the article was plagiarized from Pirenne's *Histoire de Belgique*.
The affair created an enormous sensation. Leyden students publicly protested against "an attack on Leyden." Meanwhile a committee of three professors of history of the other public universities were invited

more now. The impression created was that I was likely to prove a troublesome colleague.

The easiest way to dispose of my work on the North-South relationship was to dub it "politics." No doubt it was my profound feeling for Flanders that had inspired me to my novel interpretation of the sixteenth-century split and its causes and of the entire North-South relationship. Indeed I had always affirmed the connection of historical views and contemporary conditions, nor had I ever tried to disguise or disavow my wish to contribute by means of my historical work to the breaking down of the narrow conceptions in which the Dutch public, including the intellectuals, allowed itself to be imprisoned, conceptions concerning the foundations of Dutch nationality, concerning the Belgian state, concerning the Dutch-Flemish relationship.

But was it right on that account to attach the label "politics" to *my* views more particularly?

It is a well-known dodge to use that word to discredit the historian who goes against established opinion. It was tried on me in yet another historical field about which I made myself heard throughout those same years. I refer to my views on the conflict between the princes of Orange and the "regents," of Holland especially, in the history of the Republic. For although I said a moment ago that the Flemish question dominated my life, I did not therefore neglect the opportunity to do research work in the Public Record Office and the British Museum, and I delved deeply in seventeenth- and

---

by the Curators and the Rector of Leyden to examine the charge; after a long delay they reported that they had found it to be justified. Their report went on, however, to blame Van Eyck and myself for having rushed into publicity. To this we retorted (all these statements were published *in extenso* by the daily press) that "apparently many people in this country have a greater aversion to publicity than to deceit." The Curators publicly endorsed the report, and subsequently stated, at our request that this naturally meant: "insofar as the report related to the Leyden Professor of History."

Let me add that the retiring Utrecht Professor of Modern History, whose place I was eventually to take, had been, two years earlier, one of the committee of three.

eighteenth-century North Netherlandish history. The connection of the House of Orange with the Stuarts, and in the next century with the House of Hanover, and the way in which this influenced the party struggle in the Republic and its foreign policy—this was the theme that I dealt with in my *Orange en Stuart* (which did not appear in book form until 1939, but of which the chapters constituting the first half had already been published in various reviews[12] in the 'twenties) and also in *Willem IV* (of Orange) *en Engeland* (1734-1748), of 1924. A theme that again took me into the heart of highly controversial matter.

I had been struck, when I came to be familiar with the particulars, by the astonishing partiality toward the stadholders prevailing in our historiography. Groen's religious philosophy[13] would lead one to expect this of him, but I found the same attitude rampant even among the liberals. Later, after the second war, I have shown the effects of this bias somewhat haphazardly in the work of Fruin, and more systematically in that of Colenbrander. But it was in the early 'twenties that my opinions on this point took form. All the well-known assertions that Orange or the Orange party was identical with *national*, and States of Holland or regents' party with *egoistical*, *class*, or *provincial* interests; that the princes of Orange had prepared the way for unity while Holland did nothing but block it with her commercialism; that Orange was the people's protector, while the regents were no more than a group out for their own profit, a group outside the nation—all these assertions I learned to see as belonging to an Orangemyth at variance with past reality.

It is the historian's task to demolish myth—"in spite of those who do not like it." In this particular case too, most certainly, there were those who did not like it. The myth is, by its nature, intimately bound up with sentiment, and unyielding to reason. When my *Willem IV en Engeland*

[12] Chapters I and II in the *English Historical Review* (1923) and *Scottish Historical Review* (1923) respectively. Cf. above, pp. 152-81.
[13] See a long review by Sir Richard Lodge in the *English Historical Review*, 1925.

appeared, it was described in *The Times Literary Supplement* as a kind of anti-English pamphlet. But it is unfortunately a fact that the way in which the English government, cheered on by English opinion, treated the Dutch during the War of the Austrian Succession did not come very graciously from an ally, was indeed, frankly, rather shabby. I laid that bare in all its ugly detail—the first modern historian to do so, I believe. Does that prove me to be "anti-English"? On his part, Professor Krämer, a predecessor of mine in the Utrecht chair of modern history, at that time House-Archivist to Her Majesty the Queen, pictured me in a review in *Museum* as a bitter enemy to Orange. But could I help it if William IV was so feeble a character, unable to follow a consistent line of policy, now indulging in rabid Frisian provincialism (until 1747 he was stadholder of Friesland and Groningen only), then prepared to swallow whatever England, his father-in-law's country, dictated, and all the time more accessible to personal ambition than capable of taking a large view of the national interest? To observe these things, does that show me to be anti-Orange? There is a great deal of difference between one prince of Orange and the next. Unless, at least, you look at the lot through orange spectacles. Such spectacles were still much the fashion in those days, but I have never consented to wear them.

I am not taking these old controversies too tragically. The instinctive opposition soon proved to be really powerless. The reception of my book in the professional journals, both English and Dutch, was quite satisfactory on the whole.

The fate of my Great-Netherlands arguments and inter-pretations was not essentially different, but the opposition was more vehement, and there was quite a lengthy and to me painful intermezzo when it seemed as if it would triumph and my return to Holland be prevented. "Nothing but politics! Unscholarly!" was what the adversaries said. In fact all I had done was to take issue with a prejudice, demonstrating that it was historically untenable. As for politics, I had maintained all along that, on the contrary, this unreasoning sentiment was, with the current historical view, the product of political events, and that what my opponents used that false history for—unconsciously perhaps, but in that case so much the worse for historians—was to justify existing political arrangements and abuses (like the partial Gallicization of Flanders).

Anyhow, in 1935, when my name could not be suppressed altogether in connection with the pending appointment at Utrecht, some, or many, wanted to bar me as a rabid nationalist, a recruit, most likely, for the N.S.B.[14]

The men who talked (or muttered) like this not only knew nothing of the attitude that I had consistently taken in the Great-Netherlands movement, but even my historical work, which they industriously played off against me, they had read very carelessly. They suspected me of leanings toward National Socialism. Yet in the preface to the second volume of my *History of the Netherlands People* I had, in 1934, in dedicating the book to my particular friends the Great-Netherlands students, admonished them to remember that, according to the Netherlands tradition in both North and South, "variety, and respect for private rights" were among our most precious goods—as clear a warning against slipping down in an eastward direction as one could wish. And I quote only one utterance out of many. Had no attention been given to this evidence of my true feeling?

In the end I was appointed—against the recommendation of the Faculty,[15] and after a behind-the-scenes struggle shifting

[14] Nationaal-Socialistische Beweging—the National Socialist organization in Holland, led by Mussert.

[15] The procedure is as follows: The Faculty makes its recommendation to the Committee of Curators. This is a body of five, nowadays seven, men of standing and independence. In the last resort they represent the authority of the Minister of Education, by whom they are appointed and by whose decisions they have to abide. They will generally advocate the University's views in The Hague and will often do so with tenacity, but in the exchanges preceding the Minister's decision, they can also, and frequently do, take their own line. In the matter of professorial appointments it is they who make a recommendation to the Minister. In the large majority of cases they will make the Faculty's recommendation their own, although they are by no means bound to do so. The Minister, for his part, will generally follow the recommendation of Curators, although he, too, can depart from it.

from Utrecht to The Hague and lasting many months. Once I was there in person, however, the misunderstandings melted away like snow before the sun. My inaugural oration, in February 1936—you will understand that after all that had transpired during the long-drawn-out tussle over my appointment, it was attended and listened to in an atmosphere of

My case was an unusual one from beginning to end. The Faculty placed me third on its list of three candidates. The Curators recommended me; this decision was reached in July 1935, when months had already been spent in confabulations. But it was September before the Minister expressed a wish that I should call on him. I came over from London the next day. He then told me that he felt inclined to follow the recommendation of the Curators, but that, as I was sure to understand, there were difficulties. I told him that I did not understand at all. After which he said, in an impressive tone of voice: "Belgium of course!" He even said, incredible as it may appear, that the Great-Netherlands movement might lead to WAR!! with Belgium. I asked him whether he knew anything of my particular position within that movement and promised to let him have a memo I had drawn up earlier for our Ministry of Foreign Affairs (for I had had misgivings that there might be opposition from that quarter). He told me that he had brought the matter up in the Cabinet and that no voice had been raised against the appointment, although his suggestion that he would have a serious talk with me before coming to a decision had been welcomed. He assured me he would be glad to see the memo.

This memo did not contain any apology for past action or any promise of different conduct in the future. It consisted of a string of quotations from speeches and articles of mine over a period of twelve years or more. Its effect on the Minister was to make him write me a letter in which he told me that he was laying my name before Her Majesty the Queen. My friends in the Department congratulated me, advised me to go to Utrecht to present myself to the Secretary of Curators and to look for a house before returning to London. Next Thursday the Queen was to sign royal decrees.

In the evening of that day I was rung up by the head of the Universities Section, who told me, much embarrassed, that the Queen had not signed.

But I had the Minister's letter, and if I was not appointed I could let the world know (and meant to) how the original decision had come to be revised. The affair caused quite a commotion in political circles, without, however, being ventilated in the press. I received a good many expressions of sympathy and promises of support, from the then Prime Minister among others, but I had to wait for another painful three months before the decree was duly signed.

I entered upon my duties on January 1, 1936.

unusual tension—cleared the air. Yet I said in it no less on the delicate subject than I had done on so many earlier occasions. I well remember the warm congratulations I received, when I had concluded, from Bolkestein, the ancient history man, who had been among my antagonists. In the Faculty, where as a matter of fact I had been generally received in an unexceptionable manner, I came to be on particularly friendly terms with Bolkestein.

And since I have recalled that I was suspected of National Socialist inclinations, it is amusing to remember that not much more than a year afterward, Bolkestein and I both figured as speakers at a meeting in Utrecht of E.D.D. I am afraid that the younger generation will need to have those initials explained: they meant "Unity Through Democracy," and they represented a movement, to which men of all the democratic parties were welcome, intended to rally the Dutch people to close ranks (for the time being with a view to the general election to be held in the summer of 1937) against the dangers threatening from the N.S.B. Politics again. Bolkestein was uneasily aware of this. When we were mounting the platform together he whispered to me: "An academic scandal," pointing out that we seemed to be the only professors present in the overcrowded hall of Tivoli.

Were professors of that generation really so shy of politics? Perhaps only of taking so public a part. There were quite a few, whom the rise of National Socialism shocked out of their ivory towers. I myself spoke two more times the following year, in the huge R.A.I. Building in Amsterdam, before crowds compared with which that Tivoli audience seemed to shrink into insignificance. A popular orator! Never had I dreamed of such a thing!

An amusing aside to the story of my appointment at Utrecht is that the support I had received, in all the successive stages through which a professorial appointment has to pass, came from conservative elements. If the others were relieved when they at long last saw me in their midst, *they* were soon disagreeably surprised at the quick evolution through which I passed in the Dutch air, an evolution that nevertheless

amounted to going on in the direction of my earlier thinking
and writing; and really, I had never tried to mislead anyone
as to my political convictions. The climax came, I believe
before the year 1936 was out, when I told an archconservative
colleague of another Faculty, who had so recently employed
all his influence on my behalf, that now that I was back in the
country I did not in the circumstances prevailing in the world
want to remain an isolated intellectual but was planning to
join a party, and the party for me was the Socialist party. If
I had said "N.S.B.," he could not have been more shocked.
I did not take the step, after all; not yet, because after
exchanges of thought with leading personalities in that quarter
I came to the conclusion that the process through which the
S.D.A.P. (the Socialist party) was going at that moment, the
process of freeing itself from doctrinaire antimilitarism and
cosmopolitanism, had not gone far enough. I did join the
S.D.A.P. immediately after the war, just before it changed its
name to Labour party in order to mark the definite break with
Marxist doctrinairism. Let me just add that the explanation
that I used to give to my friends, in all sincerity, was that
I looked upon the Socialist party as the last refuge for a
liberal. For of course what I really am is a liberal. But our
present-day Liberal party, which professes to continue the
tradition of Thorbecke, strikes me as a typically Conservative
party.

The danger that threatened in the late' thirties did not arise
after all from the N.S.B. (which suffered large losses in the
election of 1937), but from Germany. Even when, in September 1939, war broke out in Europe, many people still attempted
to obscure *that* stark truth with vague talk about neutrality
being our bounden duty and about the need of being on our
guard with respect to England and France just as much as with
respect to Germany. I wrote a pamphlet pointing out the
hollowness of that view. I also went on speaking at E.D.D.
gatherings. In May 1940 the catastrophe broke over our heads.
I happened to be a member of the Senatus contractus and at
our daily conference with the Rector I could observe how even
then the situation was too much for the political acumen of

many of my colleagues. There were moments in that little group when tension ran high.

The real difficulties for the University did not begin until toward the end of that year. I was spared the painful struggle with them because I had already been seized as a hostage, in the early days of October 1940. When I came home, in February 1944, I still had nothing to do with them, for in December 1942, while still in internment, I had been dismissed by the Reichskommissar from my post at the University. The ground given was: "seeing that his general mentality does not hold out any guarantee for loyal co-operation. . . ." In May 1945 I looked upon myself, and so, naturally, did my colleagues, as reinstated. But it was not until September that the royal decree was issued in which my reinstatement was actually confirmed. Here, too, grounds were indicated; to wit, that "nothing had transpired of disloyalty towards Her Majesty the Queen or the Kingdom of the Netherlands." I could not help feeling that this was not the happiest way of putting it.

But I have strayed with my memories into a different world. Let me look back again and offer some general reflections on those years between the two wars and on my activity in connection with the Flemish and Great-Netherlands questions.

The memory of that struggle (it always was a struggle) over the Great-Netherlands versus the Little-Netherlands vision of our history and—within the Great-Netherlands and Flemish Nationalist movement—over moderation or extremism, realism or doctrinairism—that memory is very dear to me, although a certain melancholy goes with it.

No movement ever leads directly to the aim that its adherents have set for it. *This* movement was derailed in the thirties under the impact of the demoniac and powerful Nazi aberration. Even before I came to Utrecht, this development had estranged me from many whom I used to regard as engaged in the same cause. That cause was as close to my heart as ever, but in practice I was aware of a growing isolation. When, at Brussels in 1939, as speaker at a lunch of Flemish Catholic university graduates, I made a challenging appeal to the

E.H. O

democratic principle, I was cheered by other Flemings than those with whom I had been most closely allied.

My most intimate friend in the Nationalist camp, Herman Vos, a consistent democrat, had left the party as early as 1934 and had rejoined the Belgian Socialist party. I could not but understand his decision. But I had continued my friendly relations with Rik Borginon, who now led the Flemish Nationalist group in the Chamber. Only, my letters to him (which I still have) are one uninterrupted series of warnings and admonitions. Not that he personally had any leanings toward National Socialism, but I wanted him to take a stronger line with the untrustworthy members of the "fraction", and particularly I wanted him to state publicly the views he professed to me in private. The semblance of National Socialist influence inevitably weakened the recruiting capacity of the conception of Flemish Nationalism among Flemings at large and at the same time alienated Dutch opinion.

Borginon, unfortunately, did not succeed in keeping his wild men in check. He never gave in to German blandishments himself, and the sentence of twenty years' imprisonment which was pronounced against him after the liberation of Belgium was a striking instance of the way in which the triumphant Fransquillons used the repression to eliminate as many potential leaders of Flamingantism as possible. In fact, although he was set free quite soon afterwards, an active political career is no longer open to him. He is still numbered, however, among my friends. Jacob, too, went back to prison in 1944, but indeed *he* had lost his head completely under the influence of the German lunacy; he died in prison in 1948. With him I had had no contact for many years.

Vos, on the contrary, came to look me up very shortly after the liberation of Holland. A fortnight before the liberation my house had been raided, and we were now camping, my wife and I, in the one room that it had been possible, more or less, to furnish.[16] Vos came quite unexpectedly: we still

[16] The house was raided because it had transpired that we were hiding in the cellar arms and munitions of the Dutch underground forces. Also, a secret telephone had been installed in a top room overlooking the main

had hardly any means of communication with the outside world. I was quite startled to see him get out of a splendid Belgian government car driven by a uniformed chauffeur. I had heard a rumour—although it seemed hard to believe— that he was now a Cabinet minister. But there he was, both he and his chauffeur, loaded with good things that to us, in the famine from which Holland was as yet but slowly emerging, seemed simply marvellous. We embraced, French fashion— it is the only time in my life that I took part in that emotional ceremony—and tears (it must have been an extraordinary spectacle) trickled into both our beards.

My friendship with Vos was resumed on as cordial terms as ever, and yet there was no longer room for the kind of co-operation that had attended it in earlier days. Vos was now a member of the Belgian government! He was as true a Fleming as ever he had been, and I built high hopes on his new position and how he could make it serve our old ideals. In practice, not much came of this, and if I had pestered Borginon with "warnings and admonitions" in the 'thirties, it was now Vos's turn to receive reproaches and exhortations, which he laughed off—or tried to—as he had done the carpings and slanders of *Vlaanderen* twenty years earlier. In spite of my impatience, I felt his early death in 1952 as an irreparable loss to me, not only from the point of view of friendship, but also because with him there went my firmest *point d'appui* in postwar Belgium.

Not that I have no contacts there any more. The new climate would even seem particularly favourable to relations such as I have always dreamed of. The ideals that have meant so much to me and to which I have remained faithful, have partially

---

road east, and young people were regularly attending it. We had been warned in time and had gone into hiding ("dived under" was the technical term), which meant that we went to stay with friends in another part of the town. In our absence the Sten guns and hand grenades were discovered and the German military police carried off all our belongings. When we came back, a fortnight later, the house was completely empty and the dining room had been wrecked with one of "my own" hand grenades, the only use to which any of the lot was ever put.

been realized. Only—in other ways, in other forms, and I can no longer feel as intimately connected with their development as before. No doubt I have been able to do some work, but on an entirely different basis.

From 1946 on I have been a member of the then formed Mixed (that is to say, Dutch-Belgian) Commission, appointed by the two governments, for the execution of the cultural agreement between them. The promotion of cultural co-operation and exchange with the French-speaking part of Belgium belongs to the programme, and I can of course whole-heartedly accept it. My zeal for Dutch in Flanders has never meant that I want to exclude French or French culture. Such has never been my type of nationalism. It is true that I can work for relations with the Walloons only on condition that the special and natural connection existing between Holland and Flanders be admitted. In the new circumstances, after the enormous change that Belgium has gone through as a result of the linguistic laws passed about 1930, it has indeed been possible to have that principle unquestioningly observed by the Commission. The Belgian members are all Flemings, with the occasional exception of a Walloon with a perfect command of Dutch. The discussions are never carried on in French. I have always been able to take part in the work with conviction, although, frankly speaking, commissions are apt to make me impatient.

Two years ago the Commission celebrated its tenth anniversary. One precious moment stands out from that occasion— a moment full of irony. The celebration took place at The Hague. The Belgian Ambassador had invited us to lunch at the Embassy. And there, before we sat down, he started a little speech and began to distribute a few decorations. Suddenly I found myself a Commander in the Order of the Crown of Belgium. The irony was not lost upon the Flemish friends who came up to congratulate me. "Who would have thought so twenty-five or thirty years ago!" they grinned. To which I could only reply: "Yes, Belgium *has* changed!" The thought that I, too, had changed did cross my mind and caused me a little embarrassment.

Belgium changed—in itself the fact is not open to doubt. The most crying linguistic grievances have been remedied by the legislation of 1930 and the immediately following years. A generation of Flemish intellectuals schooled and educated in Dutch is beginning to take its place in Belgian life—a phenomenon that had been unknown for well over a century. And yet how many weaknesses can still be observed in the cultural and social position of the Flemish population! Just because the most crying grievances have been removed, it seems as if the reaction against remaining maladjustments—I mention only the progress of the Gallicization of the Brussels population and the formidable influence exercised by Brussels on the entire life of the Flemish-speaking region—has become less spontaneous and less strong. I sometimes regret the absence of a *movement* such as I knew it—for there is now hardly anything left that might be called a Flemish movement. And I still see dangers for the future.[17]

I sometimes ask myself, with self-reproach, what do I do to support the Flemings who are still struggling? Ought not I, also, to denounce, much more insistently than I do, the optimism of my Hollanders, who are only too much inclined to cherish the comfortable belief that Flemish grievances have now been remedied. On the whole I, too, acquiesce far too readily in a state of affairs that, in spite of the remarkable improvement I have witnessed in my lifetime, is not really satisfactory.

But life has disposed of me otherwise.

It is not only the state of affairs in Belgium, which makes a difference between then and now; it is not only the difficulty of finding points of contact for action there, as I found them in the past. Before the second world war the rise of National Socialism had already upset my view of the world. I thought and felt (and I think and feel) about Flanders, and about the significance to us of Flanders as a potential territory for the flowering of Netherlands culture, as I had thought from my youth onward; in that view I continue to find inspiration for

[17] I am glad to be able to add now, that a remarkable revival has taken place. (1961)—And is still gathering strength. (1963)

historical work. But civilization's life-and-death struggle of the last twenty-five years is set on a wider stage. From the first moment I had thrown myself into that struggle, and that too was in my mind automatically transposed into historical forms. Thus something within me, too, has changed; the change, however, when all is well considered, is not one that ought to cause me "embarrassment". I have shifted the focus of my interest, or rather, I have enlarged its field. Hence, even during the occupation, *Napoleon For and Against*;[18] hence polemical essays against Romein and Toynbee, against Butterfield and Barraclough; hence studies about great foreign historians, about Bilderdijk and Groen, and Ter Braak, about *Use and Abuse of History*.[19] Hence, also, the twenty years that have elapsed between the publication of the last original volume of the *Geschiedenis van de Nederlandse Stam* and the completion of a new volume, which I was able some time ago to entrust to my publisher.

I touch here upon a painful point in my career as a writer of history. I am deeply aware that I have put my publisher's patience to a test more severe than was permissible. That his patience has held out is more than I deserve. And there was not only the publisher: often enough readers gave utterance to impatience or annoyance—utterances that warmed my heart as evidence the work meant something to them, but that at the same time I could not read without experiencing pangs of conscience. Among my colleagues I believe that there was a fairly widespread opinion: "Geyl will never do it now; obviously he has lost the inspiration for his work."

But in reality I had never abandoned my intention to go on with the task so lightheartedly undertaken in 1927. In the midst of my other activities I sometimes worked on the *Nederlandse Stam* for months at a stretch as hard as ever. And I can say in all sincerity: with as much conviction, with as great a zest as ever. Only, every now and again, I found myself

[18] English translation 1949 (London: Jonathan Cape New Haven: Yale University Press).
[19] The Terry Lectures for 1954, published in 1955 (New Haven: Yale University Press).

in the grip of a polemic, or an essay seemed the only way to free my mind from the fascination of a problem. How many times have I said (and promised my wife): "This has been my last escapade, my last essay." And before I knew what I was doing, I found myself in the midst of one again.

The worst of it is that, warmly as I feel for my great work and deeply concerned as I am about its slow progress, I cannot declare that I regret those other activities. The reason is not in the first place that they have, to my own surprise, evoked such a response in England and the United States. But these explorations in fields into which I had never dreamed that I should venture—Shakespeare and Napoleon and the American Civil War and Russian historiography and Romein and Toynbee and what not—I have learned a great deal from all these adventures, and I have enjoyed them, too, just as much as I have the *Nederlandse Stam*.

"Give it up, that *Nederlandse Stam!*" so friends have at times advised me. "If you take another twenty years for the volume after this one, you will be ninety, and how many volumes will be still to come? And, after all, you have already made good the main thesis. Why go on driving a point that you have already made? Write essays! You have found your line. And no doubt you have more to say about historiography and the theory of history."

Certainly! much more! enough to fill another life. Yet, advice like this always rouses me to opposition. I don't in the least intend to take another twenty years for the next volume. I want to go on. I must go on. And it is not true—this at least I can swear to in any court you choose—that I have no heart for the *Nederlandse Stam* any more. I want to go on, not only because I feel obliged to, but because I am longing to give form to my conception of William I's United Kingdom and of the Belgian Revolution of 1830, and after that of the rise of the Flemish movement and . . . . But I stop. I can only bear witness to my feeling and to my will. I am not master of the future. This I can say, that writing history is still the joy of my life, and that I shall enter my retirement, not without feelings of regret certainly, but mainly with cheerfulness at the thought that I shall have so much the more time to give to "my own work." Concentration I dare not promise, but I am not without tenacity.

History "a key to life . . . in its fullness and all its aspects," that is how I put it at the beginning of these remarks. It is a phrase apt to counsel modesty when I survey what I have written so far. But I also hear in it an exhortation to persevere and ever again to delve and to search for treasure. To master life is not what history will permit us, but under history's colours to struggle with life will be our fulfilment and our prize.

(1958)

NOTE OF ACKNOWLEDGMENT

INDEX

NOTE OF ACKNOWLEDGMENT

Of the sixteen essays included in this volume, fourteen were published in *Encounters in History* as published by Meridian Books, World Publishing Company, New York, 1961. That American edition contained moreover three essays not published here: *Orange and Stuart, 1641-1650* (originally two articles published in *English Historical Review*, 1923, and *Scottish H.R.*, 1923, respectively; in 1939 republished as opening chapters of author's book *Oranje en Stuart, 1641-1672*); *The Batavian Revolution, 1795-1798; and Historical Appreciations of the Holland Regent Regime;* (the last-named essay is also to be found in *Essays in Diplomatic and Constitutional History*, presented to Dr. G. P. Gooch in 1961). For these three essays have here been substituted *Toynbee's Answer* (III 6) and *Huizinga as Accuser of his Age* (II 3).

I   *Shakespeare as a Historian: a Fragment* was published originally in Dutch in *Nieuw Vlaams Tijdschrift*, Antwerp, 1947; reprinted in the author's *Tochten en Toernooien*, 1950.

II 1   *Motley and his "Rise of the Dutch Republic"*, a talk delivered over the B.B.C., was published in *The Listener*, London, 1956.

II 2   *French Historians For and Against the Revolution*, originally two lectures delivered at Oxford in 1956, was published for the first time in *Encounters in History*.

II 3   *Huizinga as Accuser of his Age*, published in 1961, in Dutch, in the *Mededelingen* of the Dutch Academy at Amsterdam; a somewhat abridged version was published in *History and Theory*, Cambridge, Mass., U.S.A., 1963.

III 1   *Jan Romein, or Bowing to the Spirit of the Age;* originally published in *De Gids*, Amsterdam, 1947, reprinted in the author's *Tochten en Toernooien*, 1950. (The concluding part of this essay, containing criticism of detail, has not been reprinted here.)

III 2 *Othman F. Anderle, or Unreason as a Doctrine;* originally published in Meridian Books newspaper, *The Meridian*, New York, Fall 1958.

III 3 *Herbert Butterfield, or Thinking at Two Levels;* originally published in the *Historical Journal*, Cambridge, 1956.

III 4 *Geoffrey Barraclough, or the Scrapping of History;* originally published in *The Nation*, New York, April 13, 1957.

III 5 *Soviet Historians make their Bow;* originally published in *De Gids*, Dec. 1955; an abridged English version appeared in *The Nation*, N.Y., April 14, 1955.

III 6 *Toynbee's Answer*, published in 1961, in English, in the *Mededelingen* of the Amsterdam Academy.

IV 1 *The Idea of Liberty in History*, originally a lecture delivered for Studium Generale, Utrecht, published in *Nieuw Vlaams Tijdschrift*, 1957.

IV 2 *Hitler's Europe*, a talk delivered over the B.B.C., 1954, was published for the first time in *Encounters in History*.

IV 3 *Opening Lecture, October 1, 1945*, published in the author's *Historicus in de tijd*, 1954.

IV 4 *The Vitality of Western Civilization*, a valedictory oration delivered in the Aula of the University of Utrecht on the occasion of the author's retirement from the chair of Modern History, May 31, 1958, was published separately and was reprinted in his *Geschiedenis als medespeler*, 1959; the English version appeared in *Delta, a Review of Arts, Life and Thought in the Netherlands*, Amsterdam, Spring 1959.

IV 5 *The Historical Background of the Idea of European Unity*, originally two lectures given in the Aula of the University of Leyden in October 1959, published in *Viermaal Europa*, together with three other papers by experts in European federation.

V *Looking Back*, a talk given to the Utrecht Historical Students' Circle in March 1958, published in the author's *Studies en Strijdschriften*, 1959.

INDEX

Abjuration, Act of (Netherlands, 1581), 313-14, 319, 320

Action Française, 171, 178, 180, 181, 384

Acton, Lord, 252, 253-4, 255, 323

æstheticism, 217, 228

Africa, 259, 352, 357, 360, 361

Aitzema, 315

Alexander, Czar of Russia, 380

Alsace-Lorraine, 158, 161, 384

Alva, Duke of, 107, 109

America, colonial period in, 374; *see also* North America, United States

American Civil War, 196, 423

American Declaration of Independence, 313, 319, 322

American Revolution, 109, 111, 322

Amery, Leo, 269

Amsterdam, 61, 102-3, 201, 206, 218, 318

ancien régime, in France, 119, 126, 179, 327; Tocqueville on, 150; Renan on, 157; Taine on, 163, 166

Anderle, Othmar, F., 249-51

Anglomania, in France, 120, 145

anthropomorphism (regarding culture, etc.), 222, 290-1

anticlericalism, 126, 140, 155, 156, 159, 170

"anti-historian," the (Croce's phrase), 144; "anti-historicism," 260

apartheid, 303

Arab countries, 356

aristocracy: in Shakespeare, 34-5, 38, 47, 48; in Hooft, 64; in French history, 123, 151; Huizinga on, 200; theory of (Aristotle etc.), 311; civilization and, 350

Aristotle, 62, 71, 72, 80, 310-11, 365, 366

Arminians, 204, 205

asceticism, 194, 197

Asia, in history and current affairs, 259, 280, 352, 357, 360, 361, 374; Machiavelli on, 369-70

Assembly, National (in France), 120, 126, 131, 133, 137, 145, 167, 168; phase of Legislative Assembly, 126, 127; "la terrible Assemblée," 135; Assembly of 1871 (Bordeaux), 158-9

Augustine, St., 309, 325, 326, 346